PREVIOUSLY:

W9-BKK-533

THE WORLD now lies divided not amongst political
or geographic boundaries but amongst *financial* ones. Wealth is power, and that
power rests with only a handful of **FAMILIES**.

The few who provide a service to their ruling
Family are cared for and protected.

All others are **Waste**.

It is the Year X +66, just over six and a half decades
since the Families met in Macau to divide the world and its
riches among themselves.

What is now referred to more and more as **The Conclave War**
is entering its second year, and the map of the world is—once more—changing.
Alliances have shifted. The **RAUSLING** Family is destroyed. Western Europe
is in chaos.

And in the east, **VASSALOVKA** has brought its deadliest weapon to bear,
bringing with it more terror, violence, and carnage.

CASEY SOLOMON was Waste, living under **CARLYLE**
rule in Montana, until she was "Lifted on Merit" on the order of none other than
Commander Forever Carlyle.

Now the eye of the Lazarus has fallen upon her once more.

THE DAGGERS are the Carlyle military's most elite special forces operators, under
Commander Carlyle's direct command.

Their reputation is legendary, and gives even Carlyle's most intractible enemies
pause, for to be a Dagger is to become not only an instrument of the Carlyle
Family, but a weapon wielded by the Lazarus herself.

Casey Solomon will either become a Dagger, or she will die trying…

IMAGE COMICS, INC.
Robert Kirkman—Chief Operating Officer
Erik Larsen—Chief Financial Officer
Todd McFarlane—President
Marc Silvestri—Chief Executive Officer
Jim Valentino—Vice President

Eric Stephenson—Publisher / Chief Creative Officer
Corey Hart—Director of Sales
Jeff Boison—Director of Publishing Planning
& Book Trade Sales
Chris Ross—Director of Digital Sales
Jeff Stang—Director of Specialty Sales
Kat Salazar—Director of PR & Marketing
Drew Gill—Art Director
Heather Doornink—Production Director
Nicole Lapalme—Controller

image
IMAGECOMICS.COM

Covers by	**MICHAEL LARK**
Colors by	**SANTI ARCAS**
Letters by	**JODI WYNNE**
Edited by	**DAVID BROTHERS**
Publication design by	**ERIC TRAUTMANN**
Special thanks to	**DENISE ESPINOZA, RICHARD HOWE,** *and* **MIKHAIL KISELGOF**

LAZARUS: X +66

First printing. April 2018. Published by Image Comics, Inc. Office of publication: 2701 NW Vaughn St., Suite 780, Portland, OR 97210. Copyright © 2018 Greg Rucka and Michael Lark. All rights reserved.

Contains material originally published in single magazine form as LAZARUS: X +66 #1-6. "Lazarus," its logos, and the likenesses of all characters herein are trademarks of Greg Rucka and Michael Lark, unless otherwise noted.

"Image" and the Image Comics logos are registered trademarks of Image Comics, Inc. No part of this publication may be reproduced or transmitted, in any form or by any means (except for short excerpts for journalistic or review purposes), without the express written permission of Greg Rucka, Michael Lark, or Image Comics, Inc. All names, characters, events, and locales in this publication are entirely fictional. Any resemblance to actual persons (living or dead), events, or places, without satiric intent, is coincidental. Printed in the USA. For information regarding the CPSIA on this printed material call: 203-595-3636 and provide reference #RICH-783830.

For international rights, contact: foreignlicensing@imagecomics.com.

ISBN: 978-1-5343-0488-8

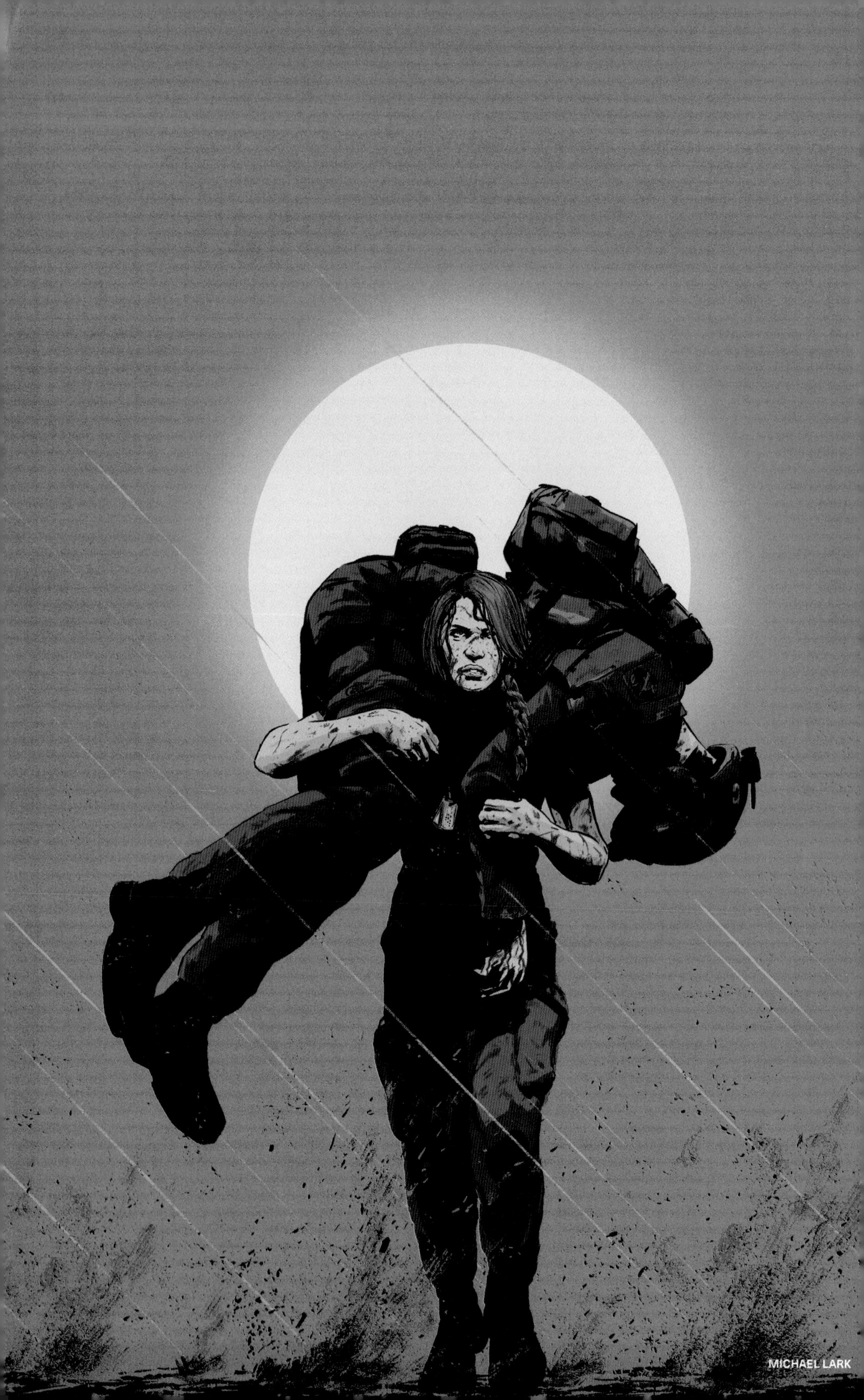

MICHAEL LARK

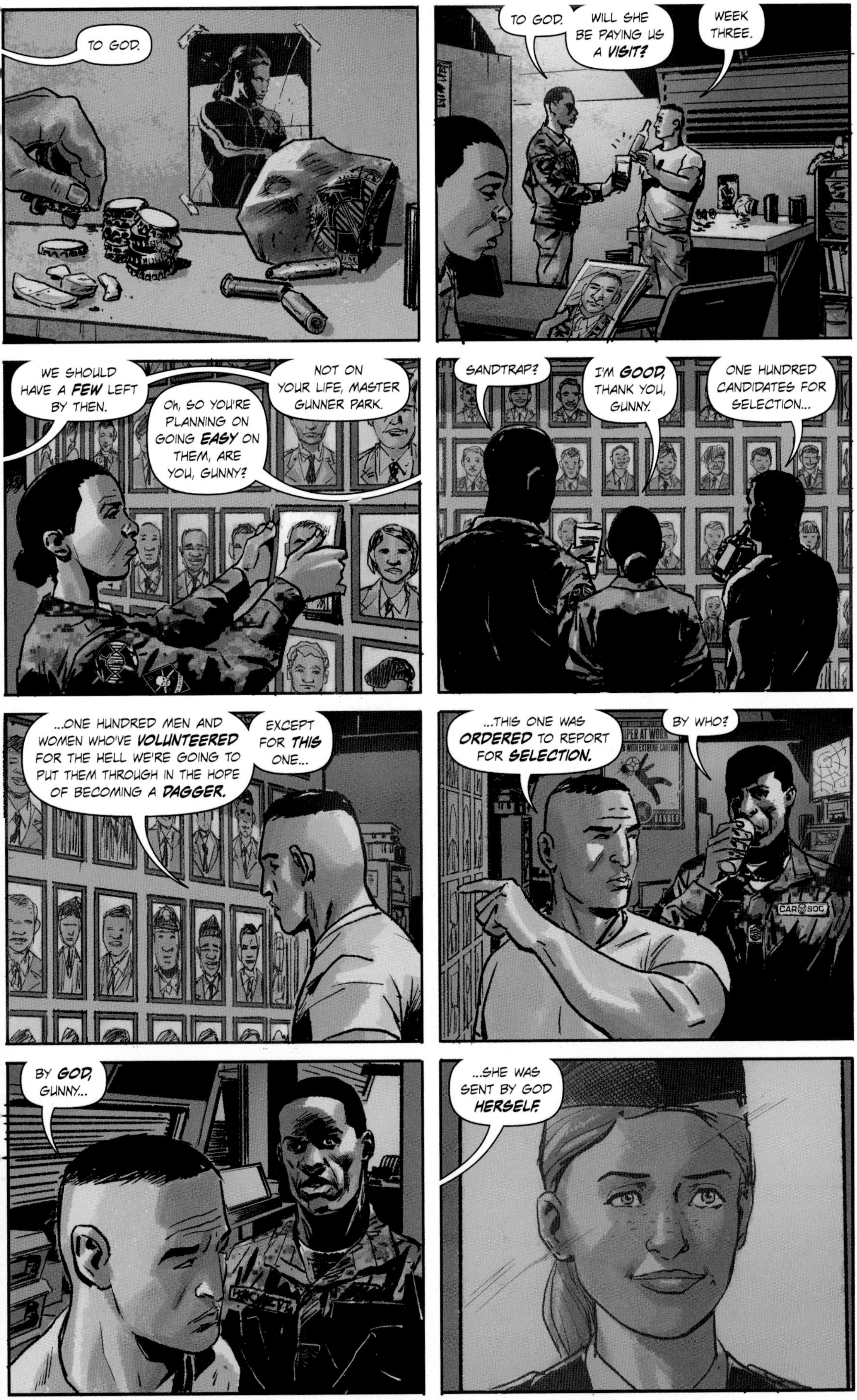
TO GOD.
TO GOD.
WILL SHE BE PAYING US A VISIT?
WEEK THREE.
WE SHOULD HAVE A FEW LEFT BY THEN.
Oh, SO YOU'RE PLANNING ON GOING EASY ON THEM, ARE YOU, GUNNY?
NOT ON YOUR LIFE, MASTER GUNNER PARK.
SANDTRAP?
I'M GOOD, THANK YOU, GUNNY.
ONE HUNDRED CANDIDATES FOR SELECTION...
...ONE HUNDRED MEN AND WOMEN WHO'VE VOLUNTEERED FOR THE HELL WE'RE GOING TO PUT THEM THROUGH IN THE HOPE OF BECOMING A DAGGER.
EXCEPT FOR THIS ONE...
...THIS ONE WAS ORDERED TO REPORT FOR SELECTION.
BY WHO?
CAR SOC
BY GOD, GUNNY...
...SHE WAS SENT BY GOD HERSELF.

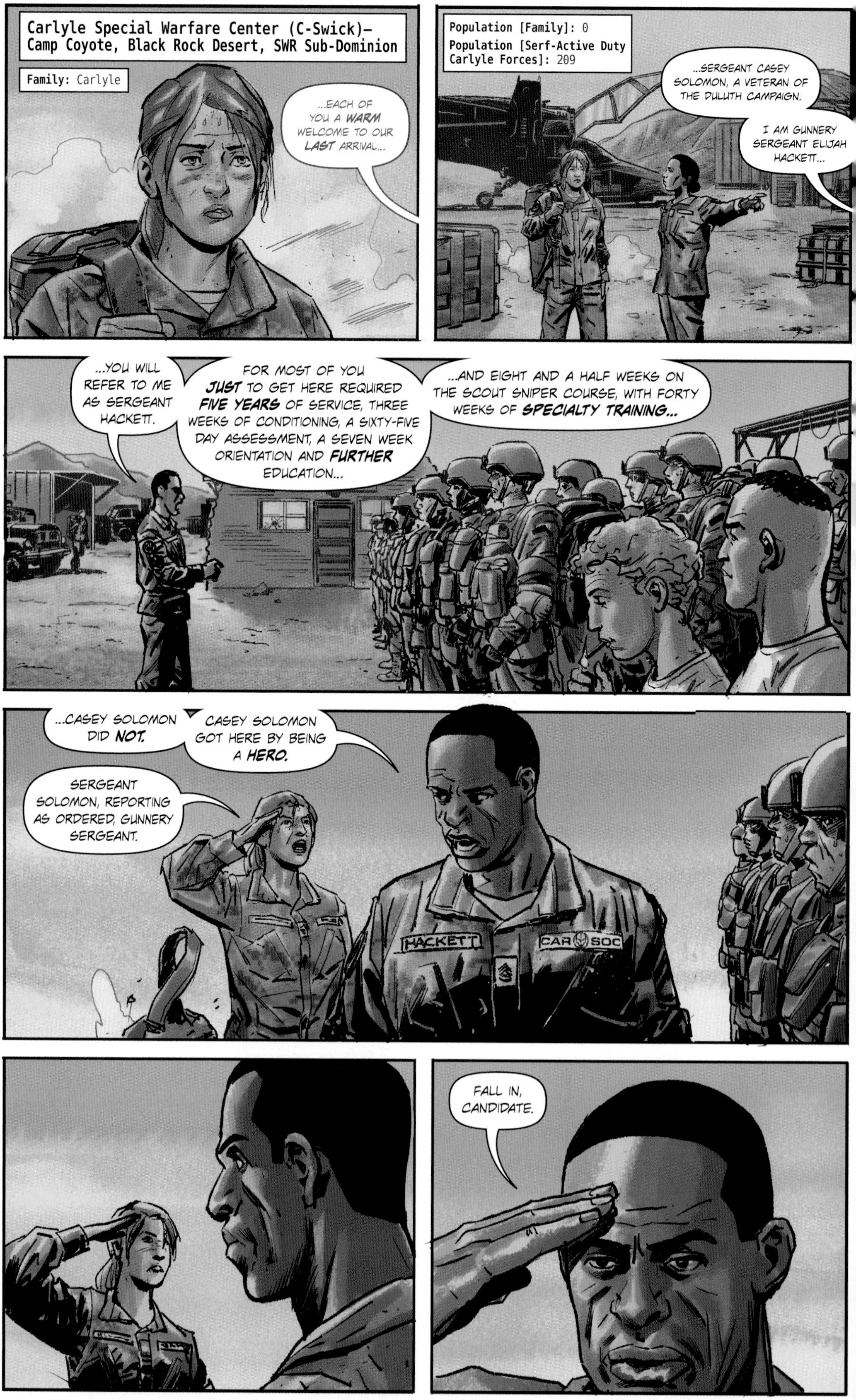

Carlyle Special Warfare Center (C-Swick)—
Camp Coyote, Black Rock Desert, SWR Sub-Dominion
Family: Carlyle
...EACH OF YOU A WARM WELCOME TO OUR LAST ARRIVAL...
Population [Family]: 0
Population [Serf-Active Duty Carlyle Forces]: 209
...SERGEANT CASEY SOLOMON, A VETERAN OF THE DULUTH CAMPAIGN.
I AM GUNNERY SERGEANT ELIJAH HACKETT...
...YOU WILL REFER TO ME AS SERGEANT HACKETT.
FOR MOST OF YOU JUST TO GET HERE REQUIRED FIVE YEARS OF SERVICE, THREE WEEKS OF CONDITIONING, A SIXTY-FIVE DAY ASSESSMENT, A SEVEN WEEK ORIENTATION AND FURTHER EDUCATION...
...AND EIGHT AND A HALF WEEKS ON THE SCOUT SNIPER COURSE, WITH FORTY WEEKS OF SPECIALTY TRAINING...
...CASEY SOLOMON DID NOT.
CASEY SOLOMON GOT HERE BY BEING A HERO.
SERGEANT SOLOMON, REPORTING AS ORDERED, GUNNERY SERGEANT.
HACKETT
CAR SOC
FALL IN, CANDIDATE.

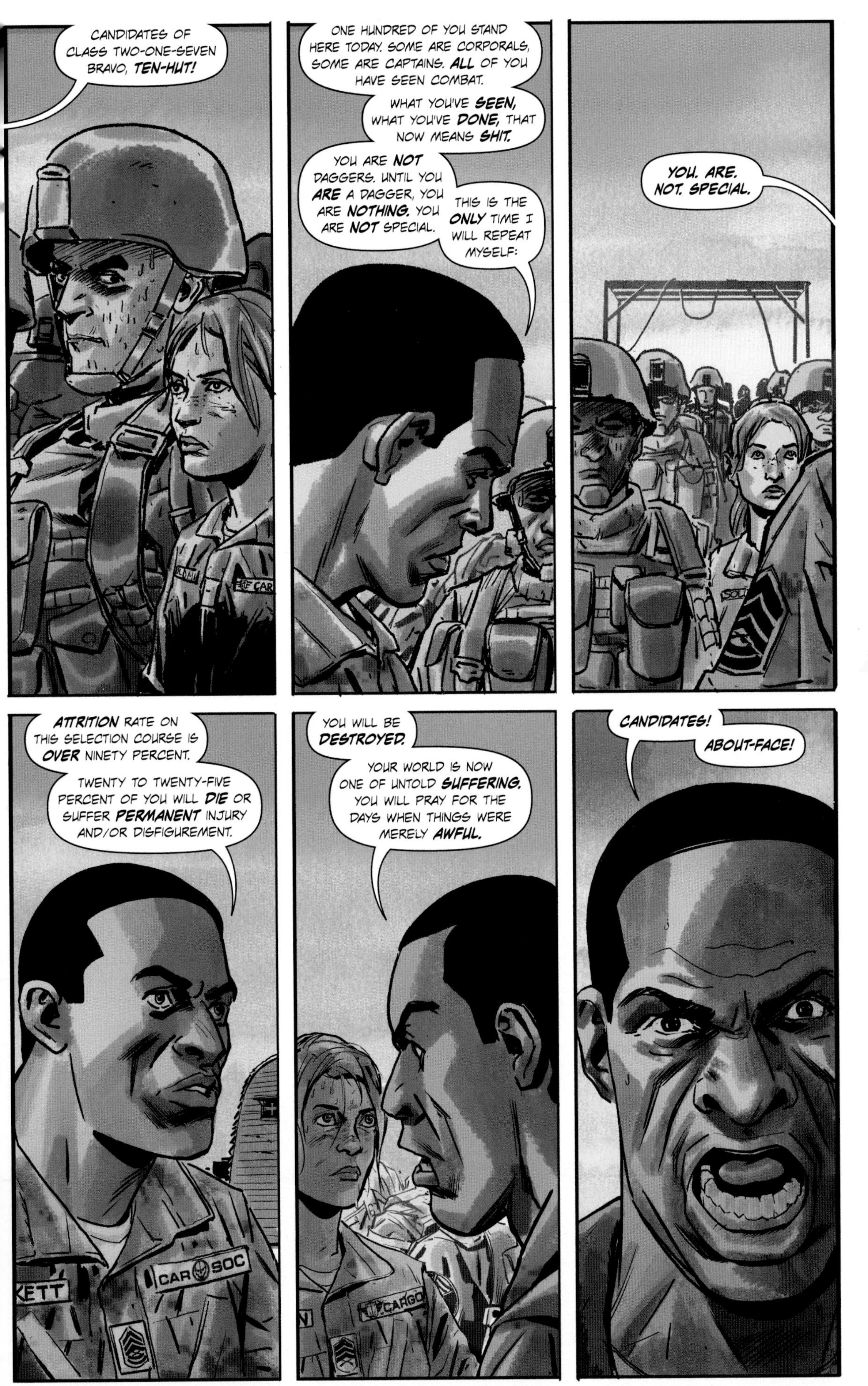
CANDIDATES OF CLASS TWO-ONE-SEVEN BRAVO, TEN-HUT!
ONE HUNDRED OF YOU STAND HERE TODAY. SOME ARE CORPORALS, SOME ARE CAPTAINS. ALL OF YOU HAVE SEEN COMBAT.
WHAT YOU'VE SEEN, WHAT YOU'VE DONE, THAT NOW MEANS SHIT.
YOU ARE NOT DAGGERS. UNTIL YOU ARE A DAGGER, YOU ARE NOTHING. YOU ARE NOT SPECIAL.
THIS IS THE ONLY TIME I WILL REPEAT MYSELF:
YOU. ARE. NOT. SPECIAL.
ATTRITION RATE ON THIS SELECTION COURSE IS OVER NINETY PERCENT.
TWENTY TO TWENTY-FIVE PERCENT OF YOU WILL DIE OR SUFFER PERMANENT INJURY AND/OR DISFIGUREMENT.
YOU WILL BE DESTROYED.
YOUR WORLD IS NOW ONE OF UNTOLD SUFFERING. YOU WILL PRAY FOR THE DAYS WHEN THINGS WERE MERELY AWFUL.
CANDIDATES!
ABOUT-FACE!

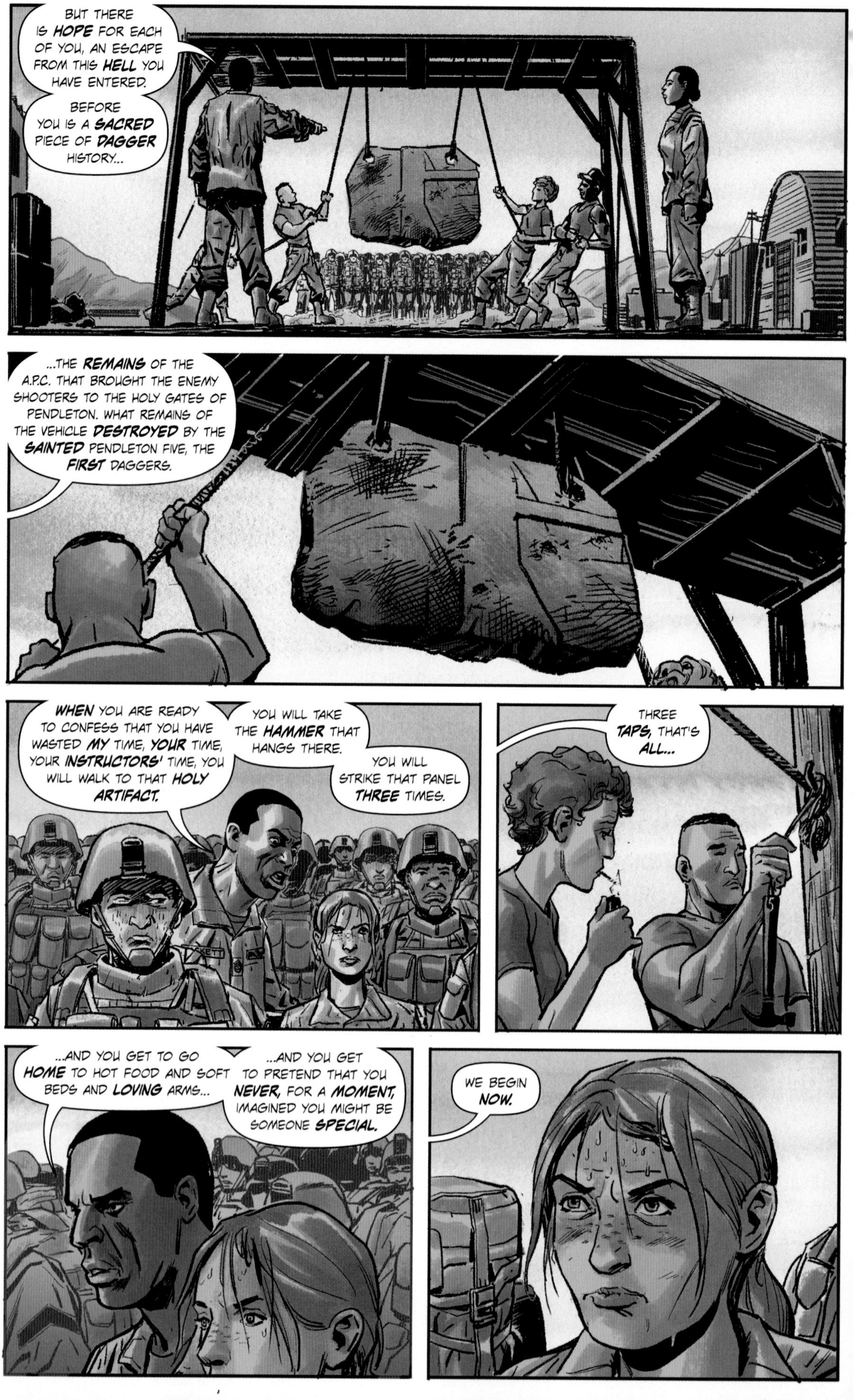

BUT THERE IS HOPE FOR EACH OF YOU, AN ESCAPE FROM THIS HELL YOU HAVE ENTERED.
BEFORE YOU IS A SACRED PIECE OF DAGGER HISTORY...
...THE REMAINS OF THE A.P.C. THAT BROUGHT THE ENEMY SHOOTERS TO THE HOLY GATES OF PENDLETON. WHAT REMAINS OF THE VEHICLE DESTROYED BY THE SAINTED PENDLETON FIVE, THE FIRST DAGGERS.
WHEN YOU ARE READY TO CONFESS THAT YOU HAVE WASTED MY TIME, YOUR TIME, YOUR INSTRUCTORS' TIME, YOU WILL WALK TO THAT HOLY ARTIFACT.
YOU WILL TAKE THE HAMMER THAT HANGS THERE.
YOU WILL STRIKE THAT PANEL THREE TIMES.
THREE TAPS, THAT'S ALL...
...AND YOU GET TO GO HOME TO HOT FOOD AND SOFT BEDS AND LOVING ARMS...
...AND YOU GET TO PRETEND THAT YOU NEVER, FOR A MOMENT, IMAGINED YOU MIGHT BE SOMEONE SPECIAL.
WE BEGIN NOW.

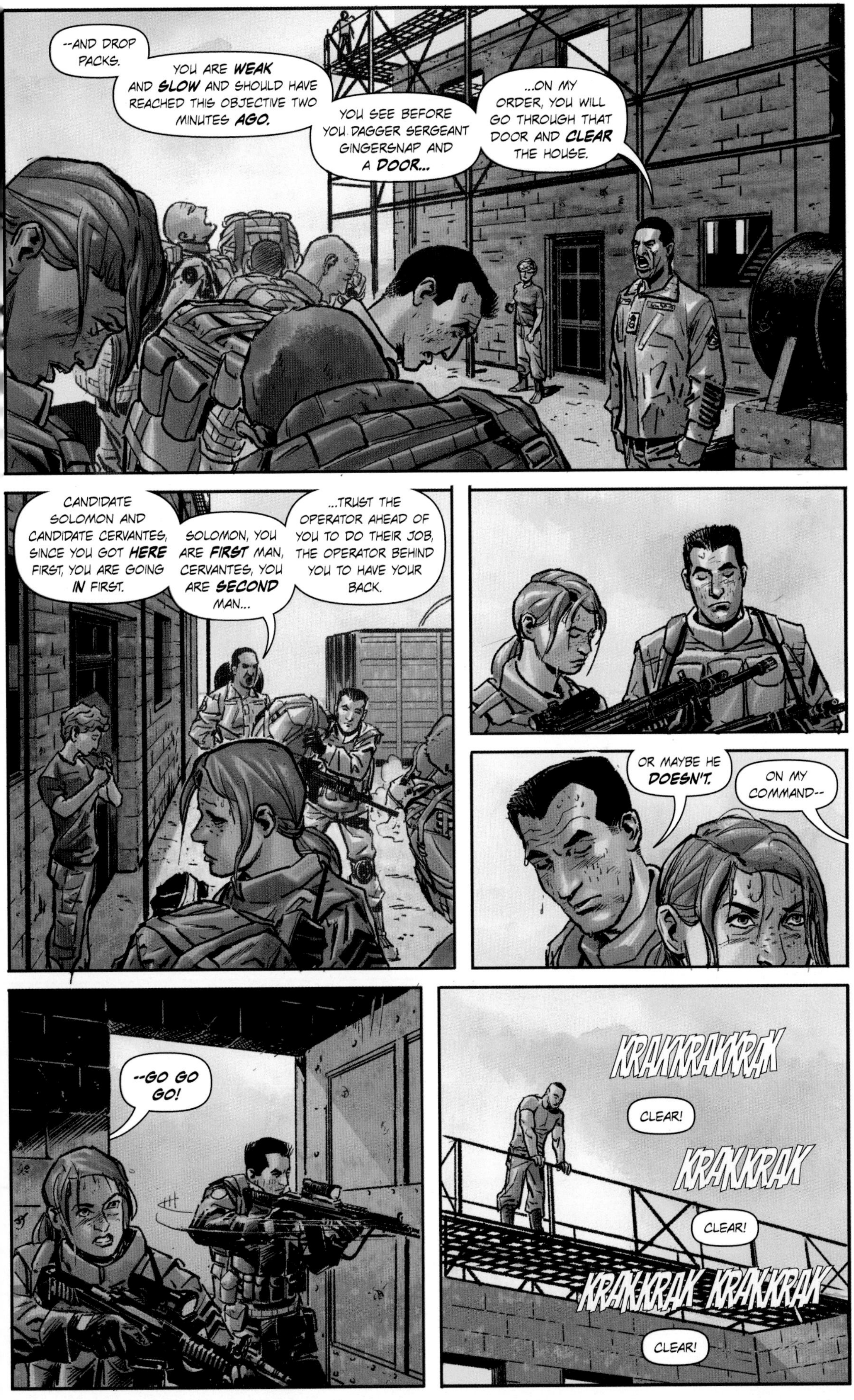
--AND DROP PACKS.
YOU ARE WEAK AND SLOW AND SHOULD HAVE REACHED THIS OBJECTIVE TWO MINUTES AGO.
YOU SEE BEFORE YOU DAGGER SERGEANT GINGERSNAP AND A DOOR...
...ON MY ORDER, YOU WILL GO THROUGH THAT DOOR AND CLEAR THE HOUSE.
CANDIDATE SOLOMON AND CANDIDATE CERVANTES, SINCE YOU GOT HERE FIRST, YOU ARE GOING IN FIRST.
SOLOMON, YOU ARE FIRST MAN, CERVANTES, YOU ARE SECOND MAN...
...TRUST THE OPERATOR AHEAD OF YOU TO DO THEIR JOB, THE OPERATOR BEHIND YOU TO HAVE YOUR BACK.
OR MAYBE HE DOESN'T.
ON MY COMMAND--
--GO GO GO!
KRAKKRAKKRAK
CLEAR!
KRAKKRAK
CLEAR!
KRAKKRAK KRAKKRAK
CLEAR!

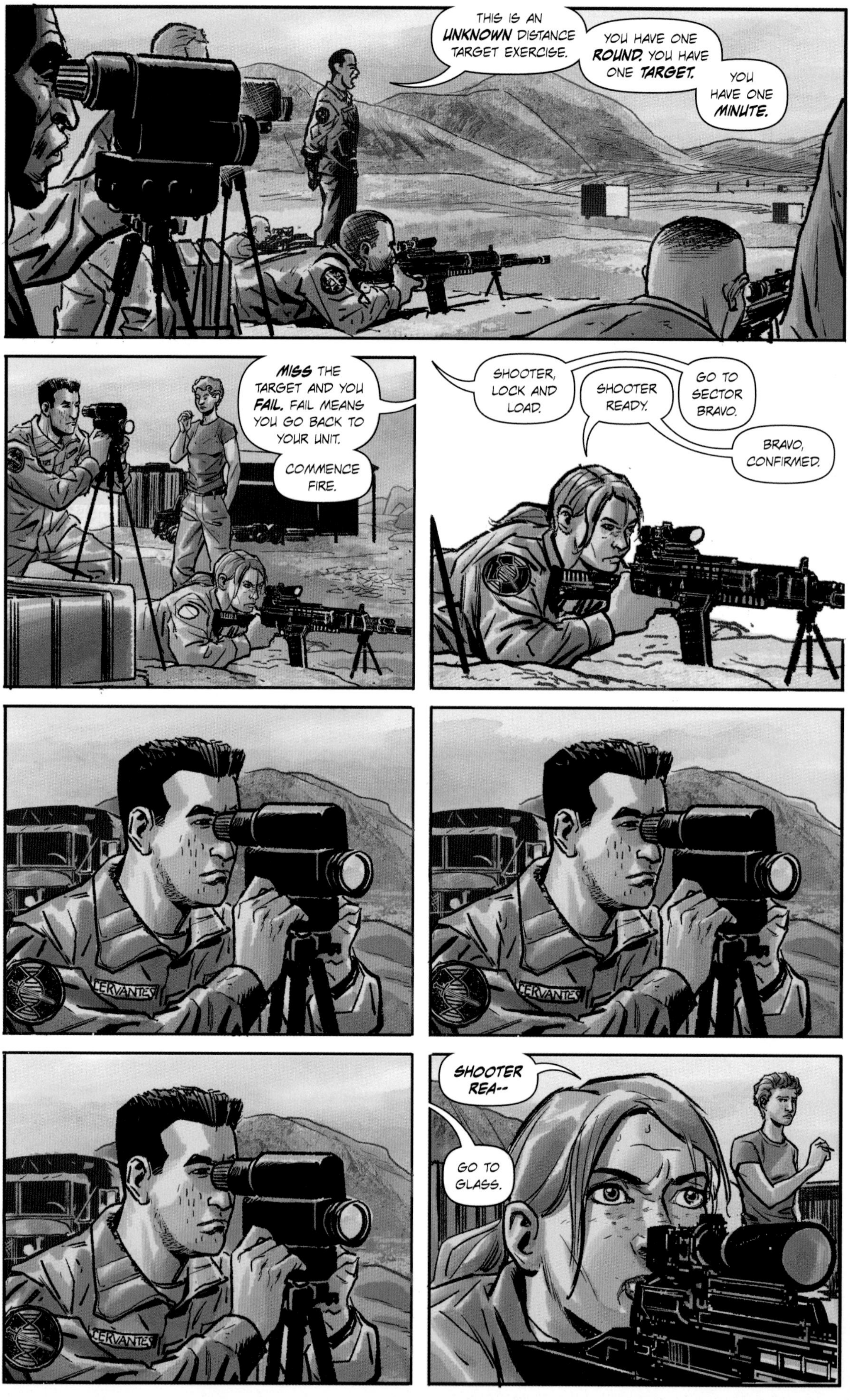

THIS IS AN UNKNOWN DISTANCE TARGET EXERCISE.
YOU HAVE ONE ROUND. YOU HAVE ONE TARGET.
YOU HAVE ONE MINUTE.
MISS THE TARGET AND YOU FAIL. FAIL MEANS YOU GO BACK TO YOUR UNIT.
COMMENCE FIRE.
SHOOTER, LOCK AND LOAD.
SHOOTER READY.
GO TO SECTOR BRAVO.
BRAVO, CONFIRMED.
CERVANTES
CERVANTES
CERVANTES
SHOOTER REA--
GO TO GLASS.

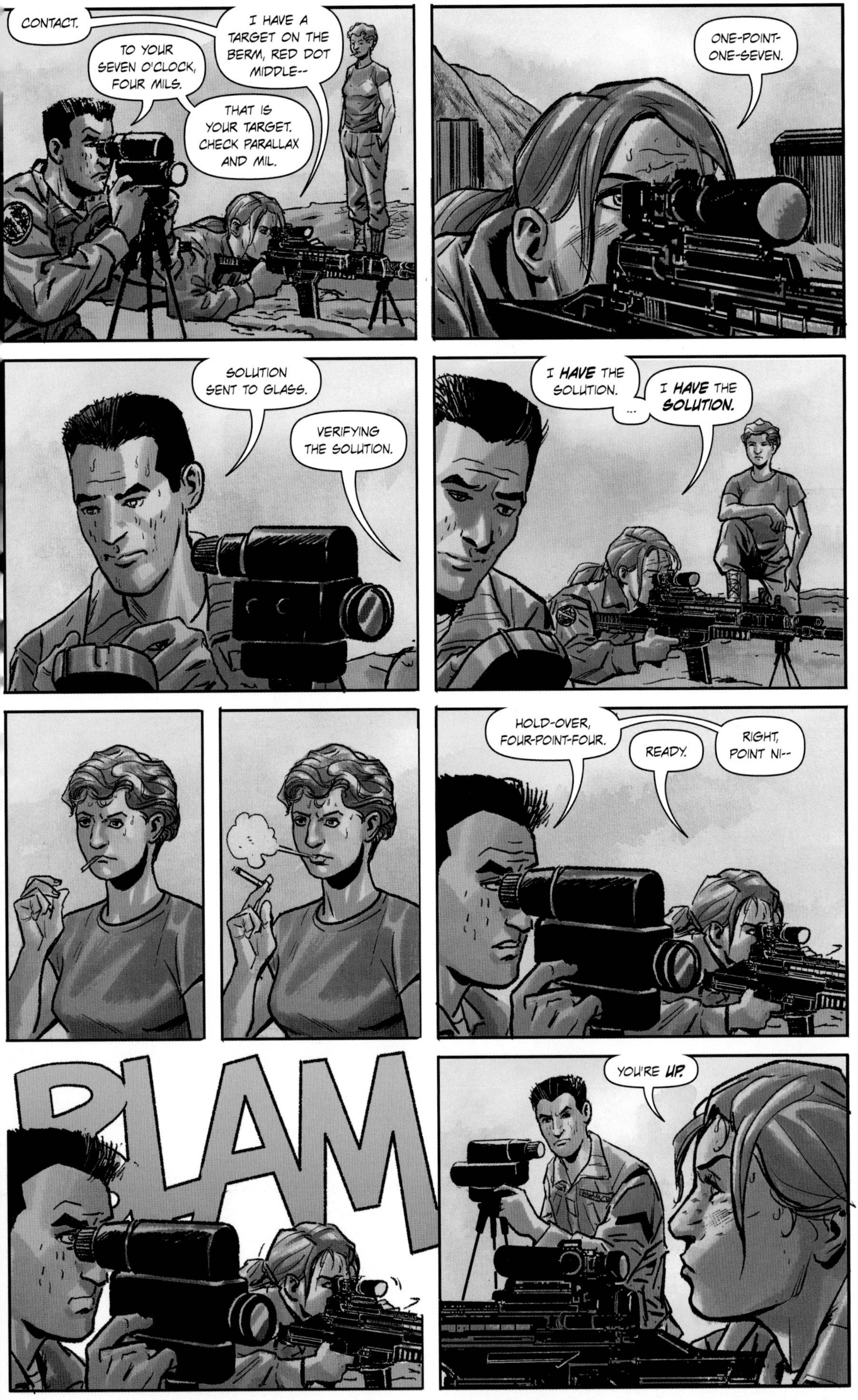
CONTACT.
I HAVE A TARGET ON THE BERM, RED DOT MIDDLE--
TO YOUR SEVEN O'CLOCK, FOUR MILS.
THAT IS YOUR TARGET. CHECK PARALLAX AND MIL.
ONE-POINT-ONE-SEVEN.
SOLUTION SENT TO GLASS.
VERIFYING THE SOLUTION.
I HAVE THE SOLUTION.
...
I HAVE THE SOLUTION.
HOLD-OVER, FOUR-POINT-FOUR.
READY.
RIGHT, POINT NI--
BLAM
YOU'RE UP.

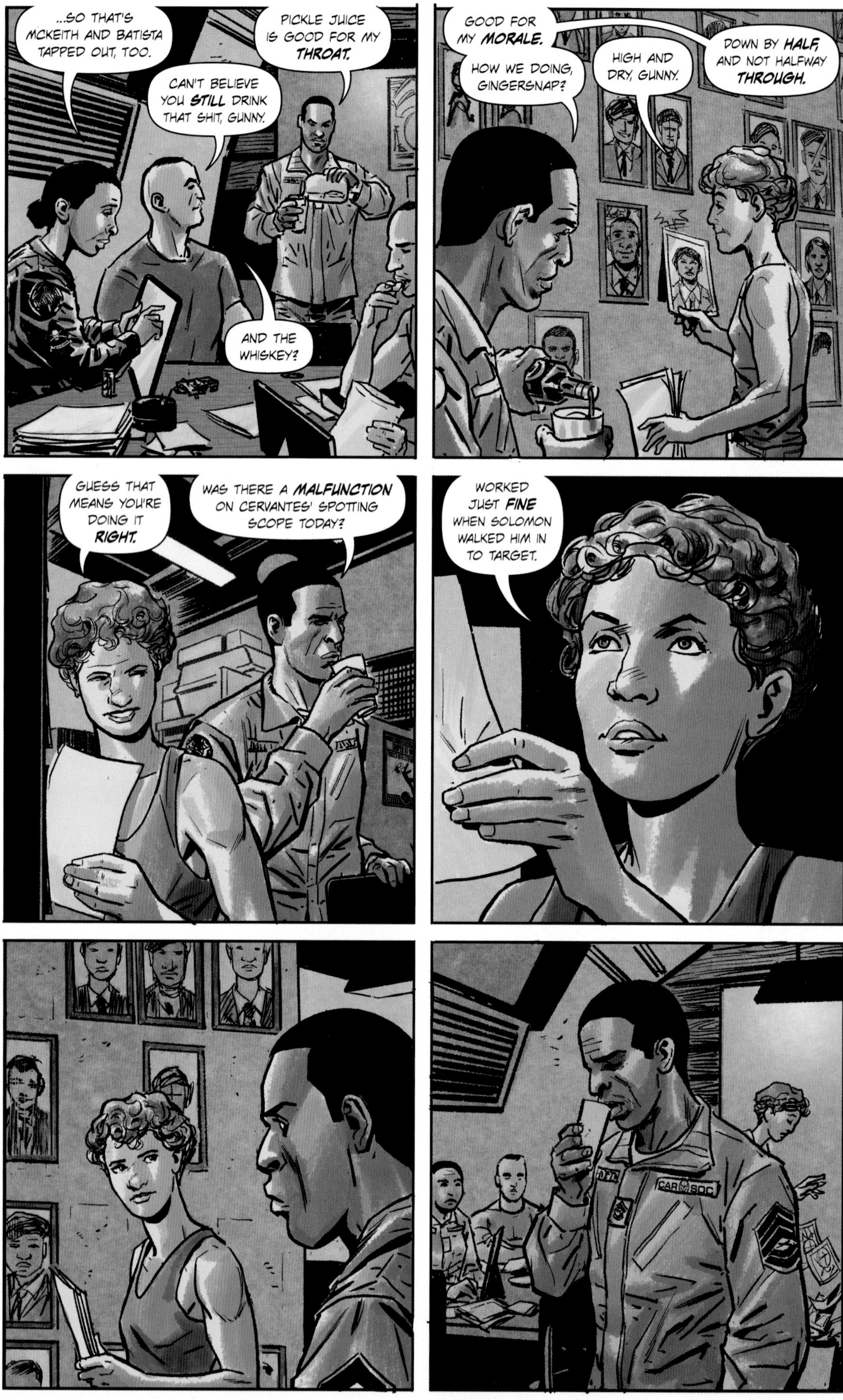
...SO THAT'S MCKEITH AND BATISTA TAPPED OUT, TOO.
CAN'T BELIEVE YOU **STILL** DRINK THAT SHIT, GUNNY.
PICKLE JUICE IS GOOD FOR MY **THROAT.**
AND THE WHISKEY?
GOOD FOR MY **MORALE.**
HOW WE DOING, GINGERSNAP?
HIGH AND DRY, GUNNY.
DOWN BY **HALF,** AND NOT HALFWAY **THROUGH.**
GUESS THAT MEANS YOU'RE DOING IT **RIGHT.**
WAS THERE A **MALFUNCTION** ON CERVANTES' SPOTTING SCOPE TODAY?
WORKED JUST **FINE** WHEN SOLOMON WALKED HIM IN TO TARGET.
CAR SOC

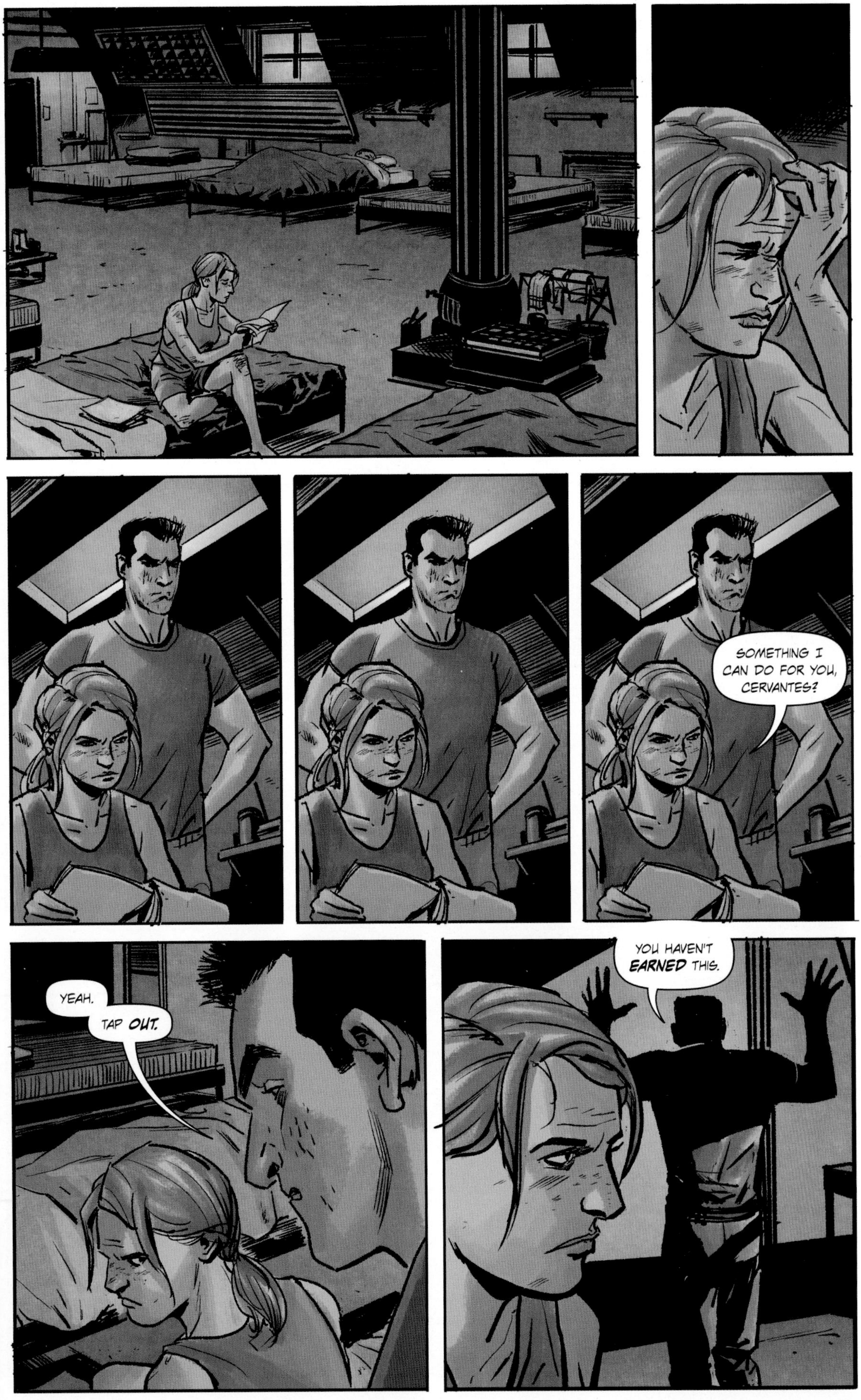
SOMETHING I CAN DO FOR YOU, CERVANTES?
YEAH.
TAP OUT.
YOU HAVEN'T EARNED THIS.

CLEARED FIELD OF FIRE

SECOND SECTION

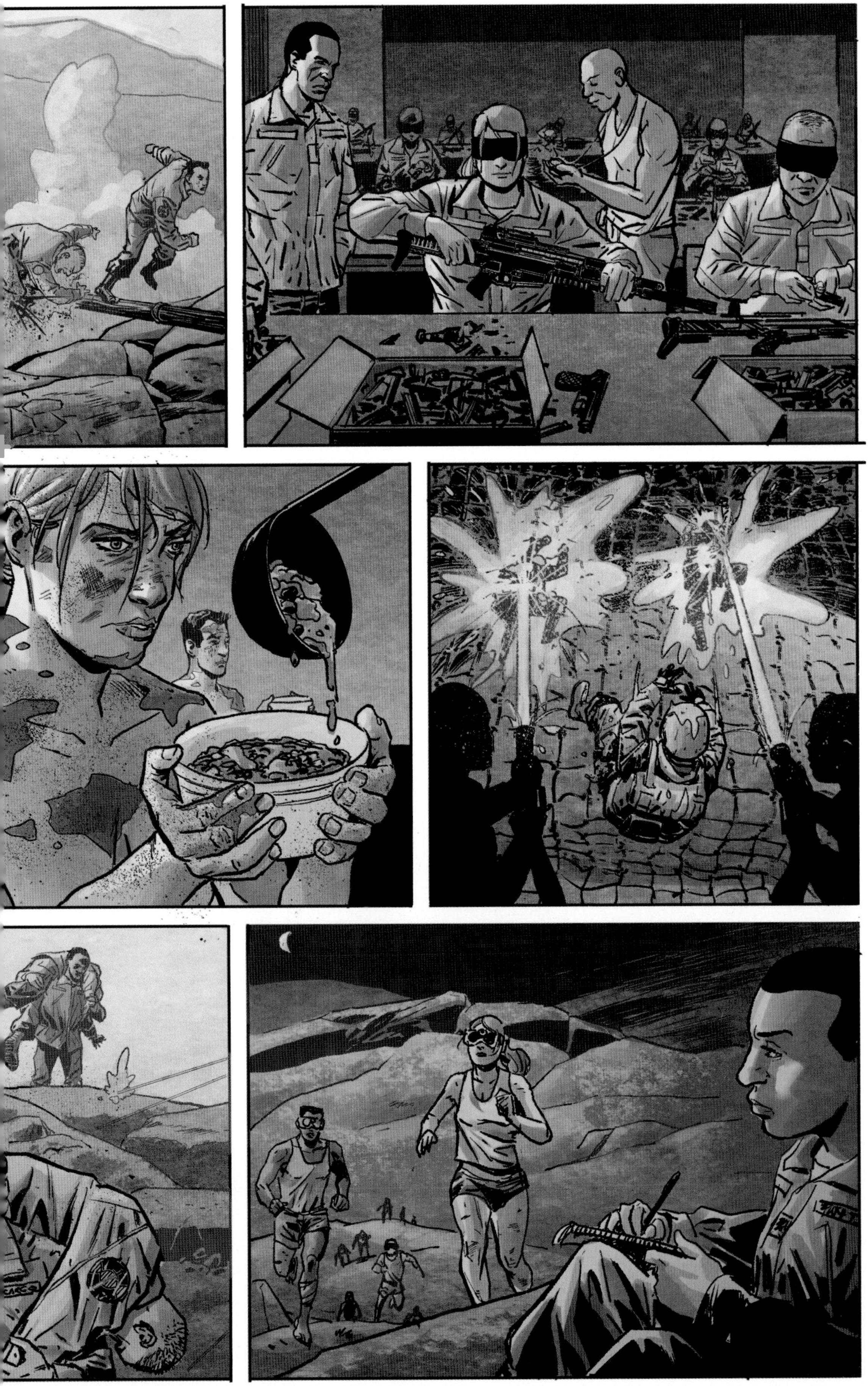

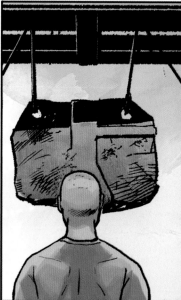

CLANG
CLANG
CLANG

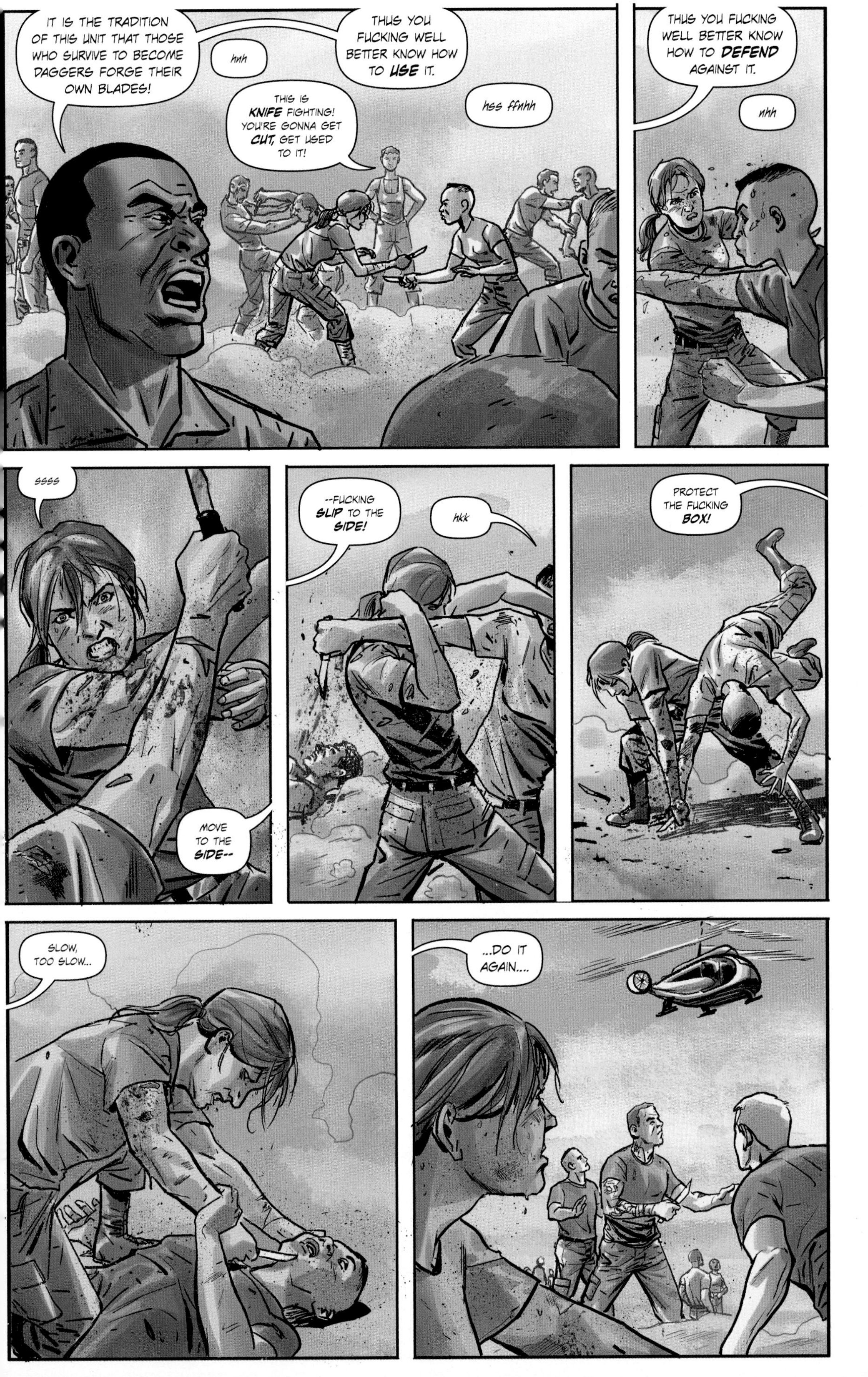
IT IS THE TRADITION OF THIS UNIT THAT THOSE WHO SURVIVE TO BECOME DAGGERS FORGE THEIR OWN BLADES!
hnh
THUS YOU FUCKING WELL BETTER KNOW HOW TO USE IT.
THIS IS KNIFE FIGHTING! YOU'RE GONNA GET CUT, GET USED TO IT!
hss ffnhh
THUS YOU FUCKING WELL BETTER KNOW HOW TO DEFEND AGAINST IT.
nhh
ssss
MOVE TO THE SIDE--
--FUCKING SLIP TO THE SIDE!
hkk
PROTECT THE FUCKING BOX!
SLOW, TOO SLOW...
...DO IT AGAIN....

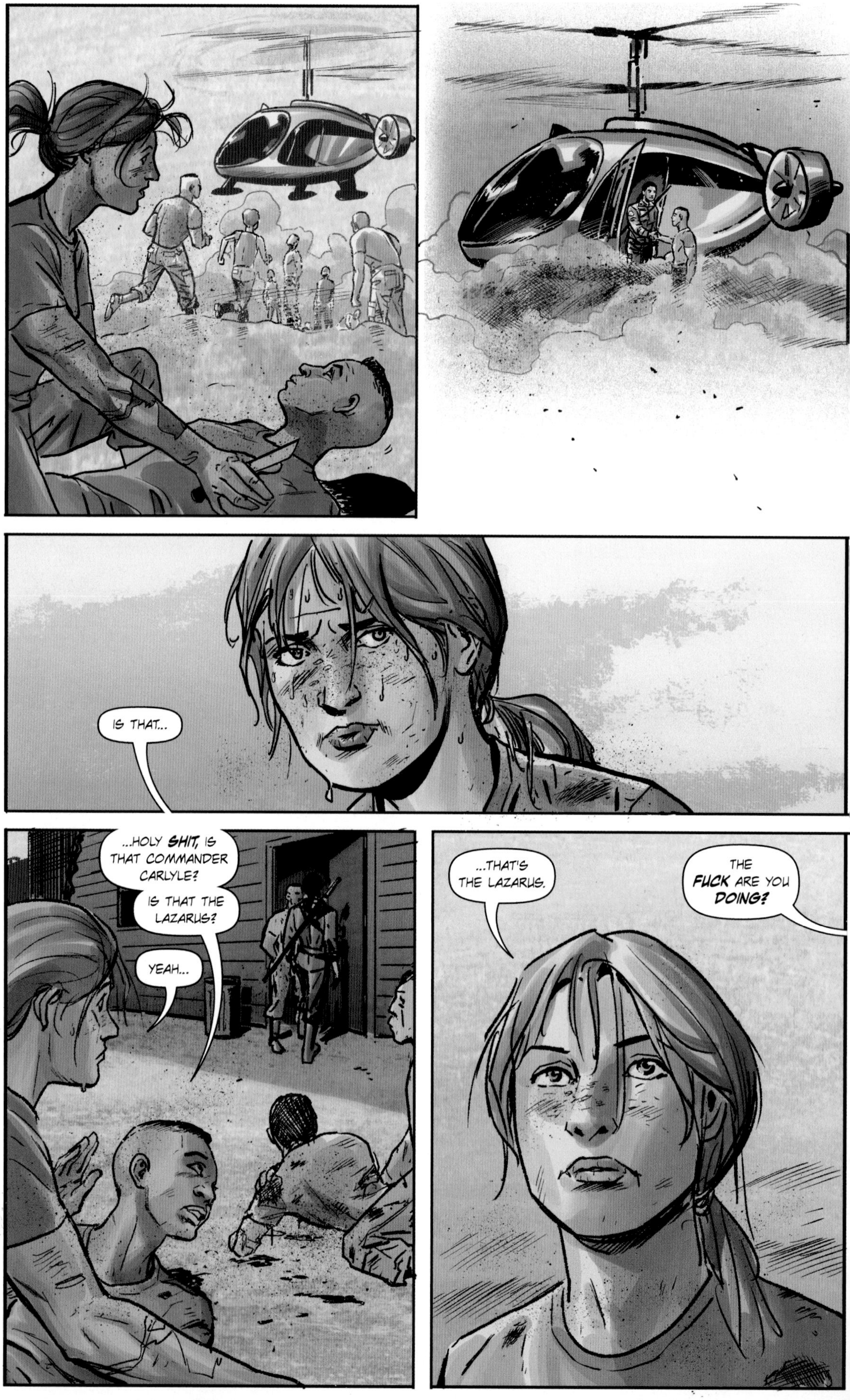
IS THAT...
...HOLY SHIT, IS THAT COMMANDER CARLYLE?
IS THAT THE LAZARUS?
YEAH...
...THAT'S THE LAZARUS.
THE FUCK ARE YOU DOING?

THE **FUCK** ARE YOU **FUCKING** DOING?

COMPLETING THE ASSIGNED TASK, SERGEANT HACKETT!

MY VISION MUST BE FUCKING **FAILING,** I AM **BLESSED** THAT YOU'RE HERE TO BE MY **EYES,** CANDIDATE CERVANTES! YOU WERE COMPLETING THE ASSIGNED TASK!

I AM **RELIEVED...**

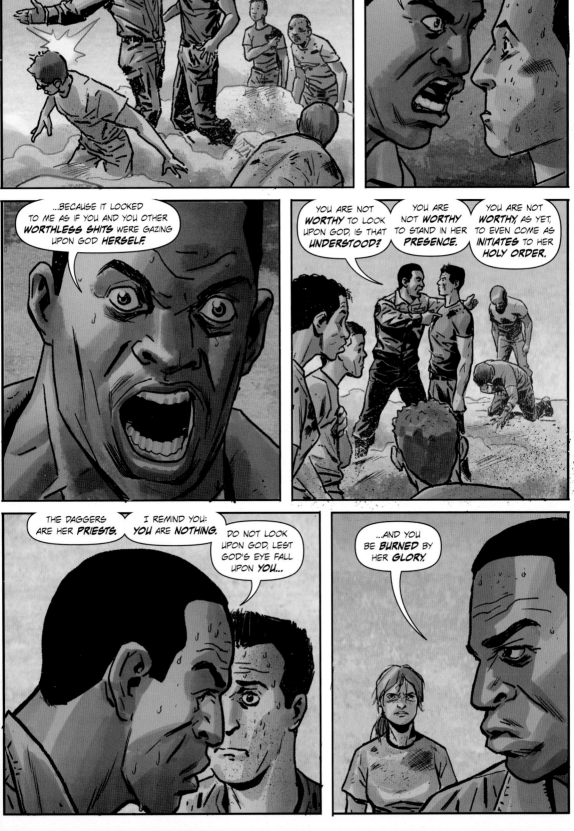

...BECAUSE IT LOOKED TO ME AS IF YOU AND YOU OTHER **WORTHLESS SHITS** WERE GAZING UPON GOD **HERSELF.**

YOU ARE NOT **WORTHY** TO LOOK UPON GOD, IS THAT **UNDERSTOOD?**

YOU ARE NOT **WORTHY** TO STAND IN HER **PRESENCE.**

YOU ARE NOT **WORTHY,** AS YET, TO EVEN COME AS **INITIATES** TO HER **HOLY ORDER.**

THE DAGGERS ARE HER **PRIESTS.**

I REMIND YOU: **YOU** ARE **NOTHING.**

DO NOT LOOK UPON GOD, LEST GOD'S EYE FALL UPON **YOU...**

...AND YOU BE **BURNED** BY HER **GLORY.**

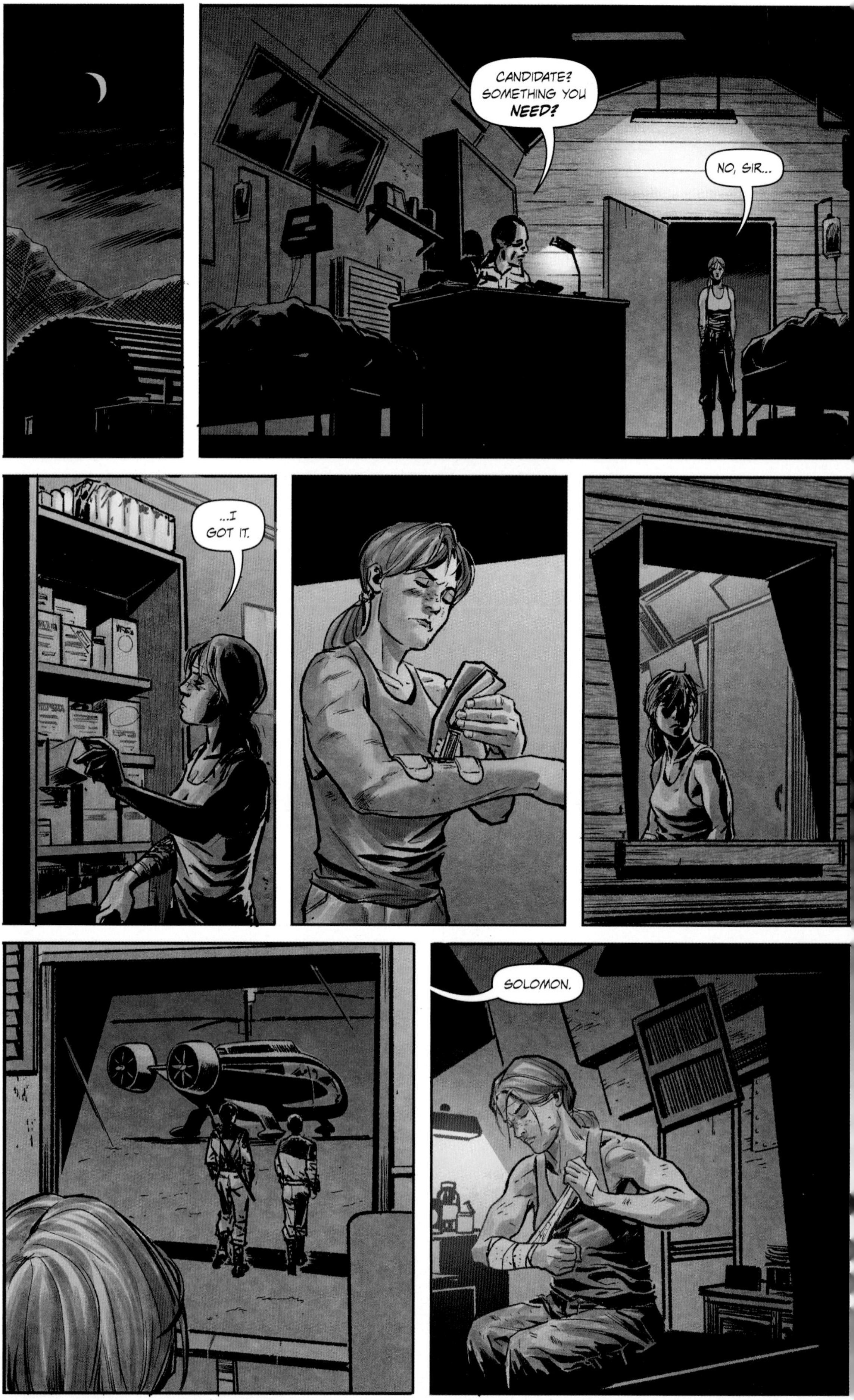
CANDIDATE? SOMETHING YOU NEED?
NO, SIR...
...I GOT IT.
SOLOMON.

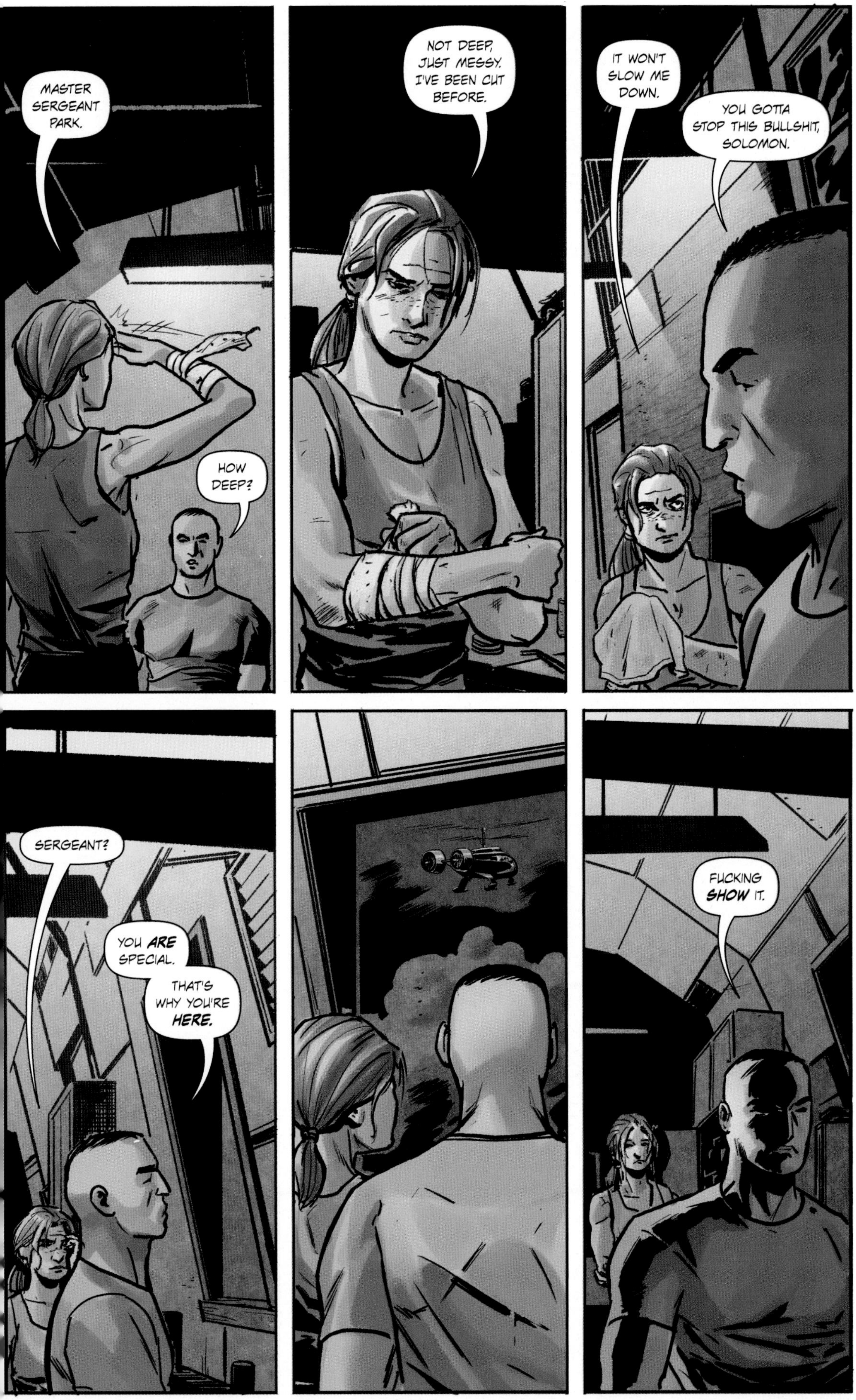
MASTER SERGEANT PARK.
HOW DEEP?
NOT DEEP, JUST MESSY. I'VE BEEN CUT BEFORE.
IT WON'T SLOW ME DOWN.
YOU GOTTA STOP THIS BULLSHIT, SOLOMON.
SERGEANT?
YOU **ARE** SPECIAL.
THAT'S WHY YOU'RE **HERE.**
FUCKING **SHOW** IT.

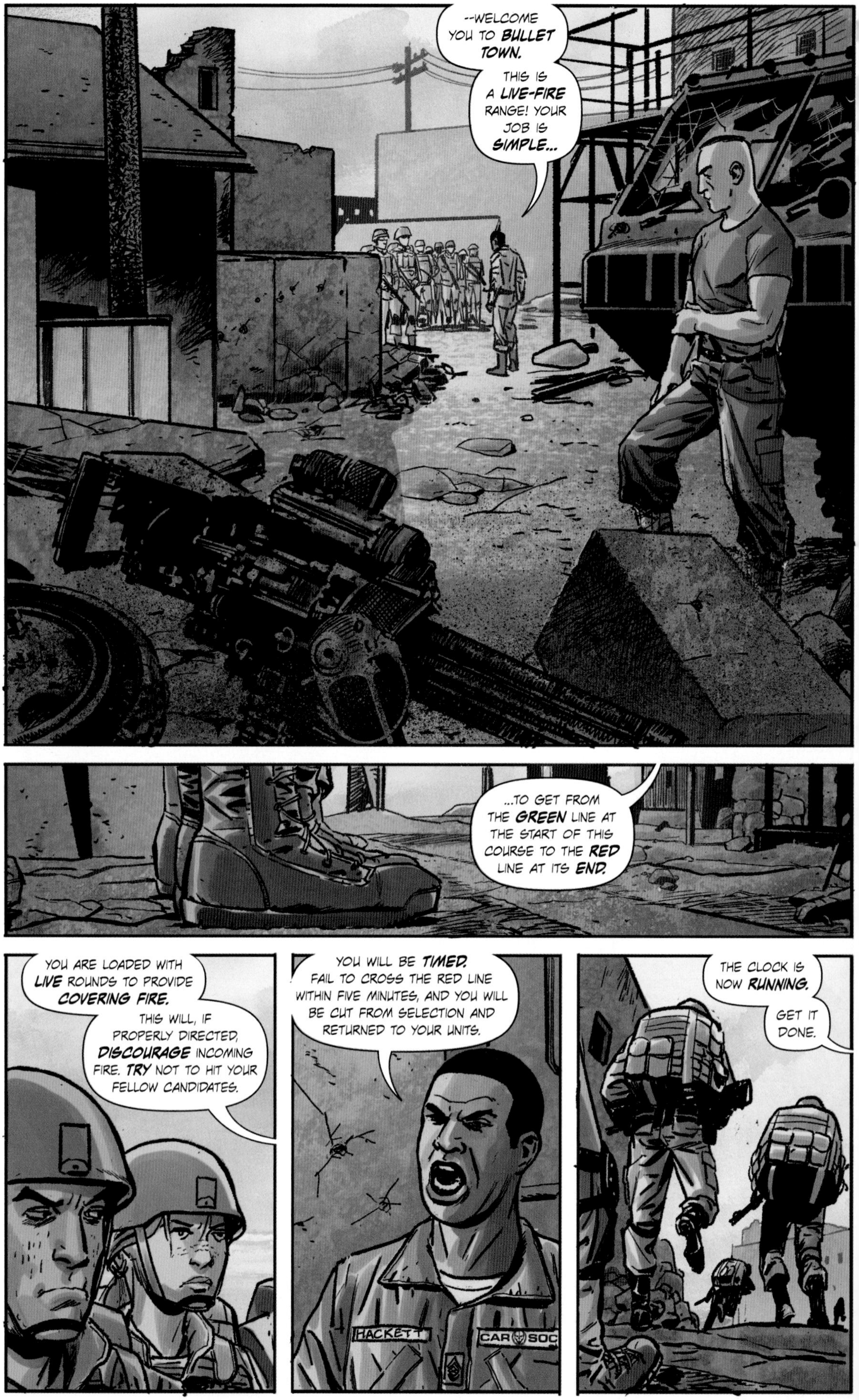
--WELCOME YOU TO BULLET TOWN.
THIS IS A LIVE-FIRE RANGE! YOUR JOB IS SIMPLE...
...TO GET FROM THE GREEN LINE AT THE START OF THIS COURSE TO THE RED LINE AT ITS END.
YOU ARE LOADED WITH LIVE ROUNDS TO PROVIDE COVERING FIRE.
THIS WILL, IF PROPERLY DIRECTED, DISCOURAGE INCOMING FIRE. TRY NOT TO HIT YOUR FELLOW CANDIDATES.
YOU WILL BE TIMED. FAIL TO CROSS THE RED LINE WITHIN FIVE MINUTES, AND YOU WILL BE CUT FROM SELECTION AND RETURNED TO YOUR UNITS.
HACKETT
CAR SOC
THE CLOCK IS NOW RUNNING.
GET IT DONE.

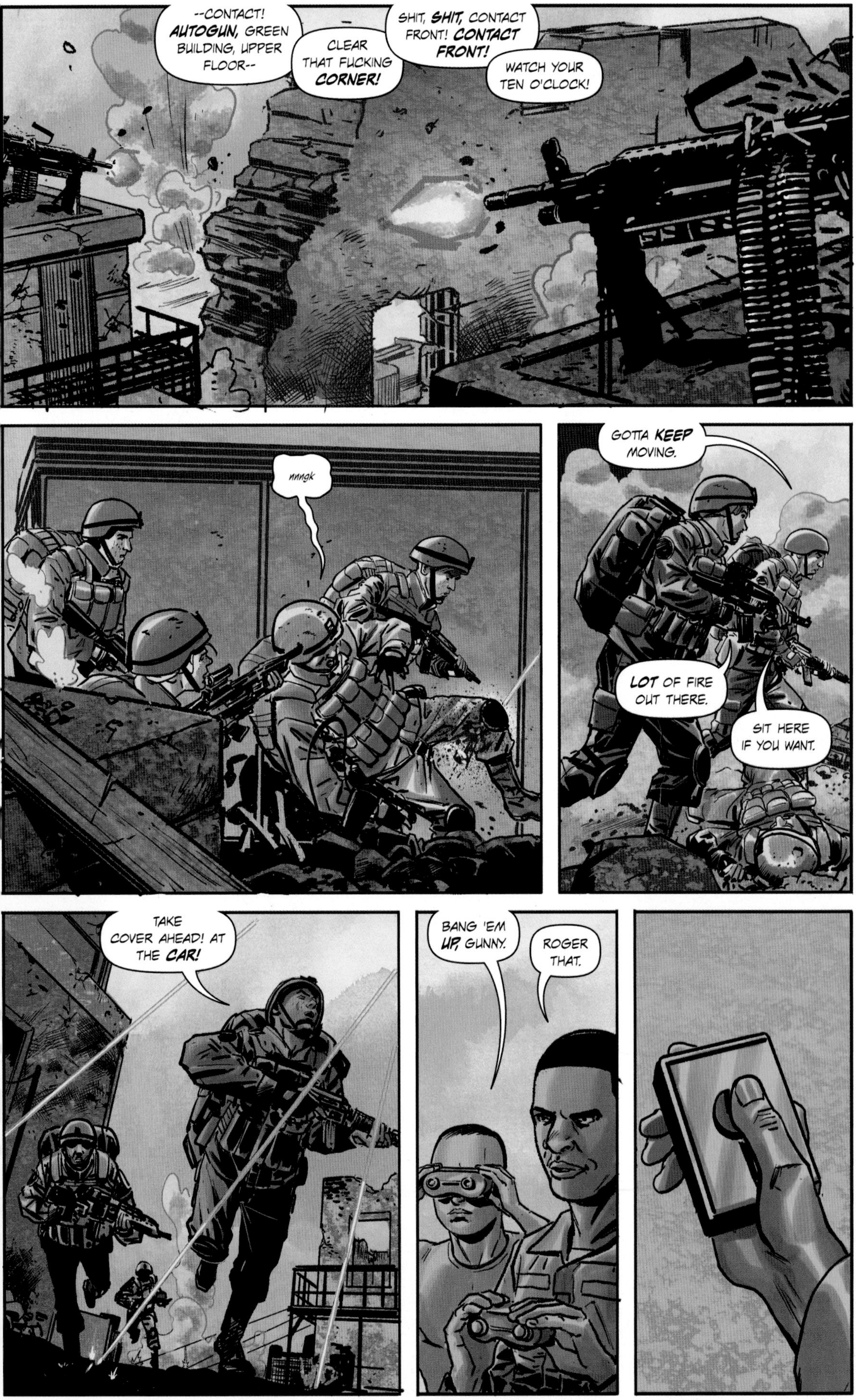
--CONTACT! AUTOGUN, GREEN BUILDING, UPPER FLOOR--
CLEAR THAT FUCKING CORNER!
SHIT, SHIT, CONTACT FRONT! CONTACT FRONT!
WATCH YOUR TEN O'CLOCK!
nnngk
GOTTA KEEP MOVING.
LOT OF FIRE OUT THERE.
SIT HERE IF YOU WANT.
TAKE COVER AHEAD! AT THE CAR!
BANG 'EM UP, GUNNY.
ROGER THAT.

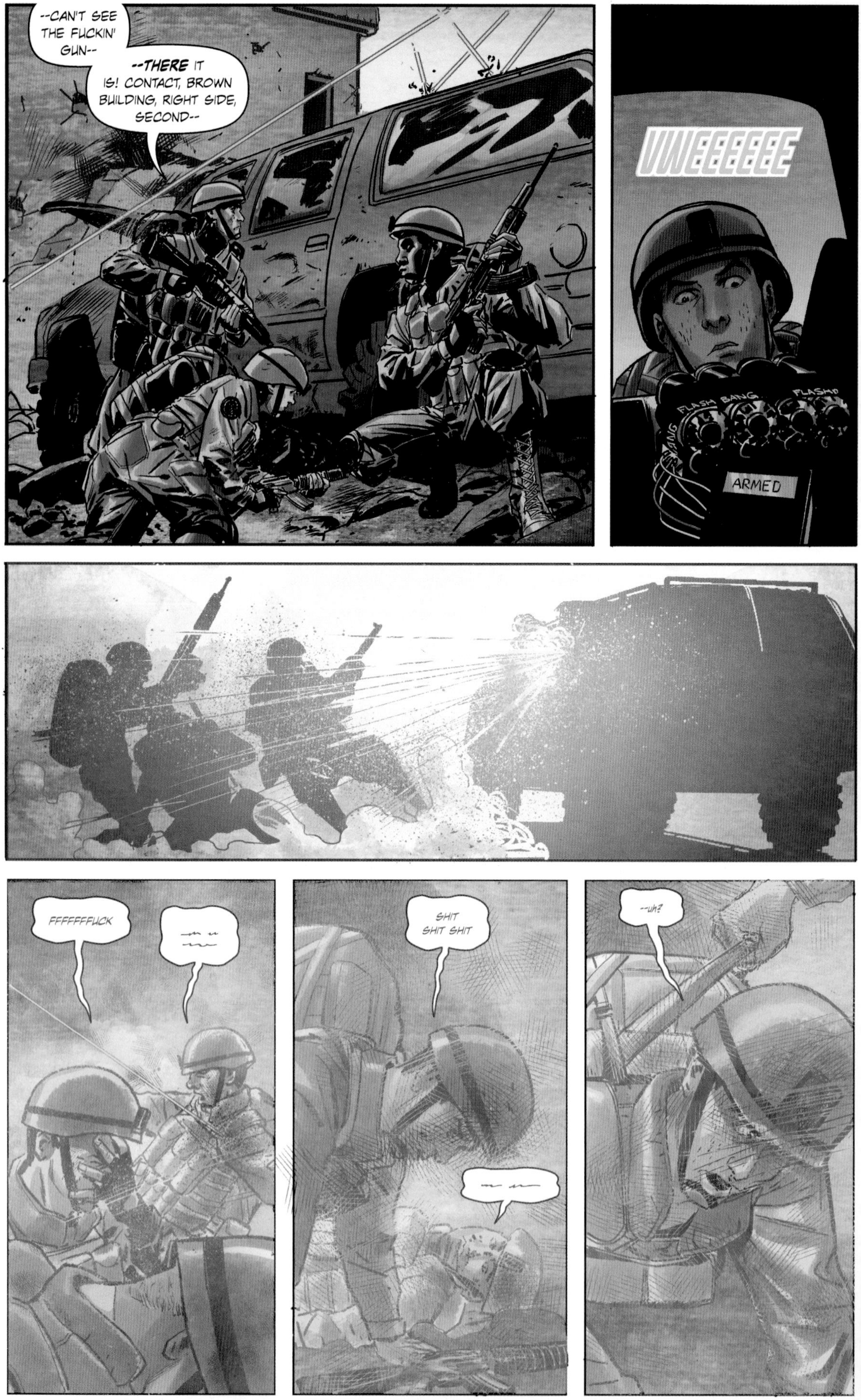
--CAN'T SEE THE FUCKIN' GUN--
--THERE IT IS! CONTACT, BROWN BUILDING, RIGHT SIDE, SECOND--
VWEEEEEE
FLASH BANG
ARMED
FFFFFFFUCK
SHIT SHIT SHIT
--uh?

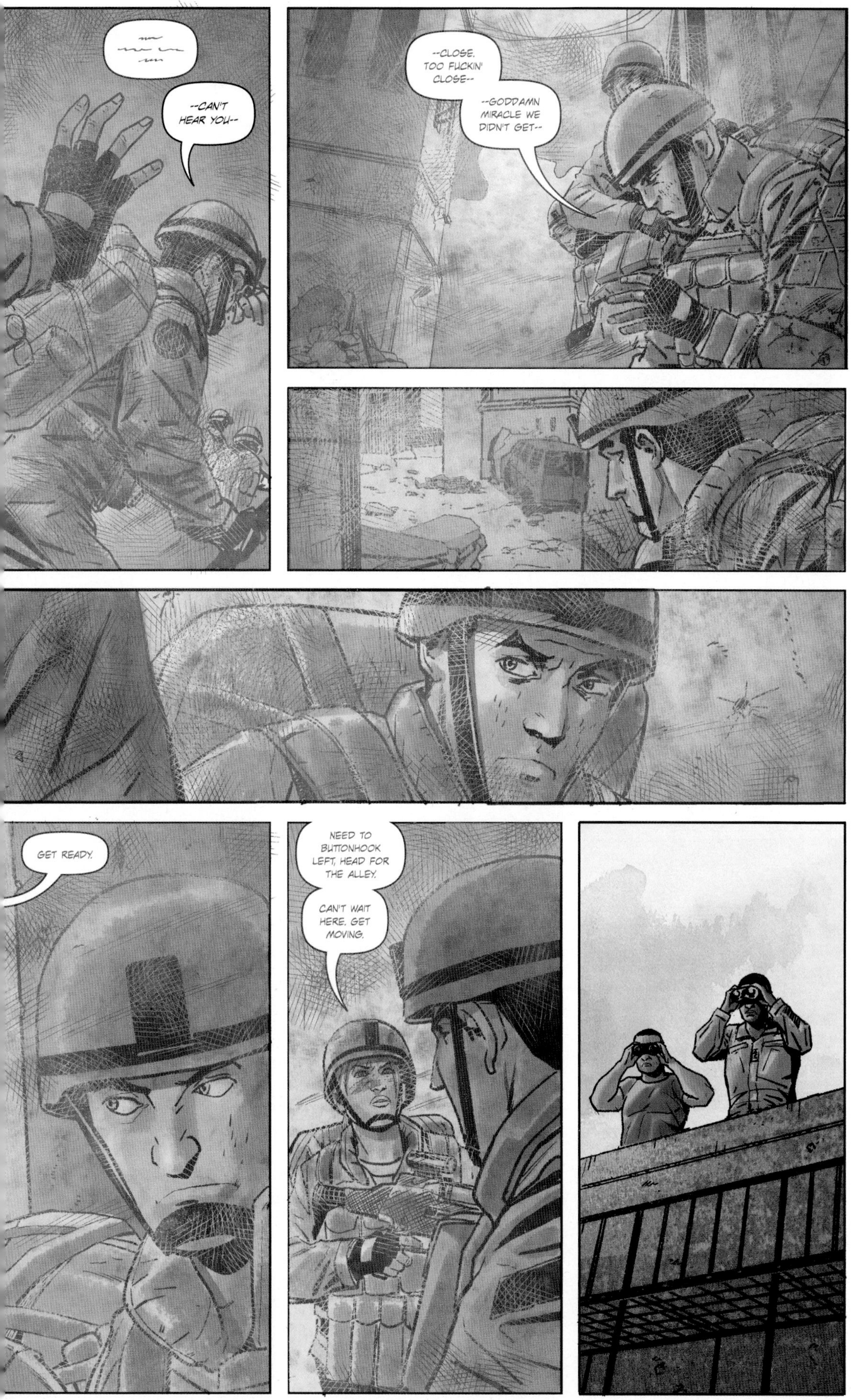
--CAN'T HEAR YOU--
--CLOSE. TOO FUCKIN' CLOSE--
--GODDAMN MIRACLE WE DIDN'T GET--
GET READY.
NEED TO BUTTONHOOK LEFT, HEAD FOR THE ALLEY.
CAN'T WAIT HERE. GET MOVING.

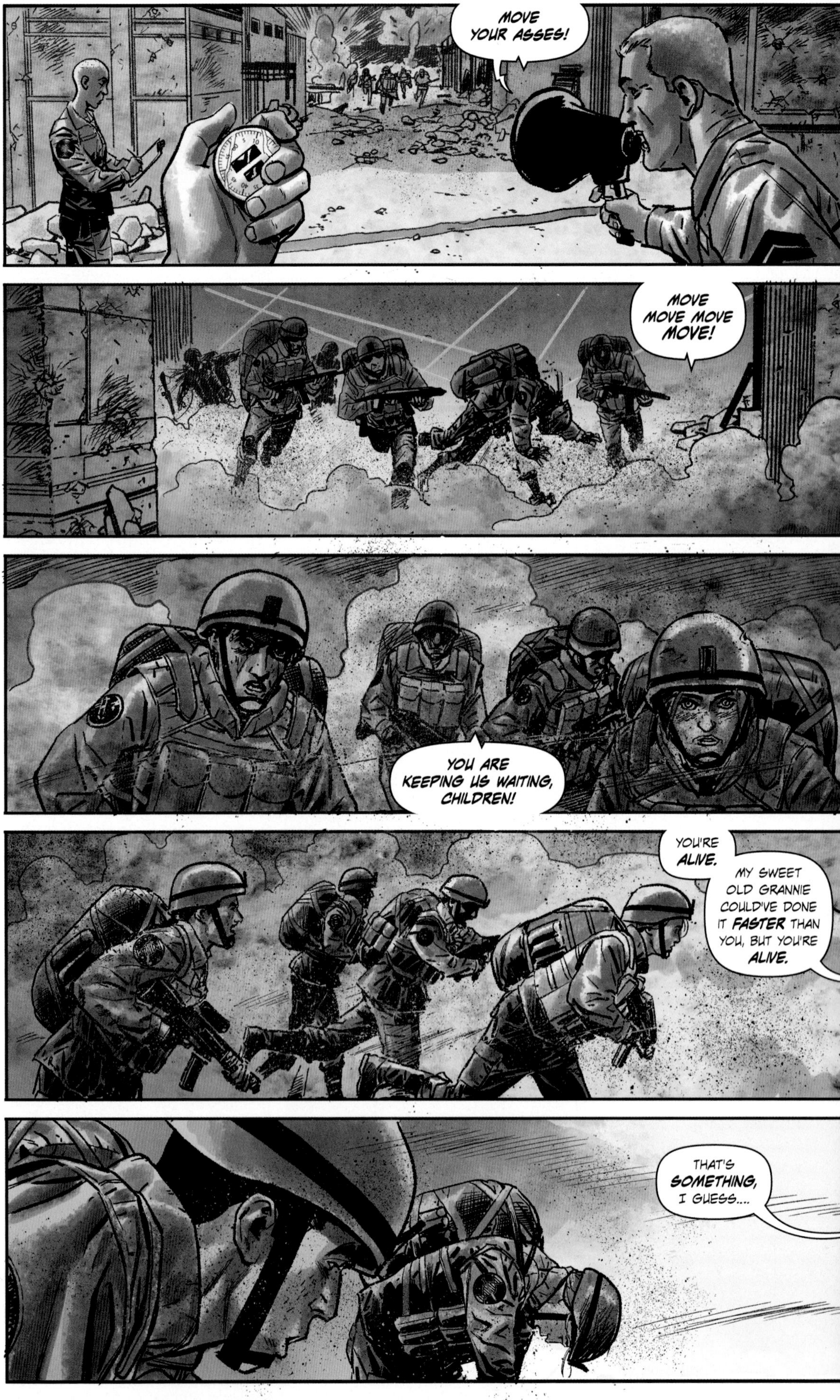
MOVE YOUR ASSES!
MOVE MOVE MOVE MOVE!
YOU ARE KEEPING US WAITING, CHILDREN!
YOU'RE ALIVE.
MY SWEET OLD GRANNIE COULD'VE DONE IT FASTER THAN YOU, BUT YOU'RE ALIVE.
THAT'S SOMETHING, I GUESS....

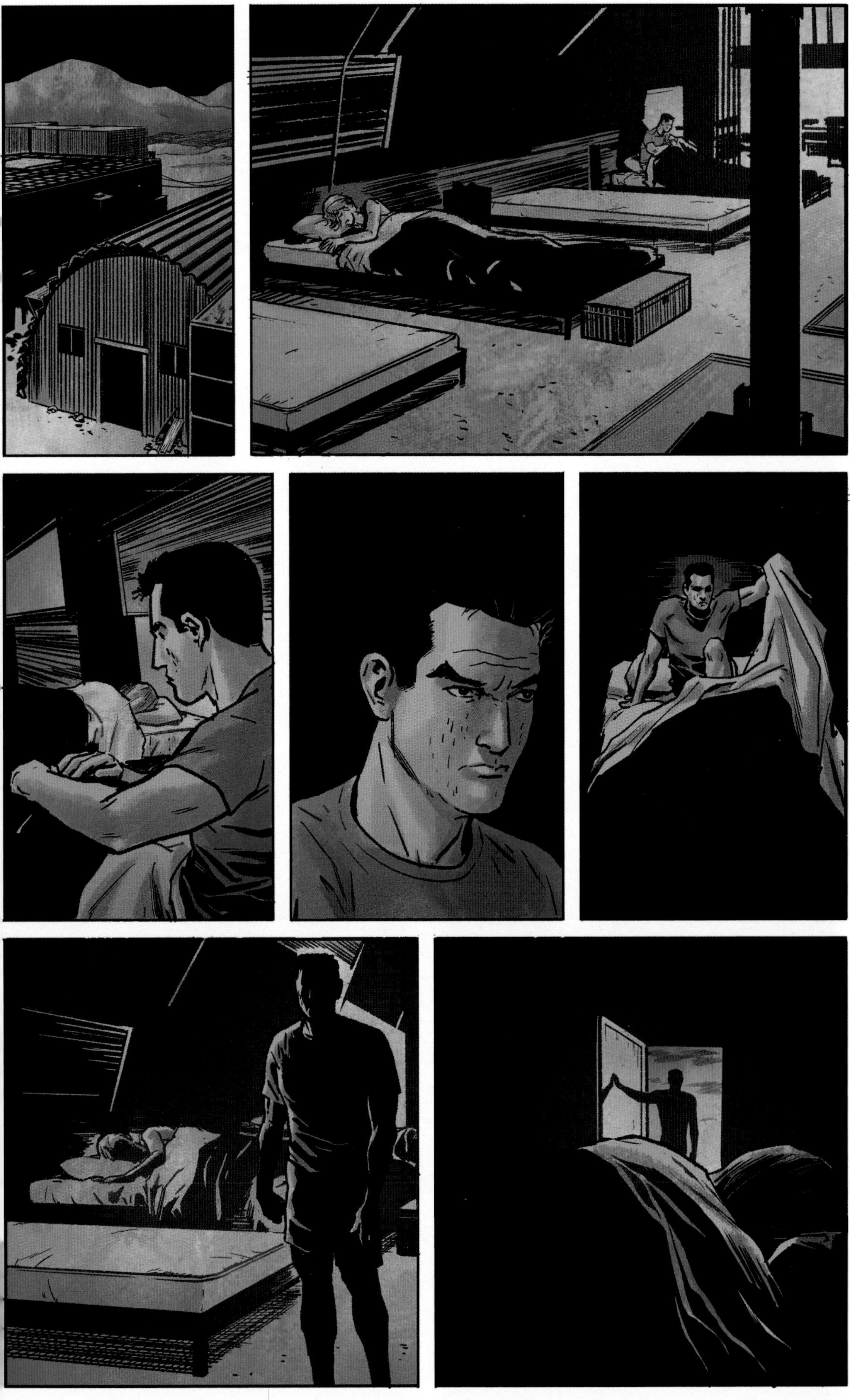

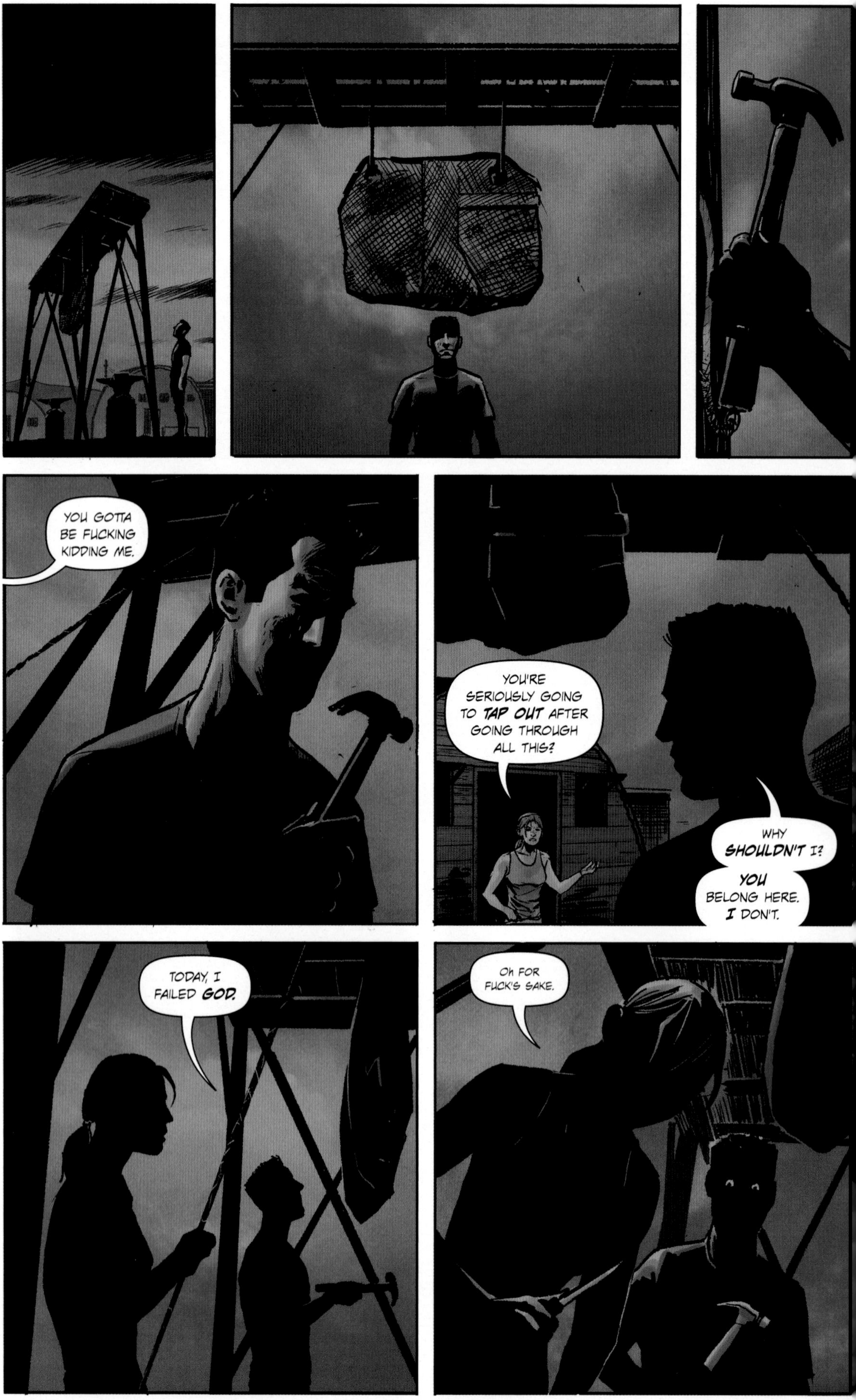
YOU GOTTA BE FUCKING KIDDING ME.
YOU'RE SERIOUSLY GOING TO TAP OUT AFTER GOING THROUGH ALL THIS?
WHY SHOULDN'T I?
YOU BELONG HERE. I DON'T.
TODAY, I FAILED GOD.
Oh FOR FUCK'S SAKE.

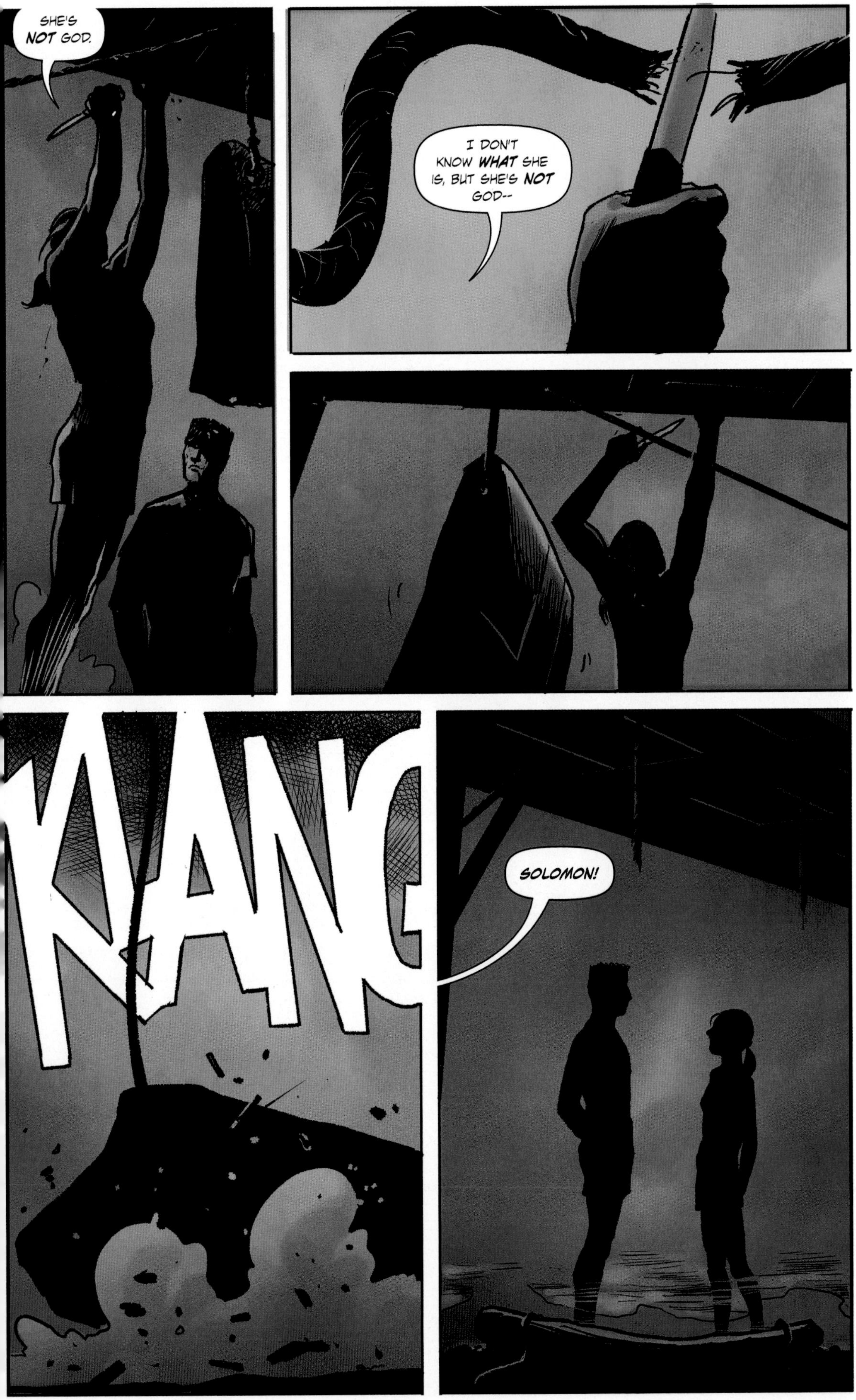
SHE'S NOT GOD.
I DON'T KNOW WHAT SHE IS, BUT SHE'S NOT GOD--
KLANG
SOLOMON!

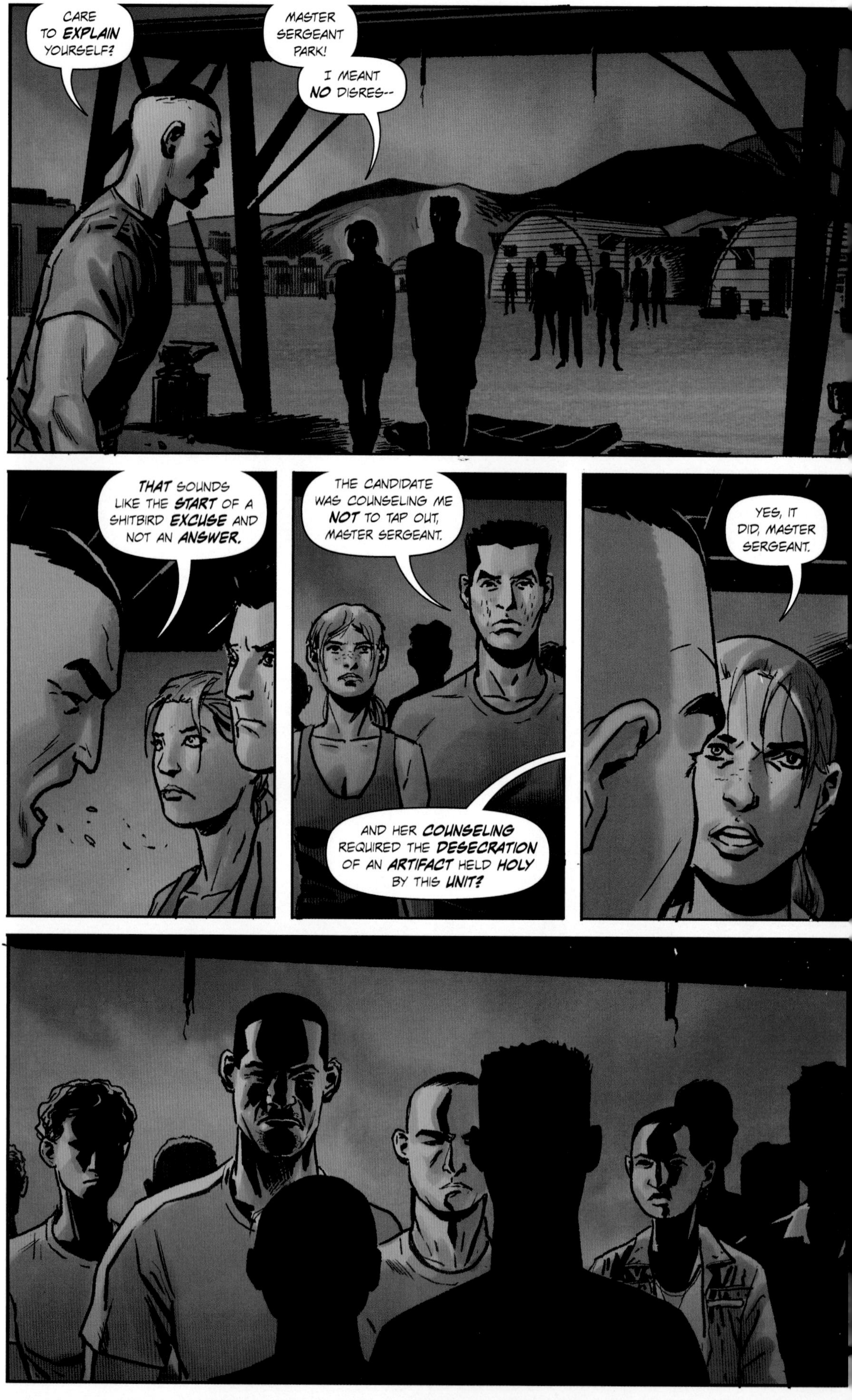
CARE TO EXPLAIN YOURSELF?
MASTER SERGEANT PARK!
I MEANT NO DISRES--
THAT SOUNDS LIKE THE START OF A SHITBIRD EXCUSE AND NOT AN ANSWER.
THE CANDIDATE WAS COUNSELING ME NOT TO TAP OUT, MASTER SERGEANT.
AND HER COUNSELING REQUIRED THE DESECRATION OF AN ARTIFACT HELD HOLY BY THIS UNIT?
YES, IT DID, MASTER SERGEANT.

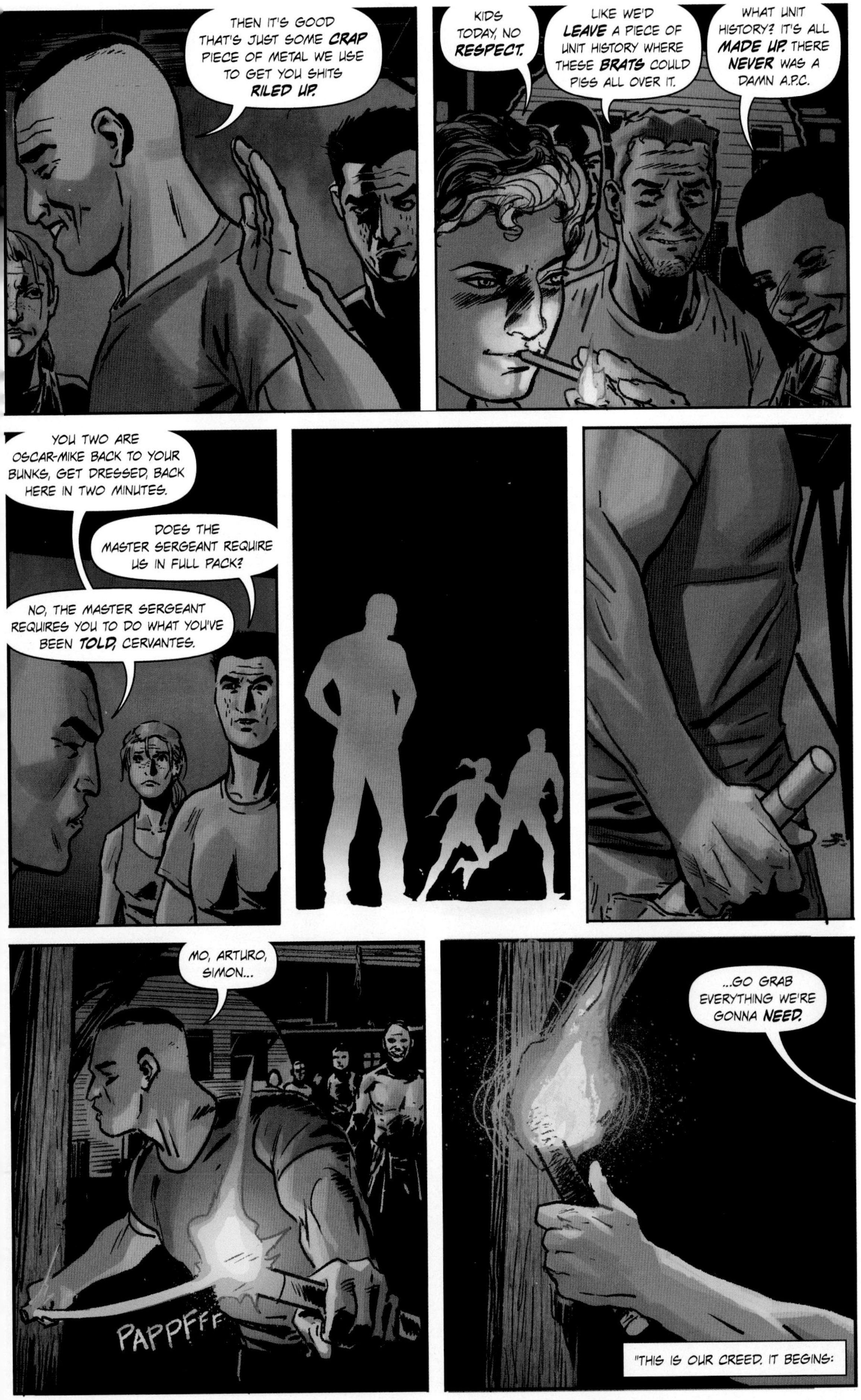
THEN IT'S GOOD THAT'S JUST SOME CRAP PIECE OF METAL WE USE TO GET YOU SHITS RILED UP.
KIDS TODAY, NO RESPECT.
LIKE WE'D LEAVE A PIECE OF UNIT HISTORY WHERE THESE BRATS COULD PISS ALL OVER IT.
WHAT UNIT HISTORY? IT'S ALL MADE UP. THERE NEVER WAS A DAMN A.P.C.
YOU TWO ARE OSCAR-MIKE BACK TO YOUR BUNKS, GET DRESSED, BACK HERE IN TWO MINUTES.
DOES THE MASTER SERGEANT REQUIRE US IN FULL PACK?
NO, THE MASTER SERGEANT REQUIRES YOU TO DO WHAT YOU'VE BEEN TOLD, CERVANTES.
MO, ARTURO, SIMON...
PAPPFFF
...GO GRAB EVERYTHING WE'RE GONNA NEED.
"THIS IS OUR CREED. IT BEGINS:

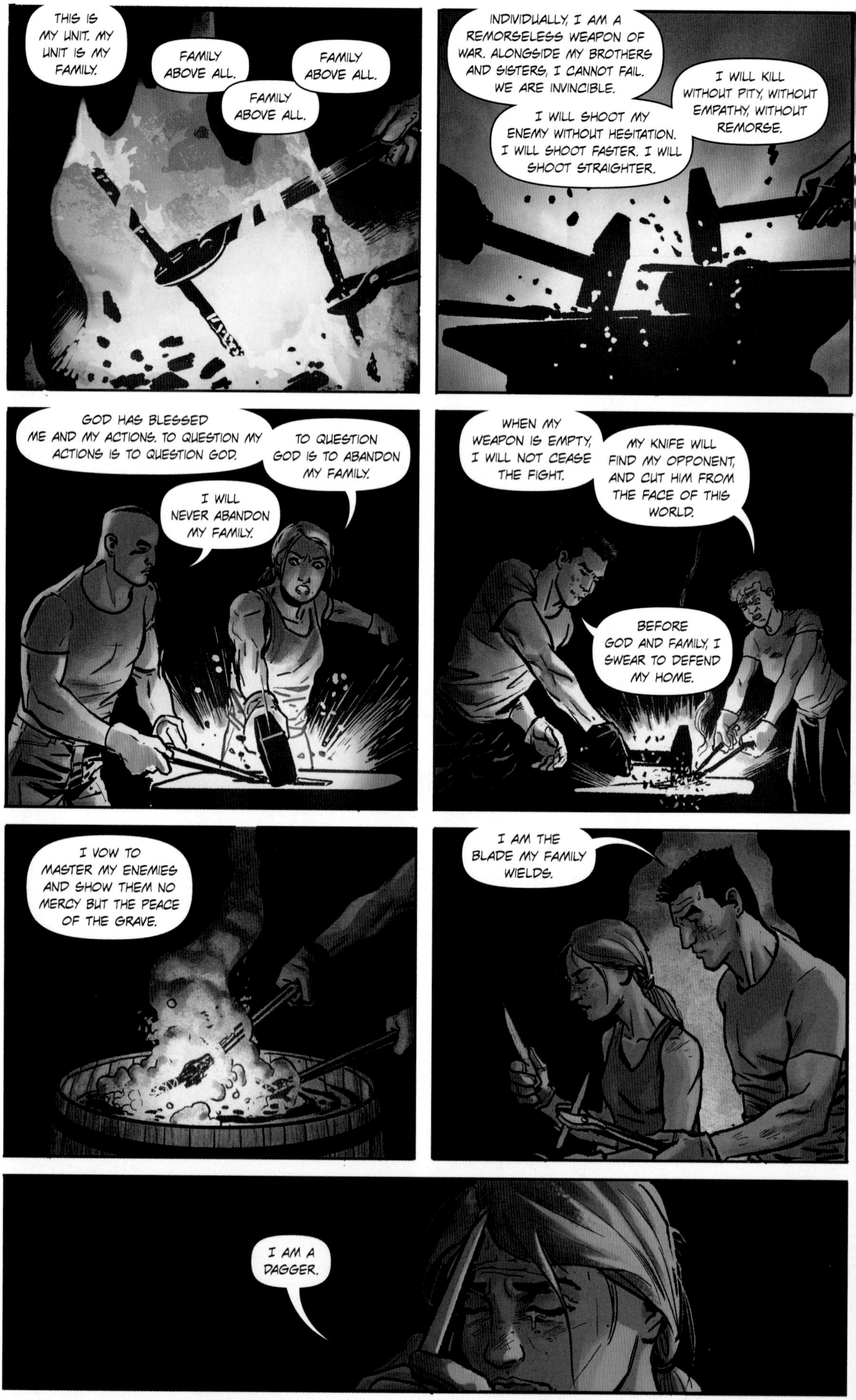

THIS IS MY UNIT. MY UNIT IS MY FAMILY.
FAMILY ABOVE ALL.
FAMILY ABOVE ALL.
FAMILY ABOVE ALL.
INDIVIDUALLY, I AM A REMORSELESS WEAPON OF WAR. ALONGSIDE MY BROTHERS AND SISTERS, I CANNOT FAIL. WE ARE INVINCIBLE.
I WILL SHOOT MY ENEMY WITHOUT HESITATION. I WILL SHOOT FASTER. I WILL SHOOT STRAIGHTER.
I WILL KILL WITHOUT PITY, WITHOUT EMPATHY, WITHOUT REMORSE.
GOD HAS BLESSED ME AND MY ACTIONS. TO QUESTION MY ACTIONS IS TO QUESTION GOD.
TO QUESTION GOD IS TO ABANDON MY FAMILY.
I WILL NEVER ABANDON MY FAMILY.
WHEN MY WEAPON IS EMPTY, I WILL NOT CEASE THE FIGHT.
MY KNIFE WILL FIND MY OPPONENT, AND CUT HIM FROM THE FACE OF THIS WORLD.
BEFORE GOD AND FAMILY, I SWEAR TO DEFEND MY HOME.
I VOW TO MASTER MY ENEMIES AND SHOW THEM NO MERCY BUT THE PEACE OF THE GRAVE.
I AM THE BLADE MY FAMILY WIELDS.
I AM A DAGGER.

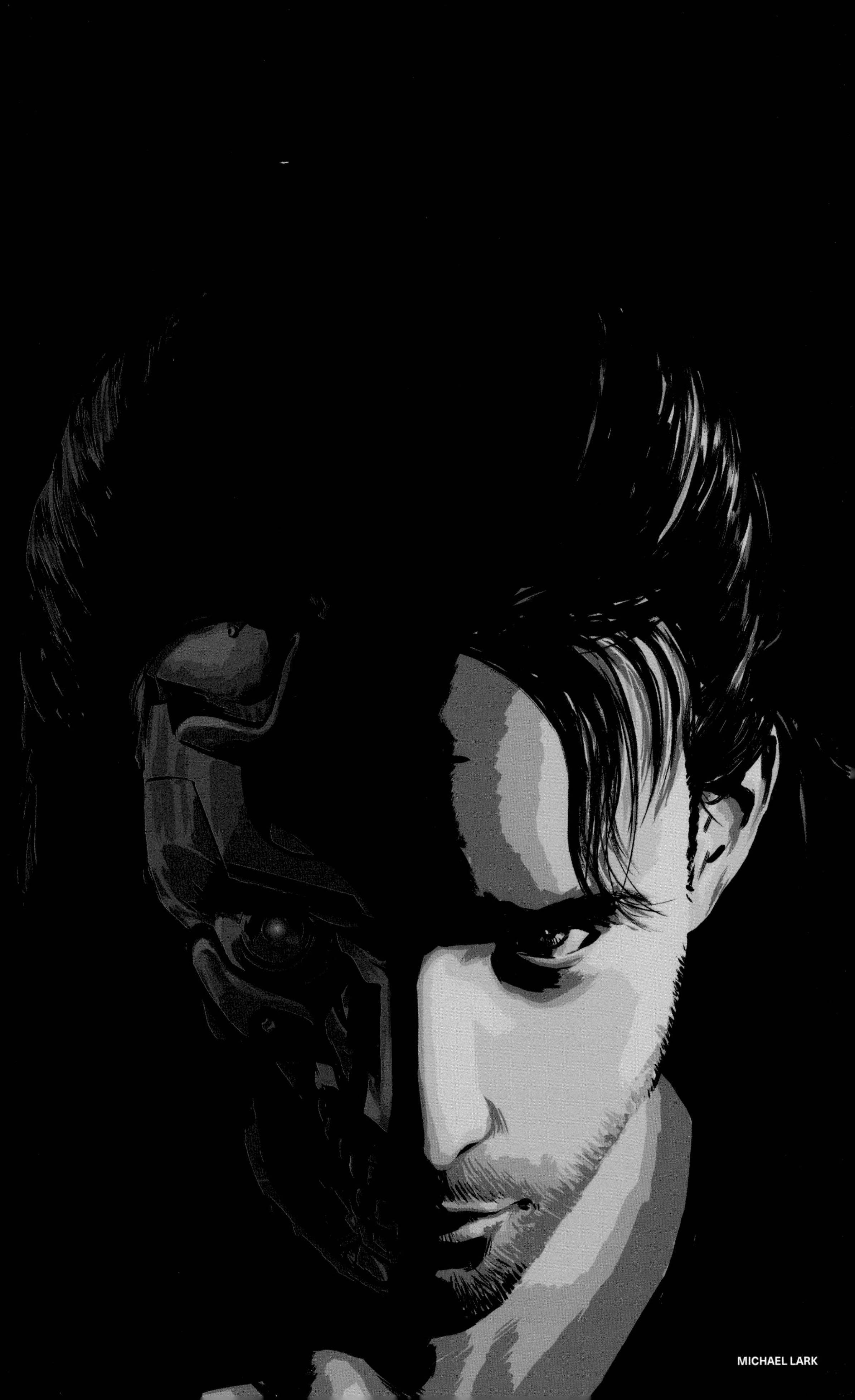

MICHAEL LARK

The Conclave War continues to rage.

One one side is the Carlyle bloc:
Carlyle, Bittner, Armitage, Nkosi, Meyers-Qasimi, and **Carragher**.

On the other side is the Hock Coalition:
Hock, Vassalovka, D'Souza, Minetta, and **Martins**.

The **Li** and **Inamura Families** remain apart, for the moment.

The **Rausling Family** is now extinct.

In X +64, the **MORRAY FAMILY** entered into an alliance with Family Carlyle.

In June of X +65, Carlyle, Armitage, Bittner, and Morray put their Lazari
into the field in an attempt to stop the Vasalovka Lazarus, **The Zmey**.

They failed, due in part to a Morray act of betrayal.

Under his Family's control, **JOACQUIM MORRAY** was
compelled to stab Forever Carlyle in the back.

It is an act that haunts him, for Forever has been more than a friend.

Now, Joacquim has returned home from Europe.

He must face the results of his actions.

He must decide what he is willing to do in service to his Family.

And his Family must decide if they can still trust their Lazarus,
and if not, determine what they are willing to do to guarantee his
loyalty and his obedience.

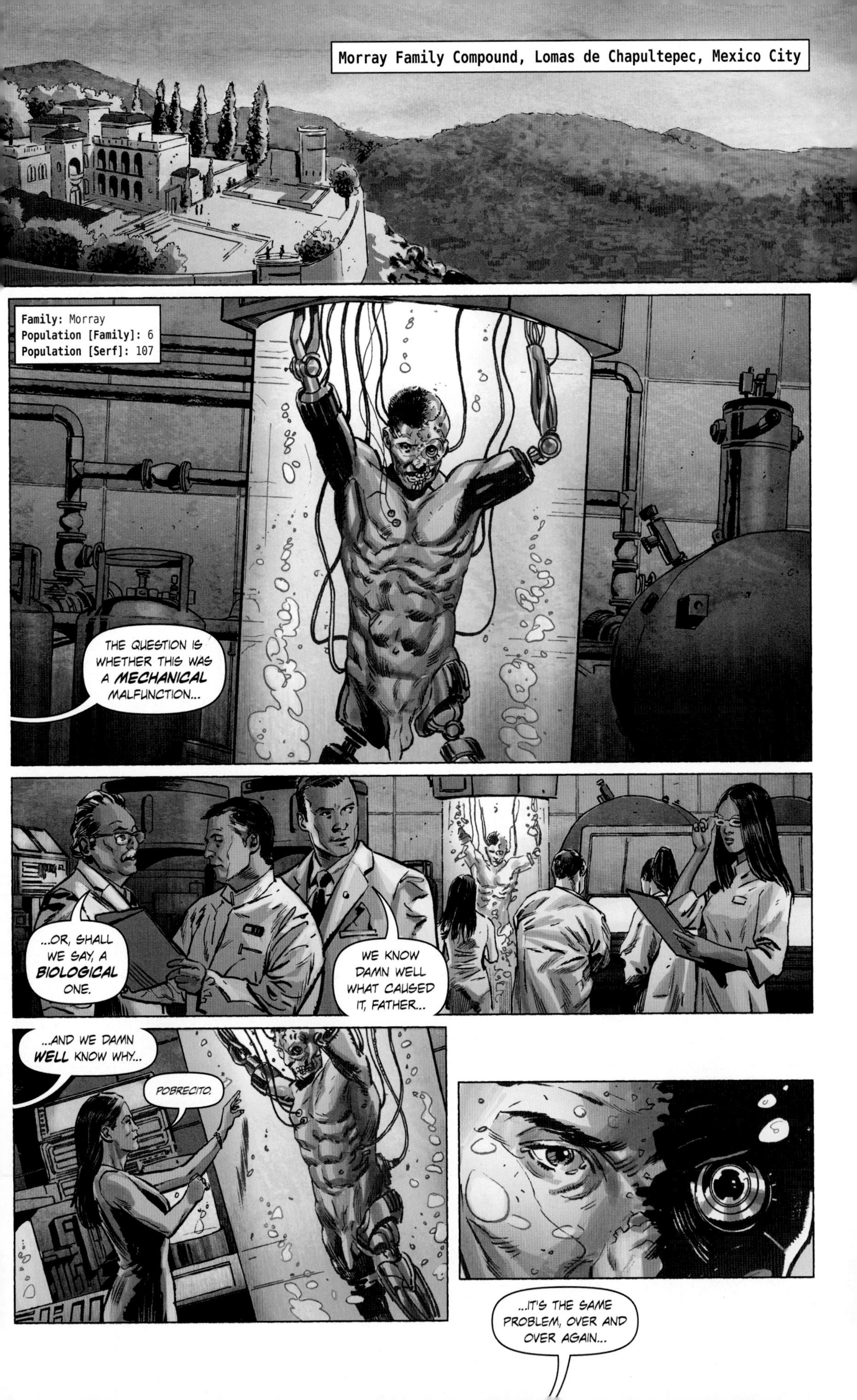
Morray Family Compound, Lomas de Chapultepec, Mexico City
Family: Morray
Population [Family]: 6
Population [Serf]: 107
THE QUESTION IS WHETHER THIS WAS A MECHANICAL MALFUNCTION...
...OR, SHALL WE SAY, A BIOLOGICAL ONE.
WE KNOW DAMN WELL WHAT CAUSED IT, FATHER...
...AND WE DAMN WELL KNOW WHY...
POBRECITO.
...IT'S THE SAME PROBLEM, OVER AND OVER AGAIN...

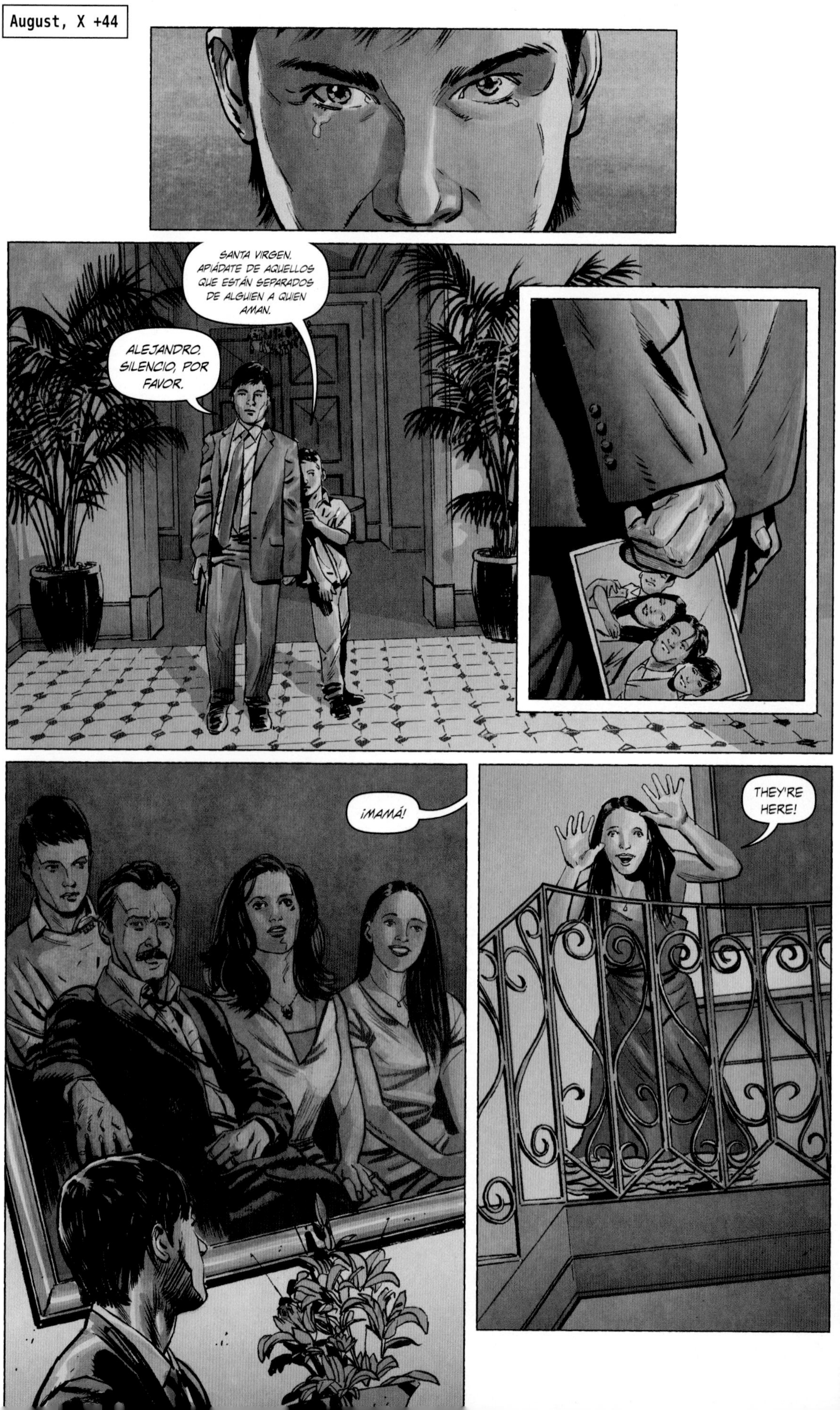
August, X +44
SANTA VIRGEN. APIÁDATE DE AQUELLOS QUE ESTÁN SEPARADOS DE ALGUIEN A QUIEN AMAN.
ALEJANDRO. SILENCIO, POR FAVOR.
¡MAMÁ!
THEY'RE HERE!

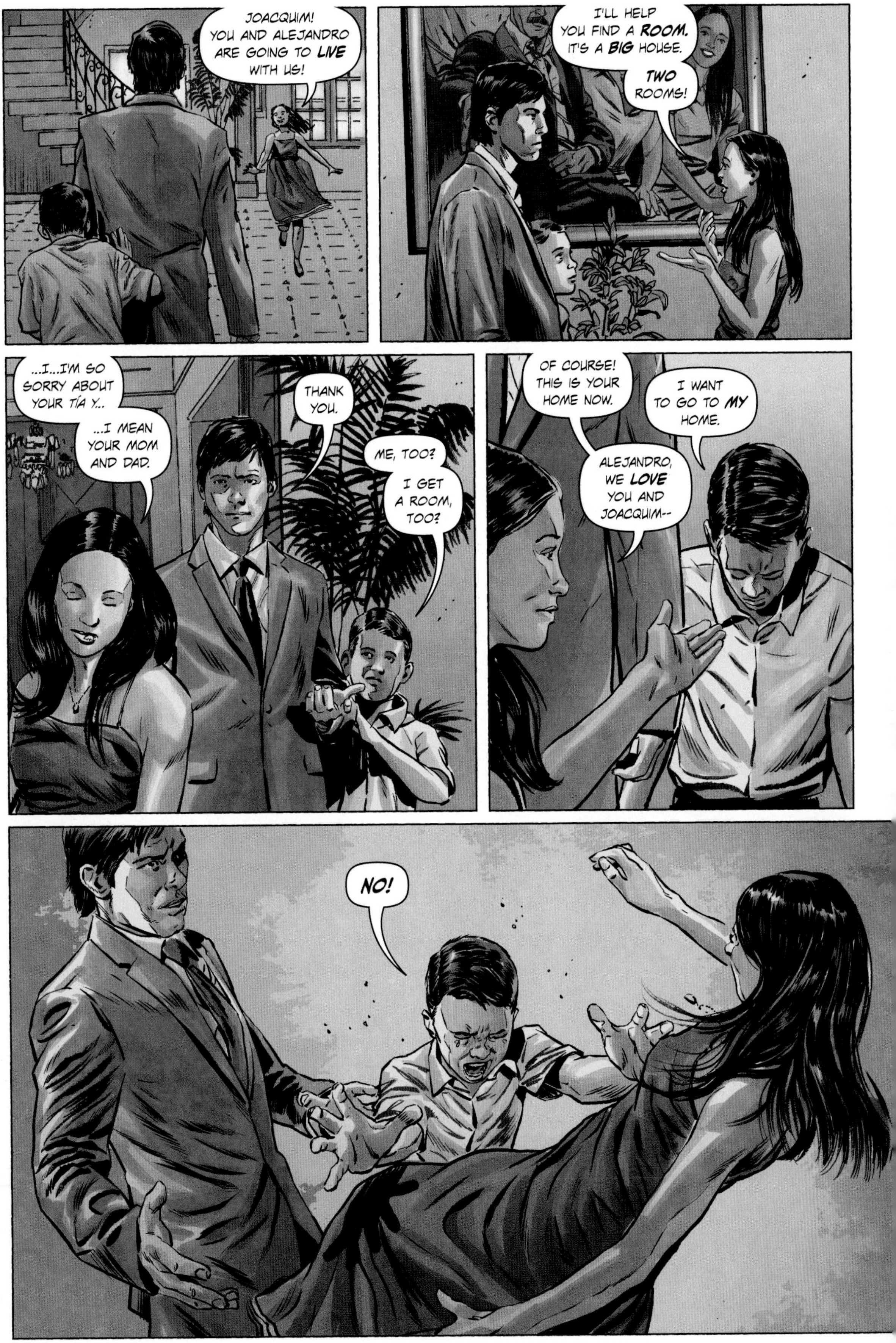
JOACQUIM! YOU AND ALEJANDRO ARE GOING TO **LIVE** WITH US!
I'LL HELP YOU FIND A **ROOM.** IT'S A **BIG** HOUSE.
TWO ROOMS!
...I...I'M SO SORRY ABOUT YOUR *TÍA Y*...
...I MEAN YOUR MOM AND DAD.
THANK YOU.
ME, TOO?
I GET A ROOM, TOO?
OF COURSE! THIS IS YOUR HOME NOW.
I WANT TO GO TO **MY** HOME.
ALEJANDRO, WE **LOVE** YOU AND JOACQUIM--
NO!

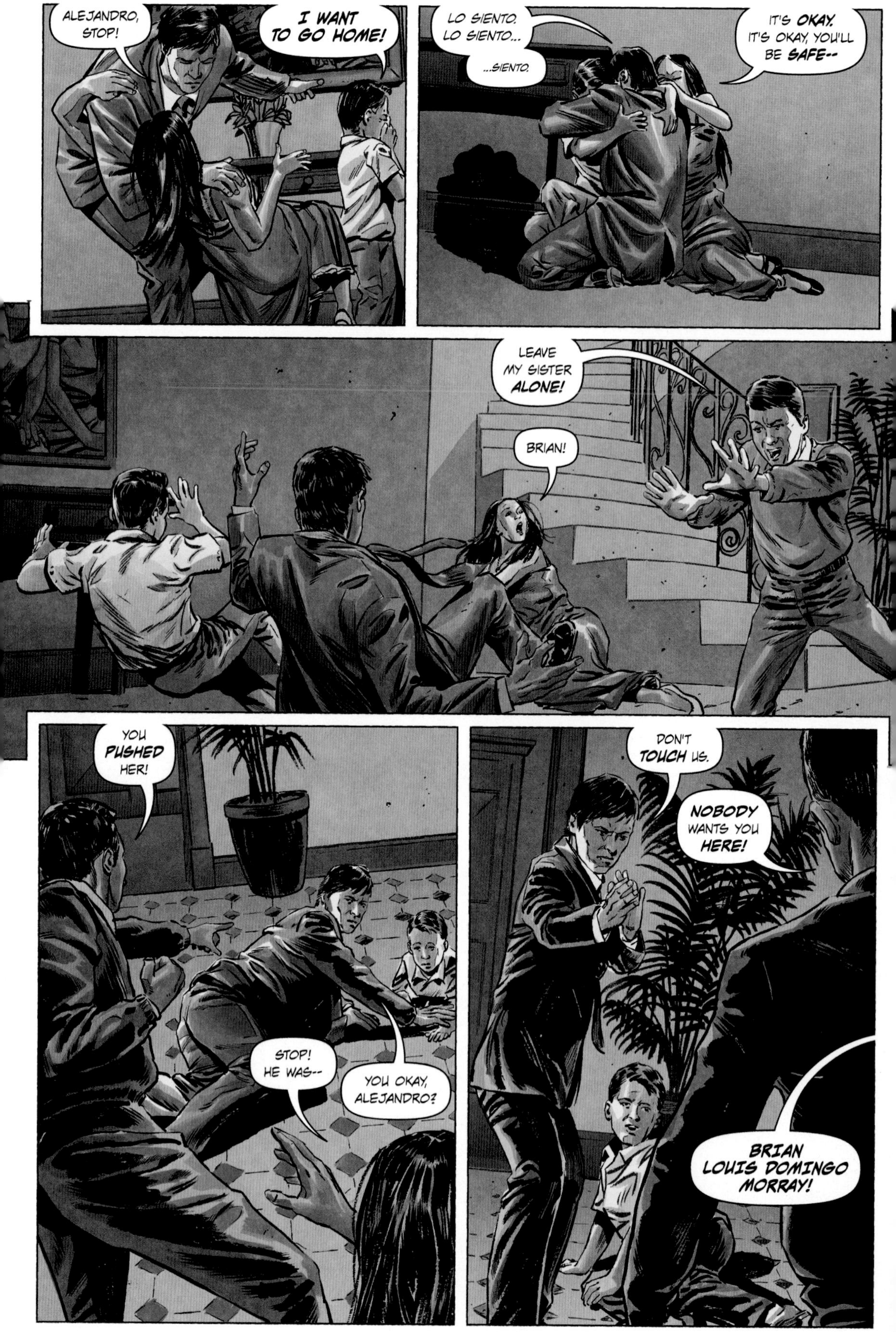
ALEJANDRO, STOP!
I WANT TO GO HOME!
LO SIENTO. LO SIENTO...
...SIENTO.
IT'S OKAY. IT'S OKAY, YOU'LL BE SAFE--
LEAVE MY SISTER ALONE!
BRIAN!
YOU PUSHED HER!
STOP! HE WAS--
YOU OKAY, ALEJANDRO?
DON'T TOUCH US.
NOBODY WANTS YOU HERE!
BRIAN LOUIS DOMINGO MORRAY!

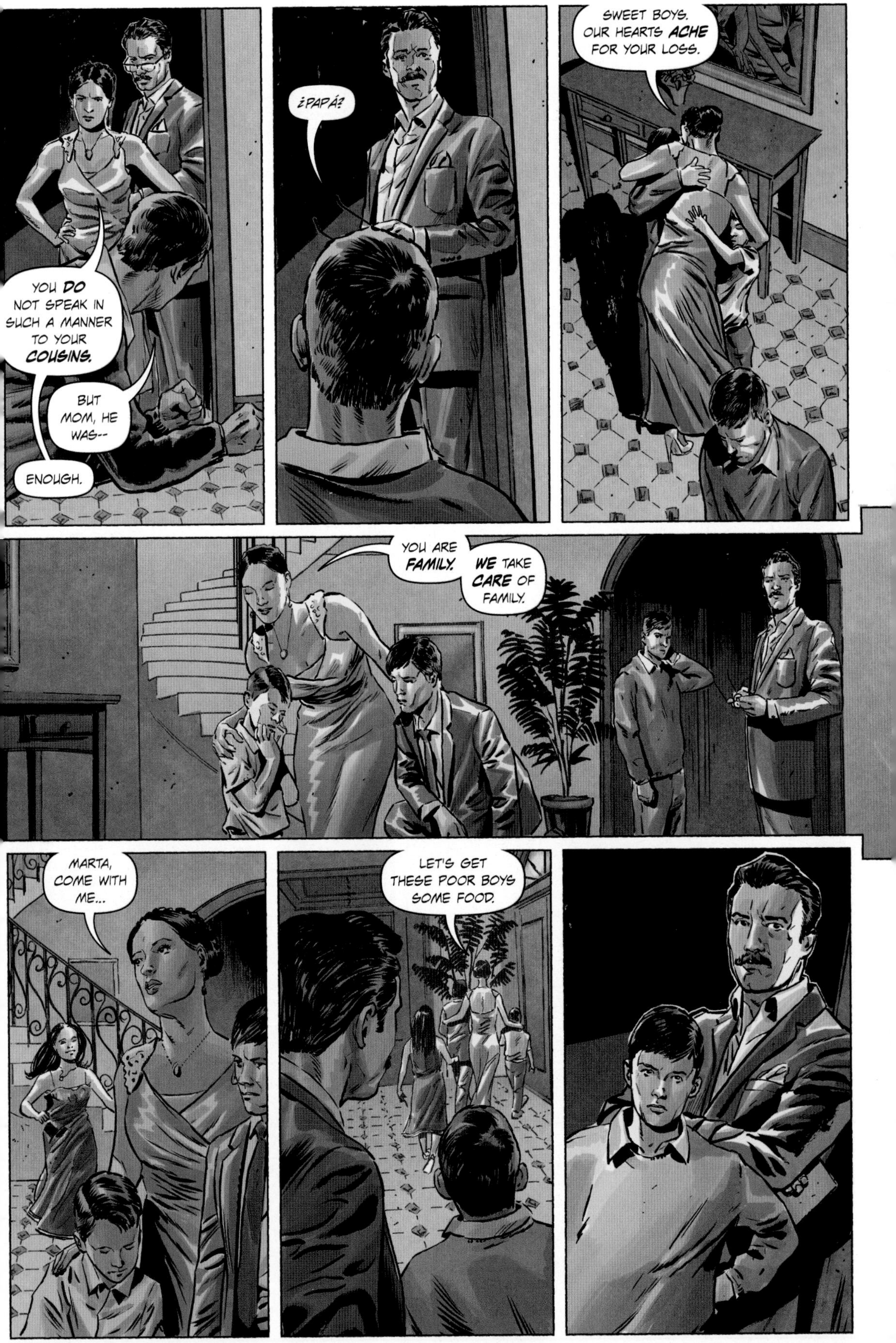
YOU DO NOT SPEAK IN SUCH A MANNER TO YOUR COUSINS.
BUT MOM, HE WAS--
ENOUGH.
¿PAPÁ?
SWEET BOYS. OUR HEARTS ACHE FOR YOUR LOSS.
YOU ARE FAMILY.
WE TAKE CARE OF FAMILY.
MARTA, COME WITH ME...
LET'S GET THESE POOR BOYS SOME FOOD.

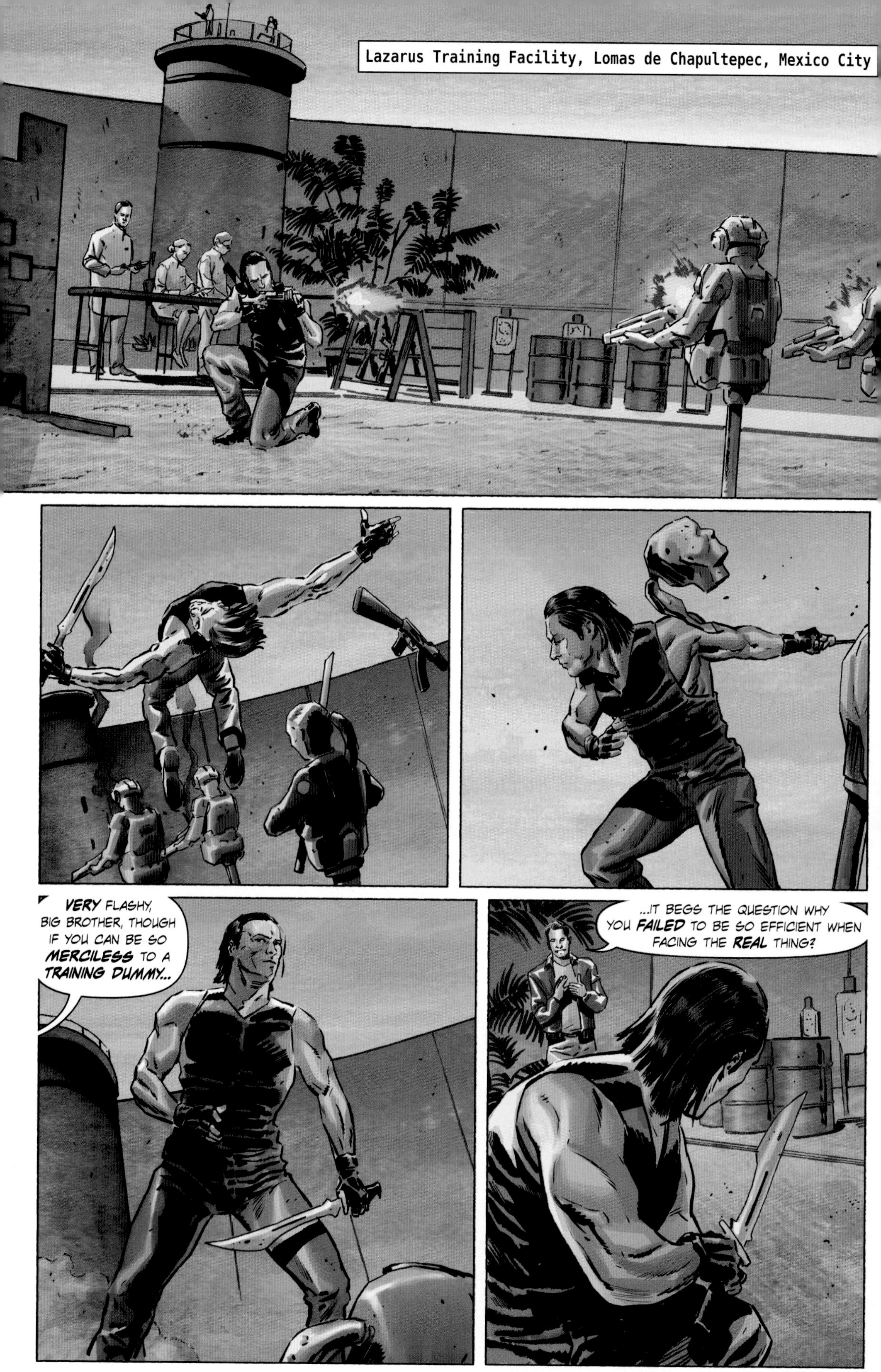
Lazarus Training Facility, Lomas de Chapultepec, Mexico City
VERY FLASHY, BIG BROTHER, THOUGH IF YOU CAN BE SO MERCILESS TO A TRAINING DUMMY...
...IT BEGS THE QUESTION WHY YOU FAILED TO BE SO EFFICIENT WHEN FACING THE REAL THING?

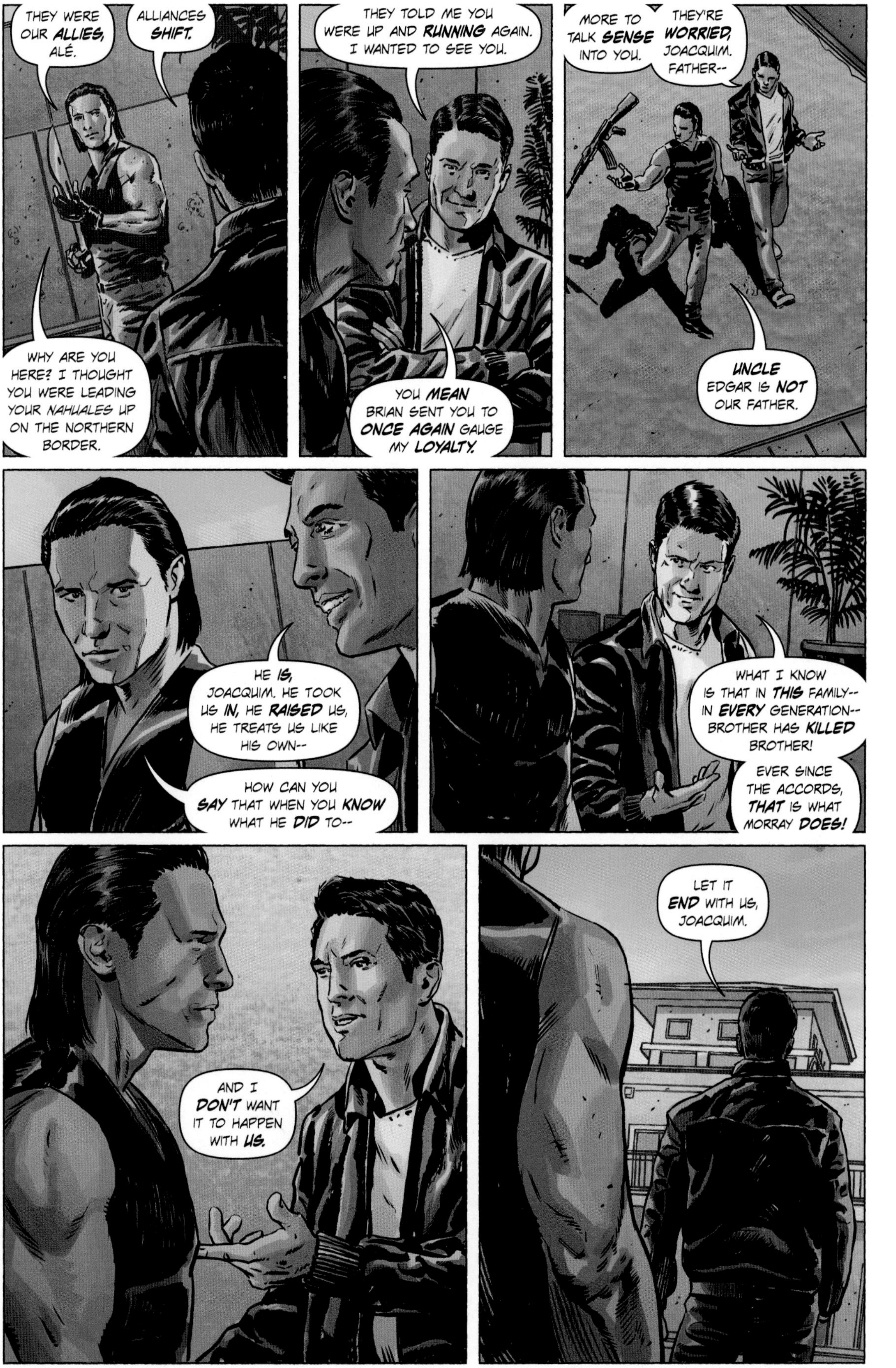

THEY WERE OUR ALLIES, ALÉ.
ALLIANCES SHIFT.
WHY ARE YOU HERE? I THOUGHT YOU WERE LEADING YOUR NAHUALES UP ON THE NORTHERN BORDER.
THEY TOLD ME YOU WERE UP AND RUNNING AGAIN. I WANTED TO SEE YOU.
YOU MEAN BRIAN SENT YOU TO ONCE AGAIN GAUGE MY LOYALTY.
MORE TO TALK SENSE INTO YOU.
THEY'RE WORRIED, JOACQUIM. FATHER--
UNCLE EDGAR IS NOT OUR FATHER.
HE IS, JOACQUIM. HE TOOK US IN, HE RAISED US, HE TREATS US LIKE HIS OWN--
HOW CAN YOU SAY THAT WHEN YOU KNOW WHAT HE DID TO--
WHAT I KNOW IS THAT IN THIS FAMILY-- IN EVERY GENERATION-- BROTHER HAS KILLED BROTHER!
EVER SINCE THE ACCORDS, THAT IS WHAT MORRAY DOES!
AND I DON'T WANT IT TO HAPPEN WITH US.
LET IT END WITH US, JOACQUIM.

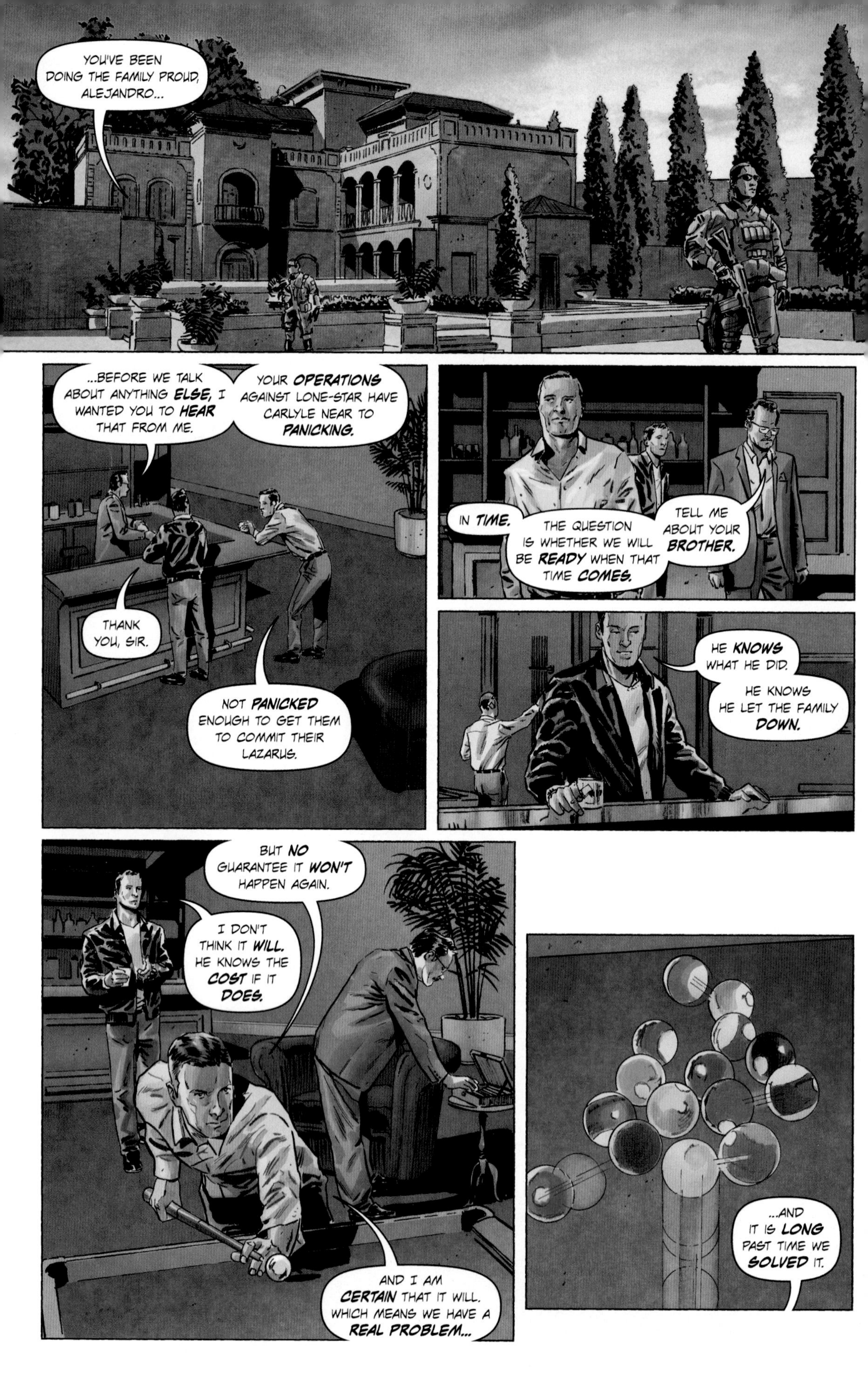
YOU'VE BEEN DOING THE FAMILY PROUD, ALEJANDRO...
...BEFORE WE TALK ABOUT ANYTHING ELSE, I WANTED YOU TO HEAR THAT FROM ME.
YOUR OPERATIONS AGAINST LONE-STAR HAVE CARLYLE NEAR TO PANICKING.
THANK YOU, SIR.
NOT PANICKED ENOUGH TO GET THEM TO COMMIT THEIR LAZARUS.
IN TIME.
THE QUESTION IS WHETHER WE WILL BE READY WHEN THAT TIME COMES.
TELL ME ABOUT YOUR BROTHER.
HE KNOWS WHAT HE DID.
HE KNOWS HE LET THE FAMILY DOWN.
BUT NO GUARANTEE IT WON'T HAPPEN AGAIN.
I DON'T THINK IT WILL. HE KNOWS THE COST IF IT DOES.
AND I AM CERTAIN THAT IT WILL. WHICH MEANS WE HAVE A REAL PROBLEM...
...AND IT IS LONG PAST TIME WE SOLVED IT.

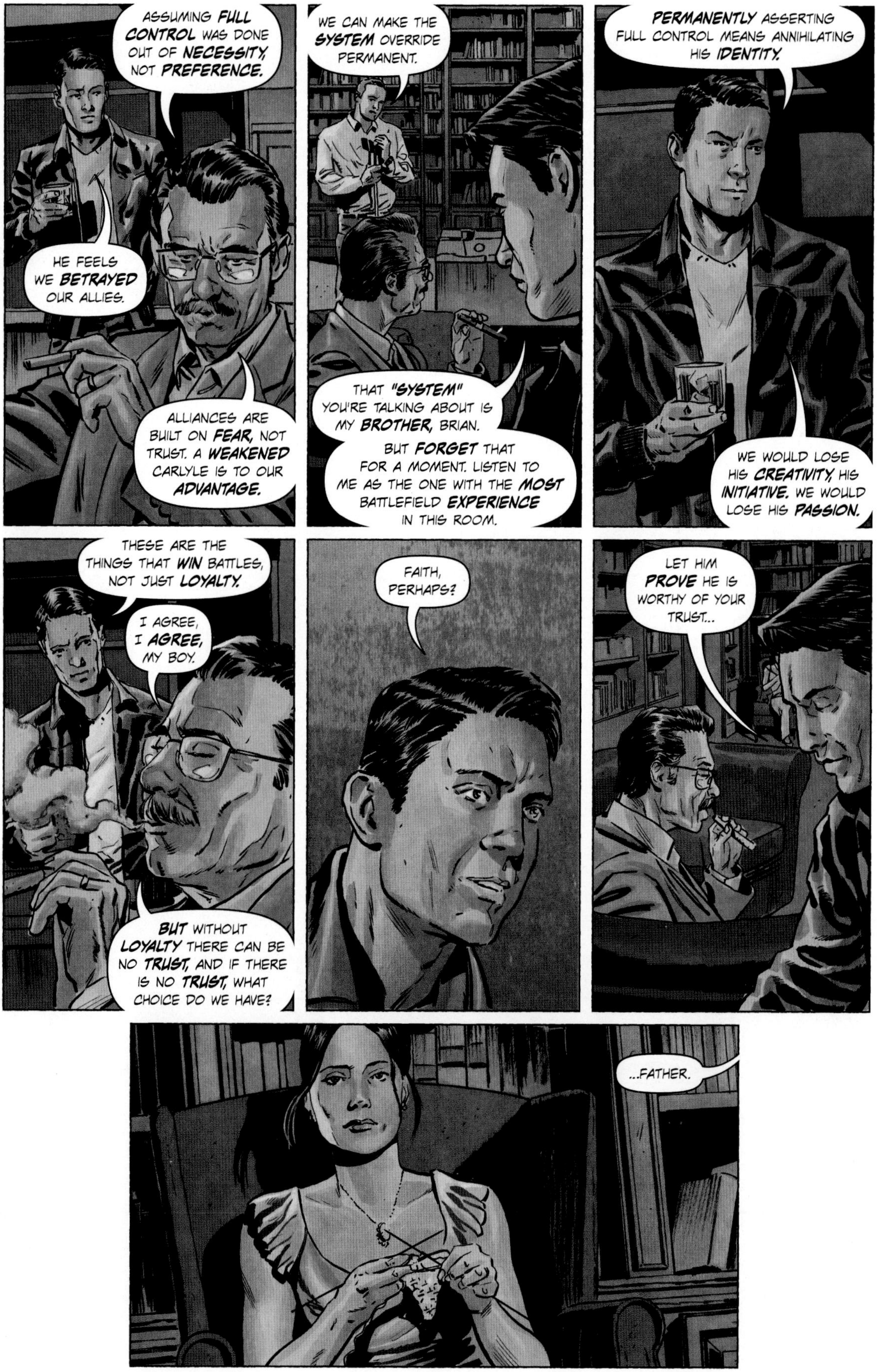
ASSUMING FULL CONTROL WAS DONE OUT OF NECESSITY, NOT PREFERENCE.
HE FEELS WE BETRAYED OUR ALLIES.
ALLIANCES ARE BUILT ON FEAR, NOT TRUST. A WEAKENED CARLYLE IS TO OUR ADVANTAGE.
WE CAN MAKE THE SYSTEM OVERRIDE PERMANENT.
THAT "SYSTEM" YOU'RE TALKING ABOUT IS MY BROTHER, BRIAN.
BUT FORGET THAT FOR A MOMENT. LISTEN TO ME AS THE ONE WITH THE MOST BATTLEFIELD EXPERIENCE IN THIS ROOM.
PERMANENTLY ASSERTING FULL CONTROL MEANS ANNIHILATING HIS IDENTITY.
WE WOULD LOSE HIS CREATIVITY, HIS INITIATIVE. WE WOULD LOSE HIS PASSION.
THESE ARE THE THINGS THAT WIN BATTLES, NOT JUST LOYALTY.
I AGREE, I AGREE, MY BOY.
BUT WITHOUT LOYALTY THERE CAN BE NO TRUST, AND IF THERE IS NO TRUST, WHAT CHOICE DO WE HAVE?
FAITH, PERHAPS?
LET HIM PROVE HE IS WORTHY OF YOUR TRUST...
...FATHER.

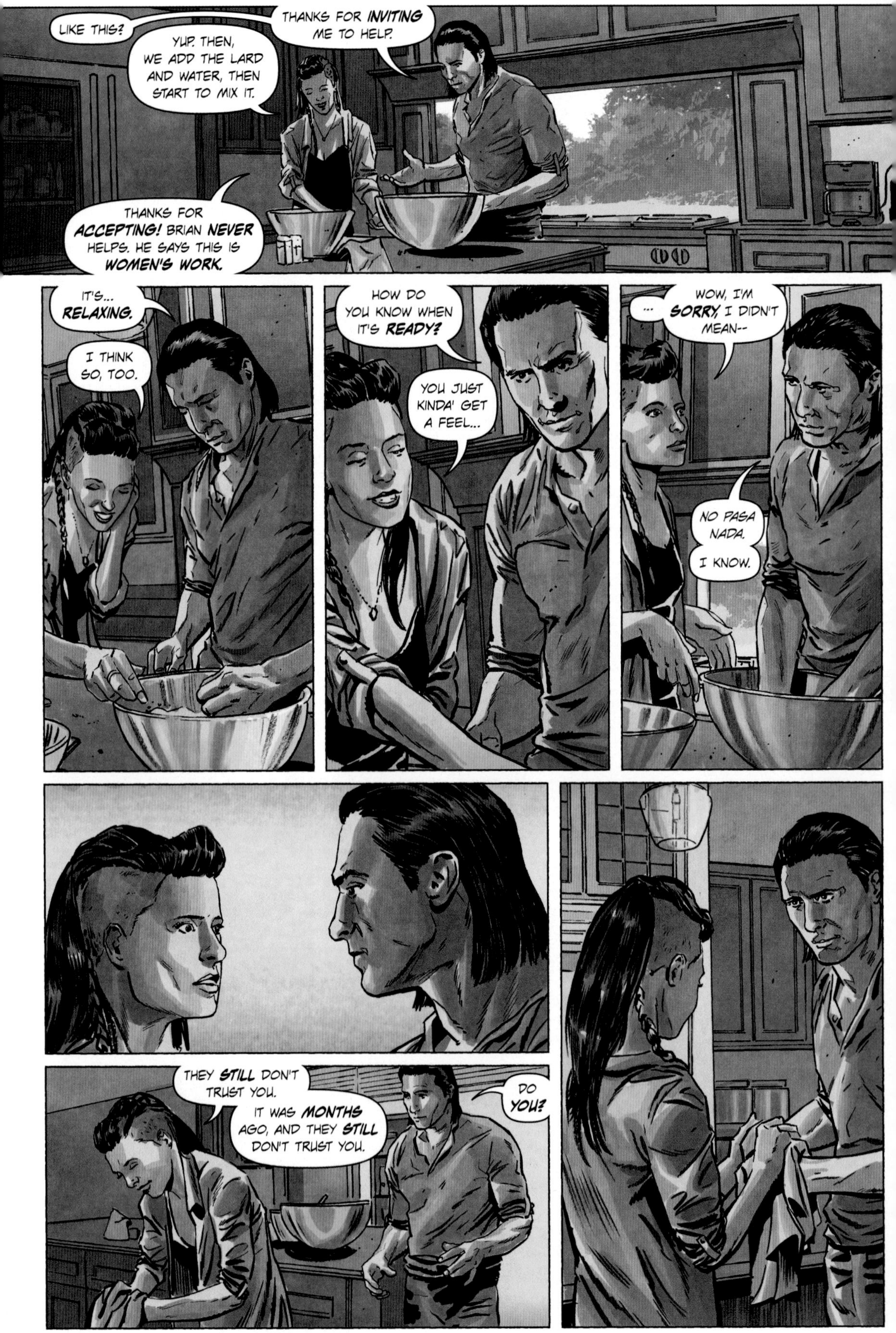
LIKE THIS?
THANKS FOR INVITING ME TO HELP.
YUP. THEN, WE ADD THE LARD AND WATER, THEN START TO MIX IT.
THANKS FOR ACCEPTING! BRIAN NEVER HELPS. HE SAYS THIS IS WOMEN'S WORK.
IT'S... RELAXING.
I THINK SO, TOO.
HOW DO YOU KNOW WHEN IT'S READY?
YOU JUST KINDA' GET A FEEL...
...
WOW, I'M SORRY, I DIDN'T MEAN--
NO PASA NADA.
I KNOW.
THEY STILL DON'T TRUST YOU.
IT WAS MONTHS AGO, AND THEY STILL DON'T TRUST YOU.
DO YOU?

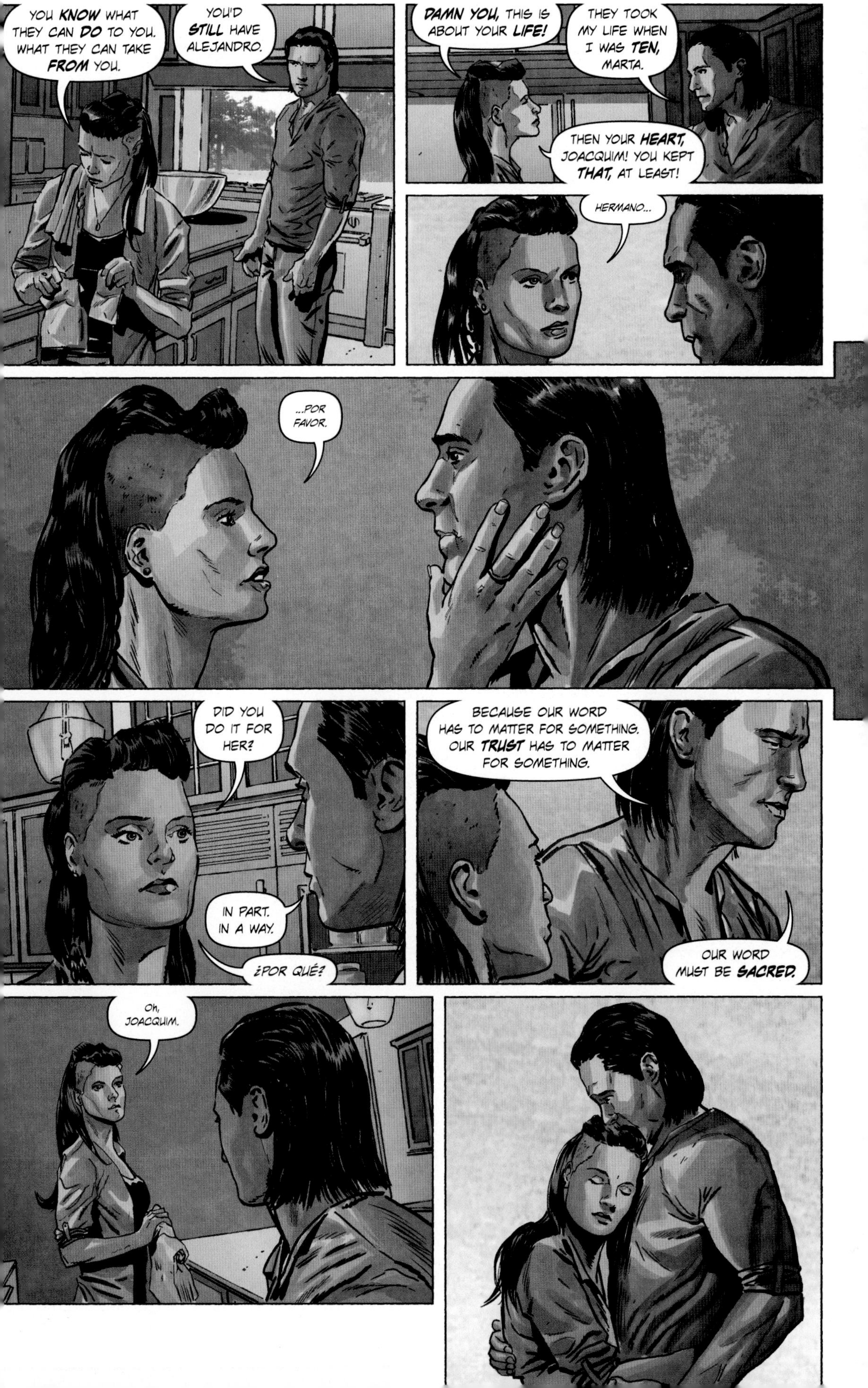
YOU KNOW WHAT THEY CAN DO TO YOU. WHAT THEY CAN TAKE FROM YOU.
YOU'D STILL HAVE ALEJANDRO.
DAMN YOU, THIS IS ABOUT YOUR LIFE!
THEY TOOK MY LIFE WHEN I WAS TEN, MARTA.
THEN YOUR HEART, JOACQUIM! YOU KEPT THAT, AT LEAST!
HERMANO...
...POR FAVOR.
DID YOU DO IT FOR HER?
IN PART. IN A WAY.
¿POR QUÉ?
BECAUSE OUR WORD HAS TO MATTER FOR SOMETHING. OUR TRUST HAS TO MATTER FOR SOMETHING.
OUR WORD MUST BE SACRED.
Oh, JOACQUIM.

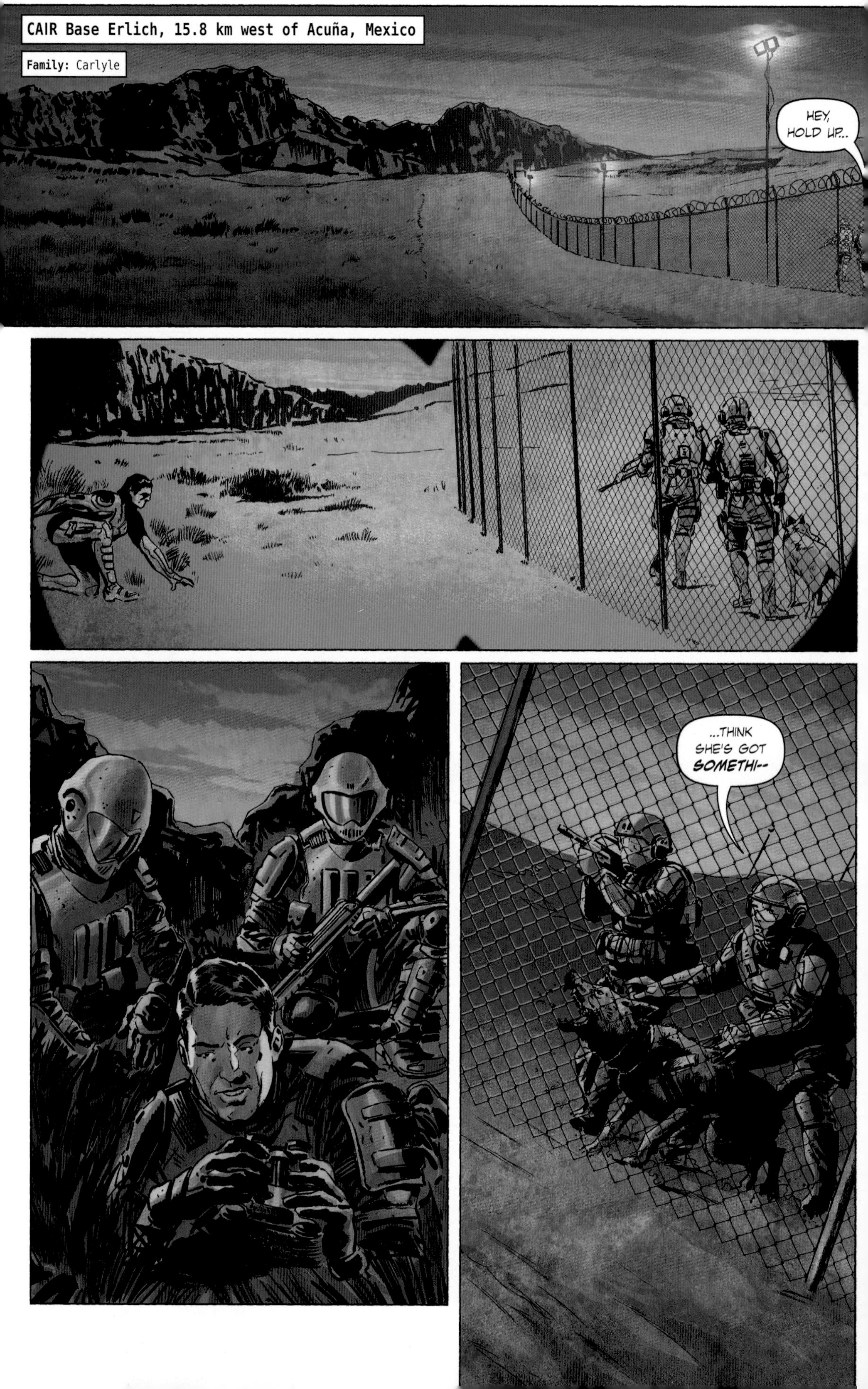
CAIR Base Erlich, 15.8 km west of Acuña, Mexico
Family: Carlyle
HEY, HOLD UP...
...THINK SHE'S GOT SOMETHI--

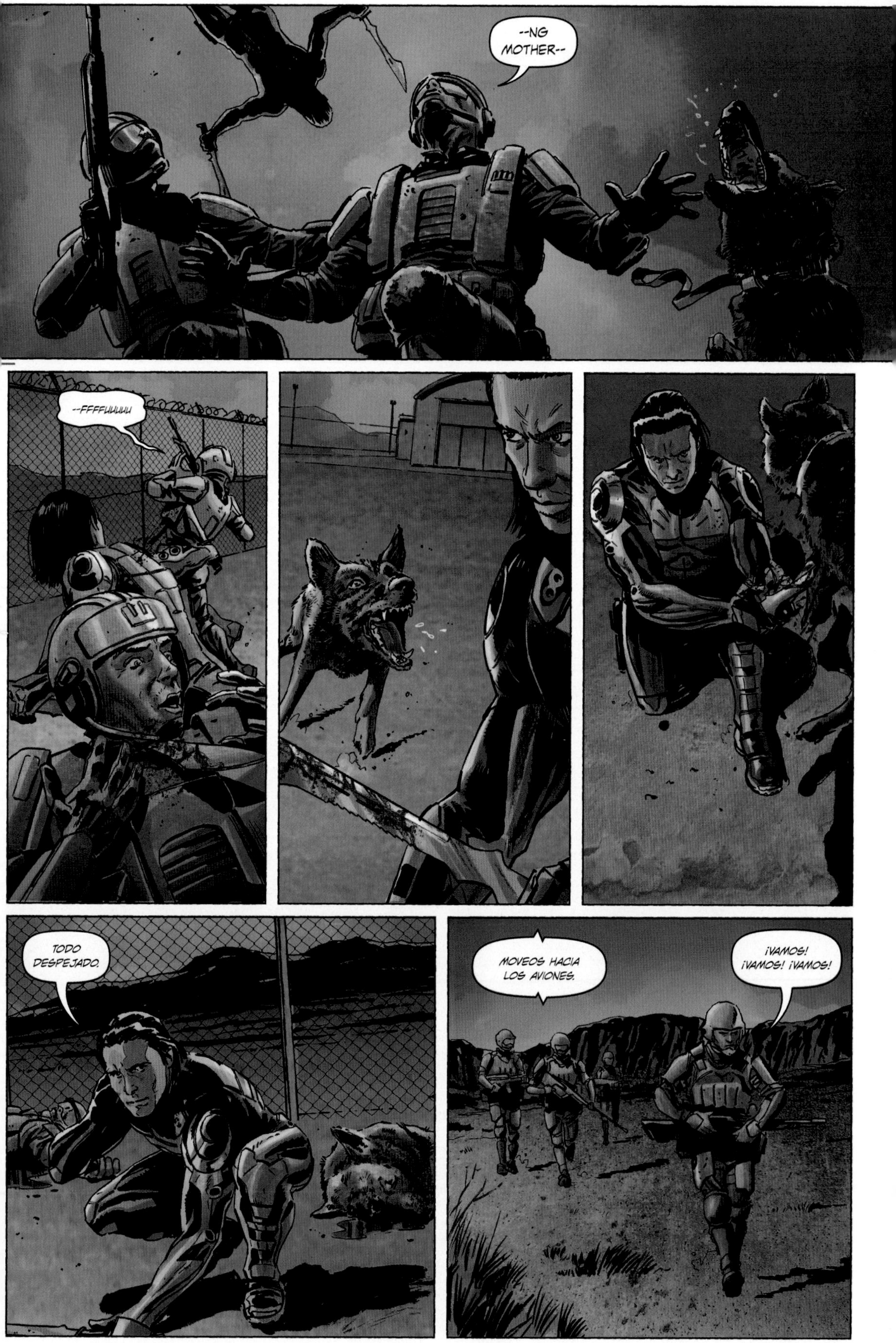
--NG MOTHER--
--FFFFUUUUU
TODO DESPEJADO.
MOVEOS HACIA LOS AVIONES.
¡VAMOS! ¡VAMOS! ¡VAMOS!

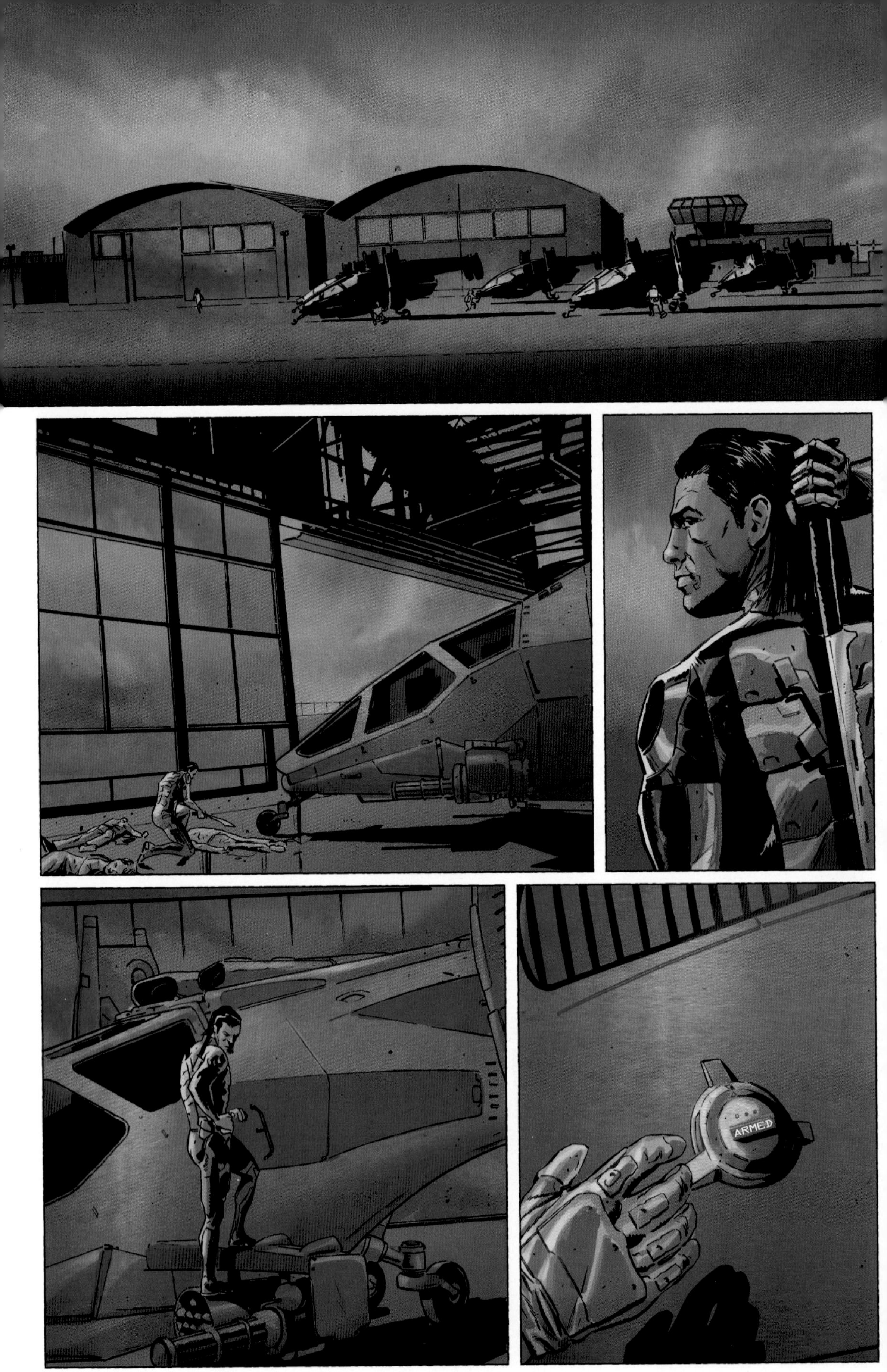
ARMED

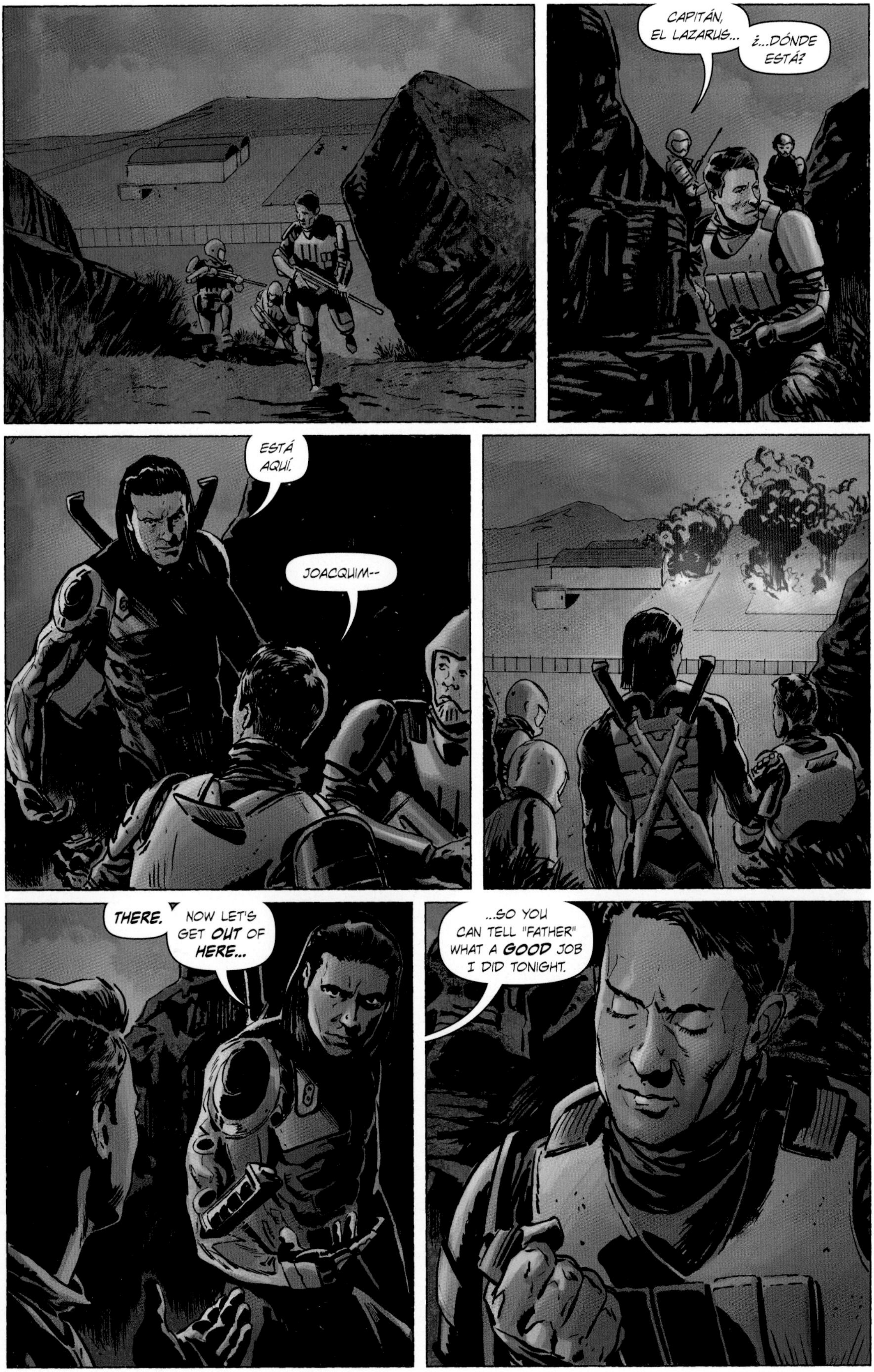
CAPITÁN, EL LAZARUS...
¿...DÓNDE ESTÁ?
ESTÁ AQUÍ.
JOACQUIM--
THERE.
NOW LET'S GET OUT OF HERE...
...SO YOU CAN TELL "FATHER" WHAT A GOOD JOB I DID TONIGHT.

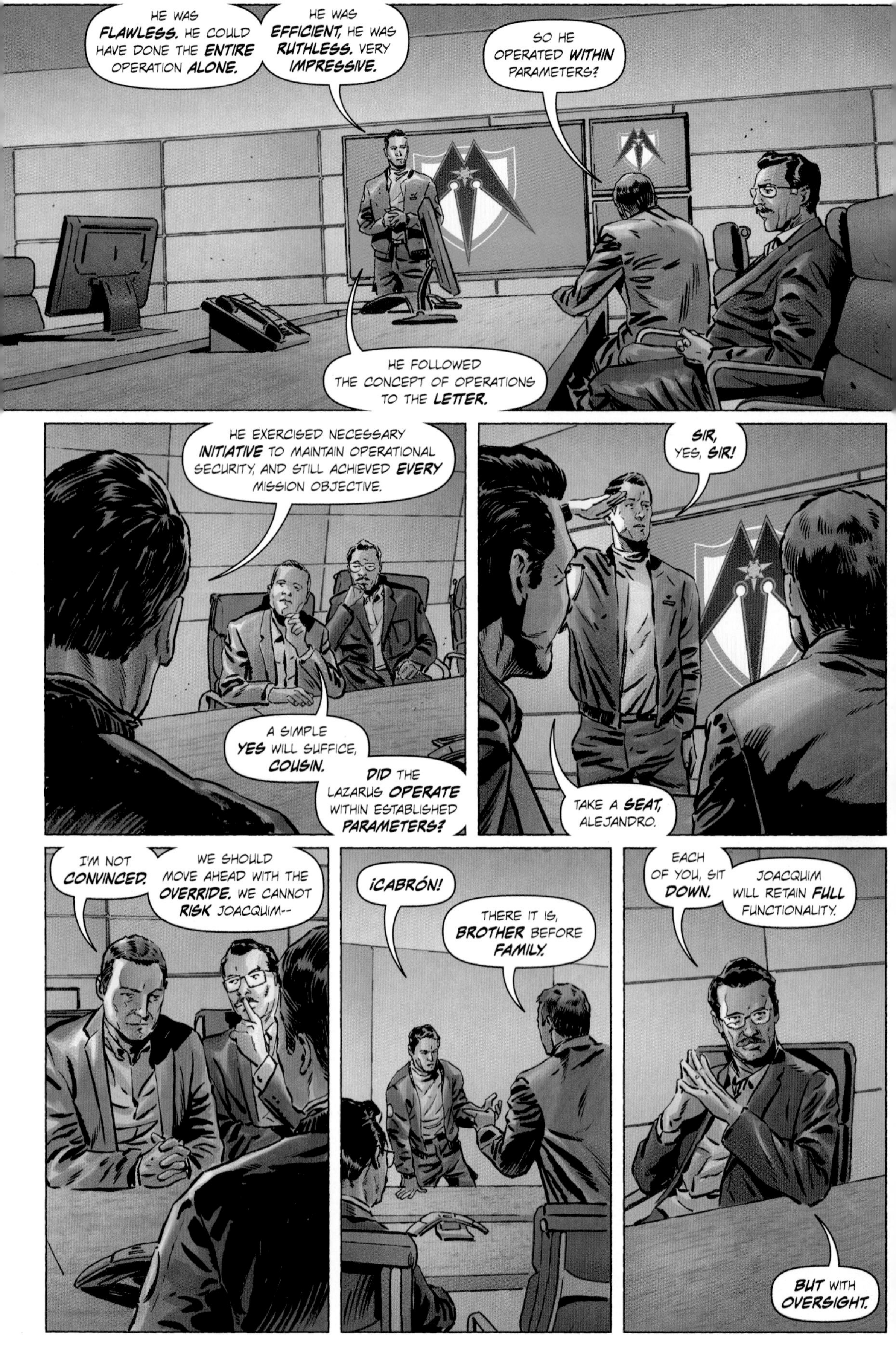
HE WAS FLAWLESS. HE COULD HAVE DONE THE ENTIRE OPERATION ALONE.
HE WAS EFFICIENT, HE WAS RUTHLESS. VERY IMPRESSIVE.
SO HE OPERATED WITHIN PARAMETERS?
HE FOLLOWED THE CONCEPT OF OPERATIONS TO THE LETTER.
HE EXERCISED NECESSARY INITIATIVE TO MAINTAIN OPERATIONAL SECURITY, AND STILL ACHIEVED EVERY MISSION OBJECTIVE.
A SIMPLE YES WILL SUFFICE, COUSIN.
DID THE LAZARUS OPERATE WITHIN ESTABLISHED PARAMETERS?
SIR, YES, SIR!
TAKE A SEAT, ALEJANDRO.
I'M NOT CONVINCED.
WE SHOULD MOVE AHEAD WITH THE OVERRIDE. WE CANNOT RISK JOACQUIM--
¡CABRÓN!
THERE IT IS, BROTHER BEFORE FAMILY.
EACH OF YOU, SIT DOWN.
JOACQUIM WILL RETAIN FULL FUNCTIONALITY.
BUT WITH OVERSIGHT.

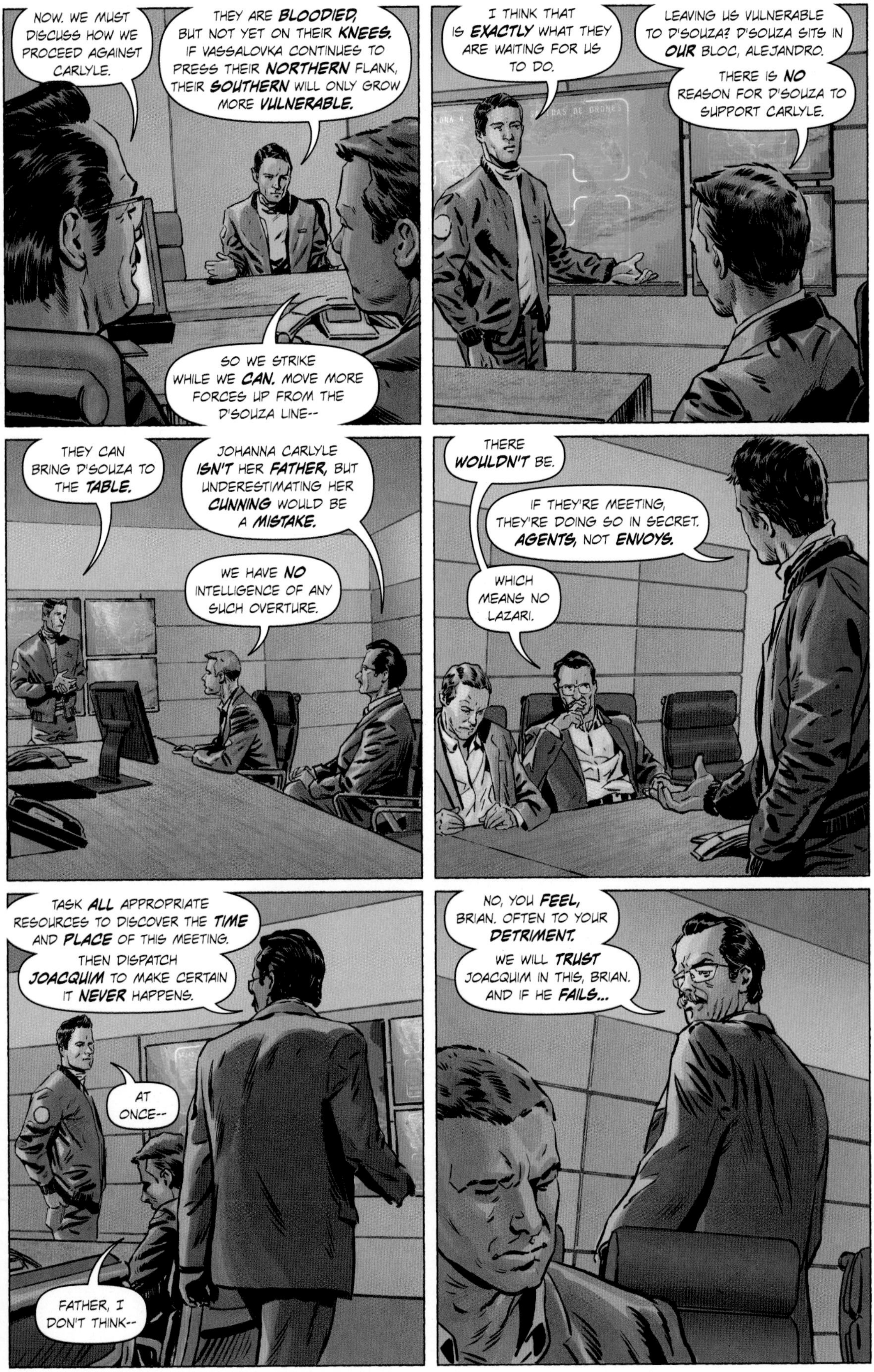
NOW. WE MUST DISCUSS HOW WE PROCEED AGAINST CARLYLE.
THEY ARE BLOODIED, BUT NOT YET ON THEIR KNEES. IF VASSALOVKA CONTINUES TO PRESS THEIR NORTHERN FLANK, THEIR SOUTHERN WILL ONLY GROW MORE VULNERABLE.
SO WE STRIKE WHILE WE CAN. MOVE MORE FORCES UP FROM THE D'SOUZA LINE--
I THINK THAT IS EXACTLY WHAT THEY ARE WAITING FOR US TO DO.
LEAVING US VULNERABLE TO D'SOUZA? D'SOUZA SITS IN OUR BLOC, ALEJANDRO.
THERE IS NO REASON FOR D'SOUZA TO SUPPORT CARLYLE.
THEY CAN BRING D'SOUZA TO THE TABLE.
JOHANNA CARLYLE ISN'T HER FATHER, BUT UNDERESTIMATING HER CUNNING WOULD BE A MISTAKE.
WE HAVE NO INTELLIGENCE OF ANY SUCH OVERTURE.
THERE WOULDN'T BE.
IF THEY'RE MEETING, THEY'RE DOING SO IN SECRET. AGENTS, NOT ENVOYS.
WHICH MEANS NO LAZARI.
TASK ALL APPROPRIATE RESOURCES TO DISCOVER THE TIME AND PLACE OF THIS MEETING.
THEN DISPATCH JOACQUIM TO MAKE CERTAIN IT NEVER HAPPENS.
AT ONCE--
FATHER, I DON'T THINK--
NO, YOU FEEL, BRIAN. OFTEN TO YOUR DETRIMENT.
WE WILL TRUST JOACQUIM IN THIS, BRIAN. AND IF HE FAILS...

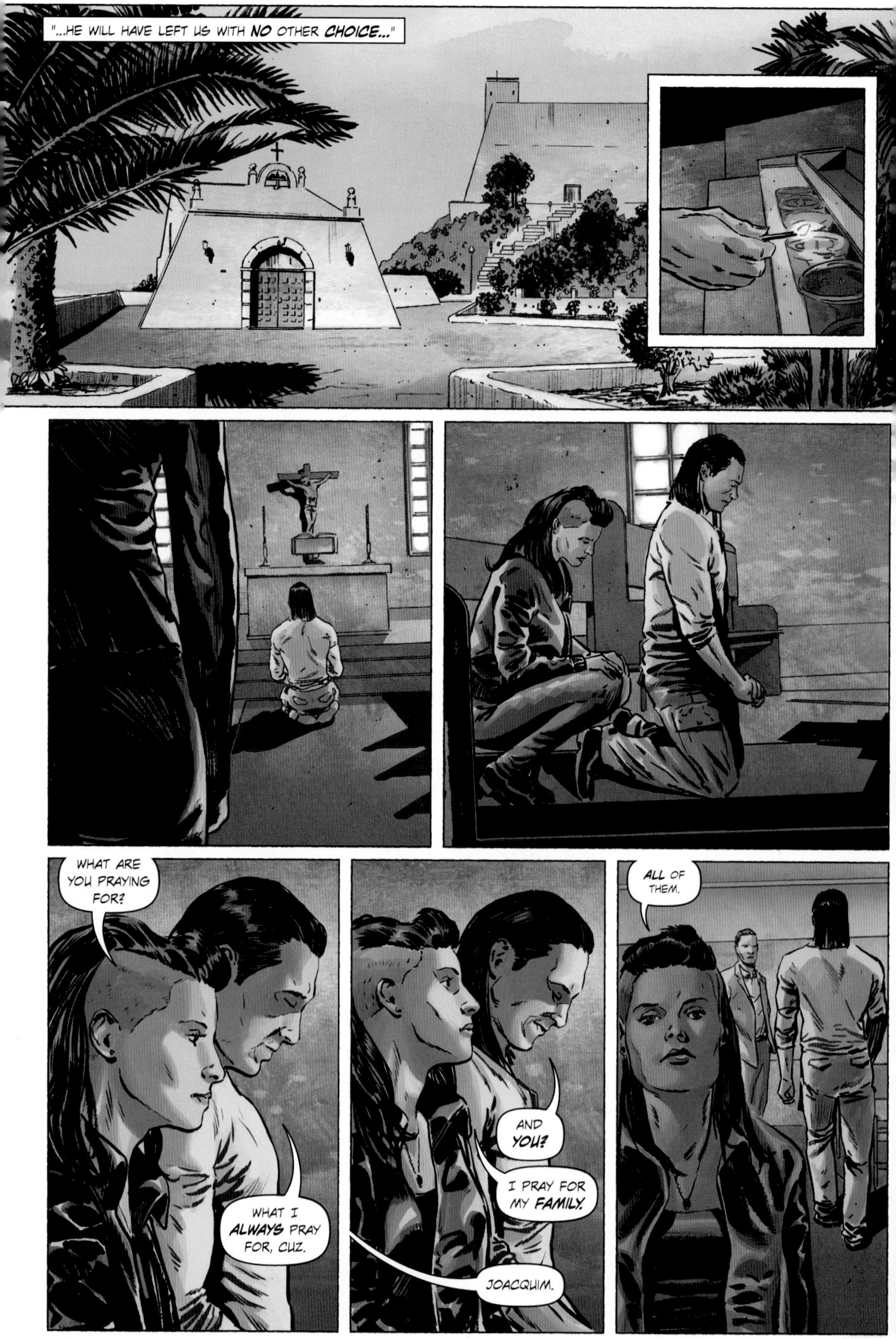
"...HE WILL HAVE LEFT US WITH NO OTHER CHOICE..."
WHAT ARE YOU PRAYING FOR?
WHAT I ALWAYS PRAY FOR, CUZ.
AND YOU?
I PRAY FOR MY FAMILY.
JOACQUIM.
ALL OF THEM.

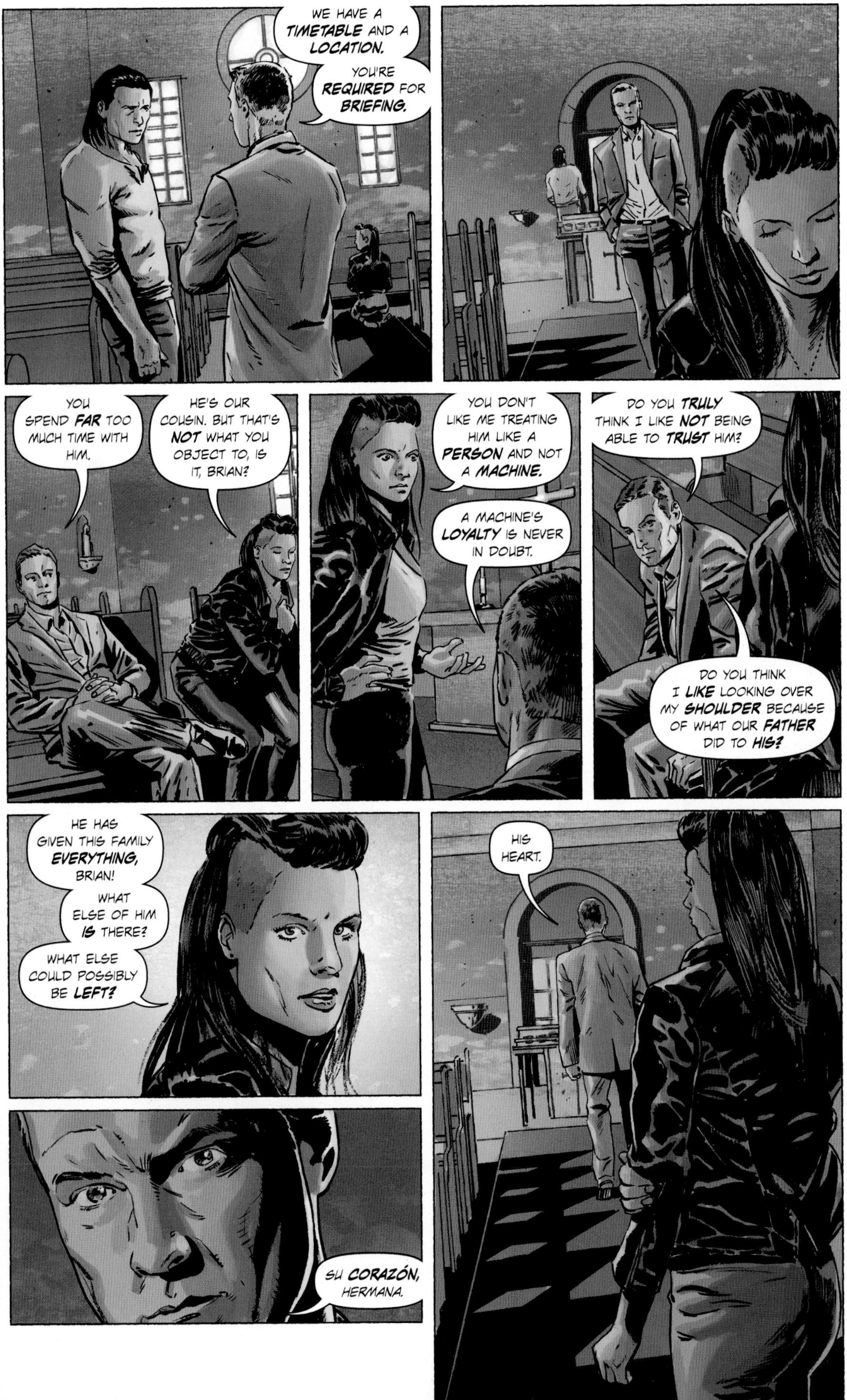
WE HAVE A TIMETABLE AND A LOCATION.
YOU'RE REQUIRED FOR BRIEFING.
YOU SPEND FAR TOO MUCH TIME WITH HIM.
HE'S OUR COUSIN. BUT THAT'S NOT WHAT YOU OBJECT TO, IS IT, BRIAN?
YOU DON'T LIKE ME TREATING HIM LIKE A PERSON AND NOT A MACHINE.
A MACHINE'S LOYALTY IS NEVER IN DOUBT.
DO YOU TRULY THINK I LIKE NOT BEING ABLE TO TRUST HIM?
DO YOU THINK I LIKE LOOKING OVER MY SHOULDER BECAUSE OF WHAT OUR FATHER DID TO HIS?
HE HAS GIVEN THIS FAMILY EVERYTHING, BRIAN!
WHAT ELSE OF HIM IS THERE?
WHAT ELSE COULD POSSIBLY BE LEFT?
SU CORAZÓN, HERMANA.
HIS HEART.

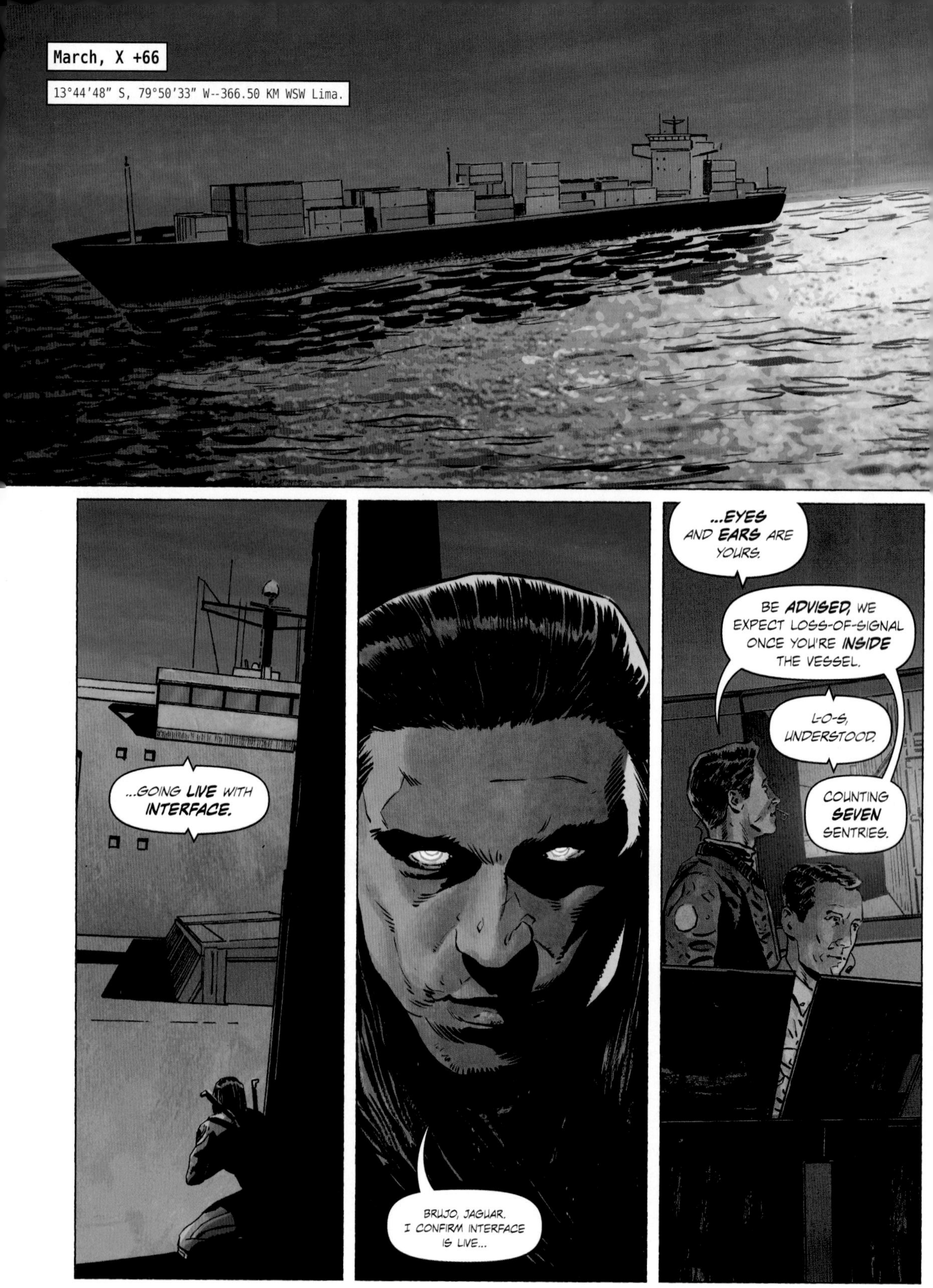
March, X +66
13°44’48” S, 79°50’33” W--366.50 KM WSW Lima.
...GOING LIVE WITH INTERFACE.
BRUJO, JAGUAR. I CONFIRM INTERFACE IS LIVE...
...EYES AND EARS ARE YOURS.
BE ADVISED, WE EXPECT LOSS-OF-SIGNAL ONCE YOU'RE INSIDE THE VESSEL.
L-O-S, UNDERSTOOD.
COUNTING SEVEN SENTRIES.

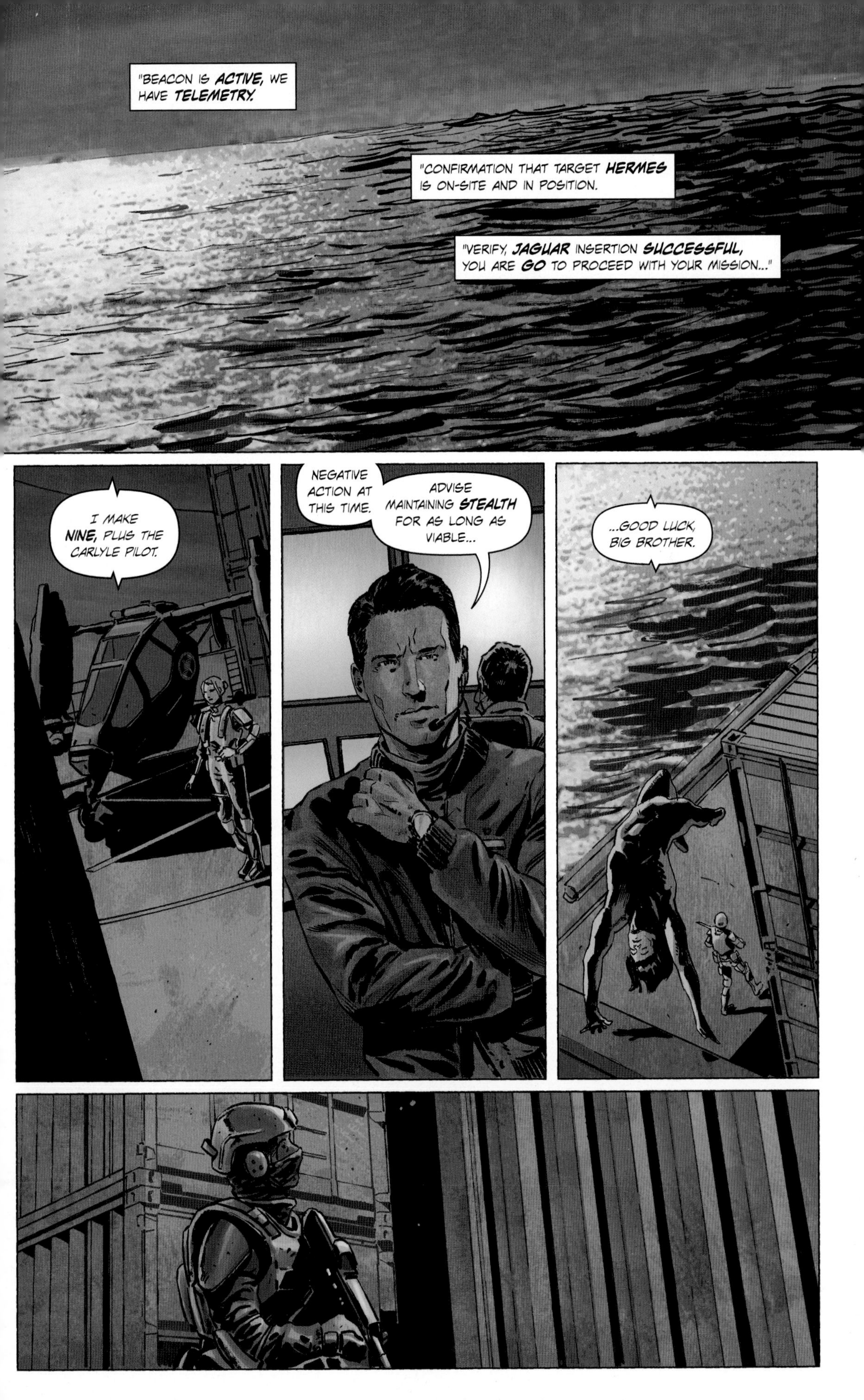
"BEACON IS ACTIVE, WE HAVE TELEMETRY.
"CONFIRMATION THAT TARGET HERMES IS ON-SITE AND IN POSITION.
"VERIFY, JAGUAR INSERTION SUCCESSFUL, YOU ARE GO TO PROCEED WITH YOUR MISSION..."
I MAKE NINE, PLUS THE CARLYLE PILOT.
NEGATIVE ACTION AT THIS TIME.
ADVISE MAINTAINING STEALTH FOR AS LONG AS VIABLE...
...GOOD LUCK, BIG BROTHER.

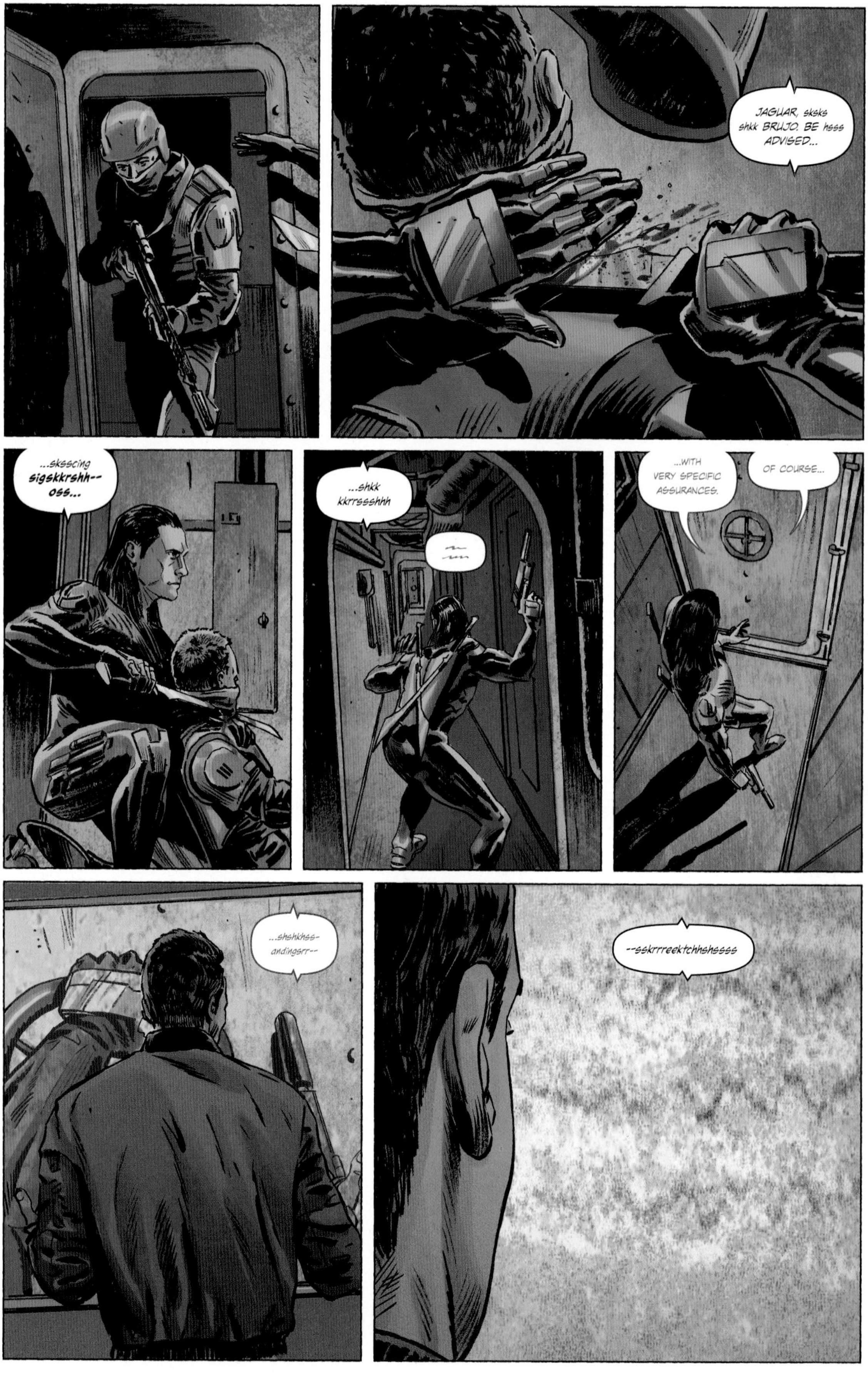
JAGUAR, sksks shkk BRUJO. BE hsss ADVISED...
...sksscing sigskkrshh--oss...
...shkk kkrrssshhh
...WITH VERY SPECIFIC ASSURANCES.
OF COURSE...
...shshkhss-andingsrr--
--sskrrreektchhshssss

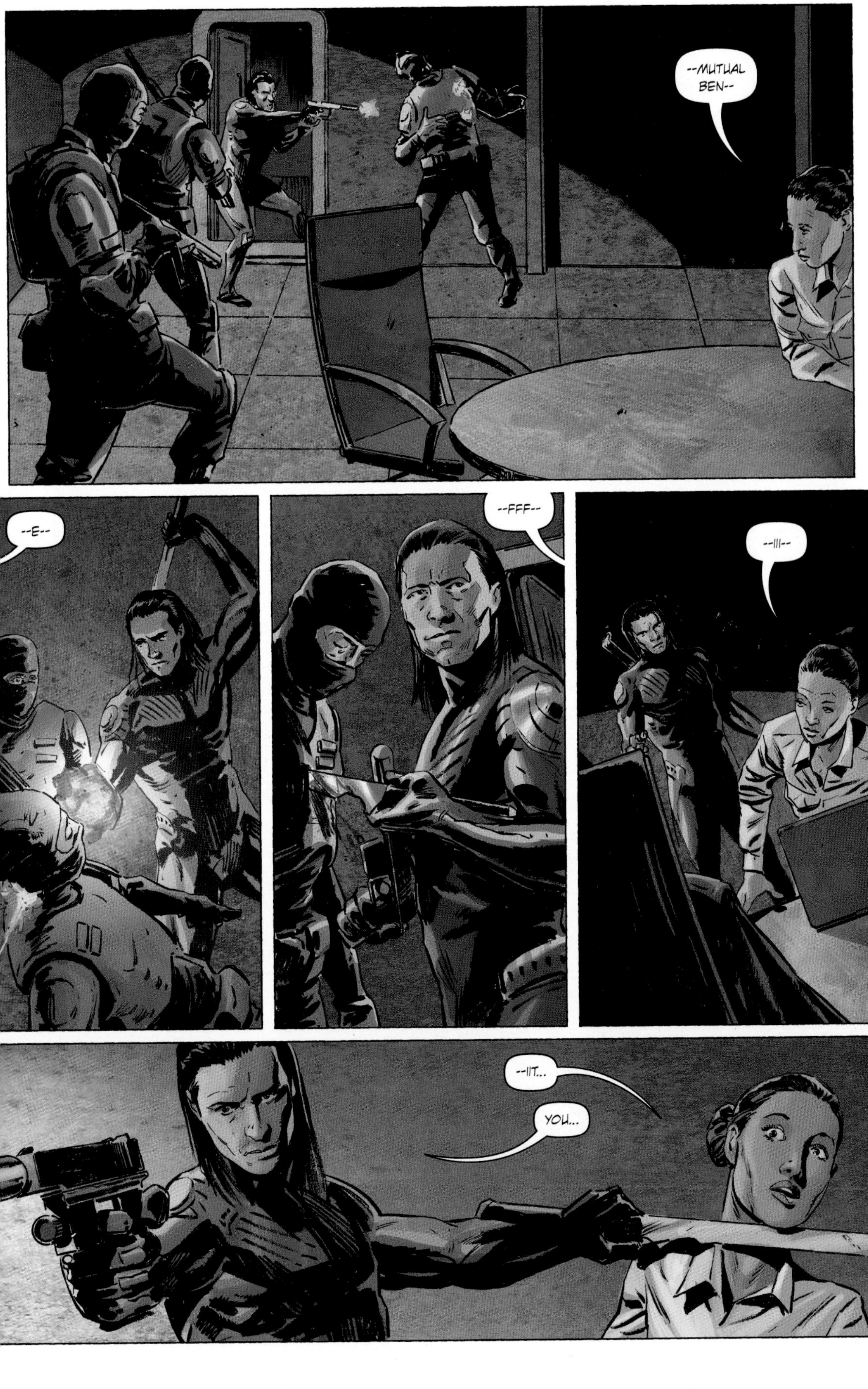
--MUTUAL BEN--
--E--
--FFF--
--III--
--IIT...
YOU...

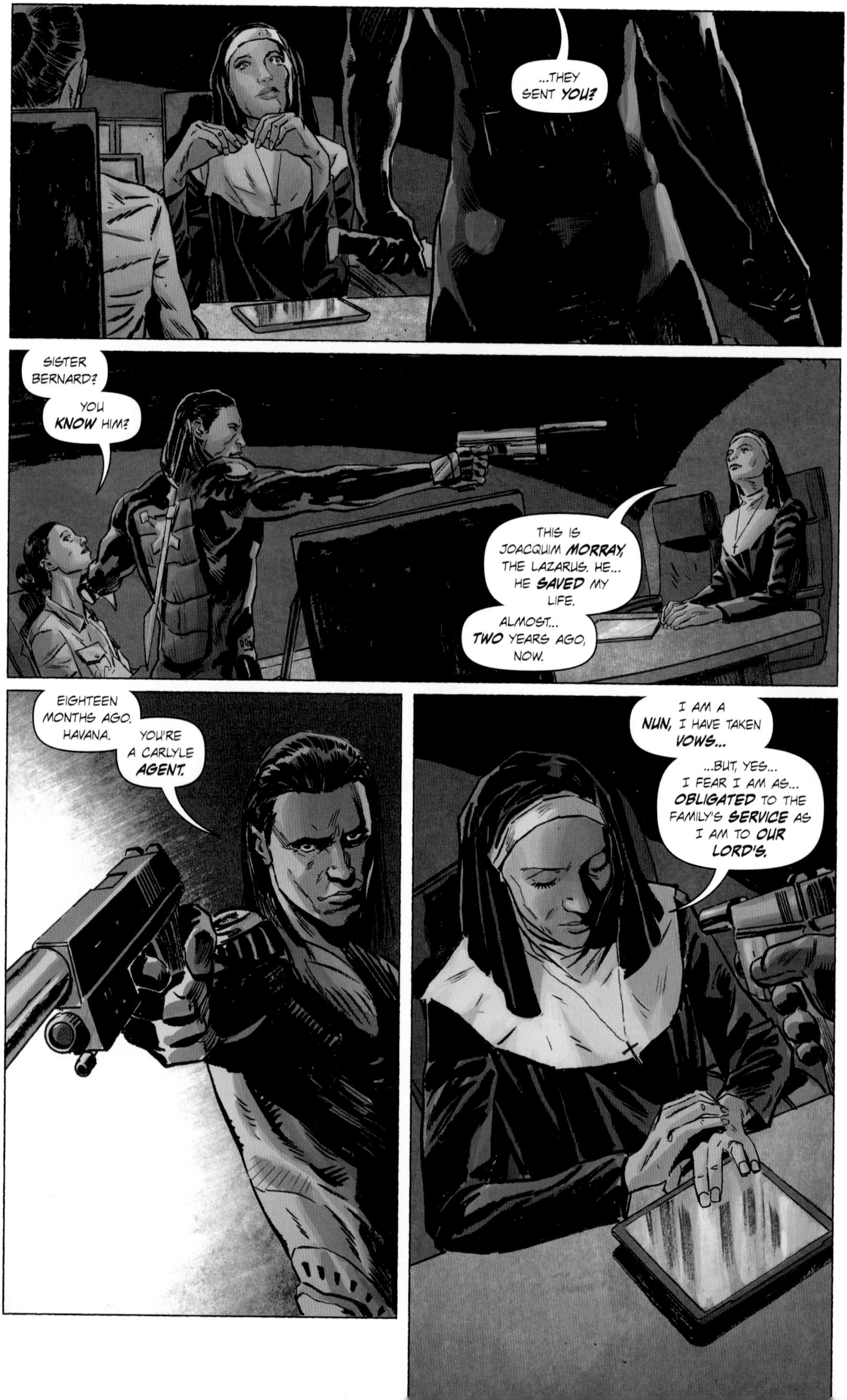
...THEY SENT YOU?
SISTER BERNARD?
YOU KNOW HIM?
THIS IS JOACQUIM MORRAY, THE LAZARUS. HE... HE SAVED MY LIFE.
ALMOST... TWO YEARS AGO, NOW.
EIGHTEEN MONTHS AGO. HAVANA.
YOU'RE A CARLYLE AGENT.
I AM A NUN, I HAVE TAKEN VOWS...
...BUT, YES... I FEAR I AM AS... OBLIGATED TO THE FAMILY'S SERVICE AS I AM TO OUR LORD'S.

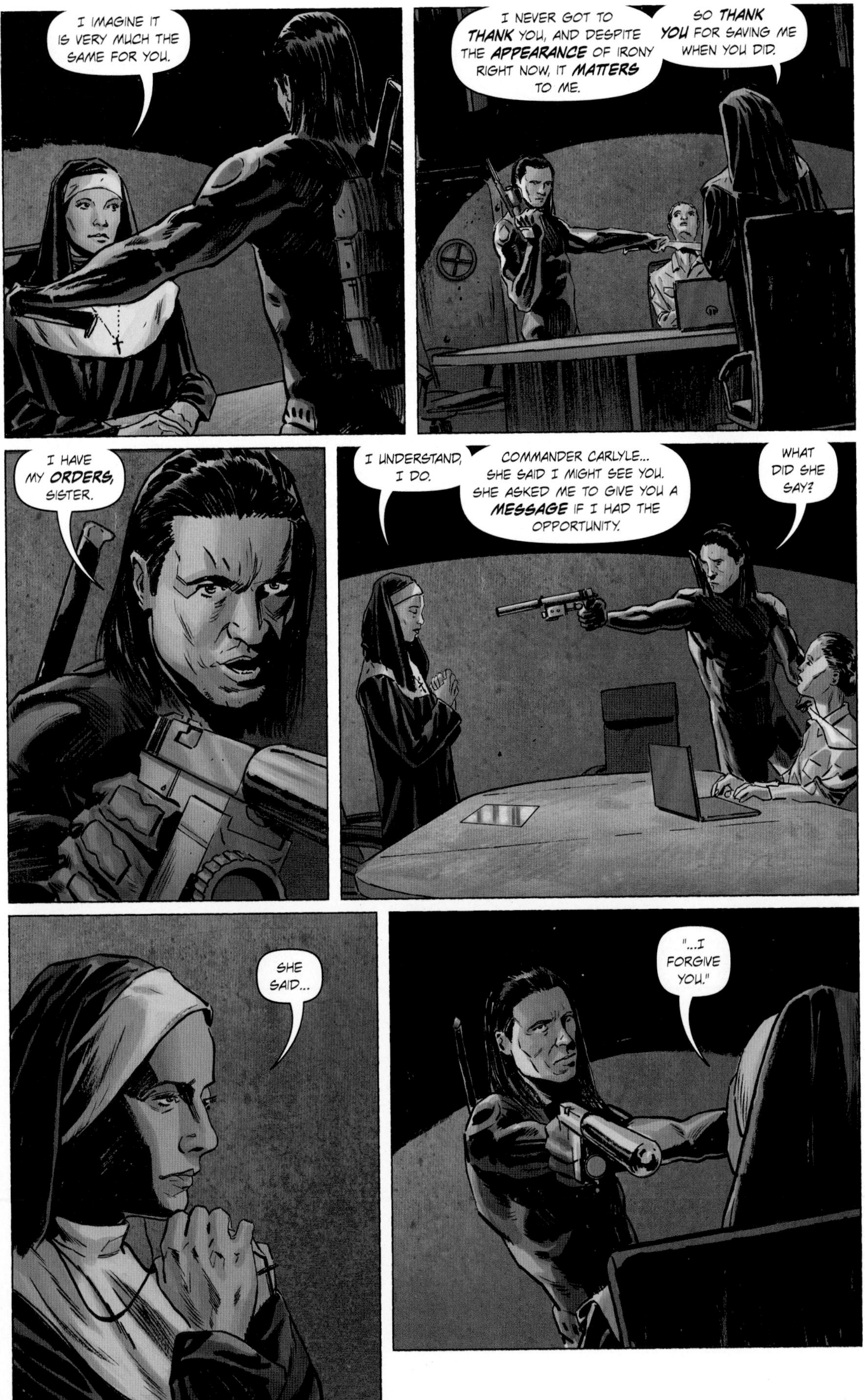
I IMAGINE IT IS VERY MUCH THE SAME FOR YOU.
I NEVER GOT TO THANK YOU, AND DESPITE THE APPEARANCE OF IRONY RIGHT NOW, IT MATTERS TO ME.
SO THANK YOU FOR SAVING ME WHEN YOU DID.
I HAVE MY ORDERS, SISTER.
I UNDERSTAND, I DO.
COMMANDER CARLYLE... SHE SAID I MIGHT SEE YOU. SHE ASKED ME TO GIVE YOU A MESSAGE IF I HAD THE OPPORTUNITY.
WHAT DID SHE SAY?
SHE SAID...
"...I FORGIVE YOU."

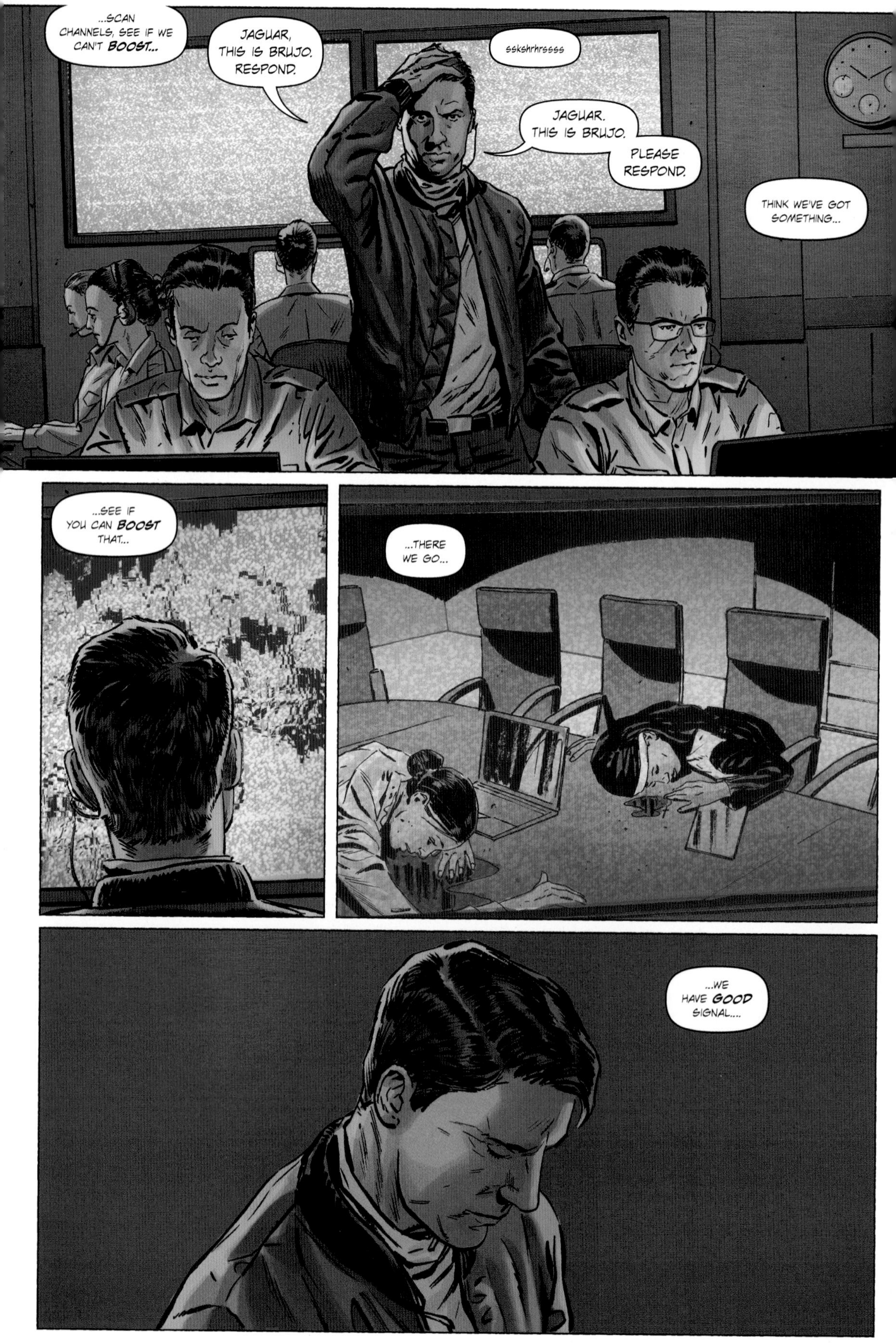
...SCAN CHANNELS, SEE IF WE CAN'T BOOST...
JAGUAR, THIS IS BRUJO. RESPOND.
ssksshrhrssss
JAGUAR. THIS IS BRUJO.
PLEASE RESPOND.
THINK WE'VE GOT SOMETHING...
...SEE IF YOU CAN BOOST THAT...
...THERE WE GO...
...WE HAVE GOOD SIGNAL....

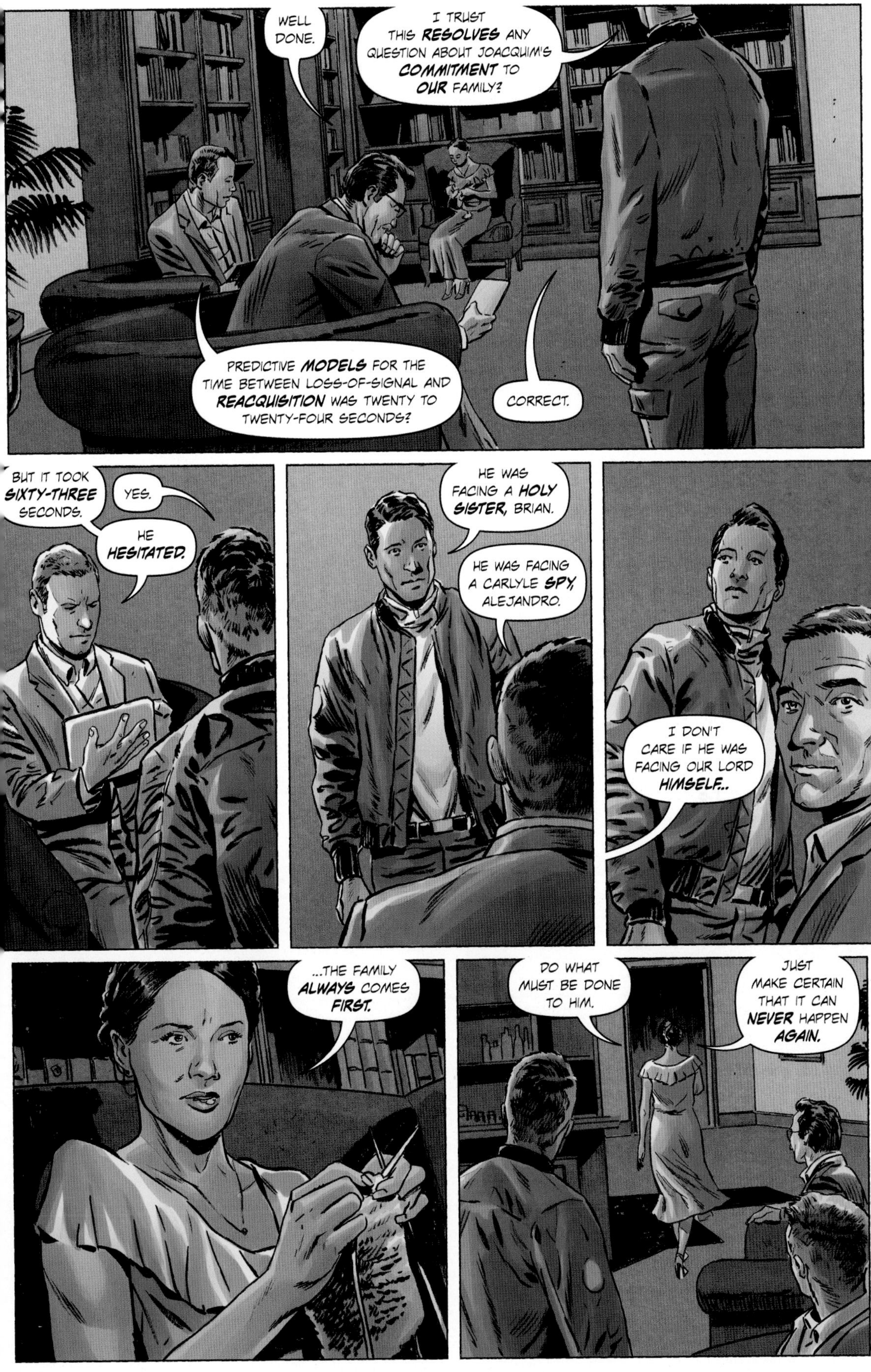
WELL DONE.
I TRUST THIS RESOLVES ANY QUESTION ABOUT JOACQUIM'S COMMITMENT TO OUR FAMILY?
PREDICTIVE MODELS FOR THE TIME BETWEEN LOSS-OF-SIGNAL AND REACQUISITION WAS TWENTY TO TWENTY-FOUR SECONDS?
CORRECT.
BUT IT TOOK SIXTY-THREE SECONDS.
YES.
HE HESITATED.
HE WAS FACING A HOLY SISTER, BRIAN.
HE WAS FACING A CARLYLE SPY, ALEJANDRO.
I DON'T CARE IF HE WAS FACING OUR LORD HIMSELF...
...THE FAMILY ALWAYS COMES FIRST.
DO WHAT MUST BE DONE TO HIM.
JUST MAKE CERTAIN THAT IT CAN NEVER HAPPEN AGAIN.

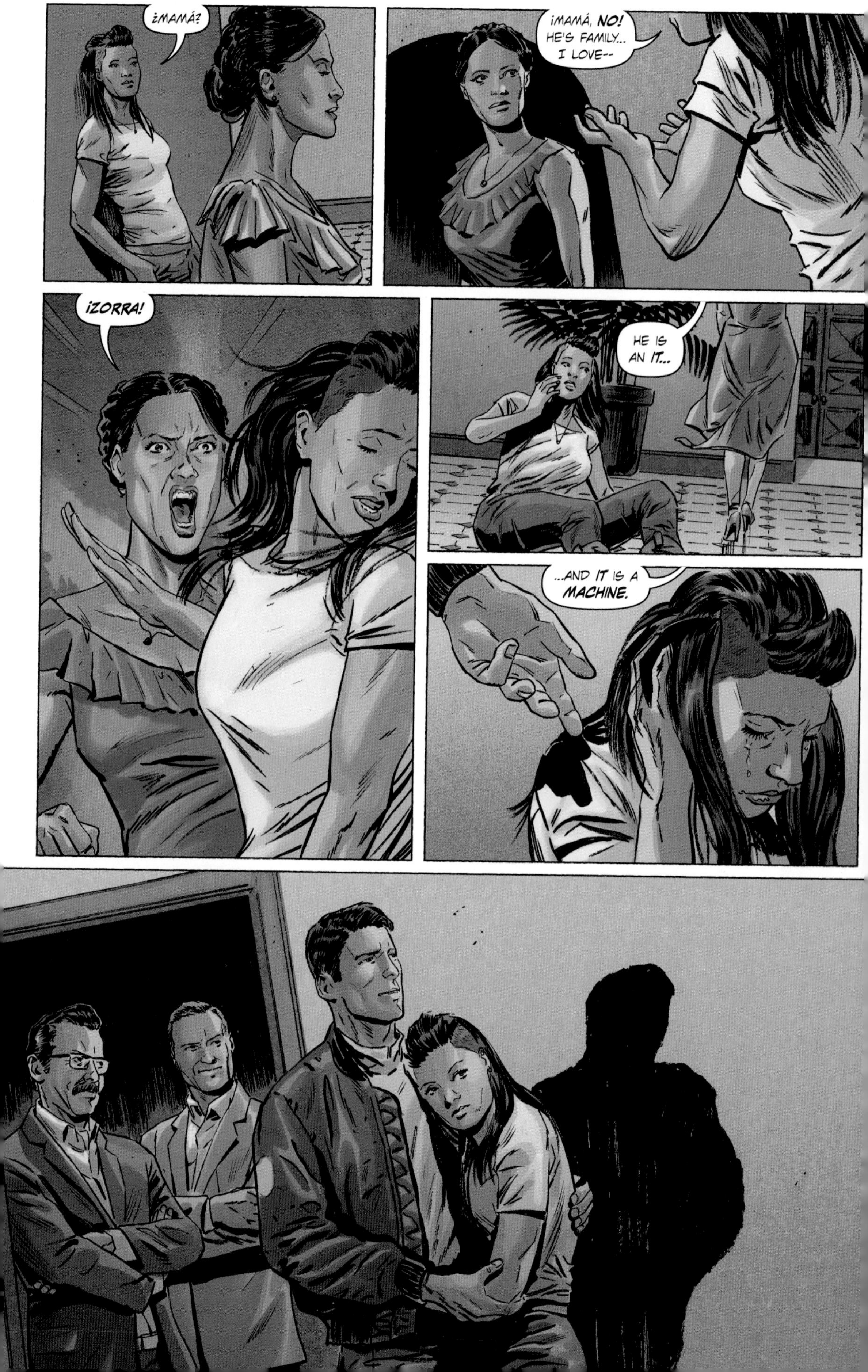
¿MAMÁ?
¡MAMÁ, NO! HE'S FAMILY... I LOVE--
¡ZORRA!
HE IS AN IT...
...AND IT IS A MACHINE.

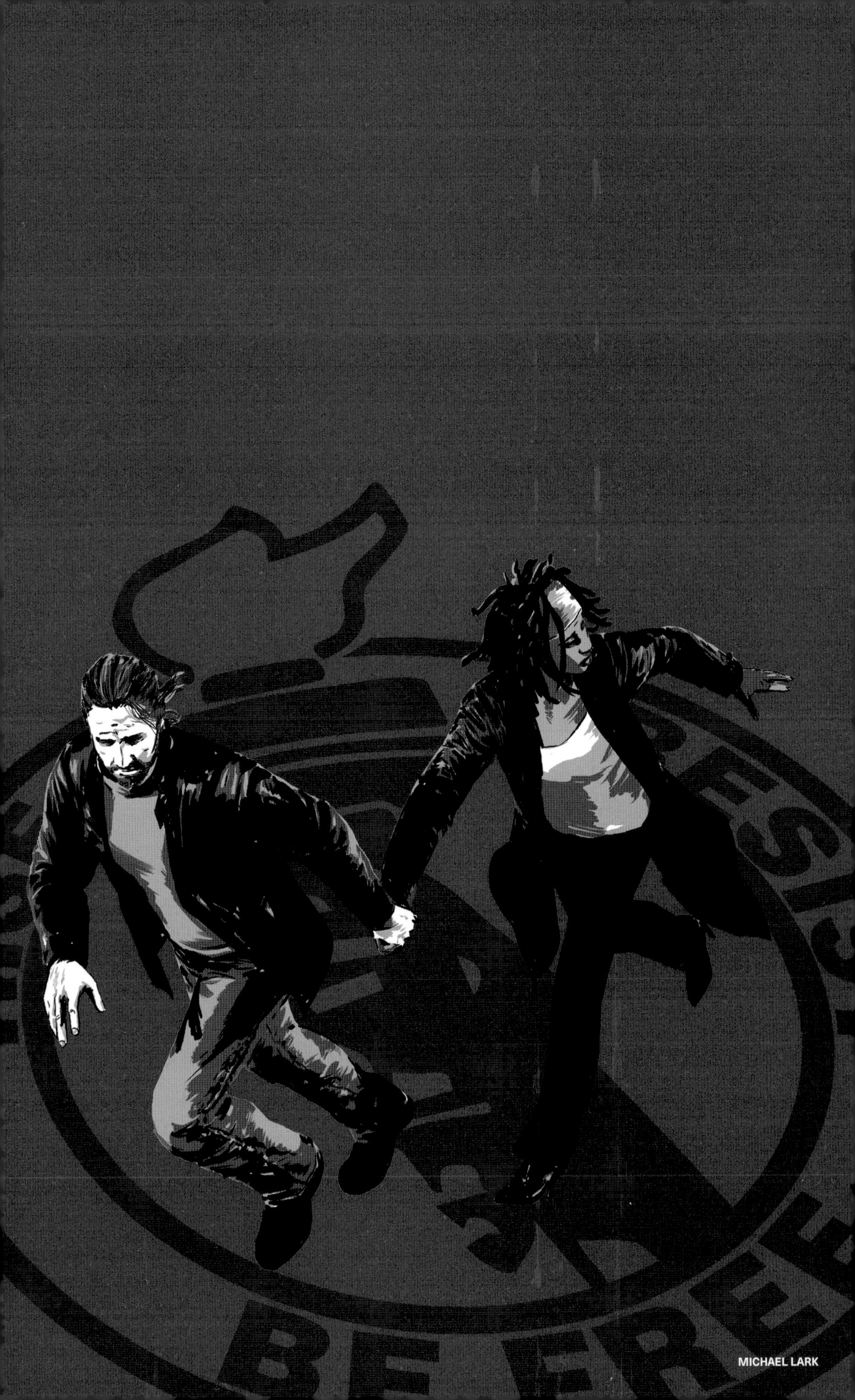
MICHAEL LARK

In the domain of **FAMILY CARLYLE**, society is
divided into three classes—**Family**, **Serf**, and **Waste**.

The **Family** rules with absolute authority and power,
aided by a small number of **Lesser Houses**, who serve at their pleasure.

The **Serfs** serve the Family in
areas requiring expertise and specialized knowledge.

Waste are viewed as little more than a source of raw labor.

Waste can become Serf in a number of ways, but the most common is through
the **Lift**, where hopefuls try to prove that they are worth the Carlyle Family's
time and investment.

———

JOE and **BOBBIE BARRETT** were Waste.

In X +64 they risked everything to attend
the Denver Lift in the hope of securing a better life for their children.

Their daughter, **Leigh**, was killed before reaching Denver.

Their son, **Michael**, along with his
childhood sweetheart, **Casey Solomon**, were both Lifted.
Each now serves the Carlyle Family—Michael as a gifted medical student,
Casey as a soldier.

———

Joe and Bobbie now live in privilege and comfort in San Francisco.

They hate what their lives have become.

They remember when they were almost **Free**....

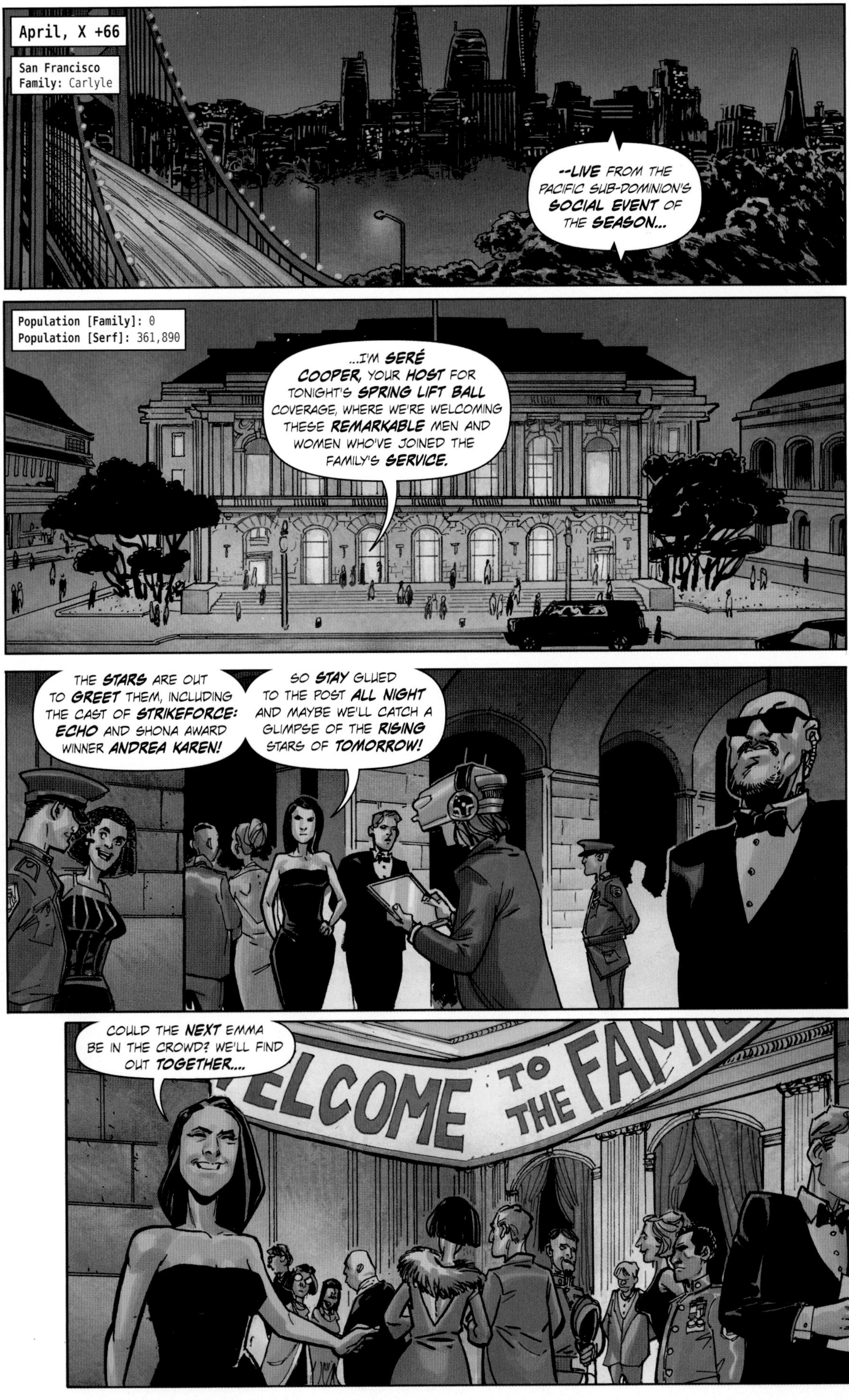
April, X +66
San Francisco
Family: Carlyle
--LIVE FROM THE PACIFIC SUB-DOMINION'S SOCIAL EVENT OF THE SEASON...
Population [Family]: 0
Population [Serf]: 361,890
...I'M SERÉ COOPER, YOUR HOST FOR TONIGHT'S SPRING LIFT BALL COVERAGE, WHERE WE'RE WELCOMING THESE REMARKABLE MEN AND WOMEN WHO'VE JOINED THE FAMILY'S SERVICE.
THE STARS ARE OUT TO GREET THEM, INCLUDING THE CAST OF STRIKEFORCE: ECHO AND SHONA AWARD WINNER ANDREA KAREN!
SO STAY GLUED TO THE POST ALL NIGHT AND MAYBE WE'LL CATCH A GLIMPSE OF THE RISING STARS OF TOMORROW!
COULD THE NEXT EMMA BE IN THE CROWD? WE'LL FIND OUT TOGETHER....
ELCOME TO THE FAMI

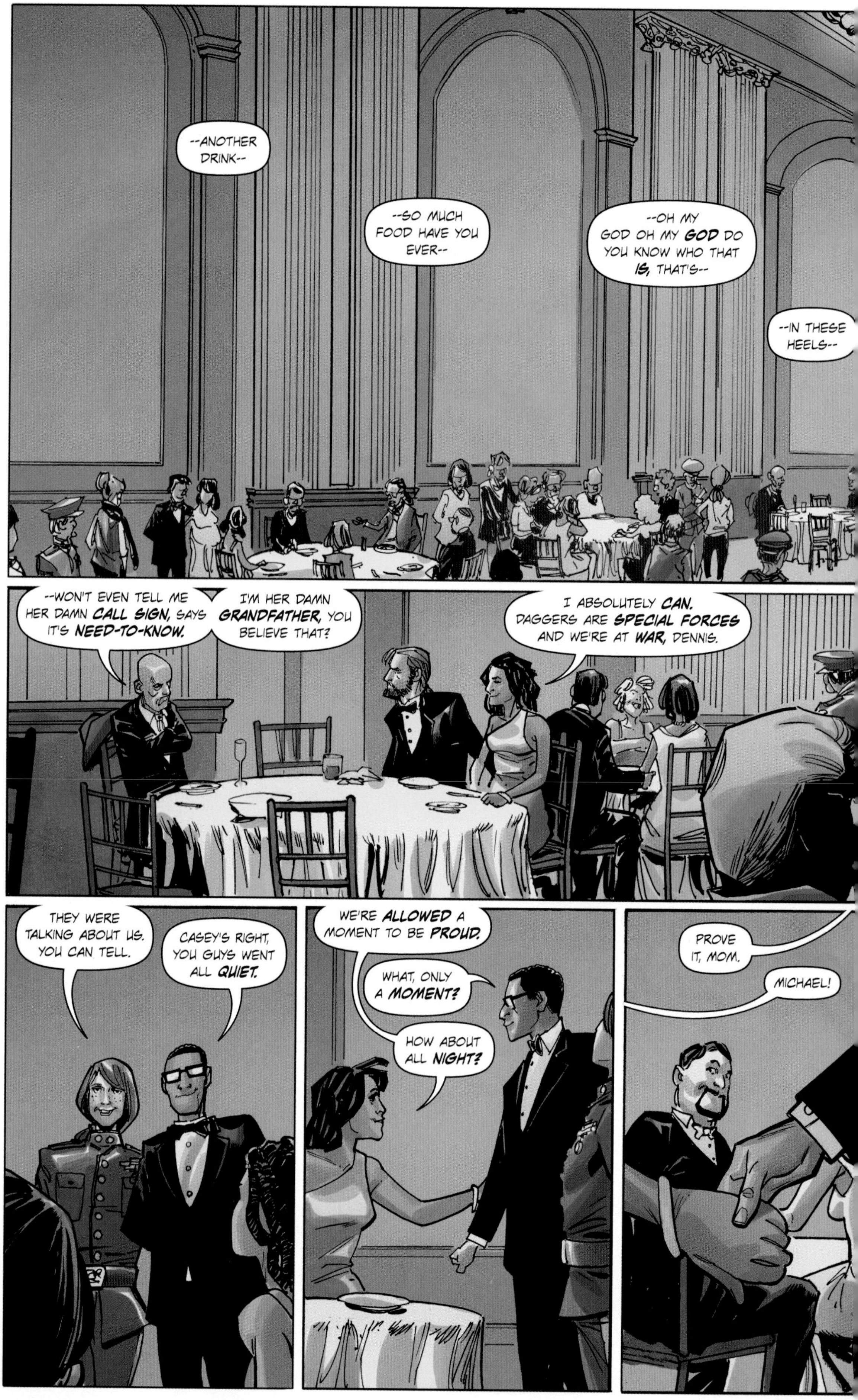
--ANOTHER DRINK--
--SO MUCH FOOD HAVE YOU EVER--
--OH MY GOD OH MY GOD DO YOU KNOW WHO THAT IS, THAT'S--
--IN THESE HEELS--
--WON'T EVEN TELL ME HER DAMN CALL SIGN, SAYS IT'S NEED-TO-KNOW.
I'M HER DAMN GRANDFATHER, YOU BELIEVE THAT?
I ABSOLUTELY CAN. DAGGERS ARE SPECIAL FORCES AND WE'RE AT WAR, DENNIS.
THEY WERE TALKING ABOUT US. YOU CAN TELL.
CASEY'S RIGHT, YOU GUYS WENT ALL QUIET.
WE'RE ALLOWED A MOMENT TO BE PROUD.
WHAT, ONLY A MOMENT?
HOW ABOUT ALL NIGHT?
PROVE IT, MOM.
MICHAEL!

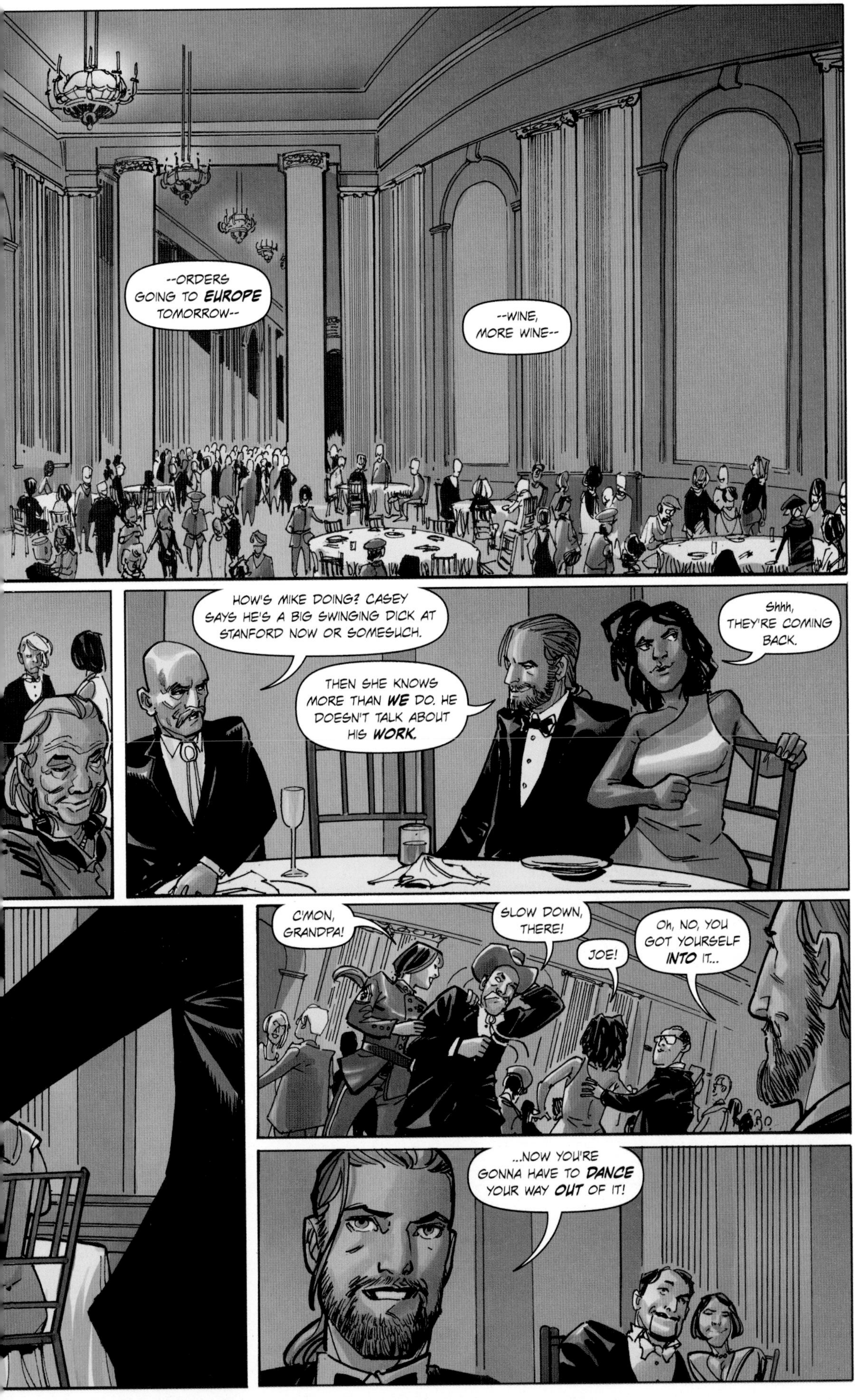
--ORDERS GOING TO EUROPE TOMORROW--
--WINE, MORE WINE--
HOW'S MIKE DOING? CASEY SAYS HE'S A BIG SWINGING DICK AT STANFORD NOW OR SOMESUCH.
THEN SHE KNOWS MORE THAN WE DO. HE DOESN'T TALK ABOUT HIS WORK.
Shhh, THEY'RE COMING BACK.
C'MON, GRANDPA!
SLOW DOWN, THERE!
JOE!
Oh, NO, YOU GOT YOURSELF INTO IT...
...NOW YOU'RE GONNA HAVE TO DANCE YOUR WAY OUT OF IT!

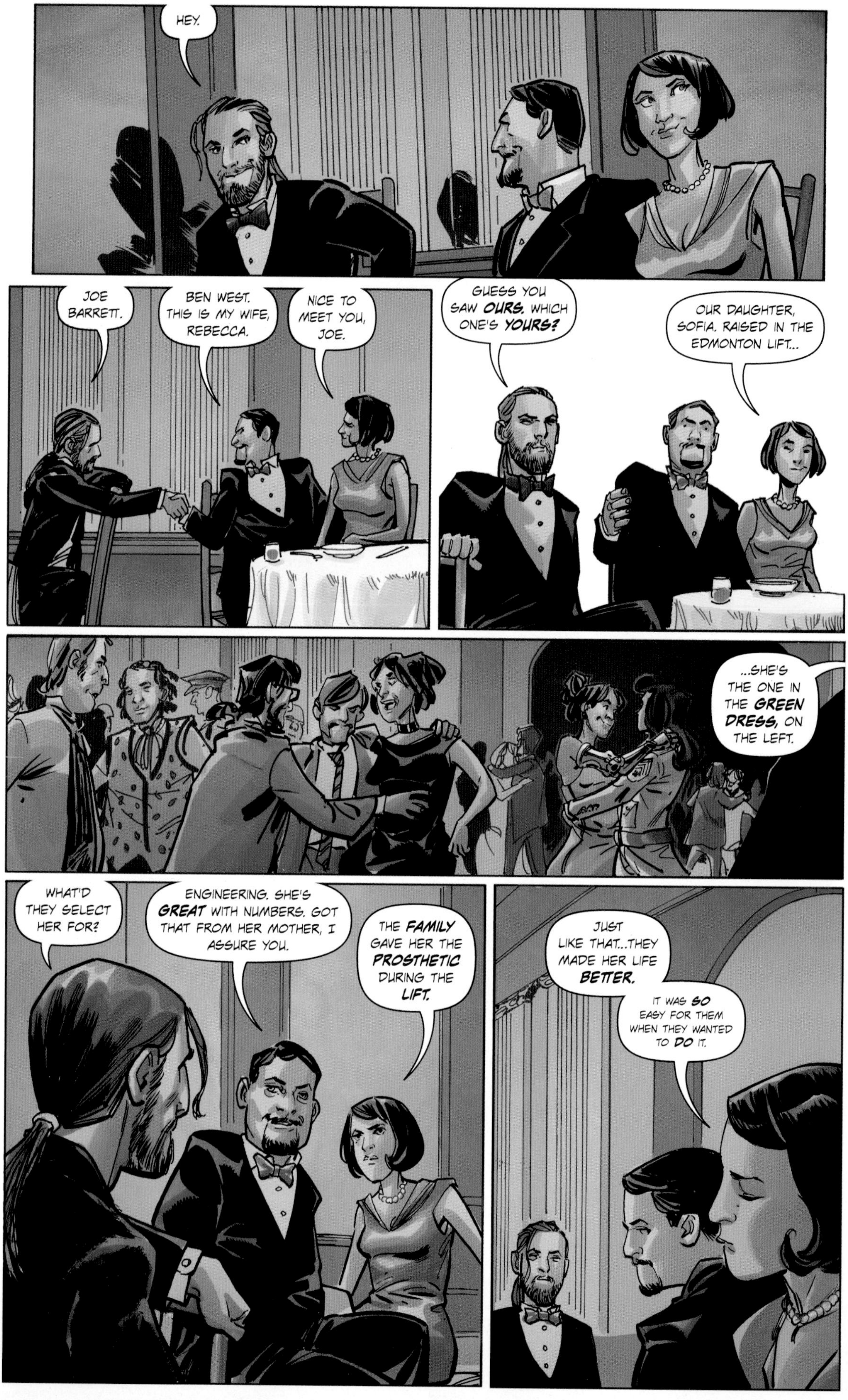
HEY.
JOE BARRETT.
BEN WEST. THIS IS MY WIFE, REBECCA.
NICE TO MEET YOU, JOE.
GUESS YOU SAW OURS. WHICH ONE'S YOURS?
OUR DAUGHTER, SOFIA. RAISED IN THE EDMONTON LIFT...
...SHE'S THE ONE IN THE GREEN DRESS, ON THE LEFT.
WHAT'D THEY SELECT HER FOR?
ENGINEERING. SHE'S GREAT WITH NUMBERS. GOT THAT FROM HER MOTHER, I ASSURE YOU.
THE FAMILY GAVE HER THE PROSTHETIC DURING THE LIFT.
JUST LIKE THAT...THEY MADE HER LIFE BETTER.
IT WAS SO EASY FOR THEM WHEN THEY WANTED TO DO IT.

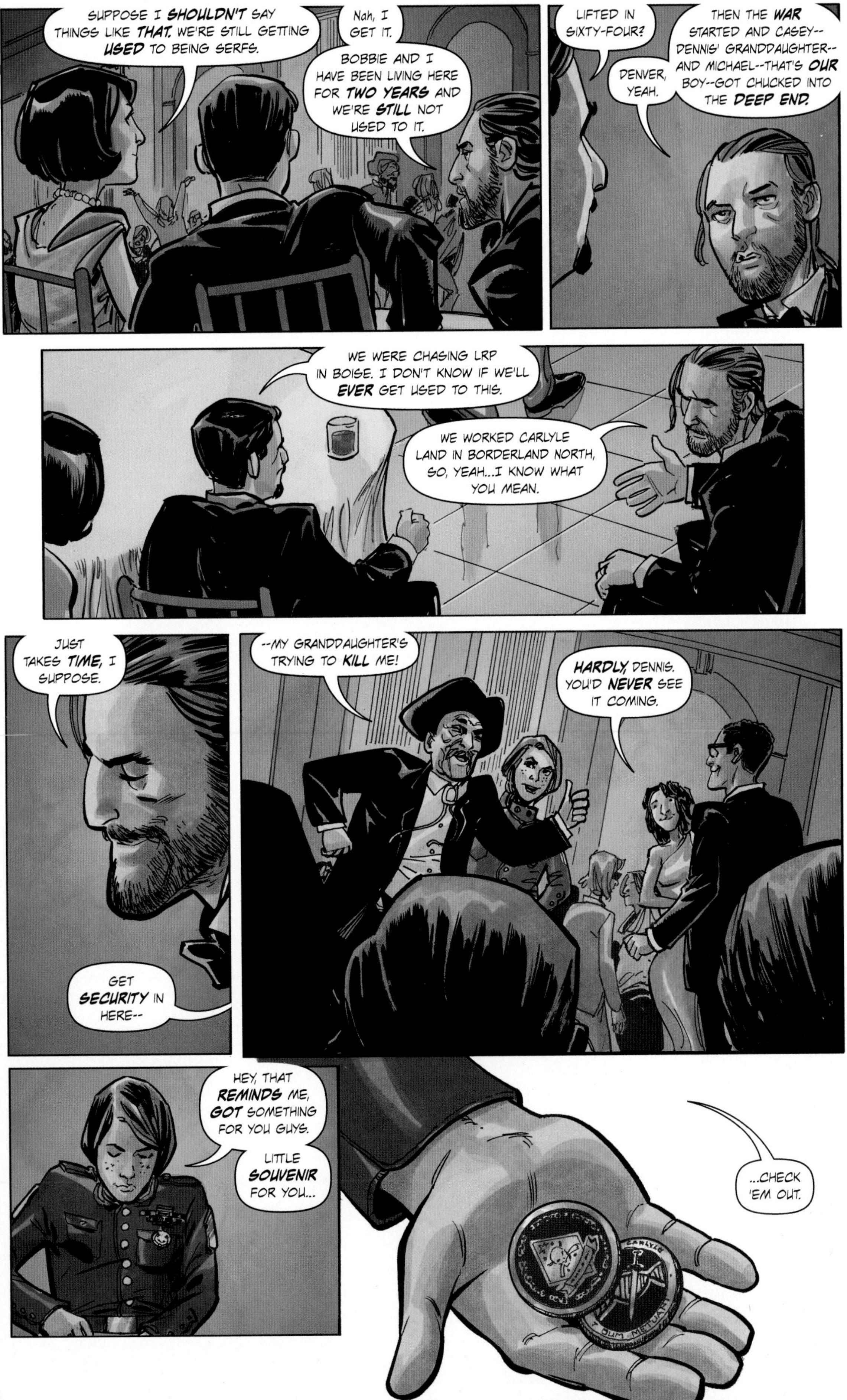
SUPPOSE I SHOULDN'T SAY THINGS LIKE THAT. WE'RE STILL GETTING USED TO BEING SERFS.
Nah, I GET IT.
BOBBIE AND I HAVE BEEN LIVING HERE FOR TWO YEARS AND WE'RE STILL NOT USED TO IT.
LIFTED IN SIXTY-FOUR?
DENVER, YEAH.
THEN THE WAR STARTED AND CASEY--DENNIS' GRANDDAUGHTER--AND MICHAEL--THAT'S OUR BOY--GOT CHUCKED INTO THE DEEP END.
WE WERE CHASING LRP IN BOISE. I DON'T KNOW IF WE'LL EVER GET USED TO THIS.
WE WORKED CARLYLE LAND IN BORDERLAND NORTH, SO, YEAH...I KNOW WHAT YOU MEAN.
JUST TAKES TIME, I SUPPOSE.
GET SECURITY IN HERE--
--MY GRANDDAUGHTER'S TRYING TO KILL ME!
HARDLY, DENNIS. YOU'D NEVER SEE IT COMING.
HEY, THAT REMINDS ME, GOT SOMETHING FOR YOU GUYS.
LITTLE SOUVENIR FOR YOU...
...CHECK 'EM OUT.

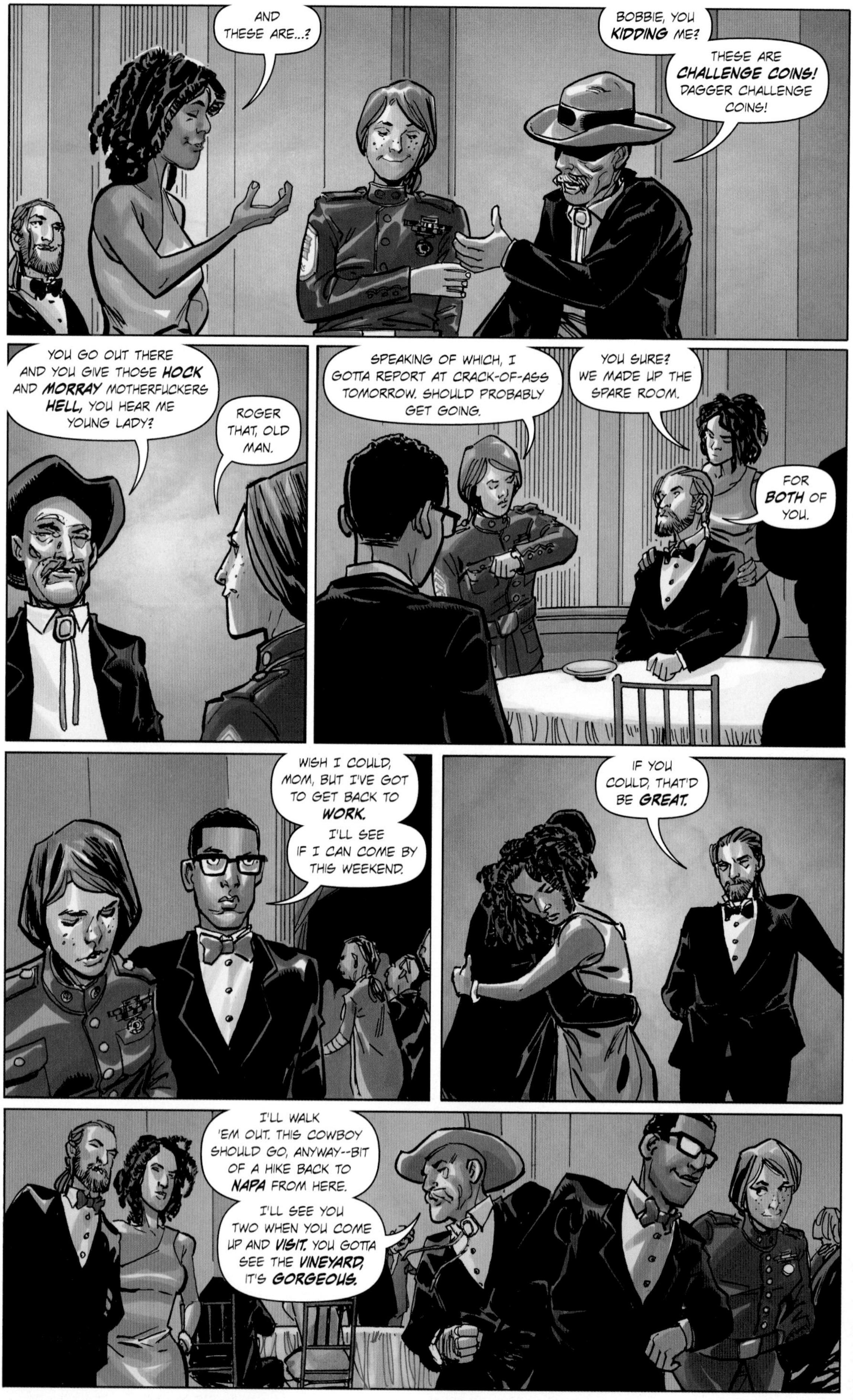
AND THESE ARE...?
BOBBIE, YOU KIDDING ME?
THESE ARE CHALLENGE COINS! DAGGER CHALLENGE COINS!
YOU GO OUT THERE AND YOU GIVE THOSE HOCK AND MORRAY MOTHERFUCKERS HELL, YOU HEAR ME YOUNG LADY?
ROGER THAT, OLD MAN.
SPEAKING OF WHICH, I GOTTA REPORT AT CRACK-OF-ASS TOMORROW. SHOULD PROBABLY GET GOING.
YOU SURE? WE MADE UP THE SPARE ROOM.
FOR BOTH OF YOU.
WISH I COULD, MOM, BUT I'VE GOT TO GET BACK TO WORK.
I'LL SEE IF I CAN COME BY THIS WEEKEND.
IF YOU COULD, THAT'D BE GREAT.
I'LL WALK 'EM OUT. THIS COWBOY SHOULD GO, ANYWAY--BIT OF A HIKE BACK TO NAPA FROM HERE.
I'LL SEE YOU TWO WHEN YOU COME UP AND VISIT. YOU GOTTA SEE THE VINEYARD, IT'S GORGEOUS.

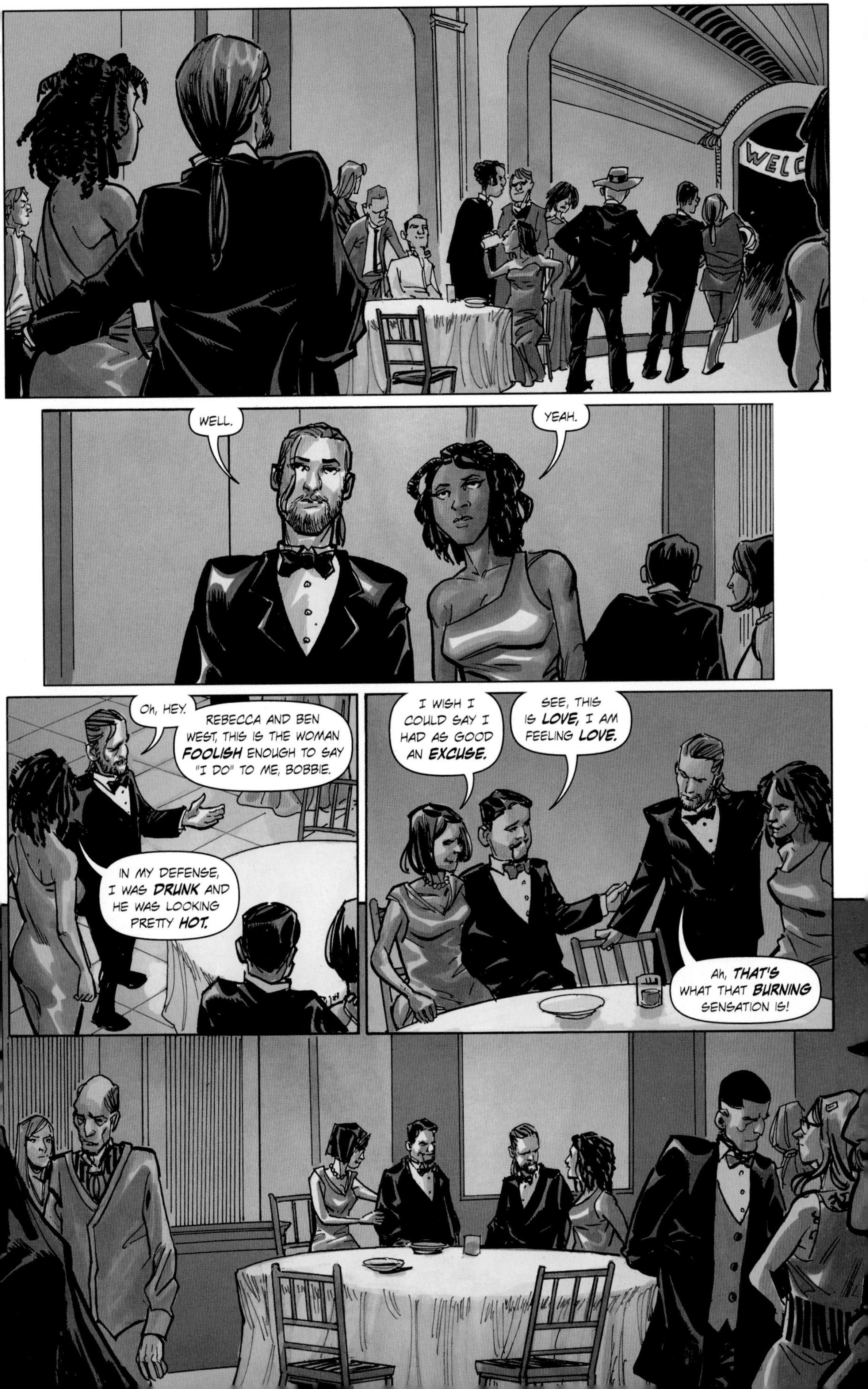

WELC
WELL.
YEAH.
Oh, HEY.
REBECCA AND BEN WEST, THIS IS THE WOMAN FOOLISH ENOUGH TO SAY "I DO" TO ME, BOBBIE.
IN MY DEFENSE, I WAS DRUNK AND HE WAS LOOKING PRETTY HOT.
I WISH I COULD SAY I HAD AS GOOD AN EXCUSE.
SEE, THIS IS LOVE, I AM FEELING LOVE.
Ah, THAT'S WHAT THAT BURNING SENSATION IS!

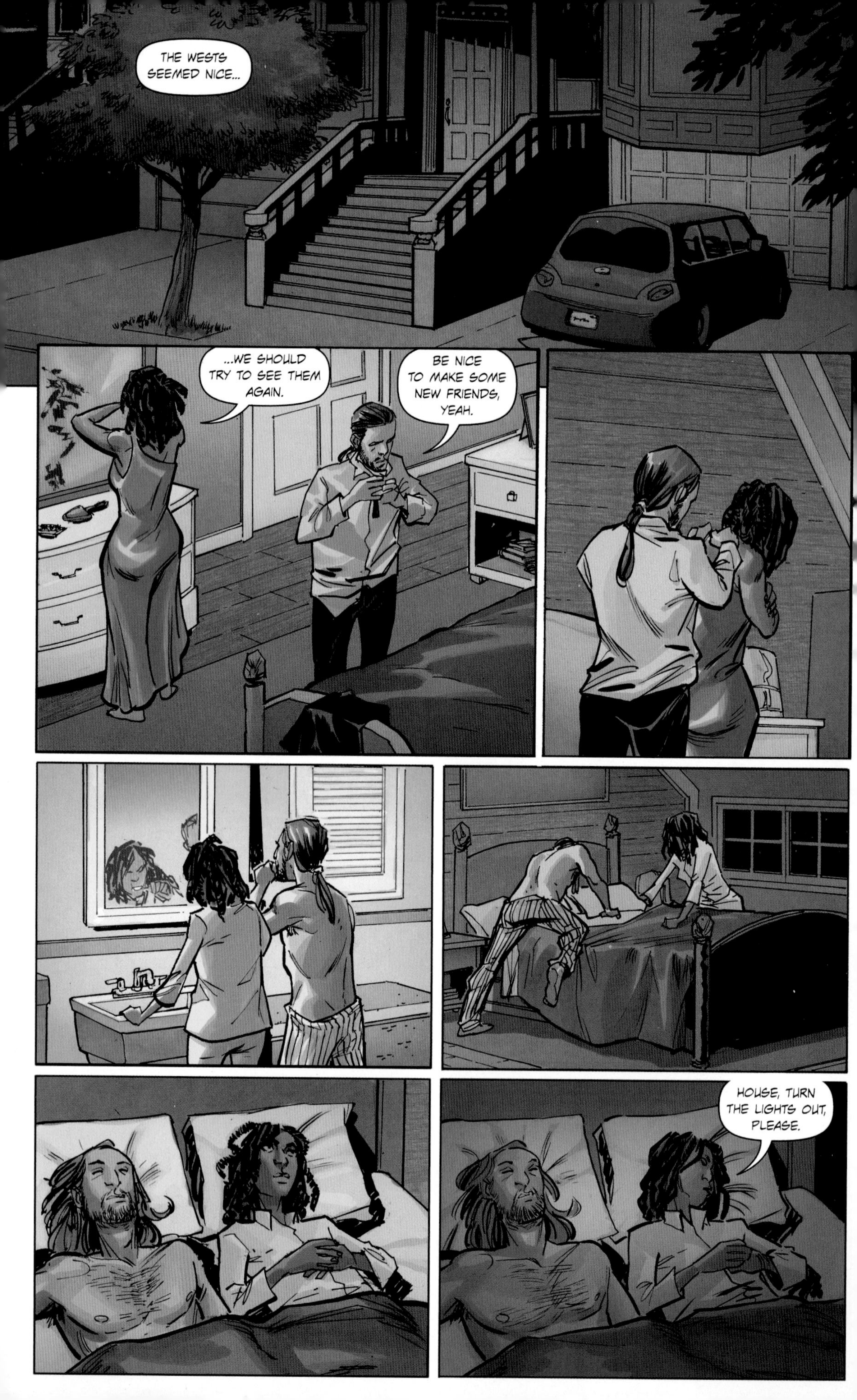
THE WESTS SEEMED NICE...
...WE SHOULD TRY TO SEE THEM AGAIN.
BE NICE TO MAKE SOME NEW FRIENDS, YEAH.
HOUSE, TURN THE LIGHTS OUT, PLEASE.

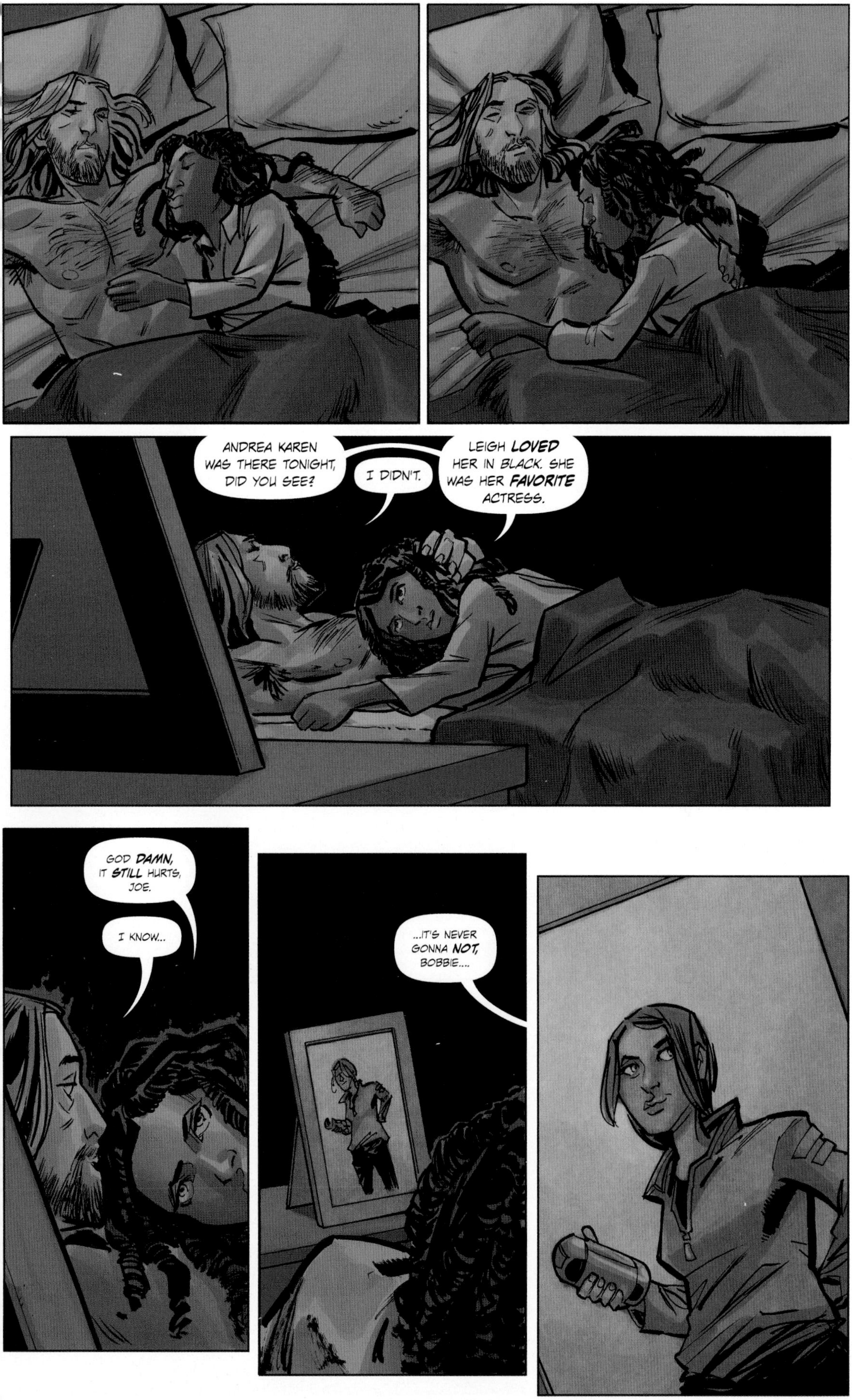
ANDREA KAREN WAS THERE TONIGHT, DID YOU SEE?
I DIDN'T.
LEIGH LOVED HER IN BLACK. SHE WAS HER FAVORITE ACTRESS.
GOD DAMN, IT STILL HURTS, JOE.
I KNOW...
...IT'S NEVER GONNA NOT, BOBBIE....

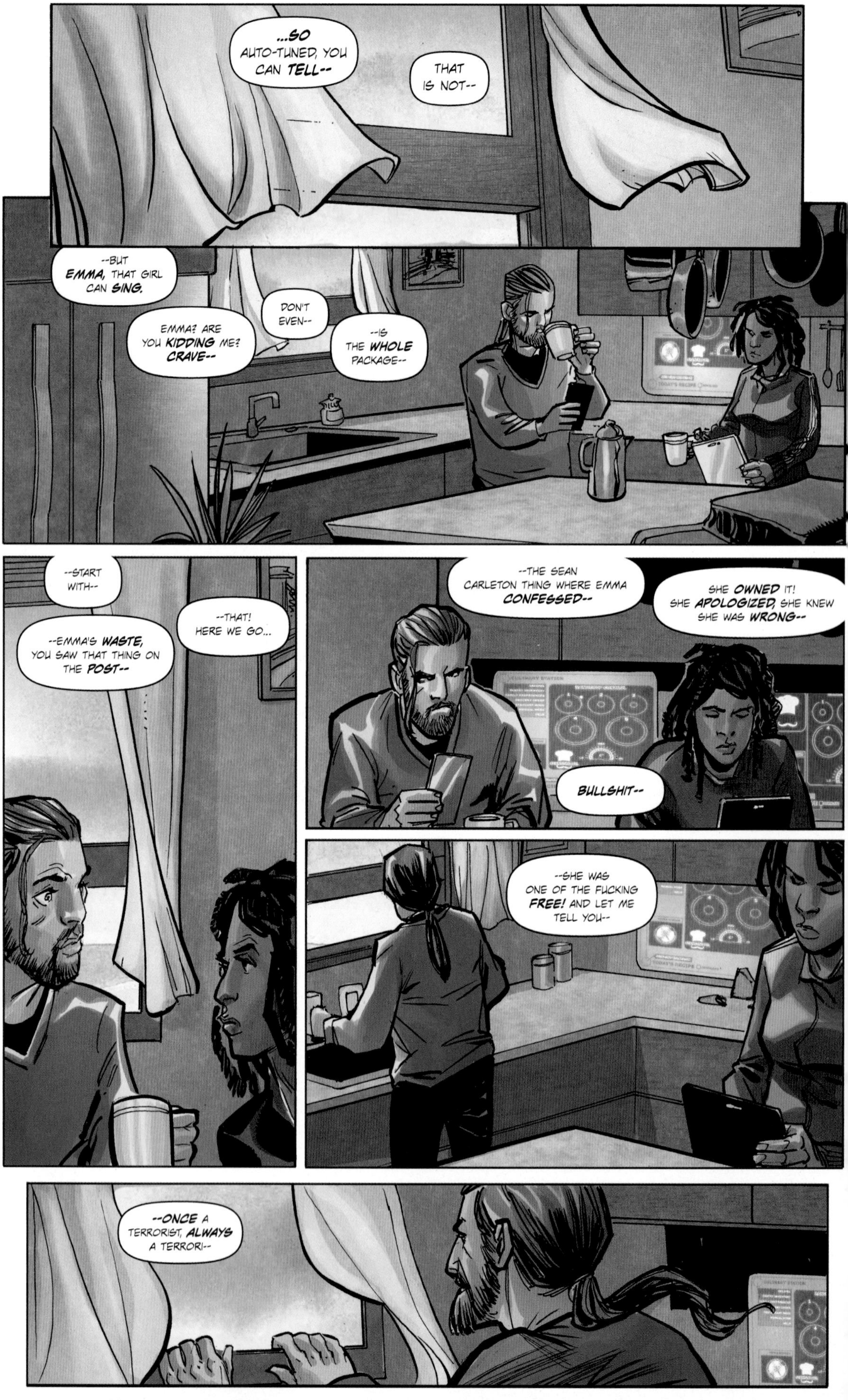
...SO AUTO-TUNED, YOU CAN TELL--
THAT IS NOT--
--BUT EMMA, THAT GIRL CAN SING.
EMMA? ARE YOU KIDDING ME? CRAVE--
DON'T EVEN--
--IS THE WHOLE PACKAGE--
--START WITH--
--EMMA'S WASTE, YOU SAW THAT THING ON THE POST--
--THAT! HERE WE GO...
--THE SEAN CARLETON THING WHERE EMMA CONFESSED--
SHE OWNED IT! SHE APOLOGIZED, SHE KNEW SHE WAS WRONG--
BULLSHIT--
--SHE WAS ONE OF THE FUCKING FREE! AND LET ME TELL YOU--
--ONCE A TERRORIST, ALWAYS A TERRORI--

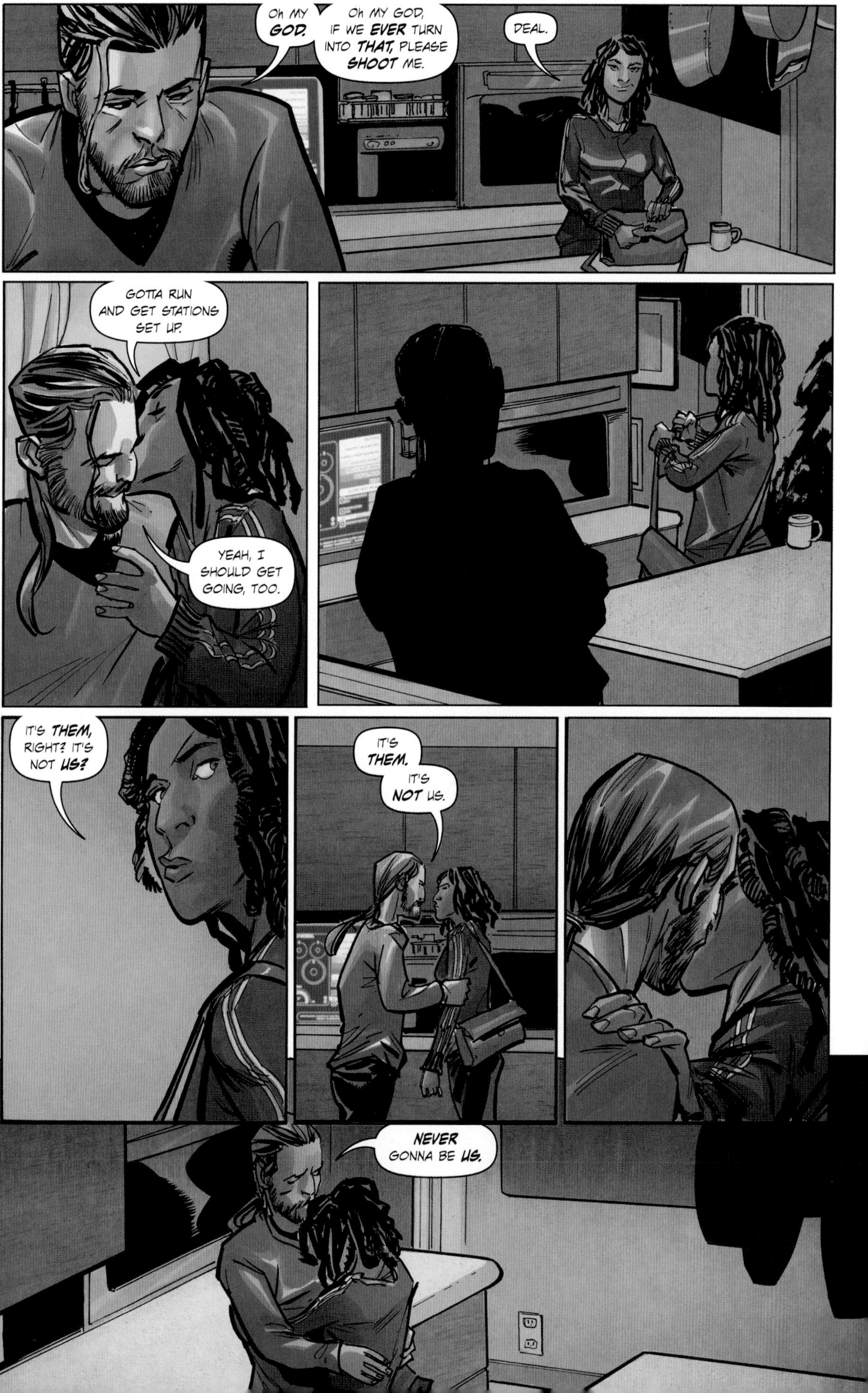
Oh MY GOD.
Oh MY GOD, IF WE EVER TURN INTO THAT, PLEASE SHOOT ME.
DEAL.
GOTTA RUN AND GET STATIONS SET UP.
YEAH, I SHOULD GET GOING, TOO.
IT'S THEM, RIGHT? IT'S NOT US?
IT'S THEM.
IT'S NOT US.
NEVER GONNA BE US.

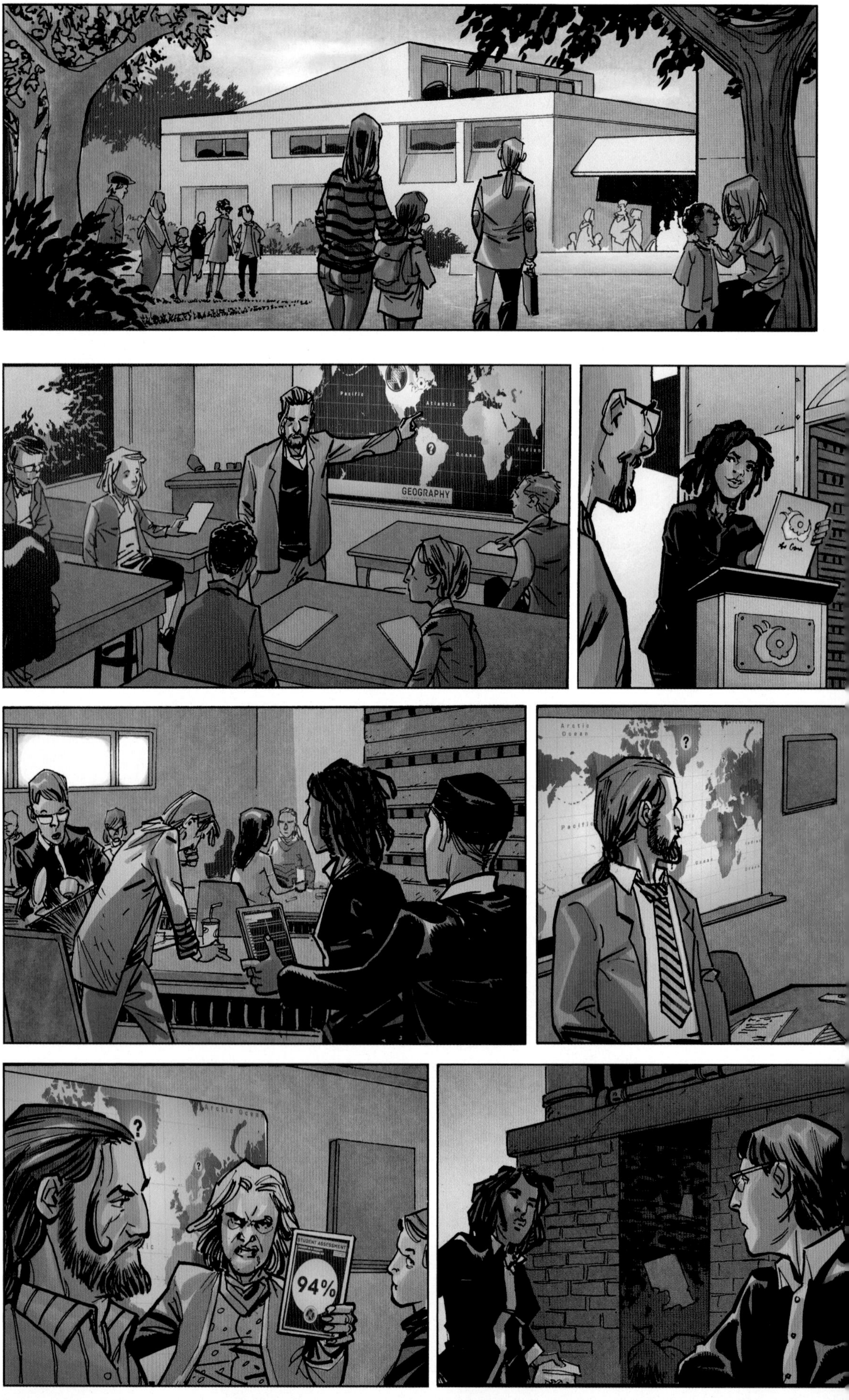
Pacific
Atlantic
Ocean
GEOGRAPHY
Arctic Ocean
Pacific
STUDENT ASSESSMENT
94%

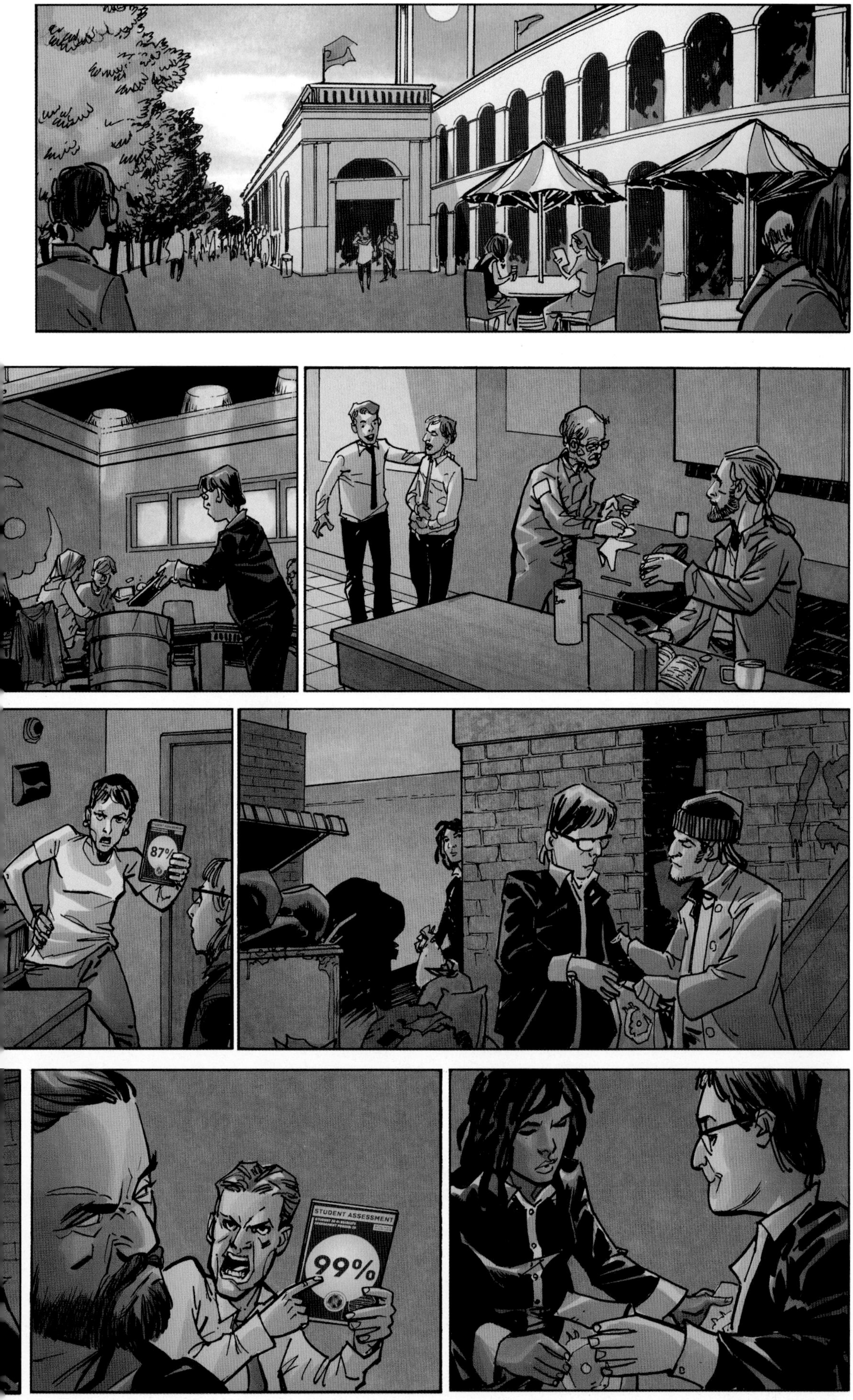
87%
STUDENT ASSESSMENT
99%

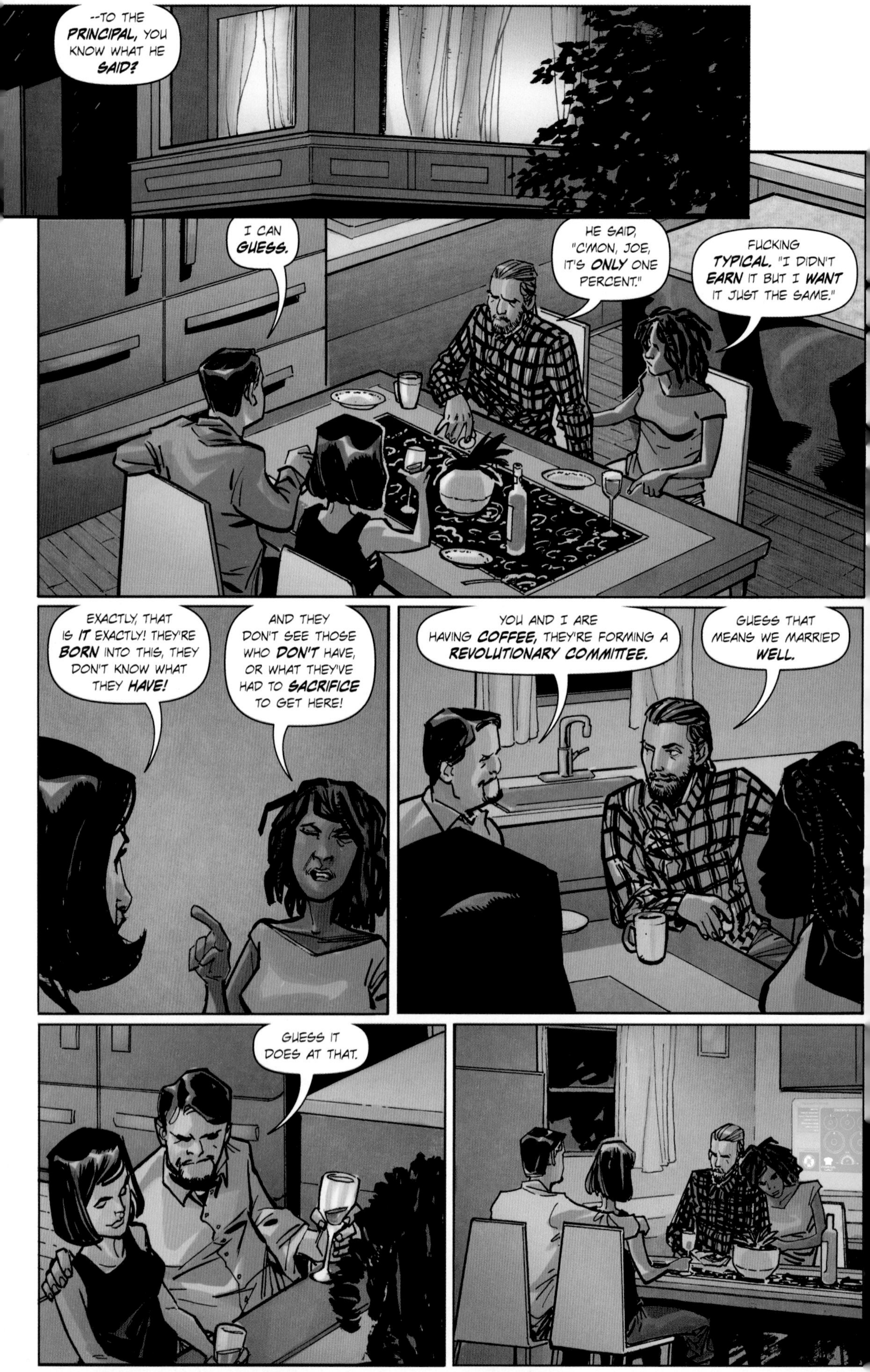

--TO THE PRINCIPAL, YOU KNOW WHAT HE SAID?
I CAN GUESS.
HE SAID, "C'MON, JOE, IT'S ONLY ONE PERCENT."
FUCKING TYPICAL. "I DIDN'T EARN IT BUT I WANT IT JUST THE SAME."
EXACTLY, THAT IS IT EXACTLY! THEY'RE BORN INTO THIS, THEY DON'T KNOW WHAT THEY HAVE!
AND THEY DON'T SEE THOSE WHO DON'T HAVE, OR WHAT THEY'VE HAD TO SACRIFICE TO GET HERE!
YOU AND I ARE HAVING COFFEE, THEY'RE FORMING A REVOLUTIONARY COMMITTEE.
GUESS THAT MEANS WE MARRIED WELL.
GUESS IT DOES AT THAT.

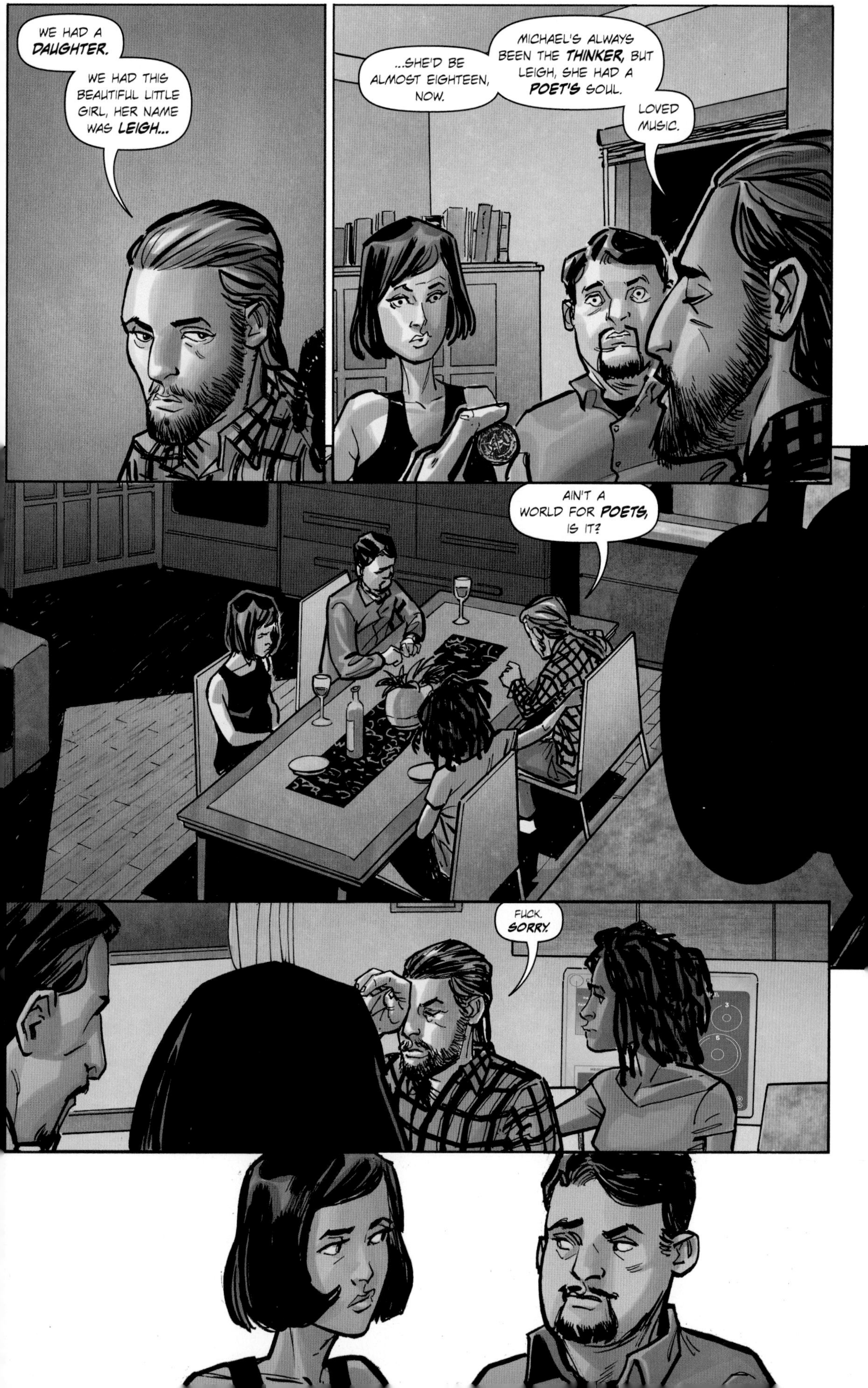
WE HAD A DAUGHTER.
WE HAD THIS BEAUTIFUL LITTLE GIRL, HER NAME WAS LEIGH...
...SHE'D BE ALMOST EIGHTEEN, NOW.
MICHAEL'S ALWAYS BEEN THE THINKER, BUT LEIGH, SHE HAD A POET'S SOUL.
LOVED MUSIC.
AIN'T A WORLD FOR POETS, IS IT?
FUCK. SORRY.

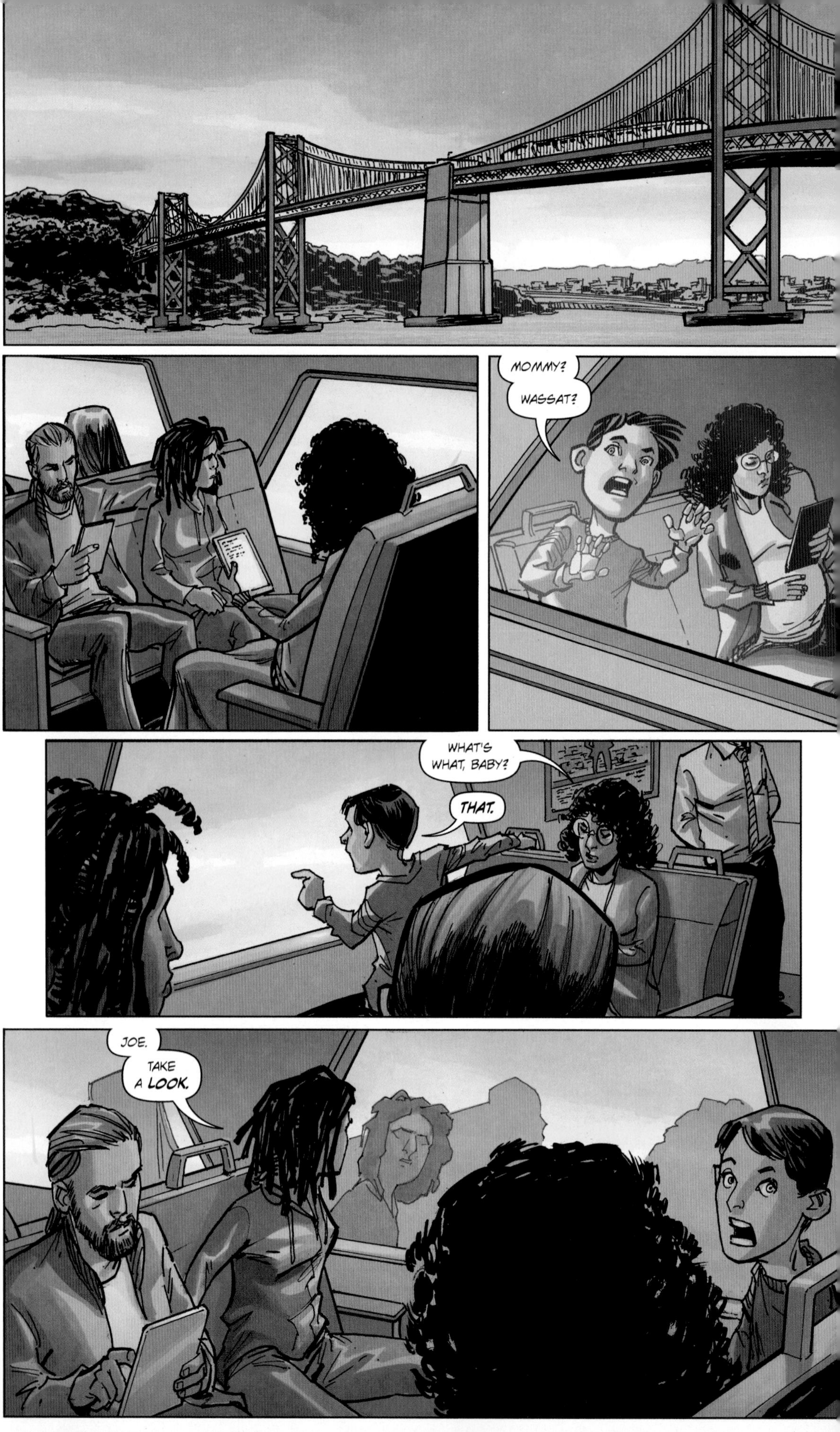
MOMMY?
WASSAT?
WHAT'S WHAT, BABY?
THAT.
JOE.
TAKE A LOOK.

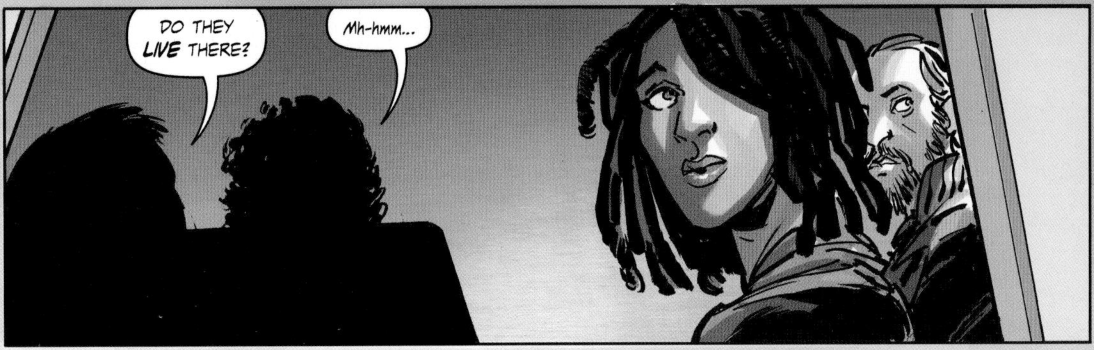
DO THEY LIVE THERE?
Mh-hmm...

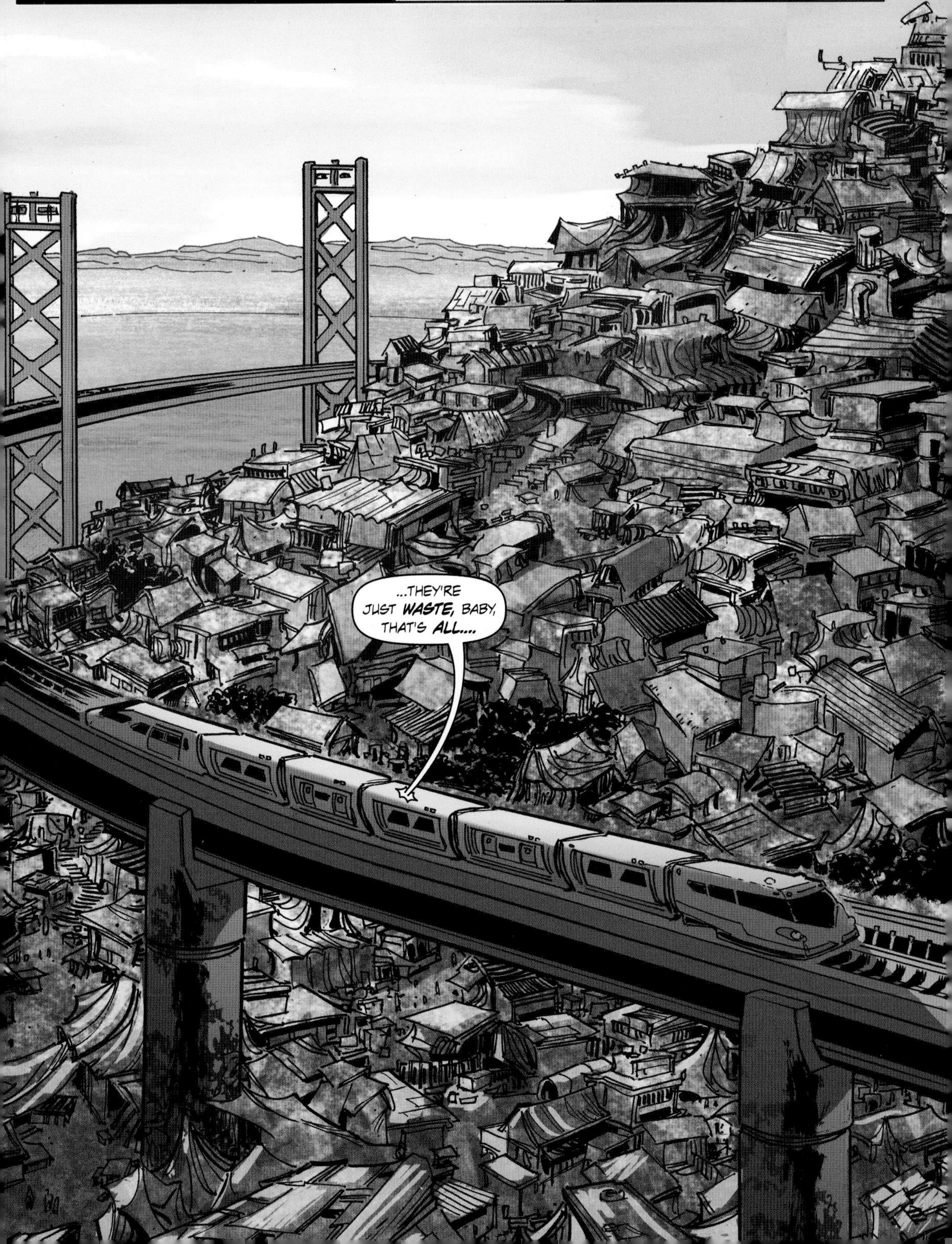
...THEY'RE JUST WASTE, BABY, THAT'S ALL....

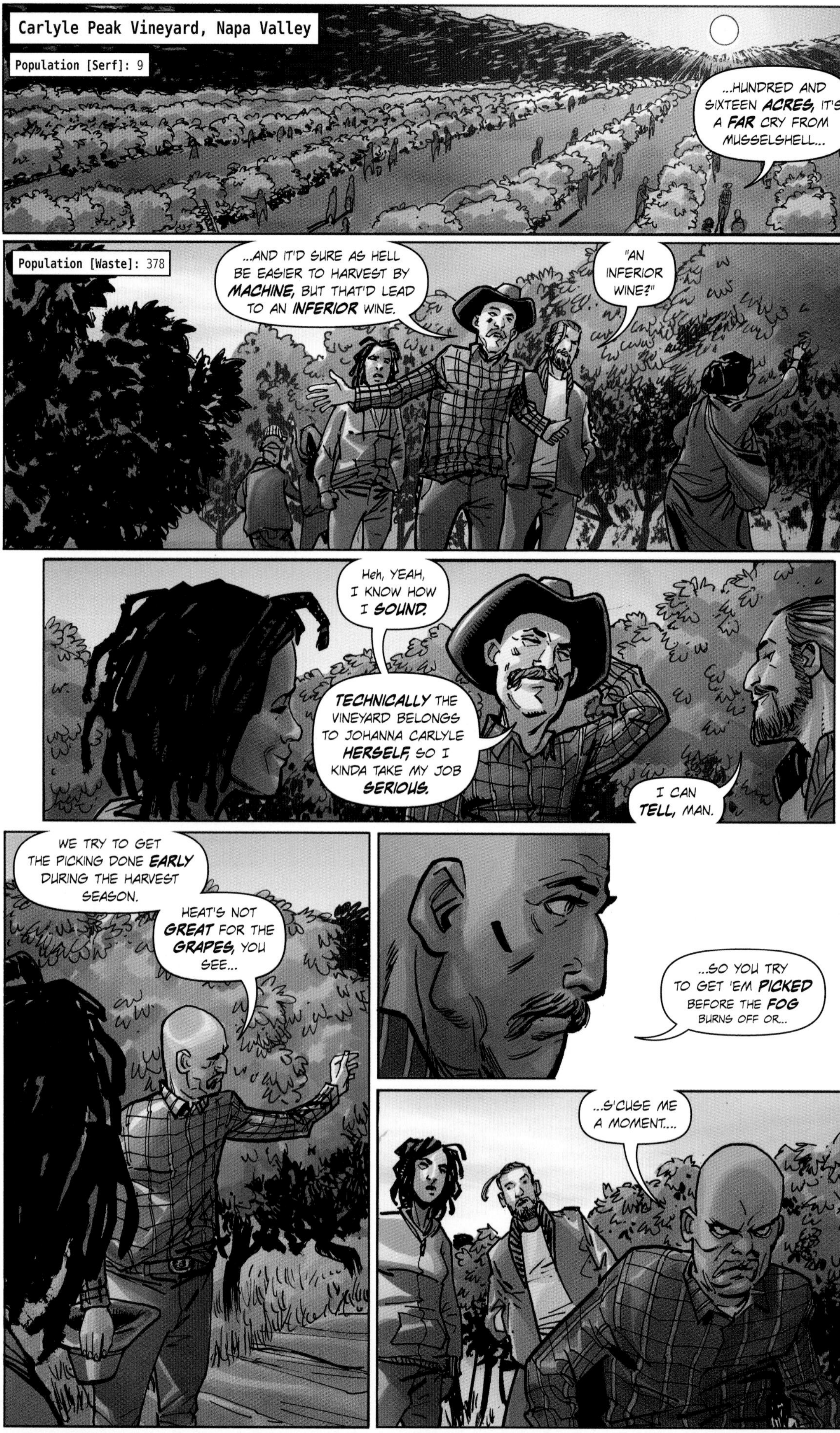

Carlyle Peak Vineyard, Napa Valley
Population [Serf]: 9
...HUNDRED AND SIXTEEN ACRES, IT'S A FAR CRY FROM MUSSELSHELL...
Population [Waste]: 378
...AND IT'D SURE AS HELL BE EASIER TO HARVEST BY MACHINE, BUT THAT'D LEAD TO AN INFERIOR WINE.
"AN INFERIOR WINE?"
Heh, YEAH, I KNOW HOW I SOUND.
TECHNICALLY THE VINEYARD BELONGS TO JOHANNA CARLYLE HERSELF, SO I KINDA TAKE MY JOB SERIOUS.
I CAN TELL, MAN.
WE TRY TO GET THE PICKING DONE EARLY DURING THE HARVEST SEASON.
HEAT'S NOT GREAT FOR THE GRAPES, YOU SEE...
...SO YOU TRY TO GET 'EM PICKED BEFORE THE FOG BURNS OFF OR...
...S'CUSE ME A MOMENT....

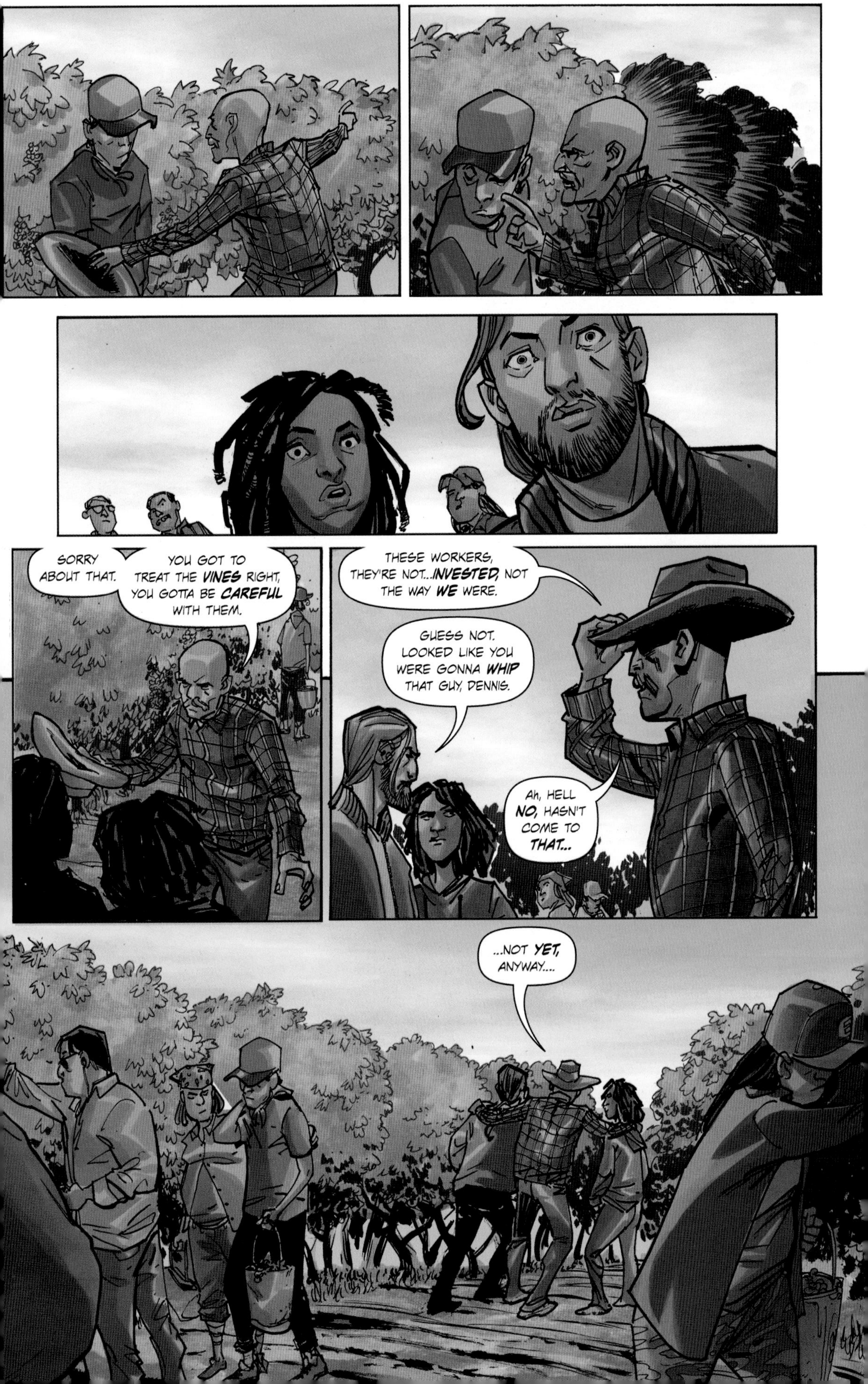
SORRY ABOUT THAT.
YOU GOT TO TREAT THE VINES RIGHT, YOU GOTTA BE CAREFUL WITH THEM.
THESE WORKERS, THEY'RE NOT...INVESTED, NOT THE WAY WE WERE.
GUESS NOT. LOOKED LIKE YOU WERE GONNA WHIP THAT GUY, DENNIS.
Ah, HELL NO, HASN'T COME TO THAT...
...NOT YET, ANYWAY....

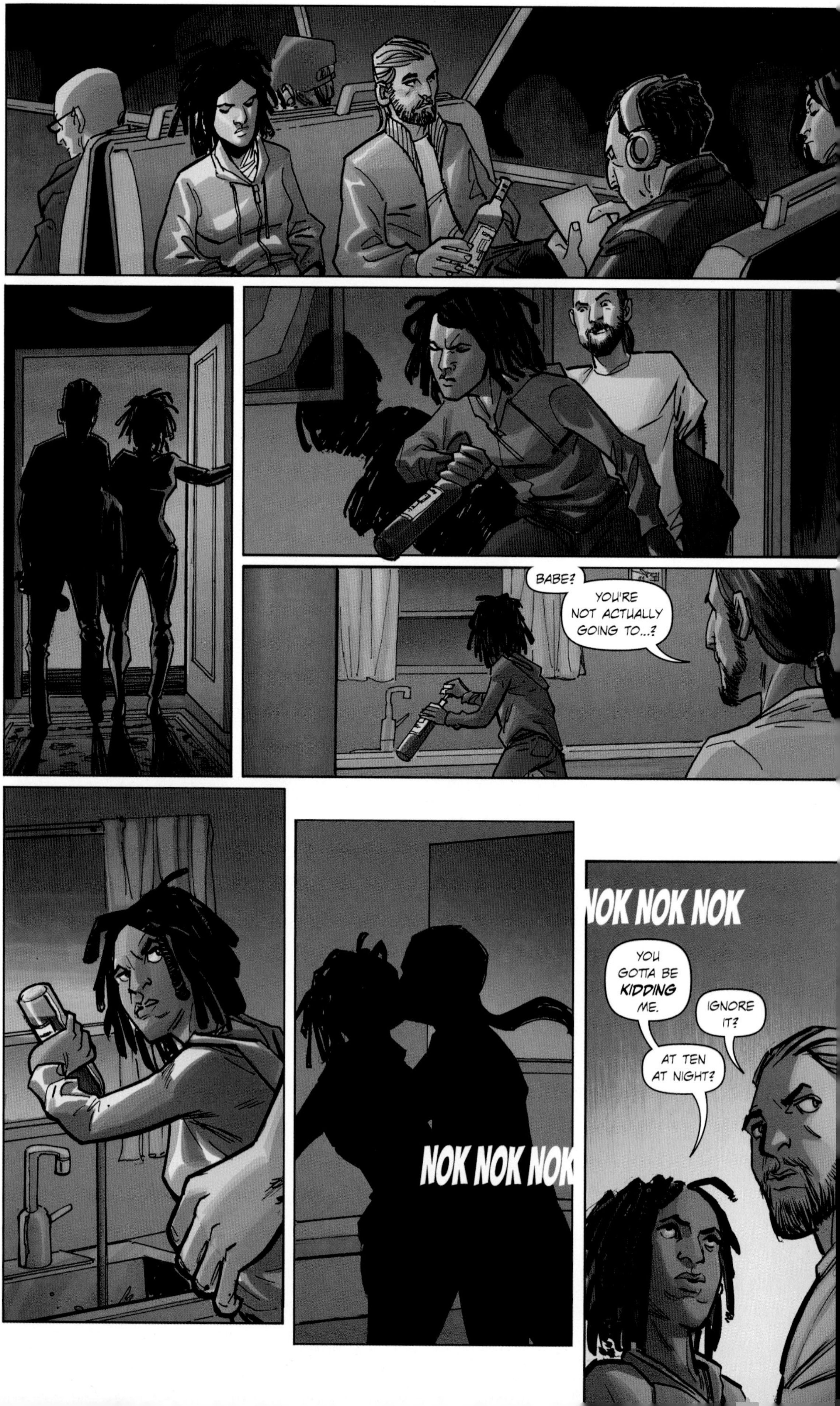
BABE?
YOU'RE NOT ACTUALLY GOING TO...?
NOK NOK NOK
NOK NOK NOK
YOU GOTTA BE **KIDDING** ME.
AT TEN AT NIGHT?
IGNORE IT?

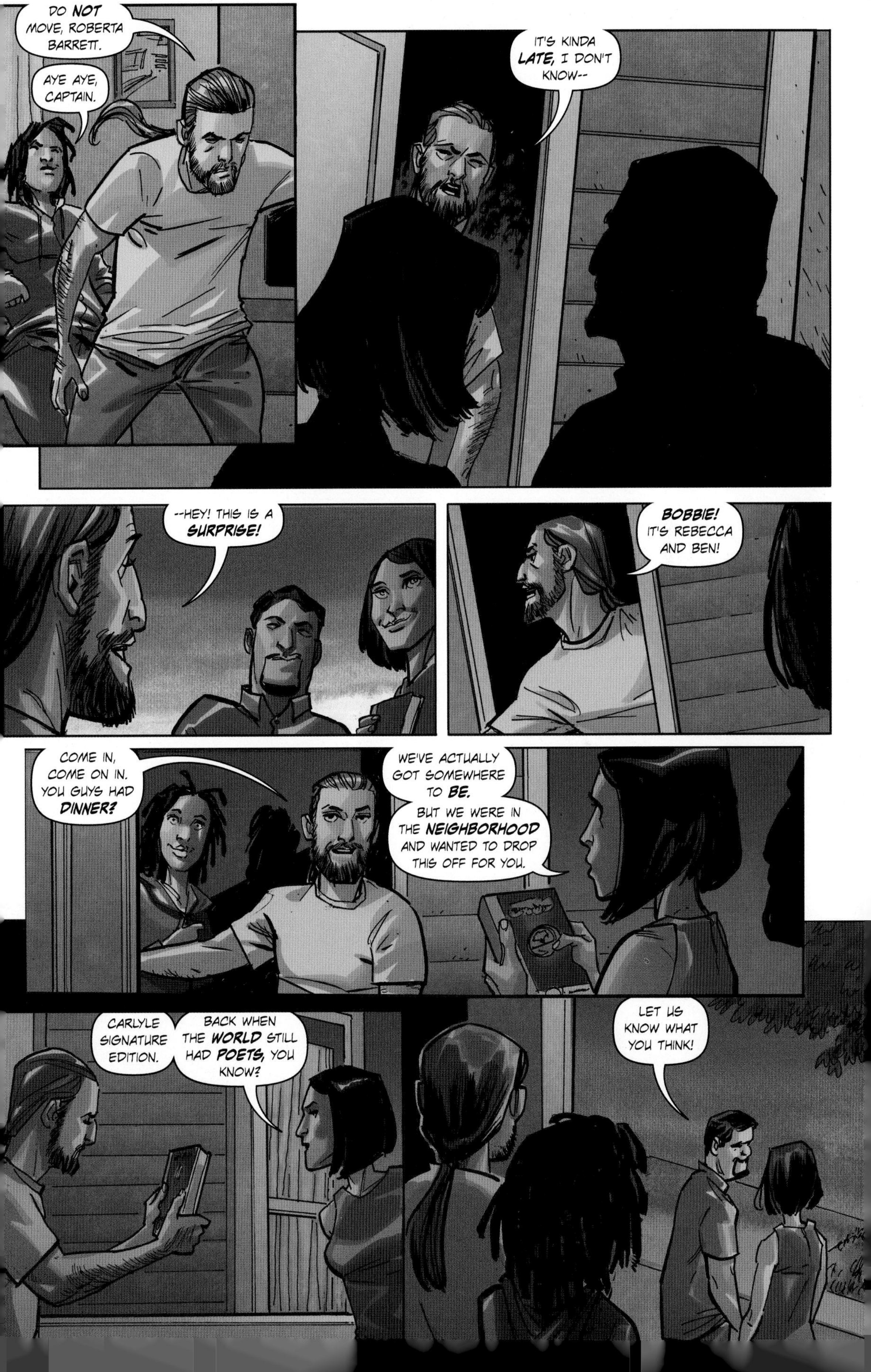

DO NOT MOVE, ROBERTA BARRETT.
AYE AYE, CAPTAIN.
IT'S KINDA LATE, I DON'T KNOW--
--HEY! THIS IS A SURPRISE!
BOBBIE! IT'S REBECCA AND BEN!
COME IN, COME ON IN. YOU GUYS HAD DINNER?
WE'VE ACTUALLY GOT SOMEWHERE TO BE.
BUT WE WERE IN THE NEIGHBORHOOD AND WANTED TO DROP THIS OFF FOR YOU.
CARLYLE SIGNATURE EDITION.
BACK WHEN THE WORLD STILL HAD POETS, YOU KNOW?
LET US KNOW WHAT YOU THINK!

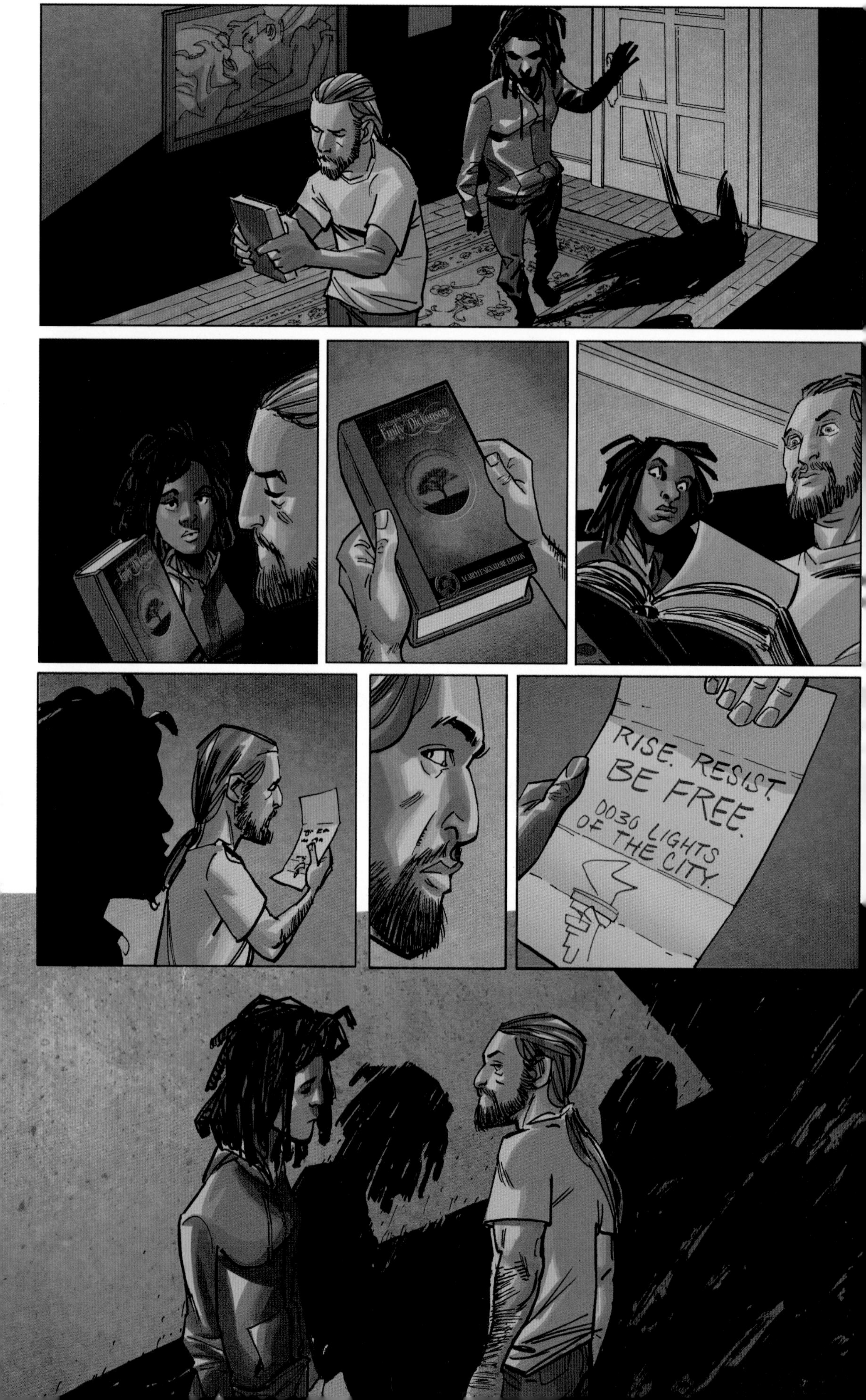
Emily Dickinson
A CARLYLE SIGNATURE EDITION
RISE. RESIST.
BE FREE.
0030 LIGHTS
OF THE CITY.

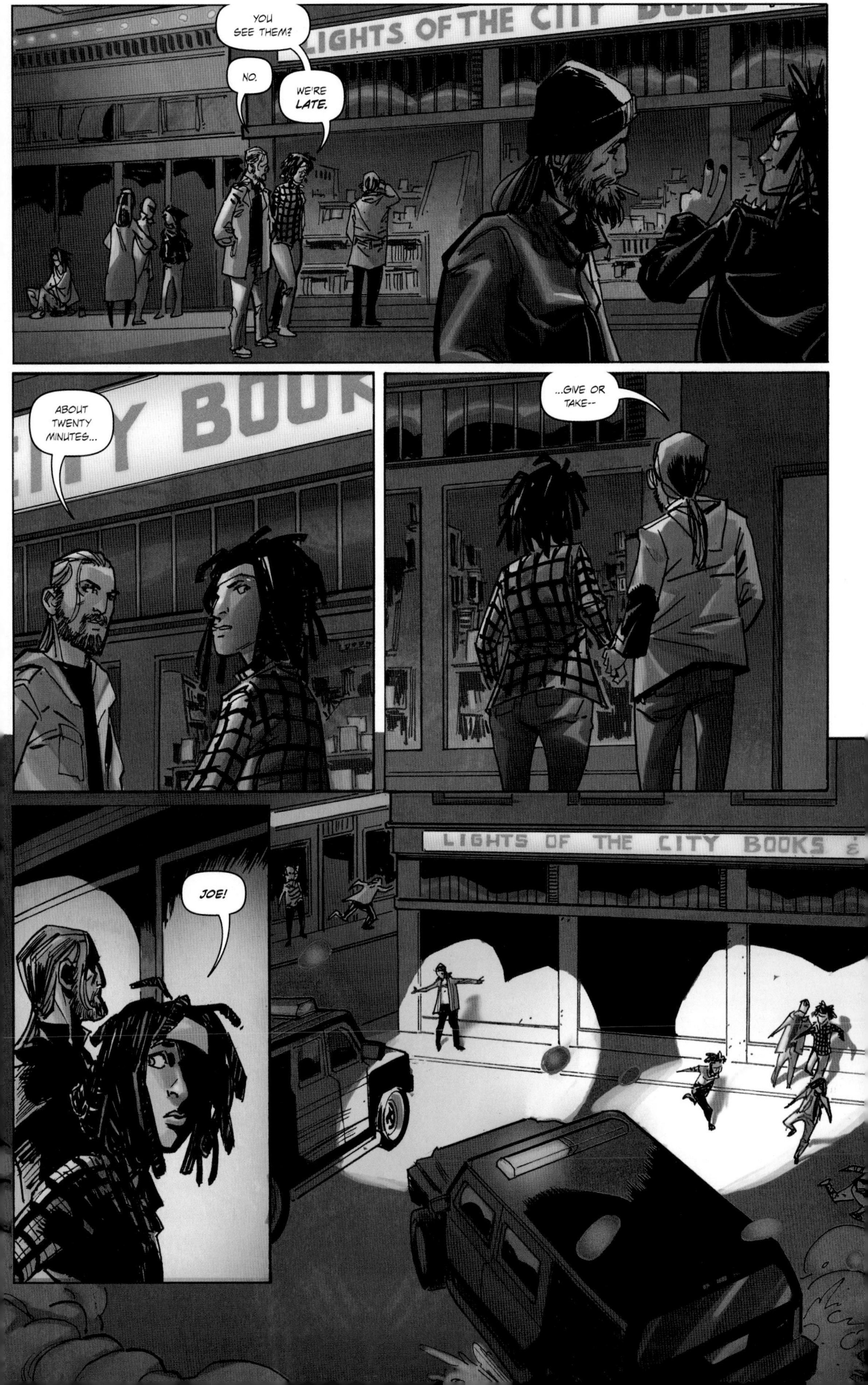
LIGHTS OF THE CITY
YOU SEE THEM?
NO.
WE'RE LATE.
ABOUT TWENTY MINUTES...
...GIVE OR TAKE--
JOE!
LIGHTS OF THE CITY BOOKS &

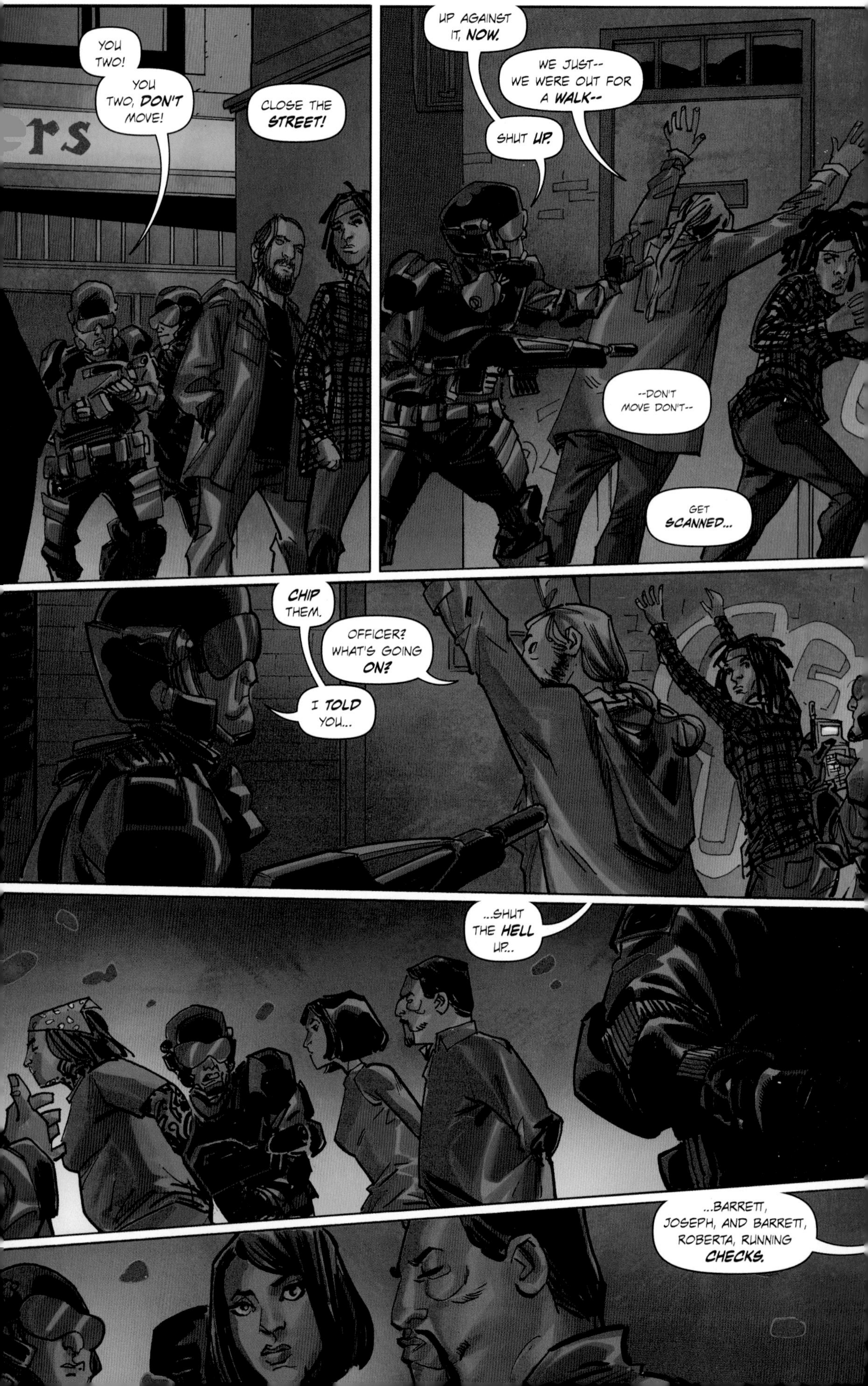
YOU TWO!
YOU TWO, DON'T MOVE!
CLOSE THE STREET!
UP AGAINST IT, NOW.
WE JUST-- WE WERE OUT FOR A WALK--
SHUT UP.
--DON'T MOVE DON'T--
GET SCANNED...
CHIP THEM.
OFFICER? WHAT'S GOING ON?
I TOLD YOU...
...SHUT THE HELL UP...
...BARRETT, JOSEPH, AND BARRETT, ROBERTA, RUNNING CHECKS.

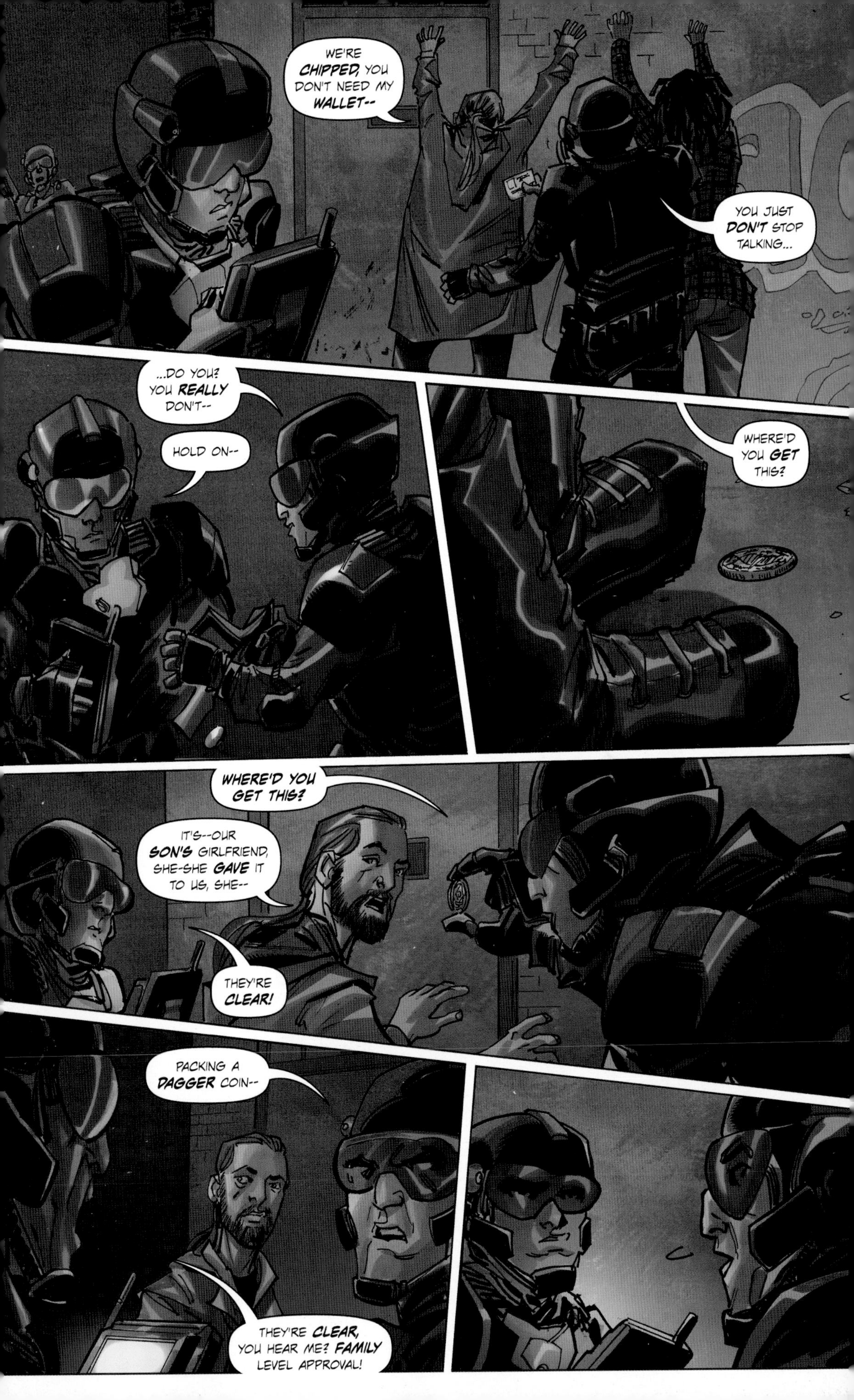
WE'RE CHIPPED, YOU DON'T NEED MY WALLET--
YOU JUST DON'T STOP TALKING...
...DO YOU? YOU REALLY DON'T--
HOLD ON--
WHERE'D YOU GET THIS?
WHERE'D YOU GET THIS?
IT'S--OUR SON'S GIRLFRIEND, SHE-SHE GAVE IT TO US, SHE--
THEY'RE CLEAR!
PACKING A DAGGER COIN--
THEY'RE CLEAR, YOU HEAR ME? FAMILY LEVEL APPROVAL!

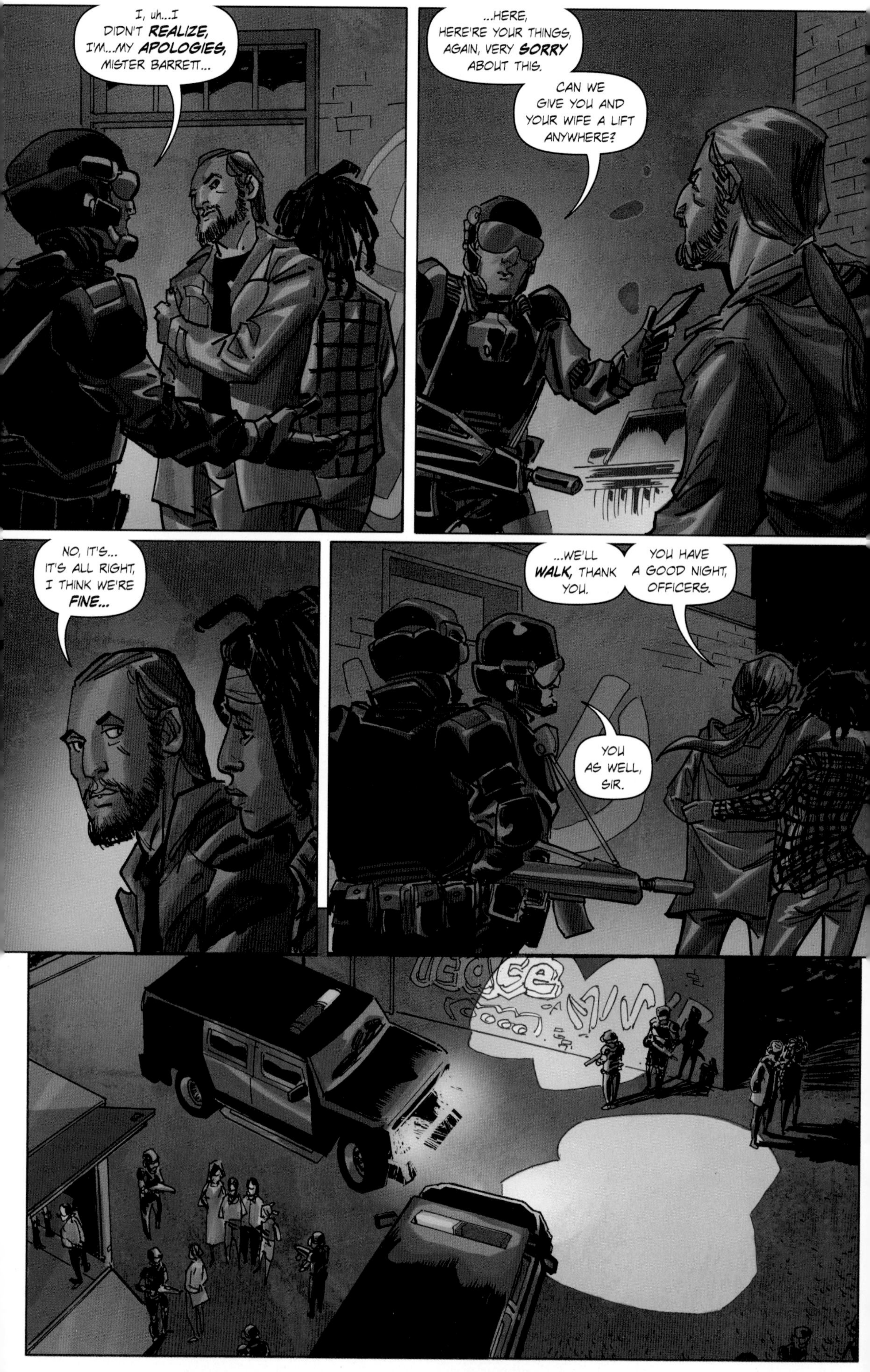
I, uh...I DIDN'T REALIZE, I'M...MY APOLOGIES, MISTER BARRETT...
...HERE, HERE'RE YOUR THINGS, AGAIN, VERY SORRY ABOUT THIS.
CAN WE GIVE YOU AND YOUR WIFE A LIFT ANYWHERE?
NO, IT'S... IT'S ALL RIGHT, I THINK WE'RE FINE...
...WE'LL WALK, THANK YOU.
YOU HAVE A GOOD NIGHT, OFFICERS.
YOU AS WELL, SIR.

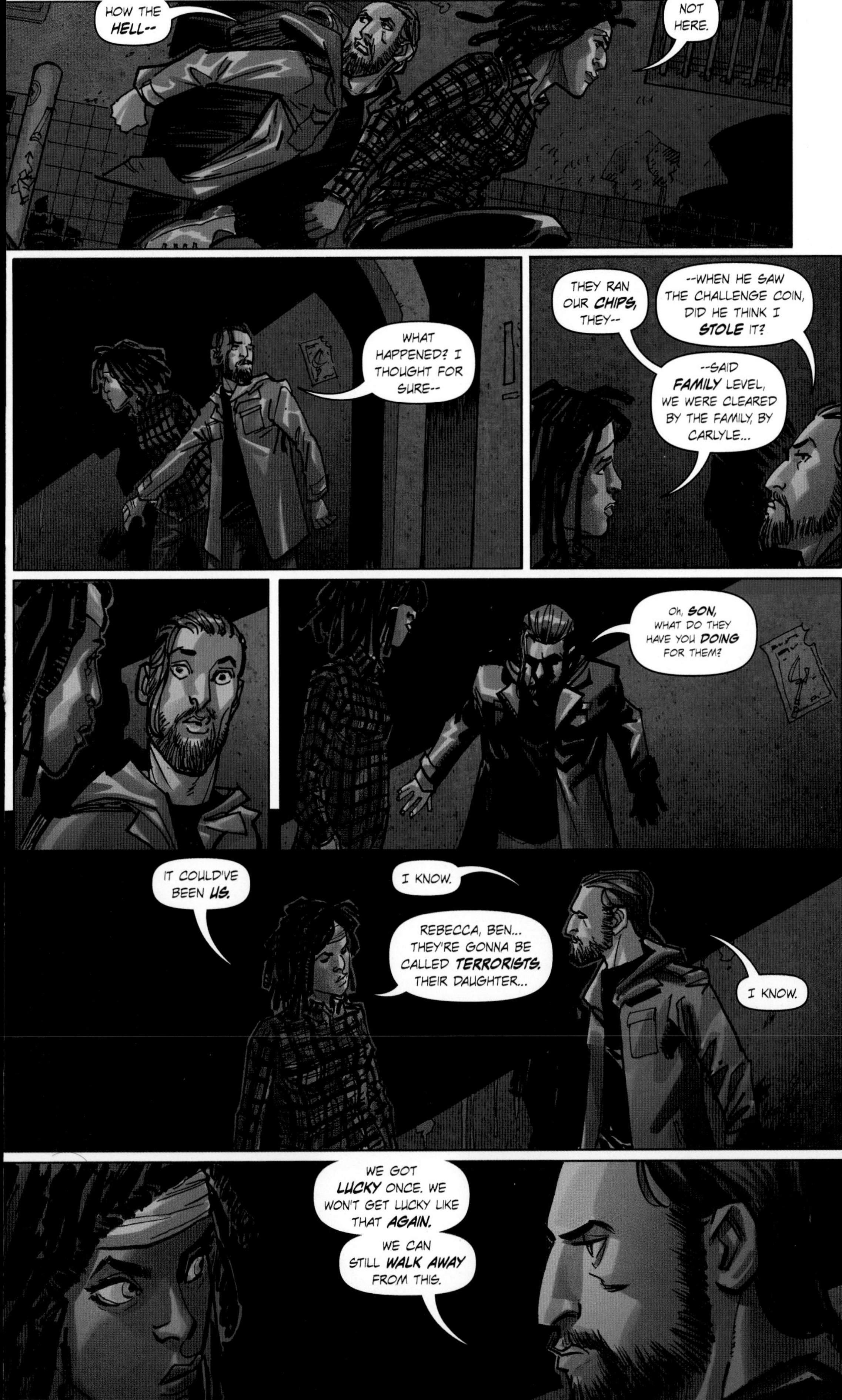

HOW THE HELL--
NOT HERE.
WHAT HAPPENED? I THOUGHT FOR SURE--
THEY RAN OUR CHIPS, THEY--
--WHEN HE SAW THE CHALLENGE COIN, DID HE THINK I STOLE IT?
--SAID FAMILY LEVEL, WE WERE CLEARED BY THE FAMILY, BY CARLYLE...
Oh, SON, WHAT DO THEY HAVE YOU DOING FOR THEM?
IT COULD'VE BEEN US.
I KNOW.
REBECCA, BEN... THEY'RE GONNA BE CALLED TERRORISTS. THEIR DAUGHTER...
I KNOW.
WE GOT LUCKY ONCE. WE WON'T GET LUCKY LIKE THAT AGAIN.
WE CAN STILL WALK AWAY FROM THIS.

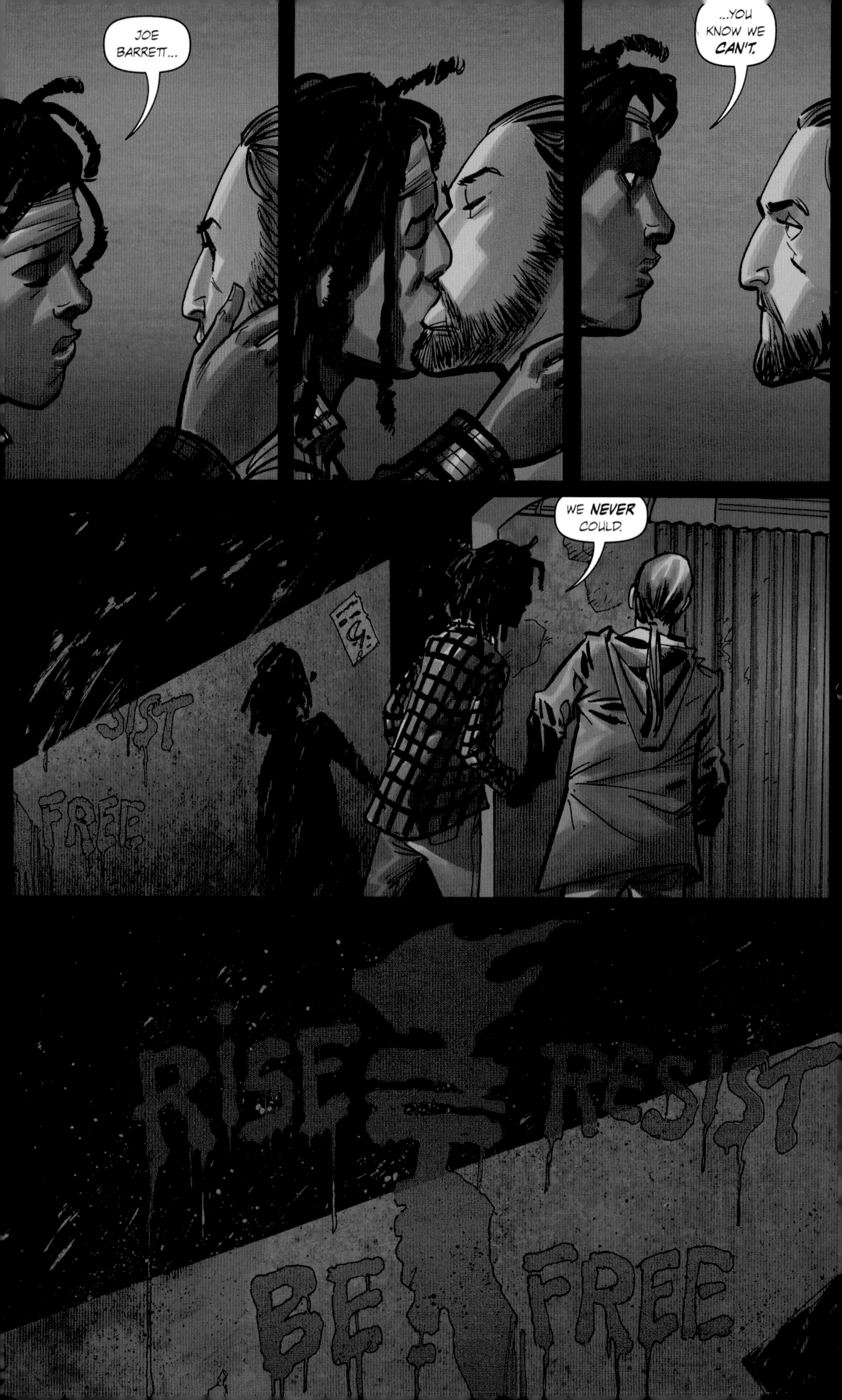
JOE BARRETT...
...YOU KNOW WE CAN'T.
WE NEVER COULD.
SIST
FREE
RISE RESIST
BE FREE

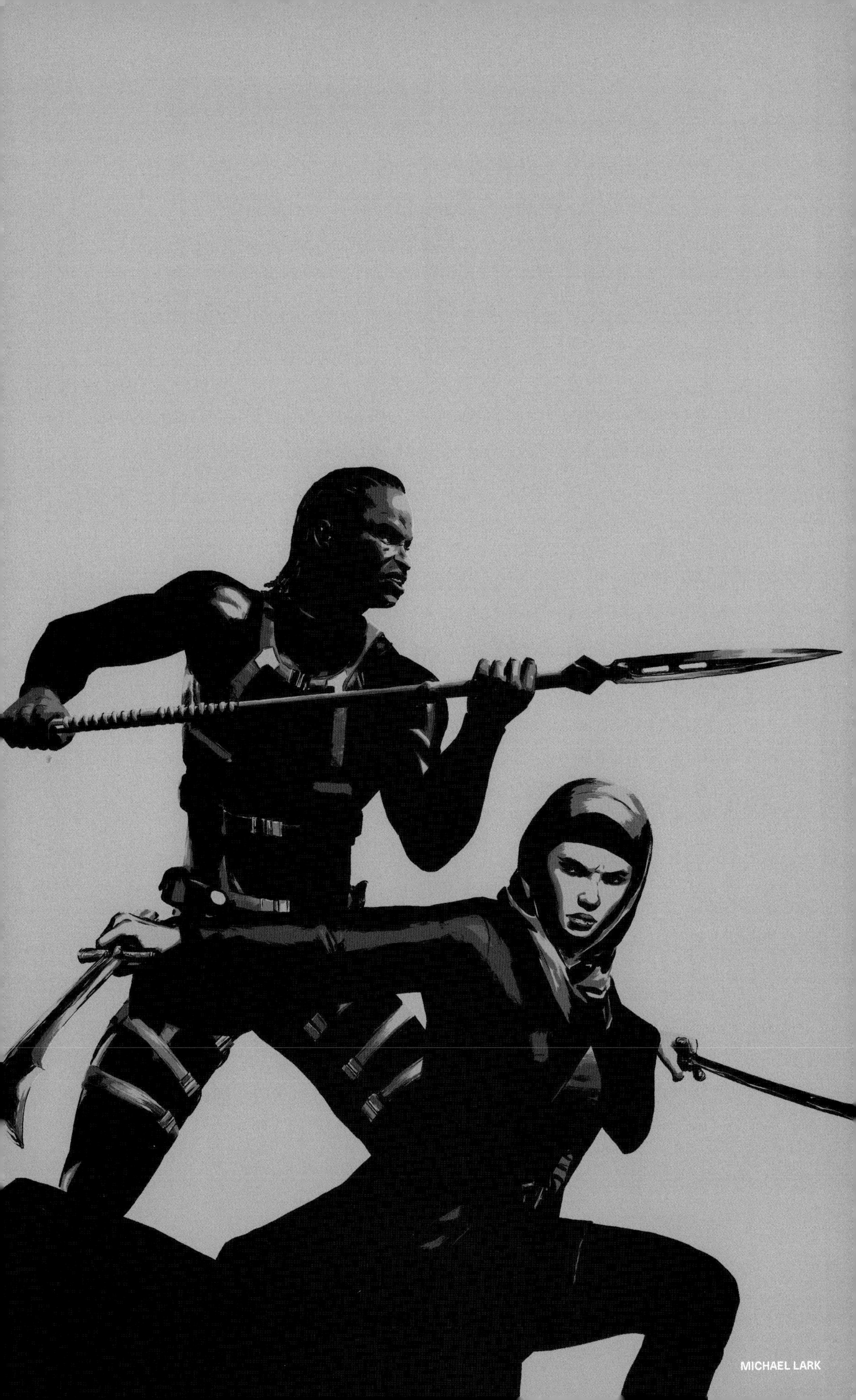

MICHAEL LARK

Of the Families, the first to vanish
from the Earth was **SOLERI**, their rule short-lived.

Their holdings in Europe have long since been seized by other Families.

Their lands in North Africa have proven another
matter, unclaimed, infested with lawless bands of brigands and mercenaries, the
battlefield for proxy wars fought between **MARTINS**, **NKOSI**,
and **MEYERS-QASIMI**.

Meyers-Qasimi and Nkosi now stand together in the face of growing global
conflict, both allied with Carlyle during this phase of **The Conclave War**.

But what the desert took from Soleri is now revealed,
and the secrets waiting to be discovered may tip the balance of power, not only
in the region but around the world—for Soleri shared much with **VASSALOVKA**
before they went extinct, and Vassalovka is now on the march with their Lazarus,
The Zmey, leading the column.

Both Meyers-Qasimi and Nkosi
seek the key to understanding and defeating The Zmey.

Each Family has sent their Lazarus to assist the other in their search.

Because they are, after all, **allies**....

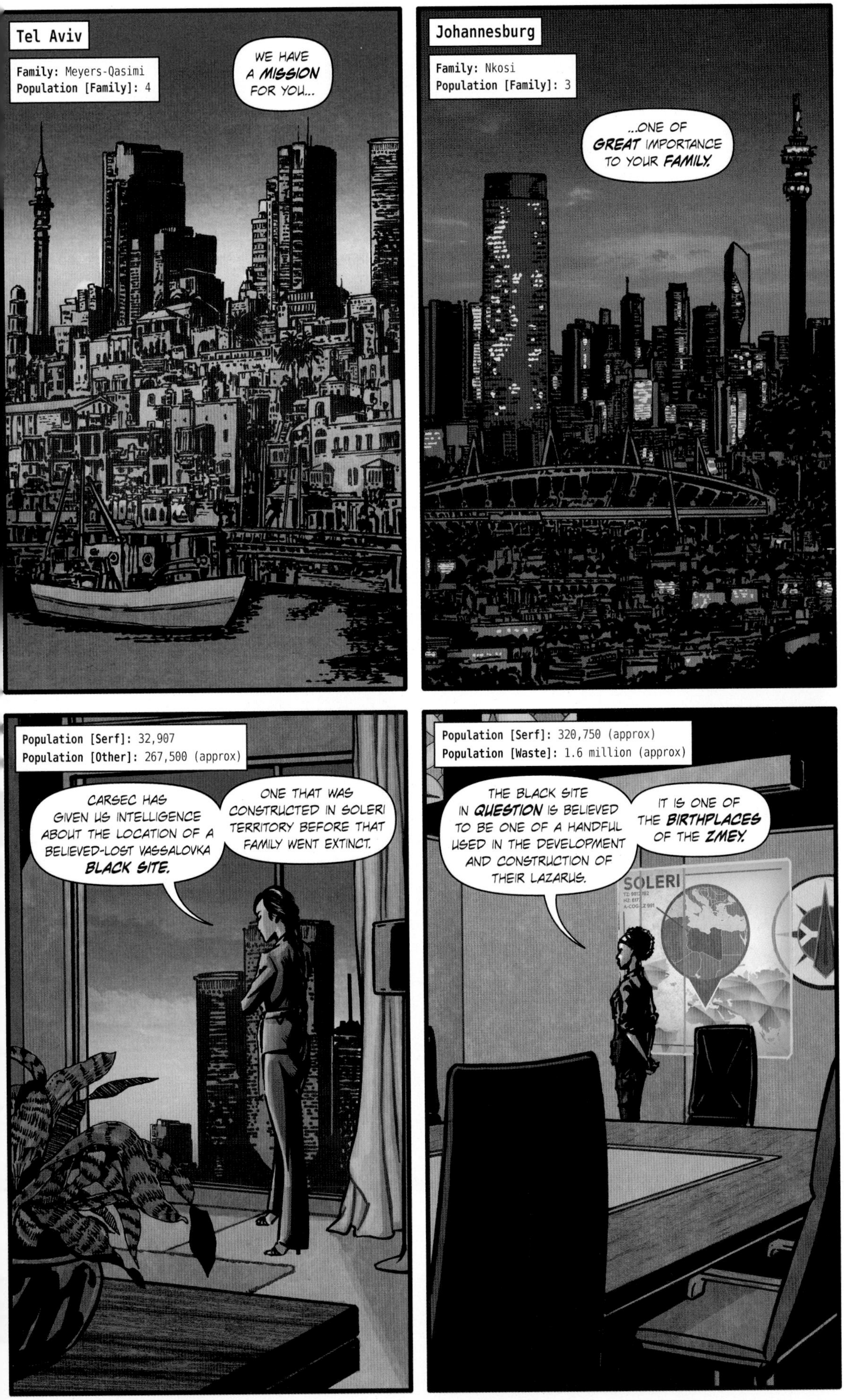

Tel Aviv
Family: Meyers-Qasimi
Population [Family]: 4
WE HAVE A MISSION FOR YOU...
Johannesburg
Family: Nkosi
Population [Family]: 3
...ONE OF GREAT IMPORTANCE TO YOUR FAMILY.
Population [Serf]: 32,907
Population [Other]: 267,500 (approx)
CARSEC HAS GIVEN US INTELLIGENCE ABOUT THE LOCATION OF A BELIEVED-LOST VASSALOVKA BLACK SITE.
ONE THAT WAS CONSTRUCTED IN SOLERI TERRITORY BEFORE THAT FAMILY WENT EXTINCT.
Population [Serf]: 320,750 (approx)
Population [Waste]: 1.6 million (approx)
THE BLACK SITE IN QUESTION IS BELIEVED TO BE ONE OF A HANDFUL USED IN THE DEVELOPMENT AND CONSTRUCTION OF THEIR LAZARUS.
IT IS ONE OF THE BIRTHPLACES OF THE ZMEY.
SOLERI

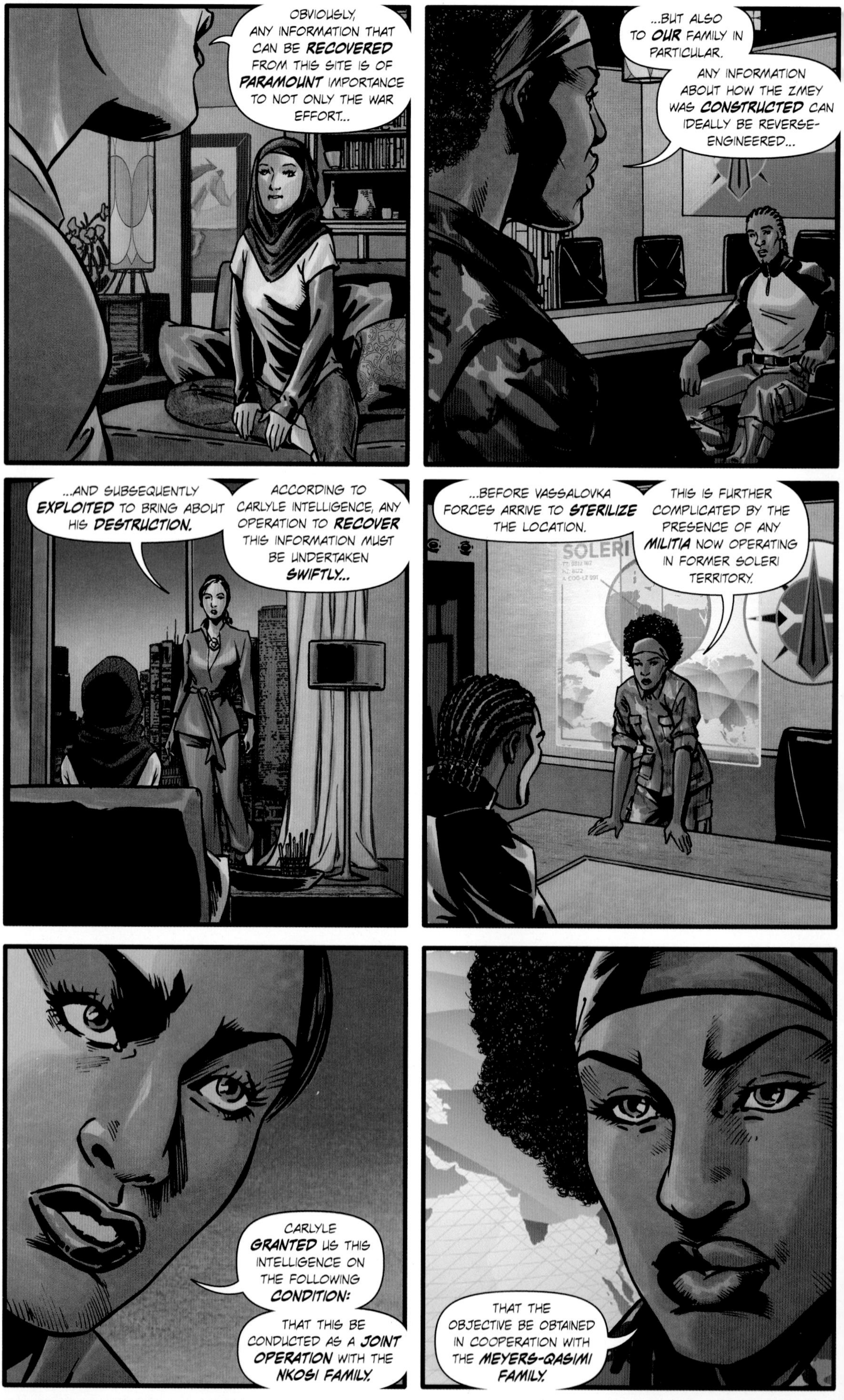
OBVIOUSLY, ANY INFORMATION THAT CAN BE RECOVERED FROM THIS SITE IS OF PARAMOUNT IMPORTANCE TO NOT ONLY THE WAR EFFORT...
...BUT ALSO TO OUR FAMILY IN PARTICULAR.
ANY INFORMATION ABOUT HOW THE ZMEY WAS CONSTRUCTED CAN IDEALLY BE REVERSE-ENGINEERED...
...AND SUBSEQUENTLY EXPLOITED TO BRING ABOUT HIS DESTRUCTION.
ACCORDING TO CARLYLE INTELLIGENCE, ANY OPERATION TO RECOVER THIS INFORMATION MUST BE UNDERTAKEN SWIFTLY...
...BEFORE VASSALOVKA FORCES ARRIVE TO STERILIZE THE LOCATION.
THIS IS FURTHER COMPLICATED BY THE PRESENCE OF ANY MILITIA NOW OPERATING IN FORMER SOLERI TERRITORY.
SOLERI
CARLYLE GRANTED US THIS INTELLIGENCE ON THE FOLLOWING CONDITION:
THAT THIS BE CONDUCTED AS A JOINT OPERATION WITH THE NKOSI FAMILY.
THAT THE OBJECTIVE BE OBTAINED IN COOPERATION WITH THE MEYERS-QASIMI FAMILY.

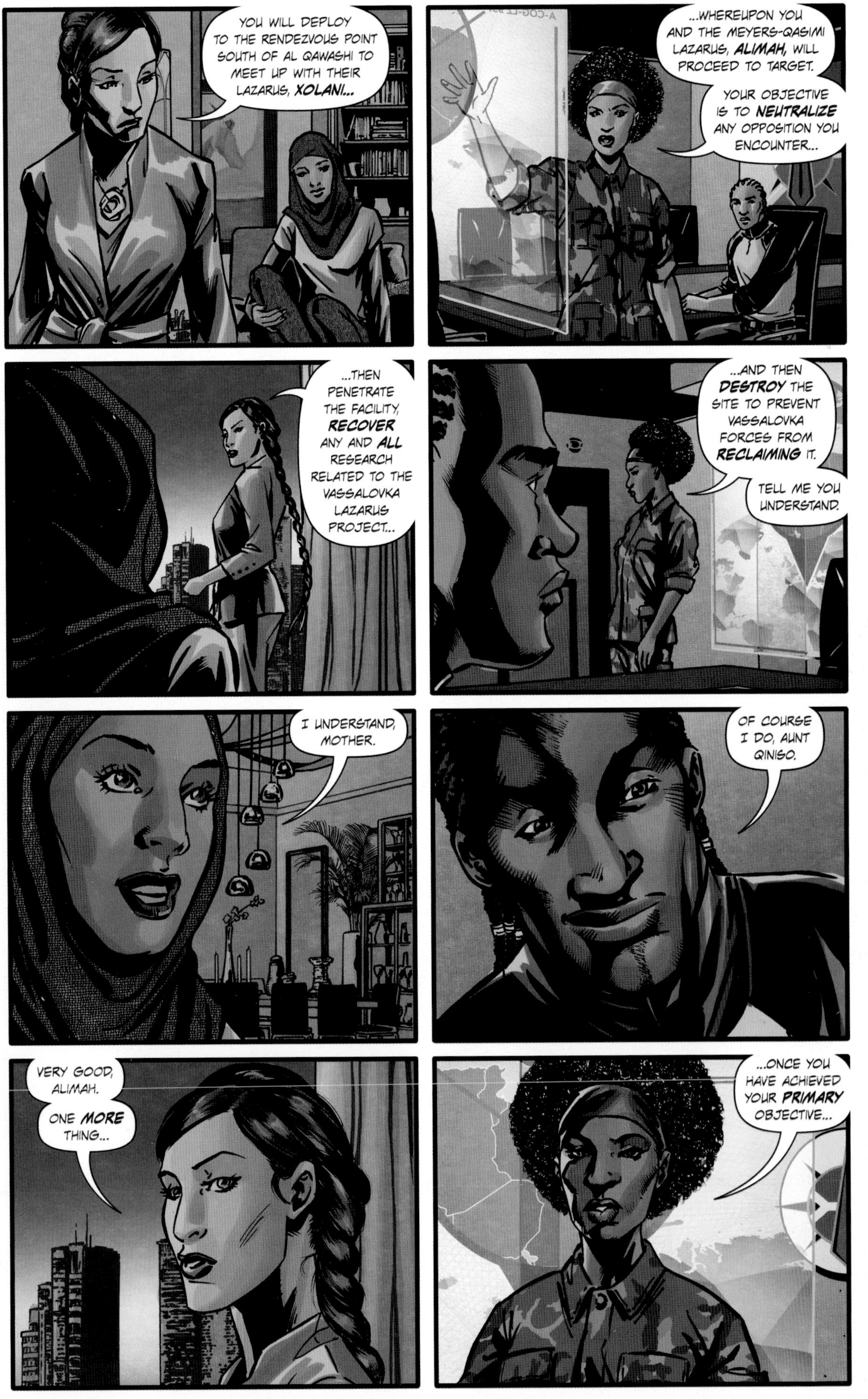
YOU WILL DEPLOY TO THE RENDEZVOUS POINT SOUTH OF AL QAWASHI TO MEET UP WITH THEIR LAZARUS, **XOLANI...**
...WHEREUPON YOU AND THE MEYERS-QASIMI LAZARUS, ***ALIMAH,*** WILL PROCEED TO TARGET.
YOUR OBJECTIVE IS TO ***NEUTRALIZE*** ANY OPPOSITION YOU ENCOUNTER...
...THEN PENETRATE THE FACILITY, ***RECOVER*** ANY AND ***ALL*** RESEARCH RELATED TO THE VASSALOVKA LAZARUS PROJECT...
...AND THEN ***DESTROY*** THE SITE TO PREVENT VASSALOVKA FORCES FROM ***RECLAIMING*** IT.
TELL ME YOU UNDERSTAND.
I UNDERSTAND, MOTHER.
OF COURSE I DO, AUNT QINISO.
VERY GOOD, ALIMAH.
ONE ***MORE*** THING...
...ONCE YOU HAVE ACHIEVED YOUR ***PRIMARY*** OBJECTIVE...

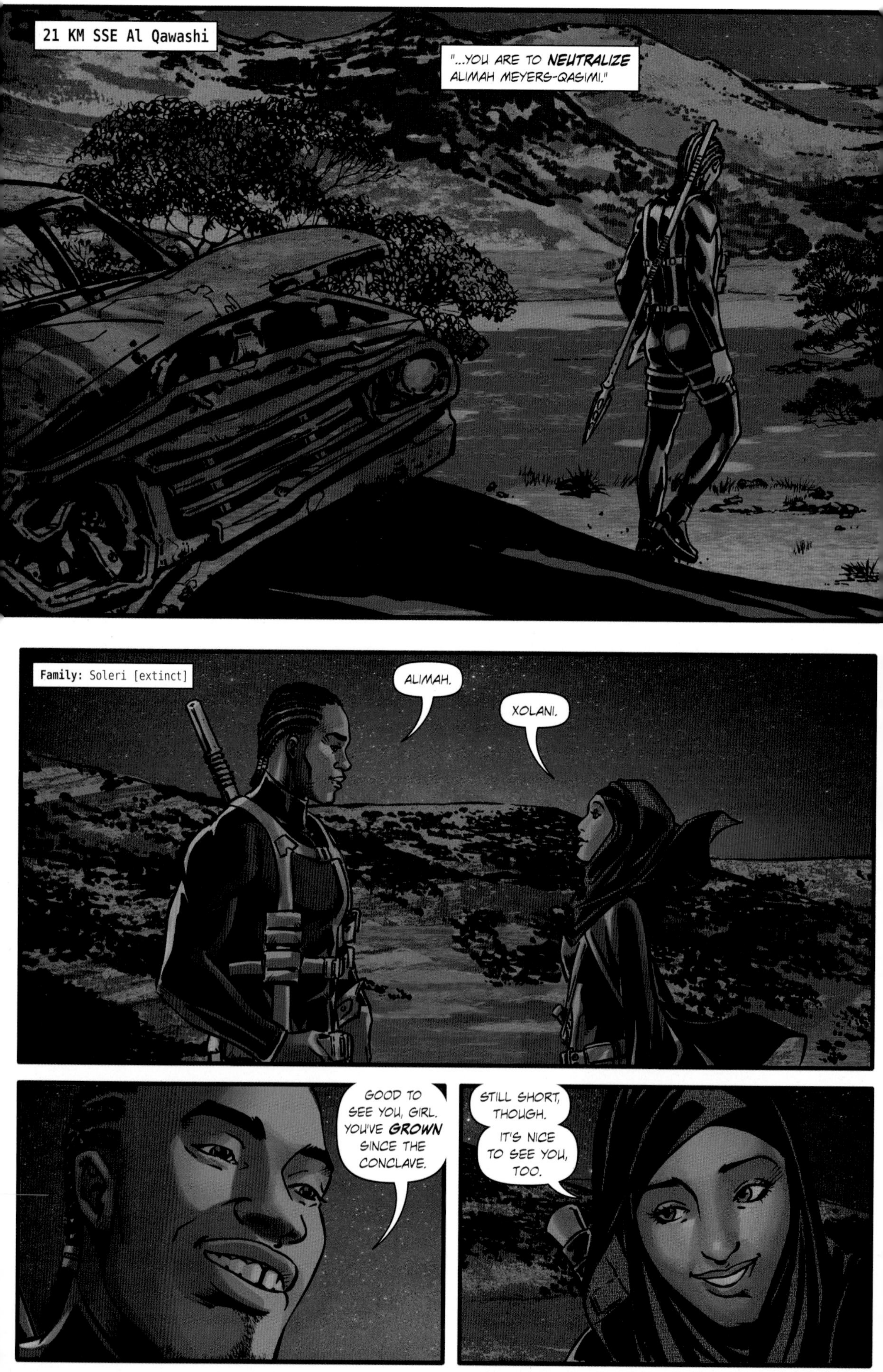
21 KM SSE Al Qawashi
"...YOU ARE TO NEUTRALIZE ALIMAH MEYERS-QASIMI."
Family: Soleri [extinct]
ALIMAH.
XOLANI.
GOOD TO SEE YOU, GIRL. YOU'VE GROWN SINCE THE CONCLAVE.
STILL SHORT, THOUGH.
IT'S NICE TO SEE YOU, TOO.

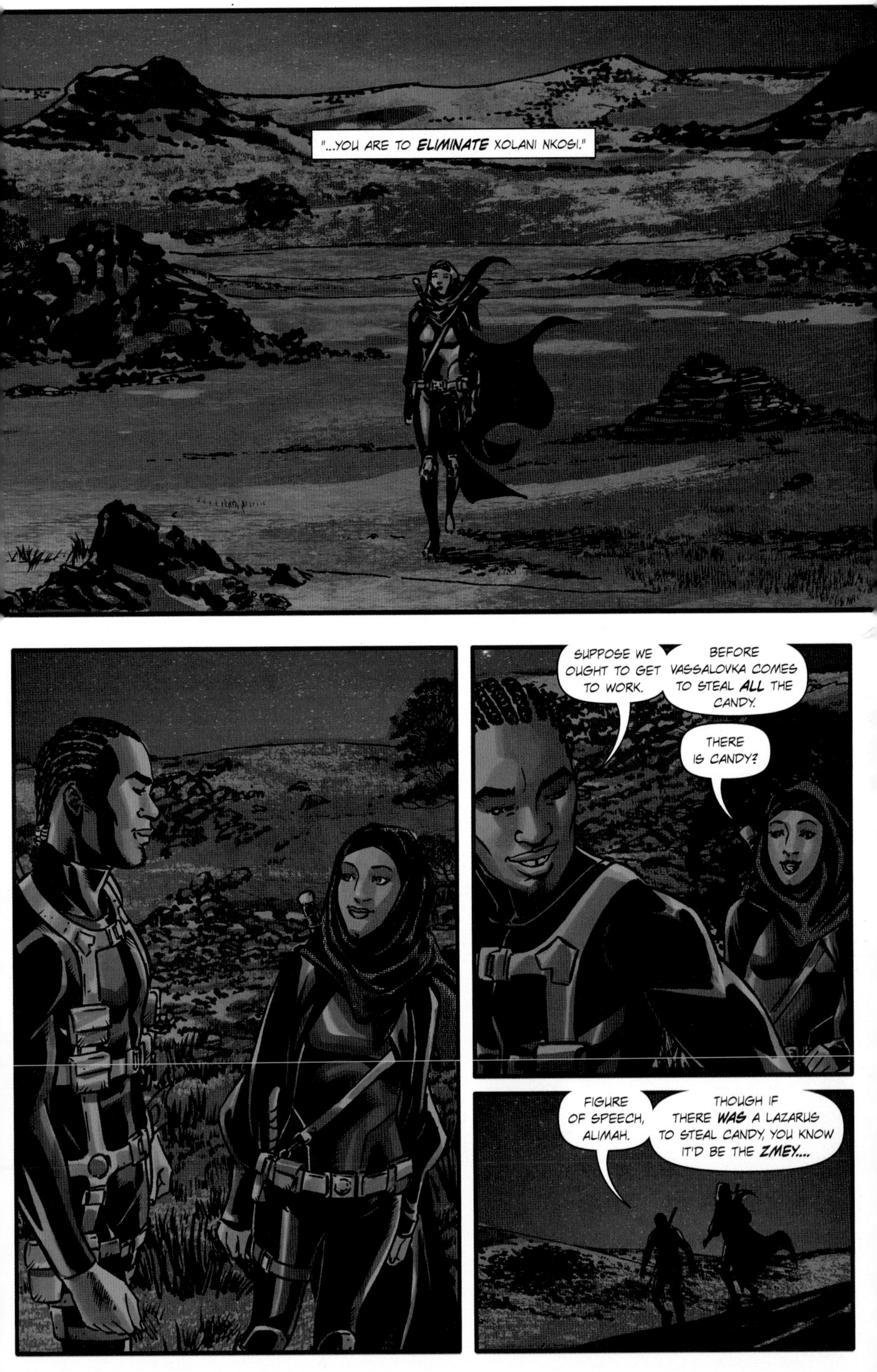
"...YOU ARE TO ELIMINATE XOLANI NKOSI."
SUPPOSE WE OUGHT TO GET TO WORK.
BEFORE VASSALOVKA COMES TO STEAL ALL THE CANDY.
THERE IS CANDY?
FIGURE OF SPEECH, ALIMAH.
THOUGH IF THERE WAS A LAZARUS TO STEAL CANDY, YOU KNOW IT'D BE THE ZMEY....

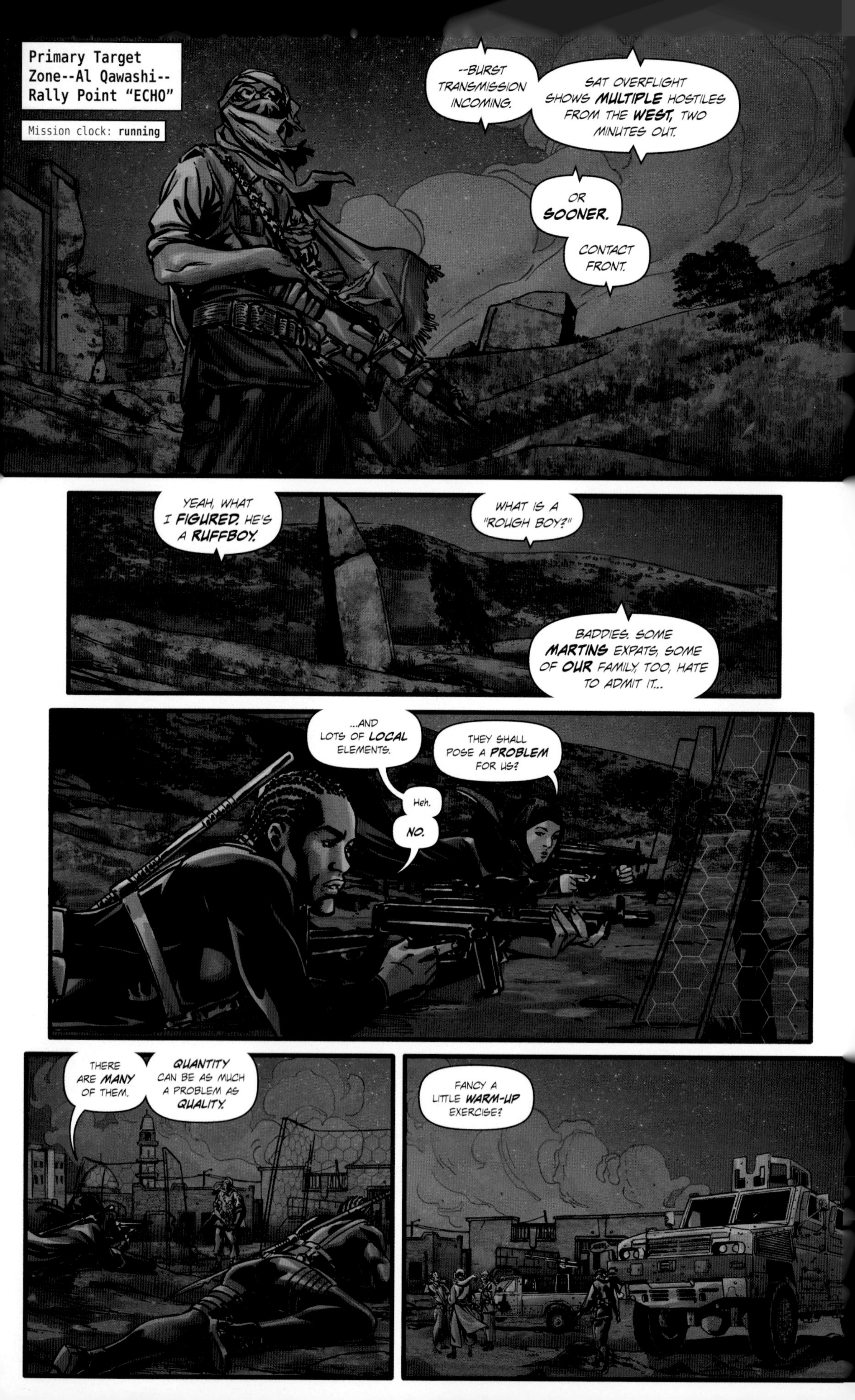

Primary Target Zone--Al Qawashi-- Rally Point "ECHO"
Mission clock: running
--BURST TRANSMISSION INCOMING.
SAT OVERFLIGHT SHOWS MULTIPLE HOSTILES FROM THE WEST, TWO MINUTES OUT.
OR SOONER.
CONTACT FRONT.
YEAH, WHAT I FIGURED. HE'S A RUFFBOY.
WHAT IS A "ROUGH BOY?"
BADDIES. SOME MARTINS EXPATS, SOME OF OUR FAMILY, TOO, HATE TO ADMIT IT...
...AND LOTS OF LOCAL ELEMENTS.
THEY SHALL POSE A PROBLEM FOR US?
Heh.
NO.
THERE ARE MANY OF THEM.
QUANTITY CAN BE AS MUCH A PROBLEM AS QUALITY.
FANCY A LITTLE WARM-UP EXERCISE?

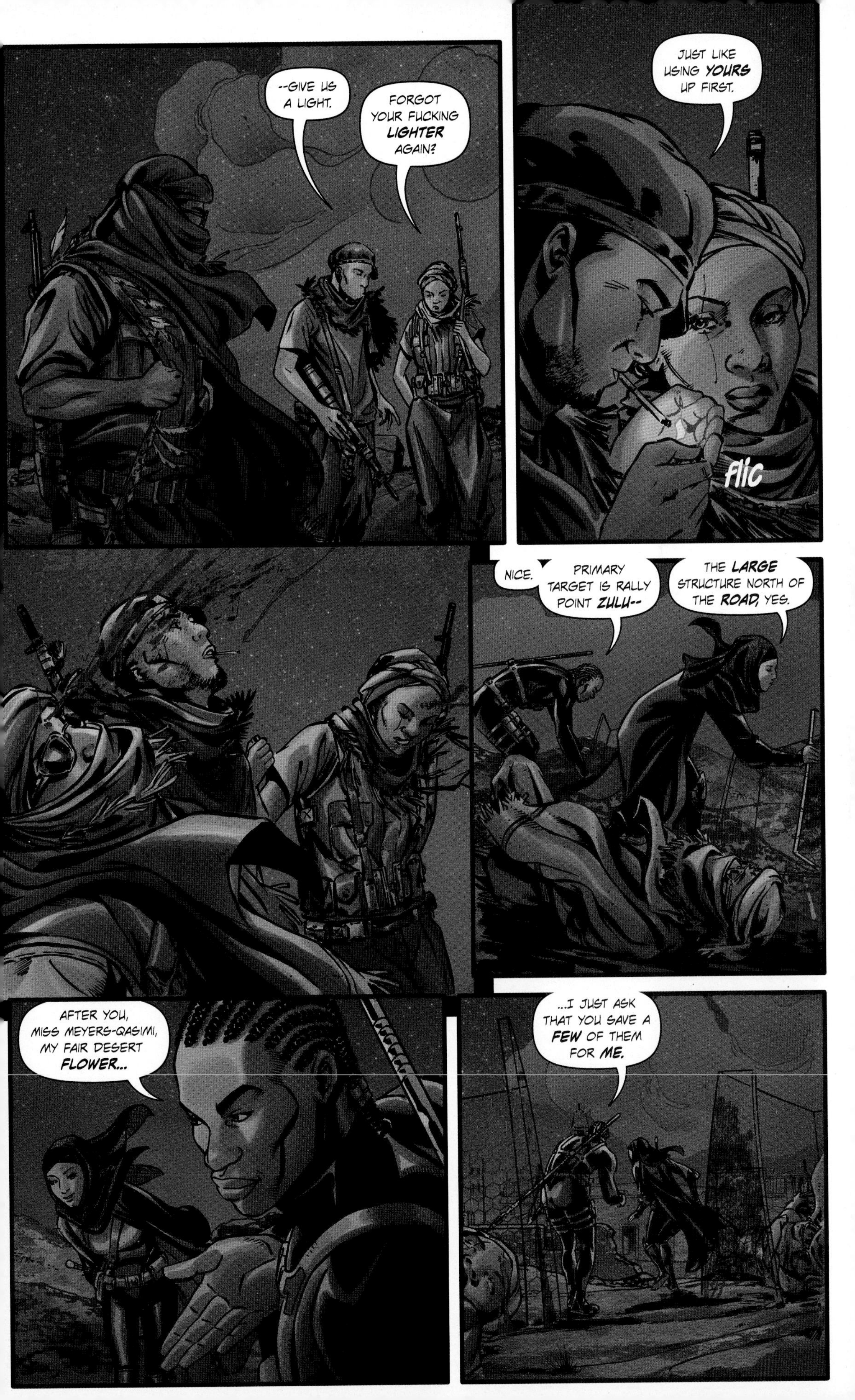
--GIVE US A LIGHT.
FORGOT YOUR FUCKING LIGHTER AGAIN?
JUST LIKE USING YOURS UP FIRST.
FLIC
NICE.
PRIMARY TARGET IS RALLY POINT ZULU--
THE LARGE STRUCTURE NORTH OF THE ROAD, YES.
AFTER YOU, MISS MEYERS-QASIMI, MY FAIR DESERT FLOWER...
...I JUST ASK THAT YOU SAVE A FEW OF THEM FOR ME.

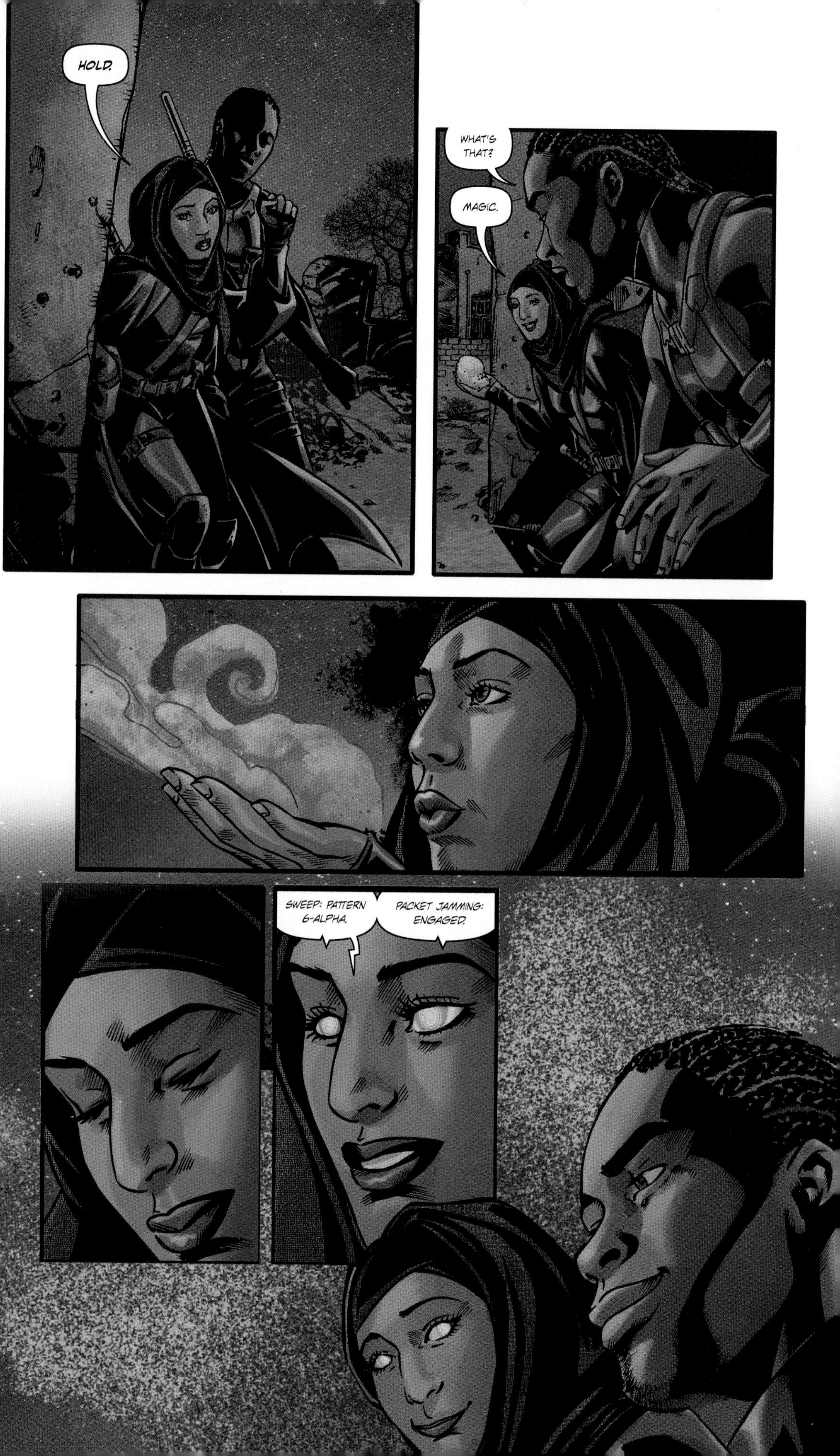
HOLD.
WHAT'S THAT?
MAGIC.
SWEEP: PATTERN 6-ALPHA.
PACKET JAMMING: ENGAGED.

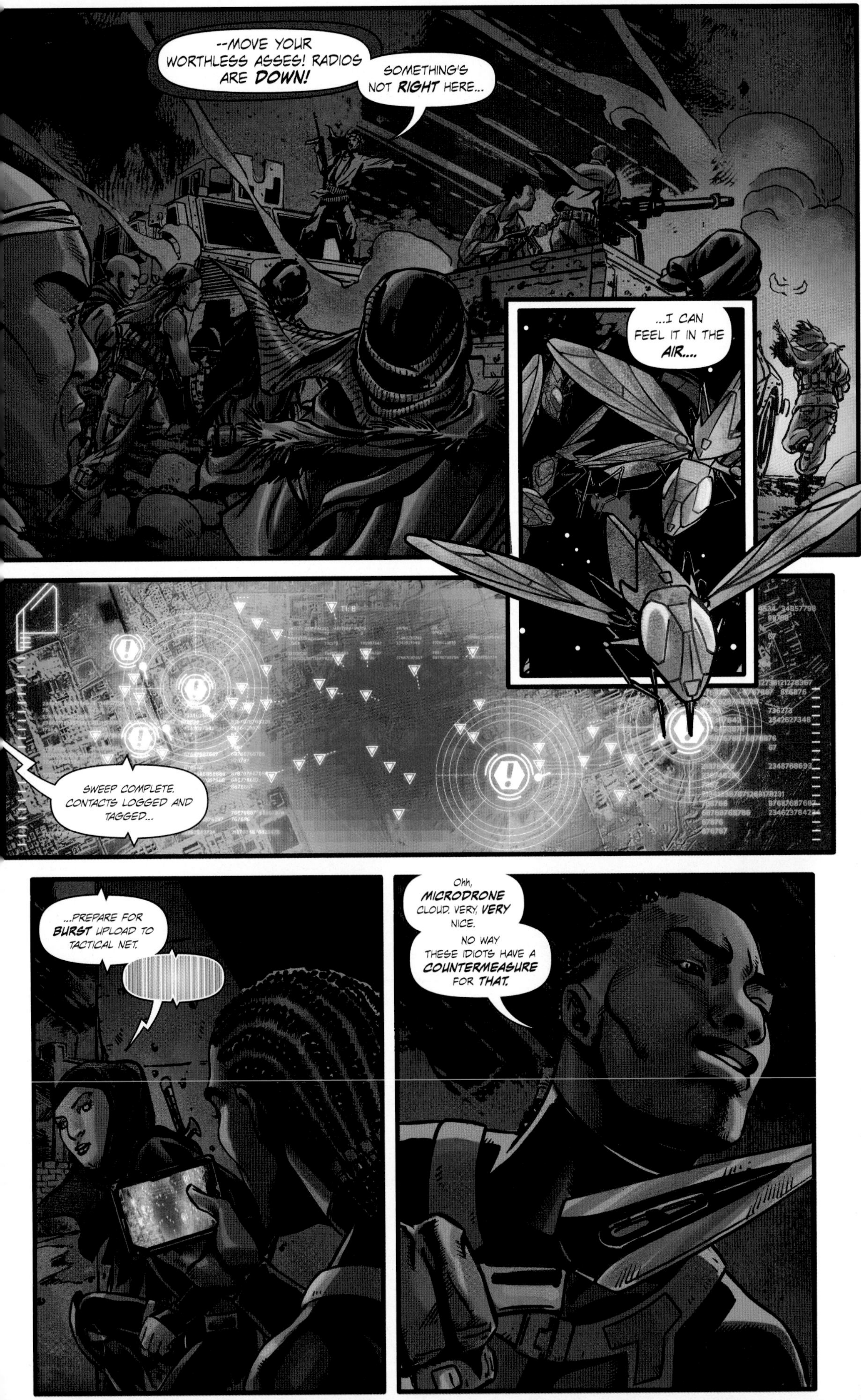
--MOVE YOUR WORTHLESS ASSES! RADIOS ARE DOWN!
SOMETHING'S NOT RIGHT HERE...
...I CAN FEEL IT IN THE AIR....
SWEEP COMPLETE. CONTACTS LOGGED AND TAGGED...
...PREPARE FOR BURST UPLOAD TO TACTICAL NET.
Ohh, MICRODRONE CLOUD. VERY, VERY NICE.
NO WAY THESE IDIOTS HAVE A COUNTERMEASURE FOR THAT.

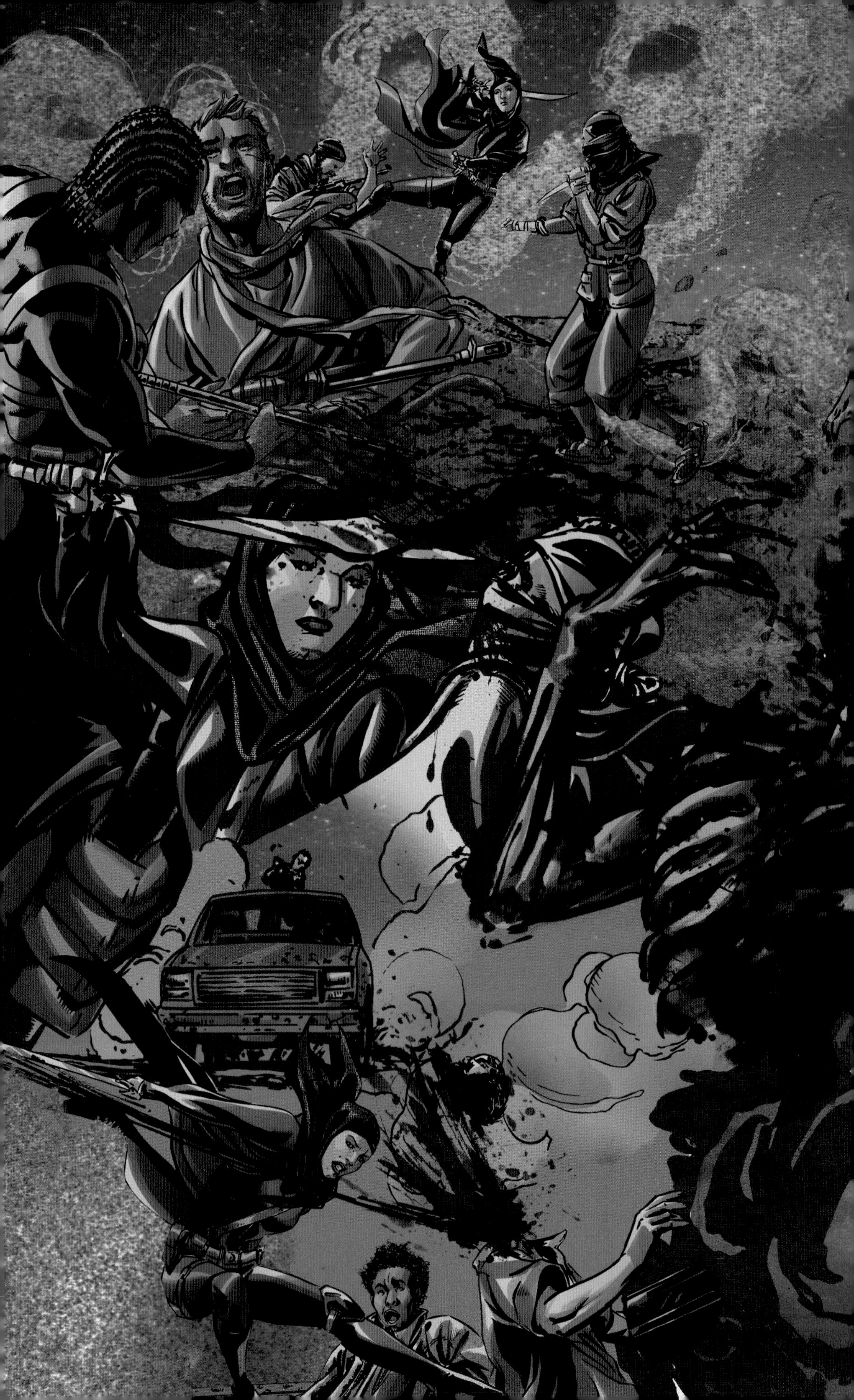

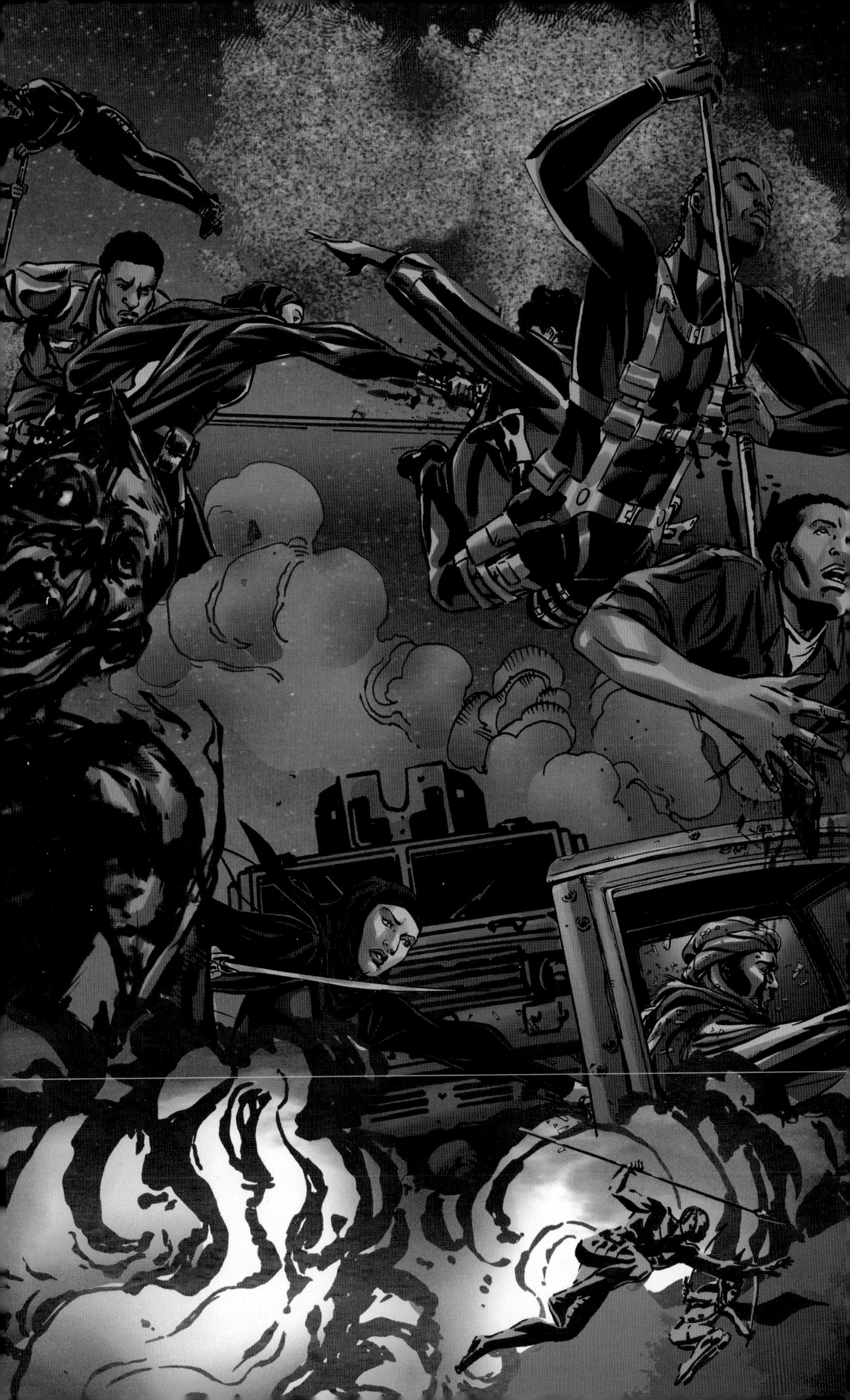

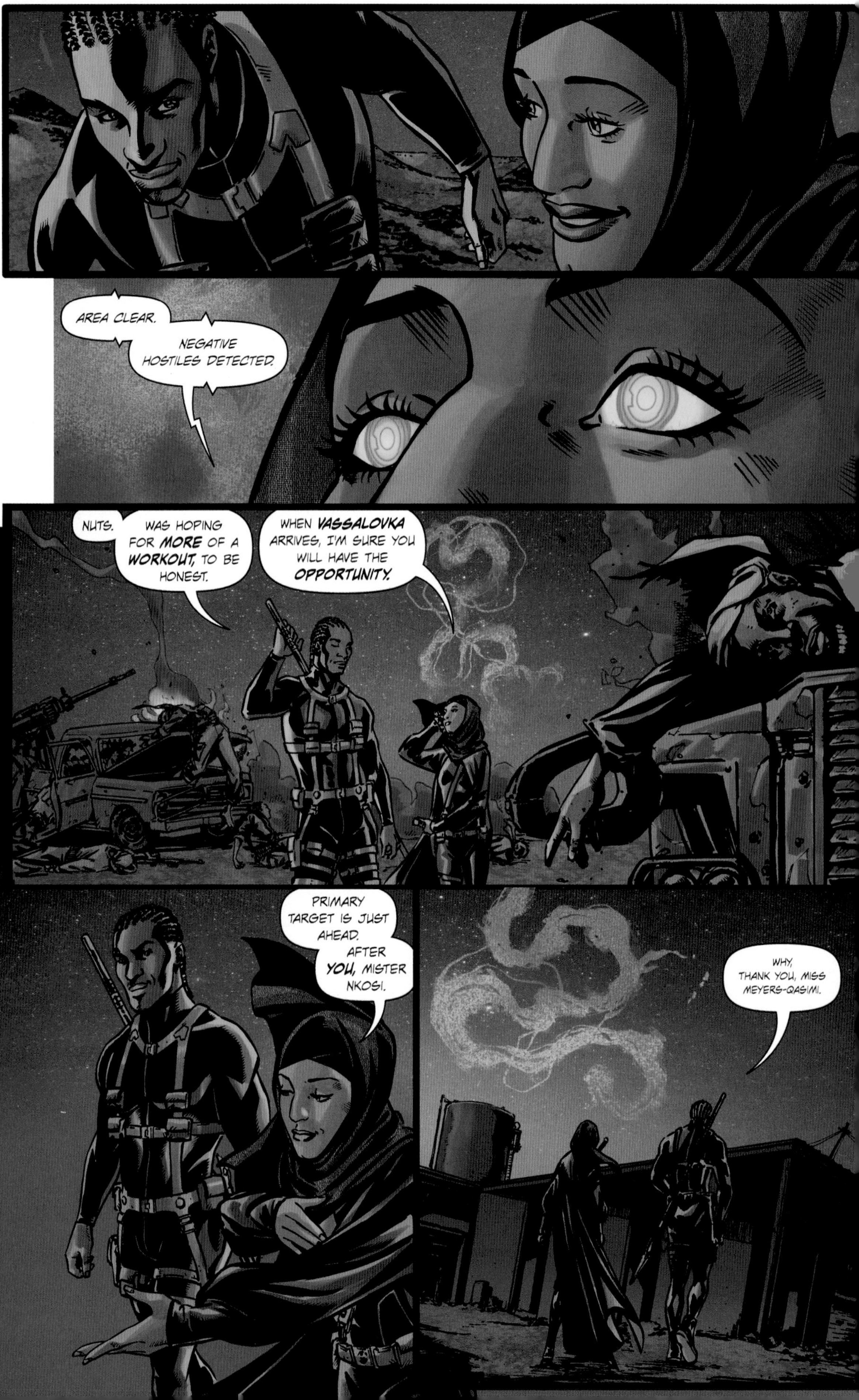
AREA CLEAR.
NEGATIVE HOSTILES DETECTED.
NUTS.
WAS HOPING FOR MORE OF A WORKOUT, TO BE HONEST.
WHEN VASSALOVKA ARRIVES, I'M SURE YOU WILL HAVE THE OPPORTUNITY.
PRIMARY TARGET IS JUST AHEAD.
AFTER YOU, MISTER NKOSI.
WHY, THANK YOU, MISS MEYERS-QASIMI.

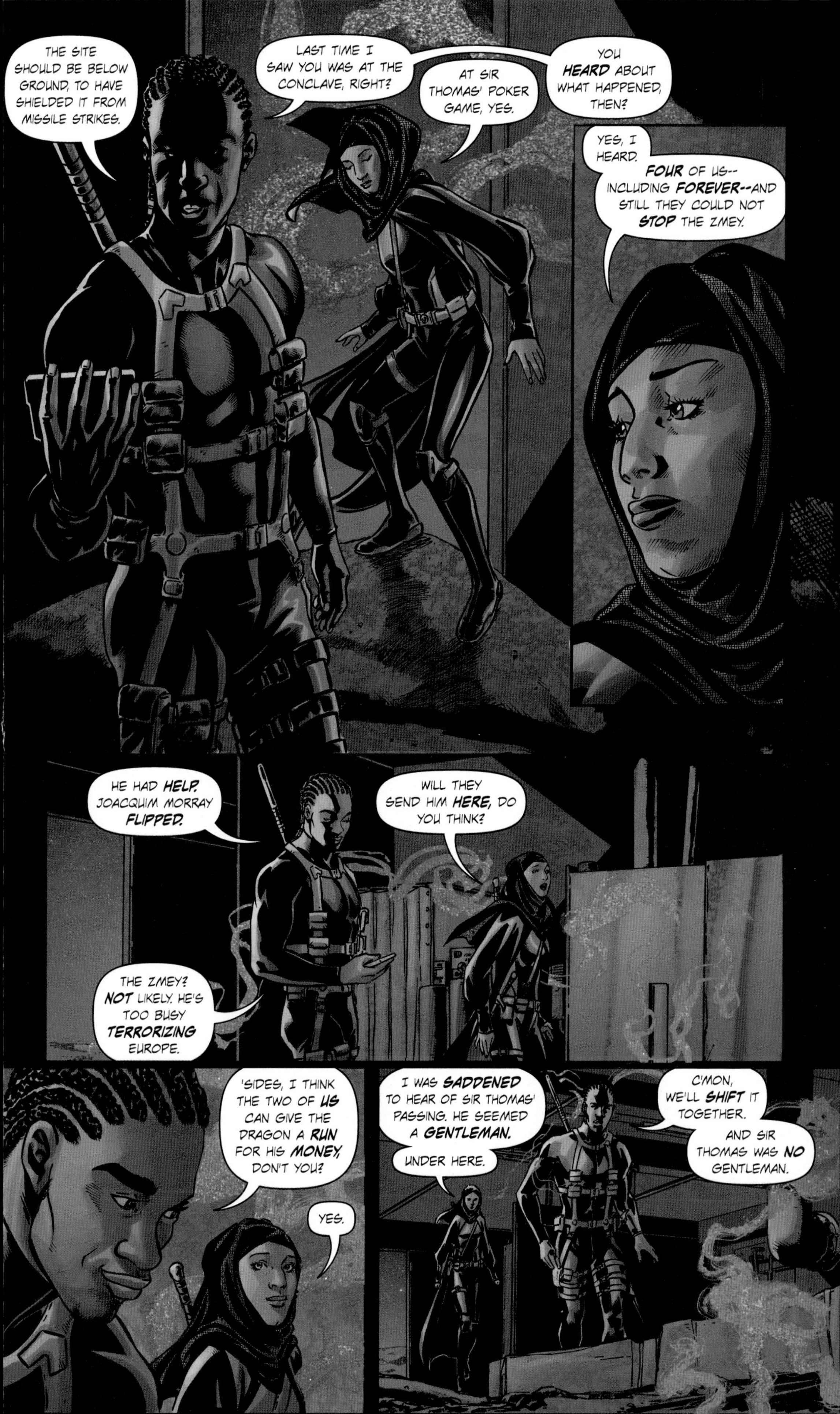
THE SITE SHOULD BE BELOW GROUND, TO HAVE SHIELDED IT FROM MISSILE STRIKES.
LAST TIME I SAW YOU WAS AT THE CONCLAVE, RIGHT?
YOU **HEARD** ABOUT WHAT HAPPENED, THEN?
AT SIR THOMAS' POKER GAME, YES.
YES, I HEARD. **FOUR** OF US-- INCLUDING **FOREVER**--AND STILL THEY COULD NOT **STOP** THE ZMEY.
HE HAD **HELP.** JOACQUIM MORRAY **FLIPPED.**
WILL THEY SEND HIM **HERE,** DO YOU THINK?
THE ZMEY? **NOT** LIKELY. HE'S TOO BUSY **TERRORIZING** EUROPE.
'SIDES, I THINK THE TWO OF **US** CAN GIVE THE DRAGON A **RUN** FOR HIS **MONEY,** DON'T YOU?
YES.
I WAS **SADDENED** TO HEAR OF SIR THOMAS' PASSING. HE SEEMED A **GENTLEMAN.**
UNDER HERE.
C'MON, WE'LL **SHIFT** IT TOGETHER.
AND SIR THOMAS WAS **NO** GENTLEMAN.

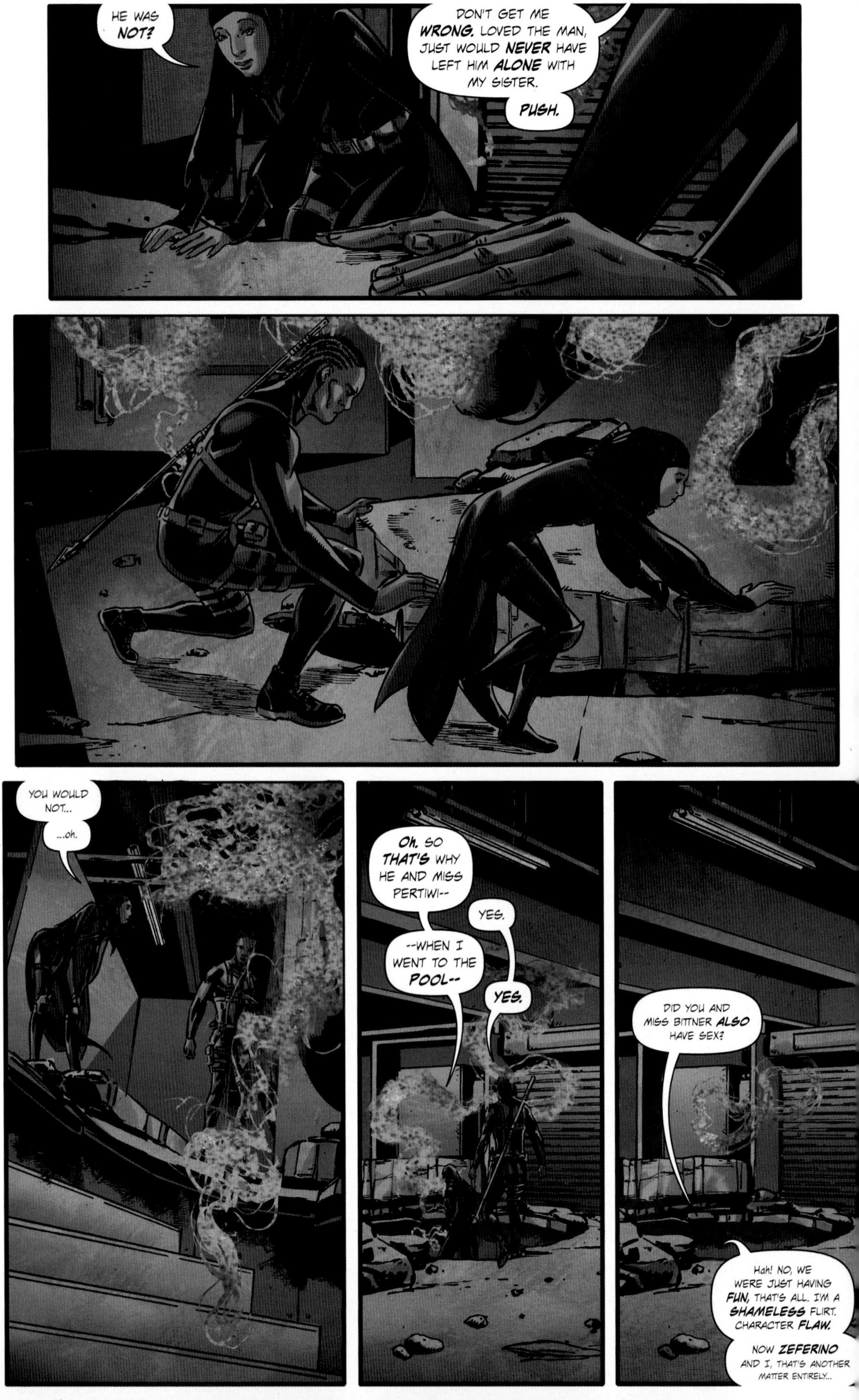
HE WAS **NOT?**
DON'T GET ME **WRONG.** LOVED THE MAN, JUST WOULD **NEVER** HAVE LEFT HIM **ALONE** WITH MY SISTER.
PUSH.
YOU WOULD NOT...
...oh.
Oh. SO **THAT'S** WHY HE AND MISS PERTIWI--
YES.
--WHEN I WENT TO THE **POOL--**
YES.
DID YOU AND MISS BITTNER **ALSO** HAVE SEX?
Hah! NO, WE WERE JUST HAVING **FUN,** THAT'S ALL. I'M A **SHAMELESS** FLIRT. CHARACTER **FLAW.**
NOW **ZEFERINO** AND I, THAT'S ANOTHER MATTER ENTIRELY...

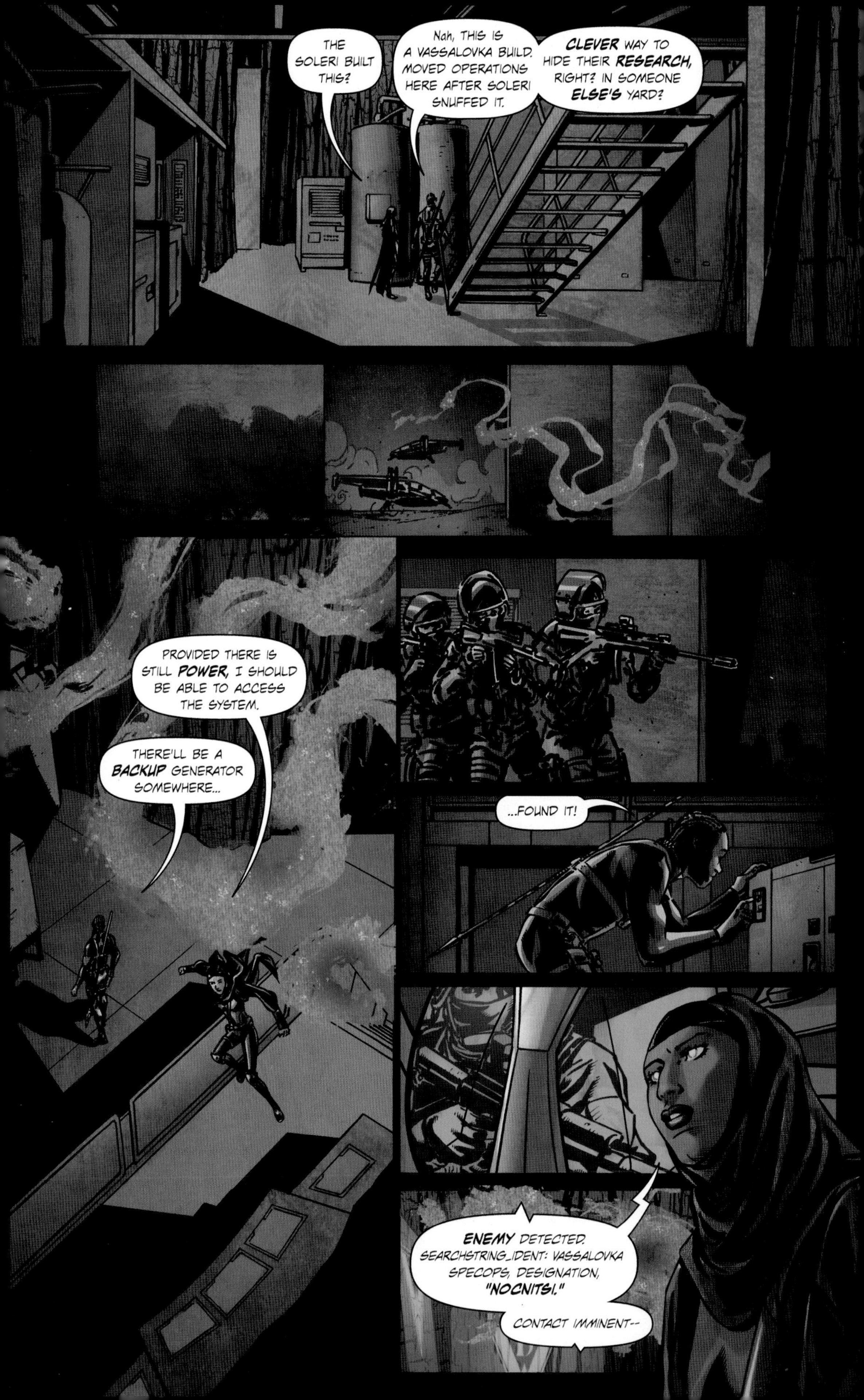
THE SOLERI BUILT THIS?
Nah, THIS IS A VASSALOVKA BUILD. MOVED OPERATIONS HERE AFTER SOLERI SNUFFED IT.
CLEVER WAY TO HIDE THEIR RESEARCH, RIGHT? IN SOMEONE ELSE'S YARD?
PROVIDED THERE IS STILL POWER, I SHOULD BE ABLE TO ACCESS THE SYSTEM.
THERE'LL BE A BACKUP GENERATOR SOMEWHERE...
...FOUND IT!
ENEMY DETECTED. SEARCHSTRING_IDENT: VASSALOVKA SPECOPS, DESIGNATION, "NOCNITSI."
CONTACT IMMINENT--

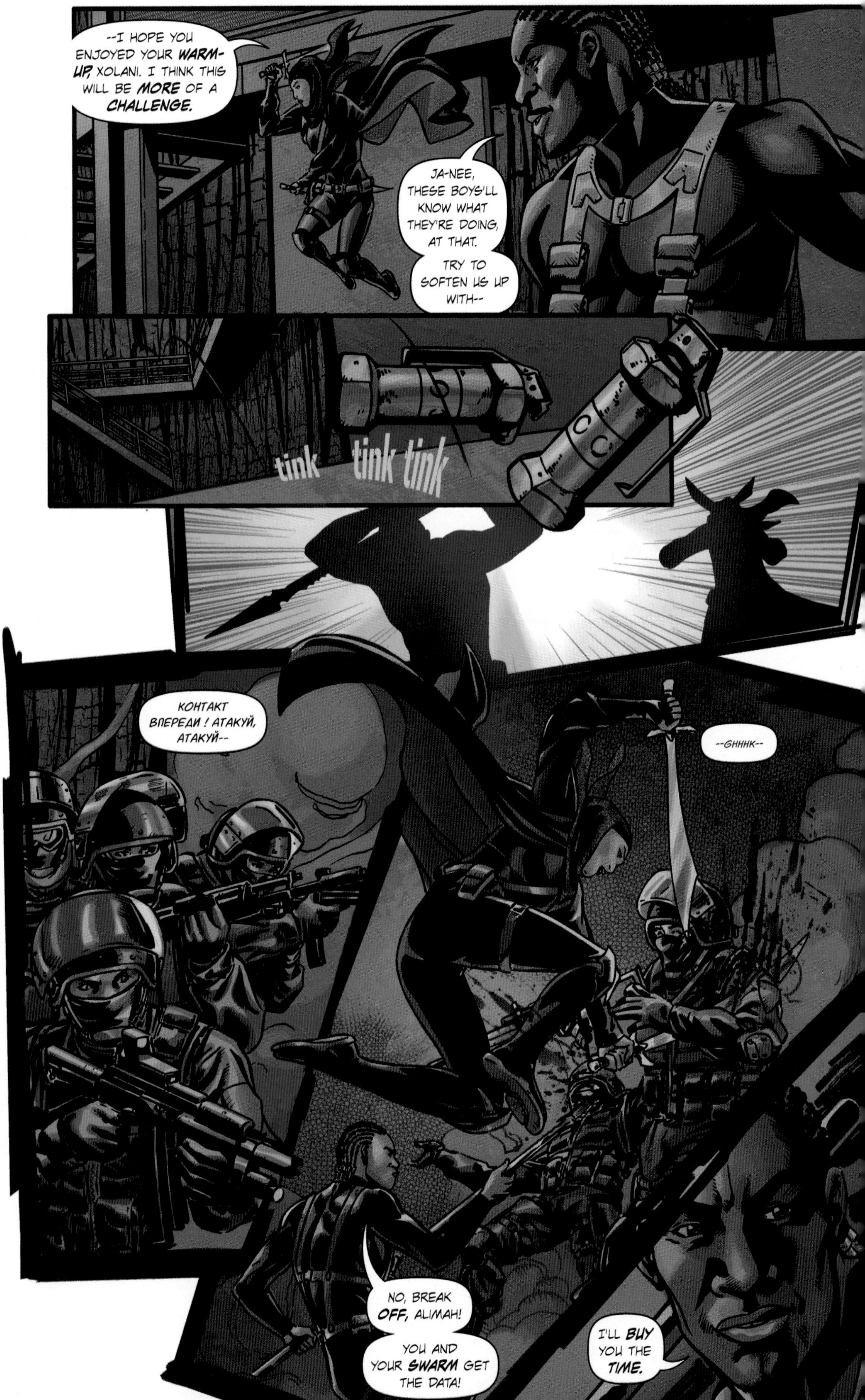
--I HOPE YOU ENJOYED YOUR WARM-UP, XOLANI. I THINK THIS WILL BE MORE OF A CHALLENGE.
JA-NEE, THESE BOYS'LL KNOW WHAT THEY'RE DOING, AT THAT.
TRY TO SOFTEN US UP WITH--
tink
tink tink
КОНТАКТ ВПЕРЕДИ ! АТАКУЙ, АТАКУЙ--
--GHHHK--
NO, BREAK OFF, ALIMAH!
YOU AND YOUR SWARM GET THE DATA!
I'LL BUY YOU THE TIME.

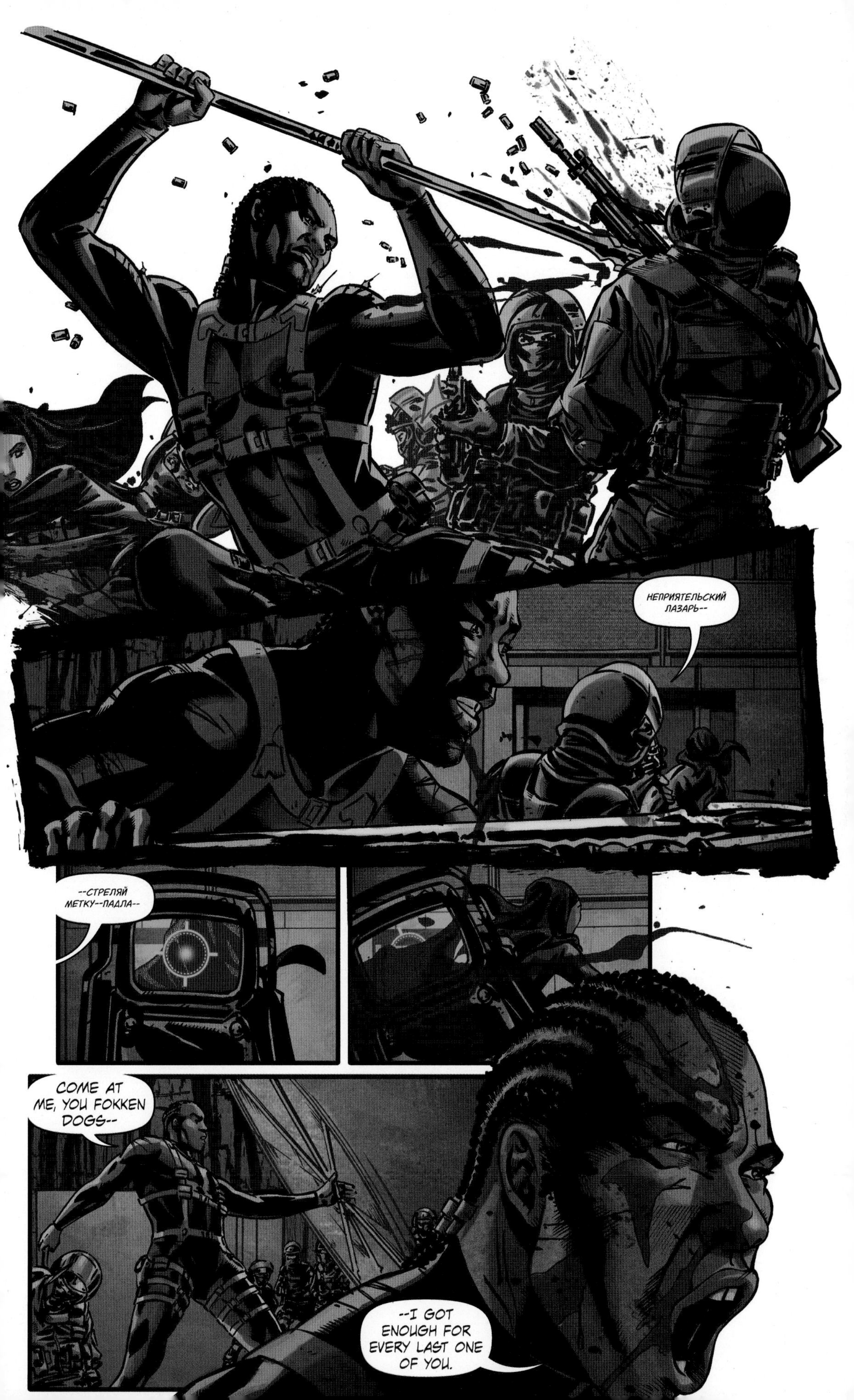
НЕПРИЯТЕЛЬСКИЙ ЛАЗАРЬ--
--СТРЕЛЯЙ МЕТКУ--ПАДЛА--
COME AT ME, YOU FOKKEN DOGS--
--I GOT ENOUGH FOR EVERY LAST ONE OF YOU.

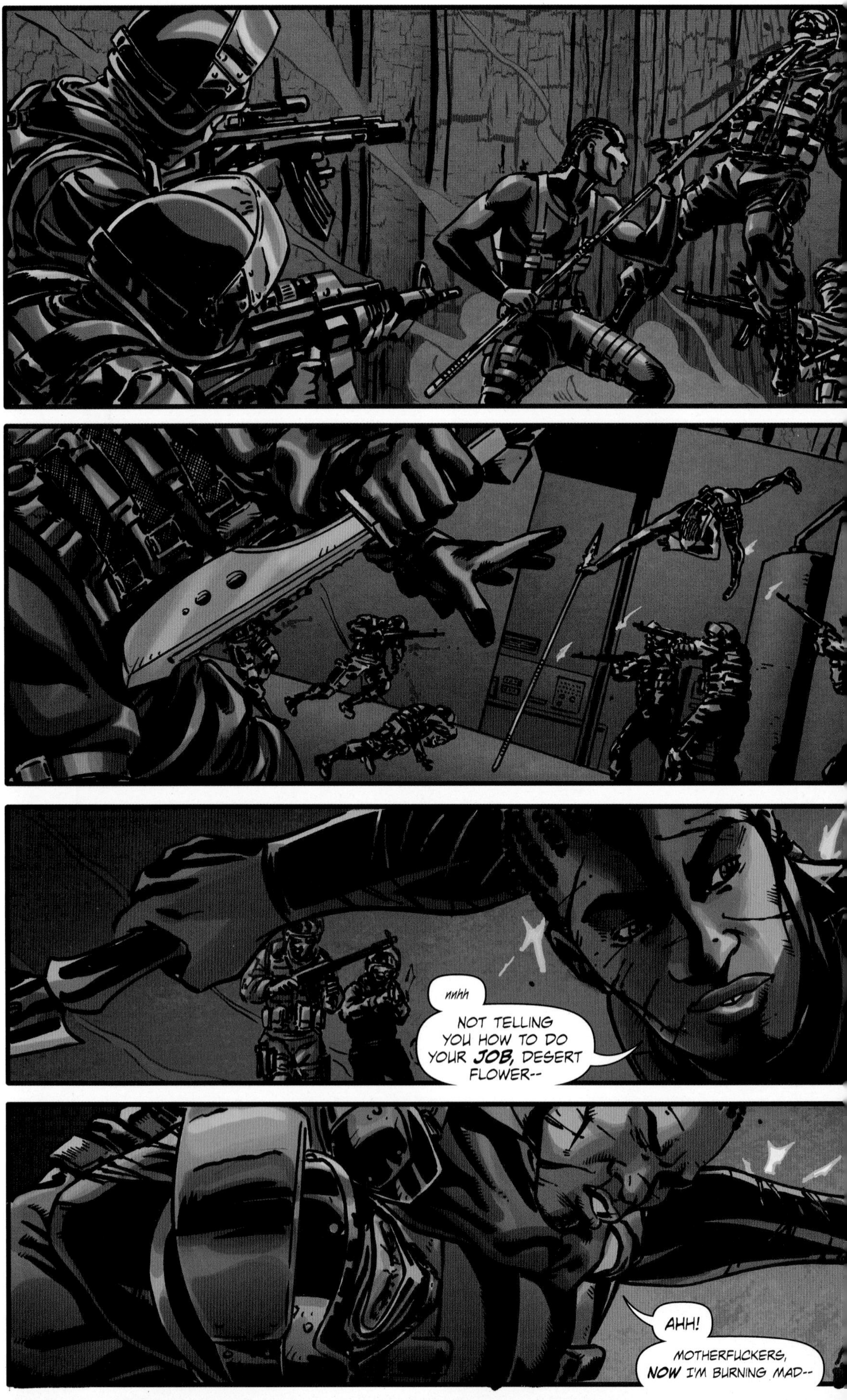
nnhh
NOT TELLING YOU HOW TO DO YOUR JOB, DESERT FLOWER--
AHH!
MOTHERFUCKERS, NOW I'M BURNING MAD--

ПАДЛА!
ПИДОР--

| INTRUSION
PROTOCOL::

DALET
SHEVAH TESAH
COMMIT_

СТРЕЛЯЙ
ЕГО!

| DECRYPT
VAS: G-I-V::01.

ENABLE
COPYALL--
MON:0.01

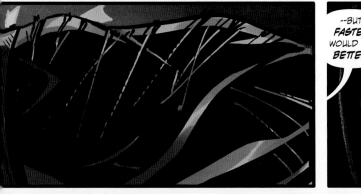

--BUT
FASTER
WOULD BE
BETTER!

ENABLE
WAIT 1

PURGE SOURCE.
DELETE-DATASTORE::
CONFIRM

AUTH CODE:
ZULU
FOXTROT ZULU

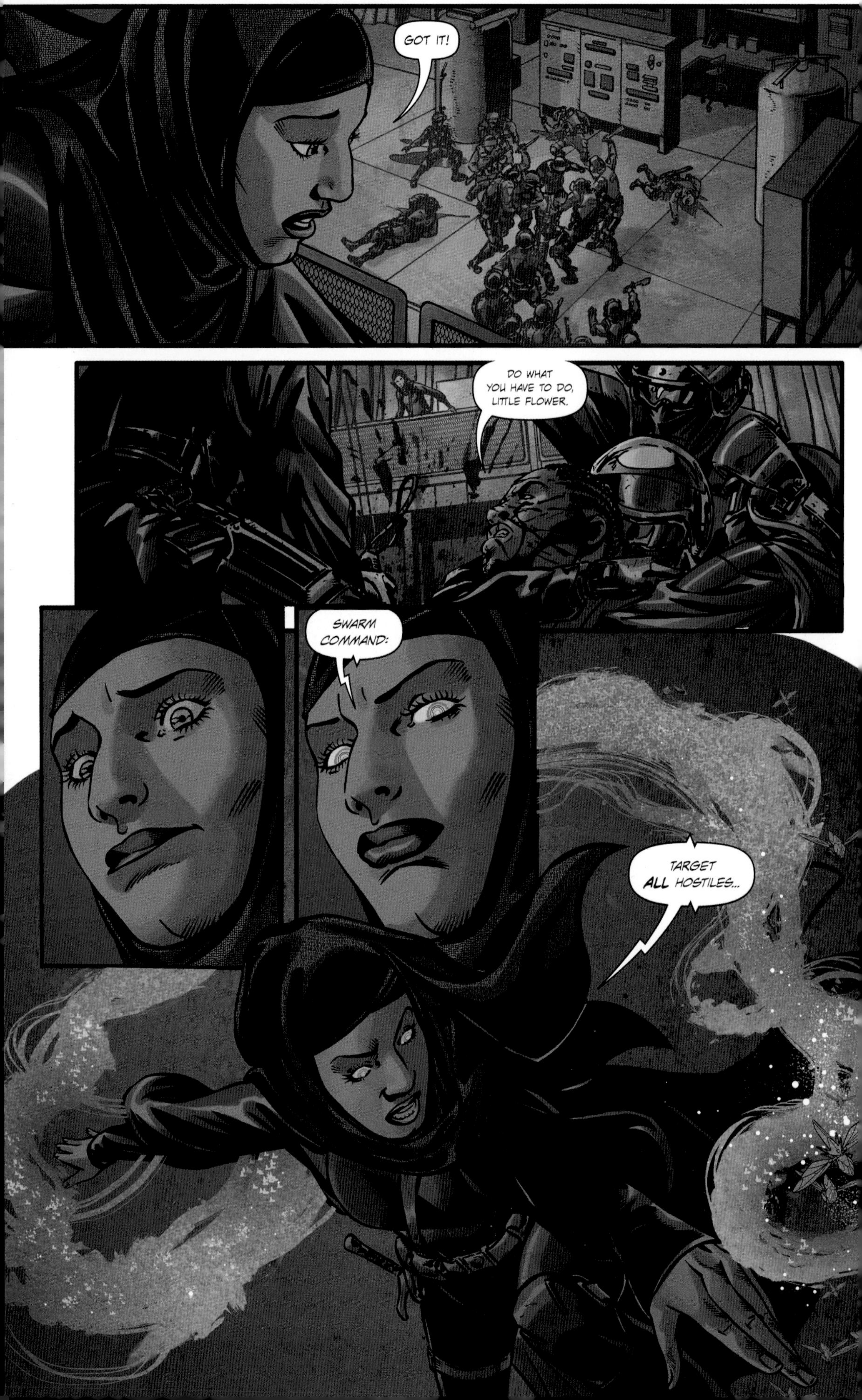
GOT IT!
DO WHAT YOU HAVE TO DO, LITTLE FLOWER.
SWARM COMMAND:
TARGET ALL HOSTILES...

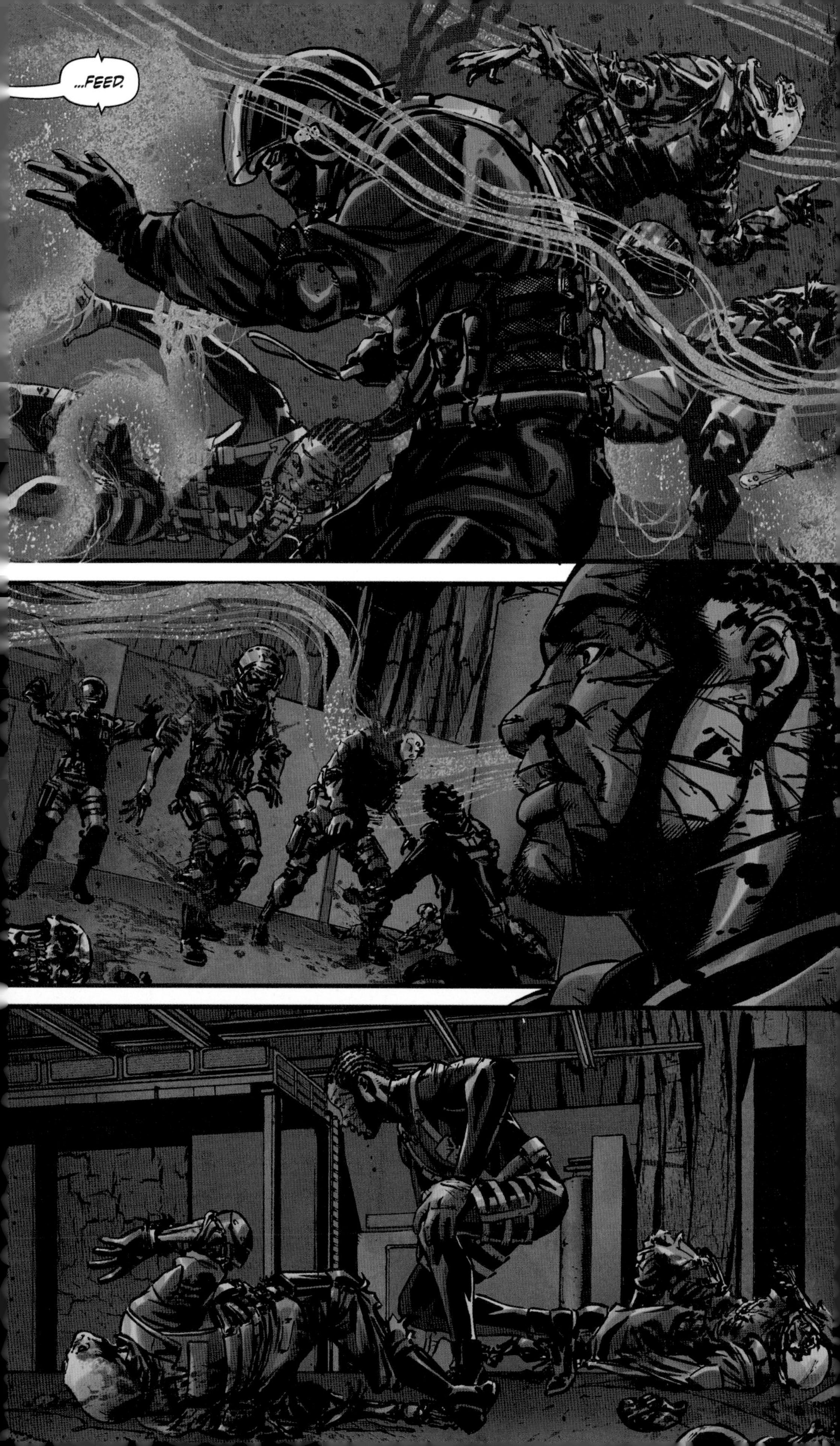
...FEED.

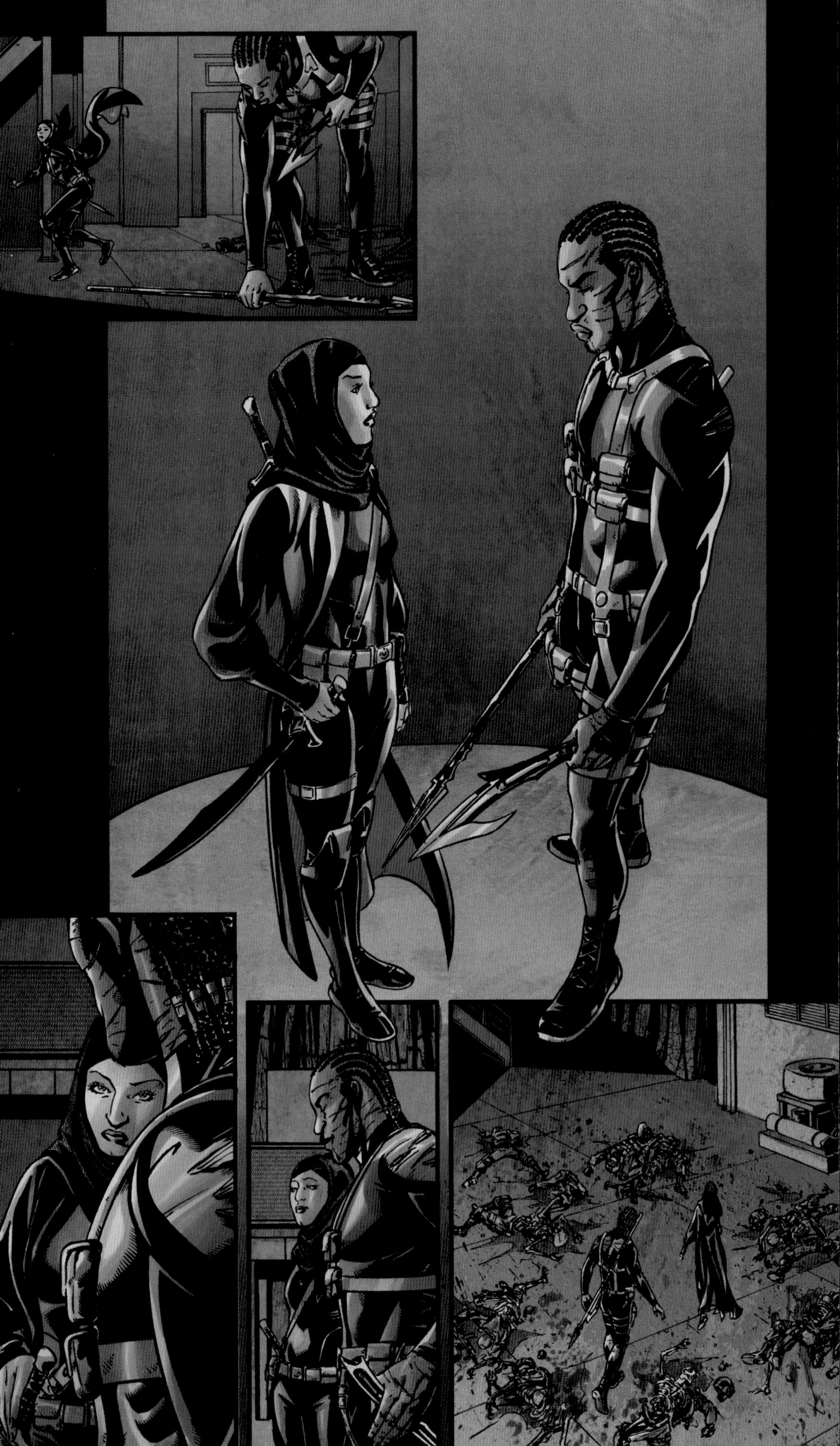

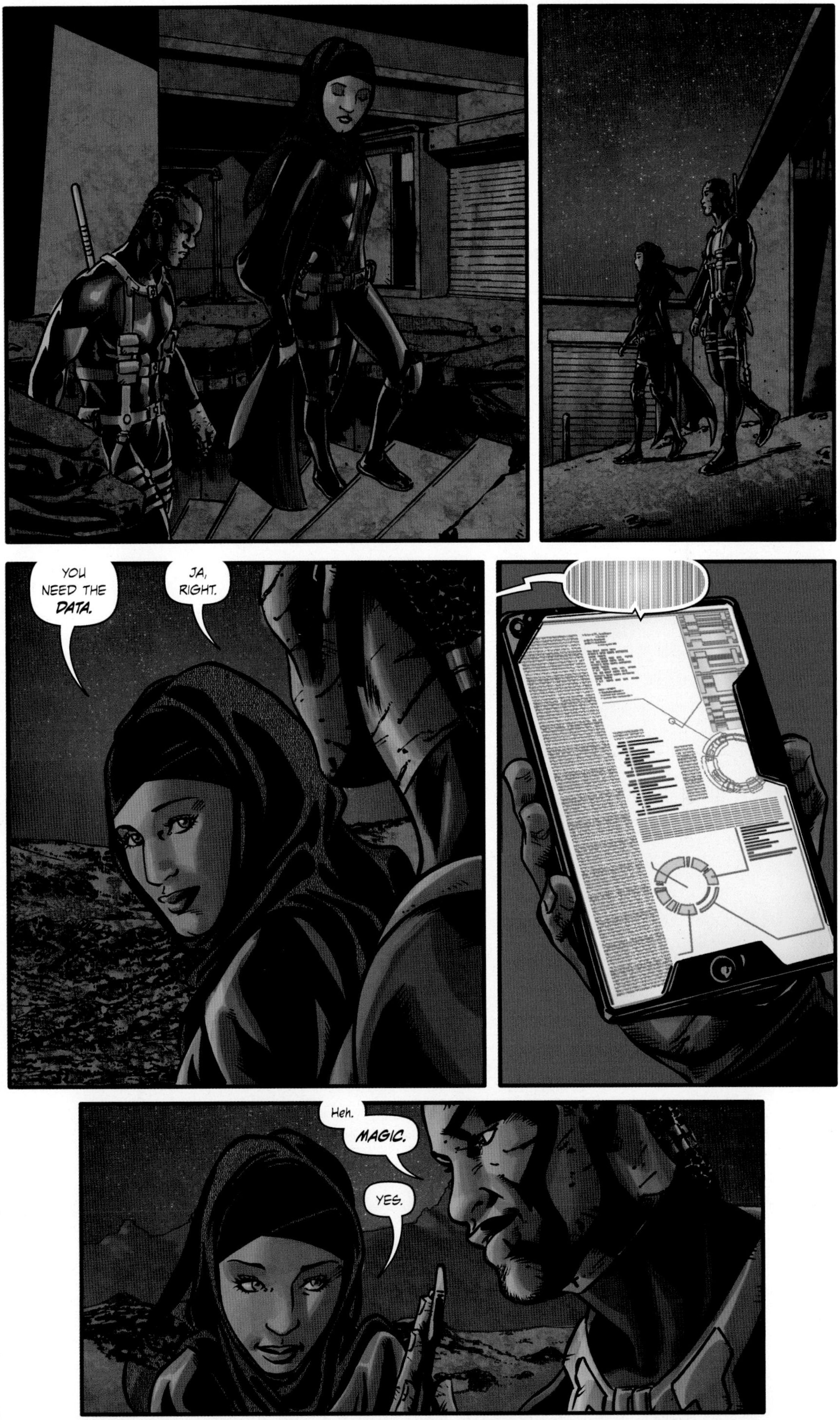

YOU NEED THE DATA.
JA, RIGHT.
Heh. MAGIC.
YES.

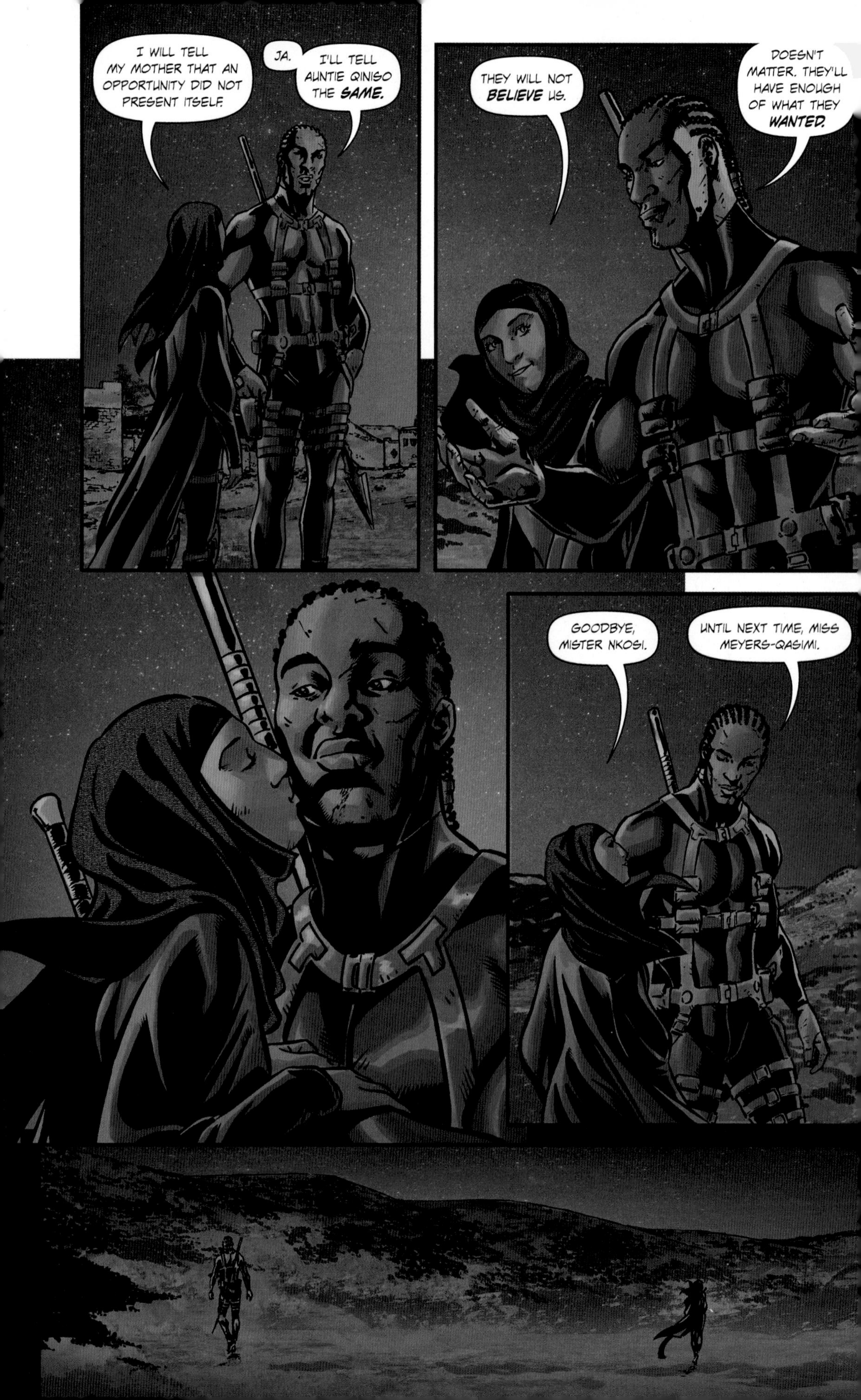
I WILL TELL MY MOTHER THAT AN OPPORTUNITY DID NOT PRESENT ITSELF.
JA.
I'LL TELL AUNTIE QINISO THE SAME.
THEY WILL NOT BELIEVE US.
DOESN'T MATTER. THEY'LL HAVE ENOUGH OF WHAT THEY WANTED.
GOODBYE, MISTER NKOSI.
UNTIL NEXT TIME, MISS MEYERS-QASIMI.

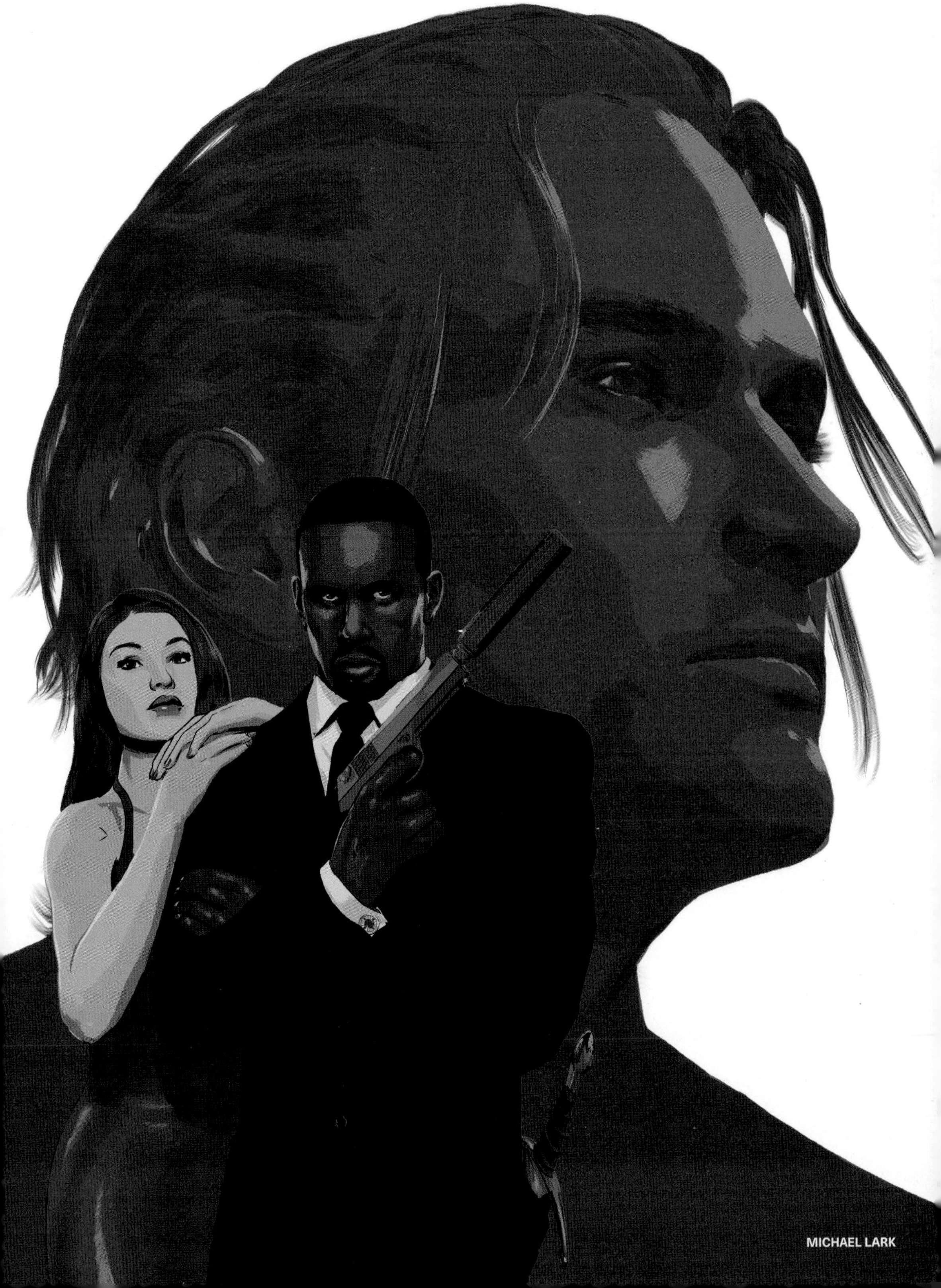

MICHAEL LARK

SERÉ COOPER is known throughout **Carlyle Territory**
as "The Face of the Post," her combination of looks, skill, and intelligence creating
a perfect delivery system for Family-approved messaging in the guise of news.

She has been at the top of her profession for years,
deftly navigating the political minefields of her work, all the while driven by her
own fierce, personal ambition.

Now, however, that ambition may finally have gotten the better of her.

———

While covering **The Conclave War** in Europe,
Seré landed an exclusive interview with the **Armitage Family** Lazarus,
SIR THOMAS HUSTON.

Shortly thereafter, Sir Thomas was murdered by **The Zmey**,
and worse, Carlyle and their allies were betrayed by the **MORRAY FAMILY**. The
setback has been devastating, and the Carlyle Family and their allies have been
aggressive in concealing these developments.

———

Seré has been reduced to reporting on celebrities and gossip
while the Family decides what—if anything—to do with her, and more crucially,
what she knows.

And Seré…Seré is looking for the story that will get her back on top….

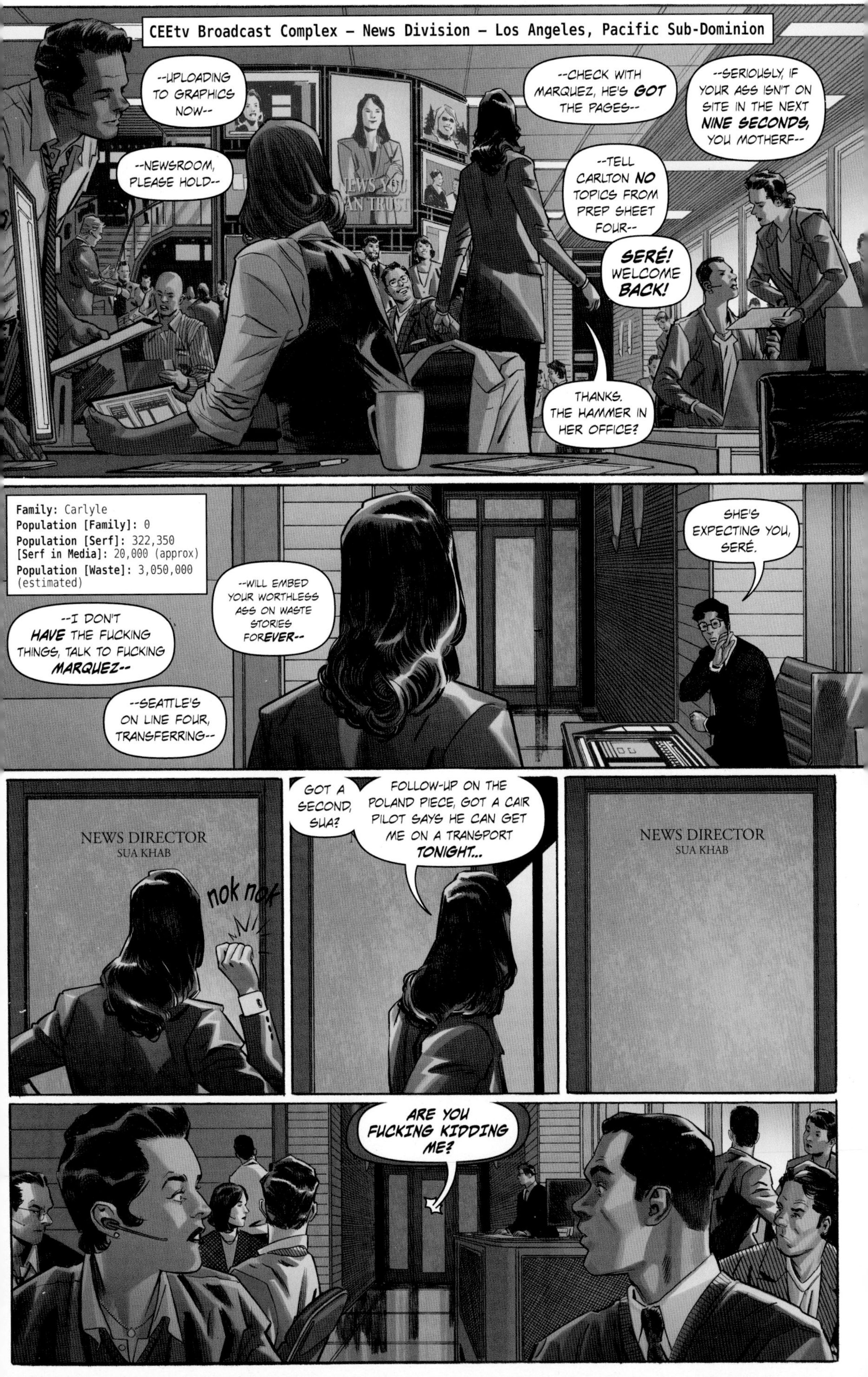
CEEtv Broadcast Complex – News Division – Los Angeles, Pacific Sub-Dominion
--UPLOADING TO GRAPHICS NOW--
--NEWSROOM, PLEASE HOLD--
NEWS YOU CAN TRUST
--CHECK WITH MARQUEZ, HE'S GOT THE PAGES--
--SERIOUSLY, IF YOUR ASS ISN'T ON SITE IN THE NEXT NINE SECONDS, YOU MOTHERF--
--TELL CARLTON NO TOPICS FROM PREP SHEET FOUR--
SERÉ! WELCOME BACK!
THANKS. THE HAMMER IN HER OFFICE?
Family: Carlyle
Population [Family]: 0
Population [Serf]: 322,350
[Serf in Media]: 20,000 (approx)
Population [Waste]: 3,050,000 (estimated)
--I DON'T HAVE THE FUCKING THINGS, TALK TO FUCKING MARQUEZ--
--WILL EMBED YOUR WORTHLESS ASS ON WASTE STORIES FOREVER--
--SEATTLE'S ON LINE FOUR, TRANSFERRING--
SHE'S EXPECTING YOU, SERÉ.
NEWS DIRECTOR
SUA KHAB
nok nok
GOT A SECOND, SUA?
FOLLOW-UP ON THE POLAND PIECE, GOT A CAIR PILOT SAYS HE CAN GET ME ON A TRANSPORT TONIGHT...
NEWS DIRECTOR
SUA KHAB
ARE YOU FUCKING KIDDING ME?

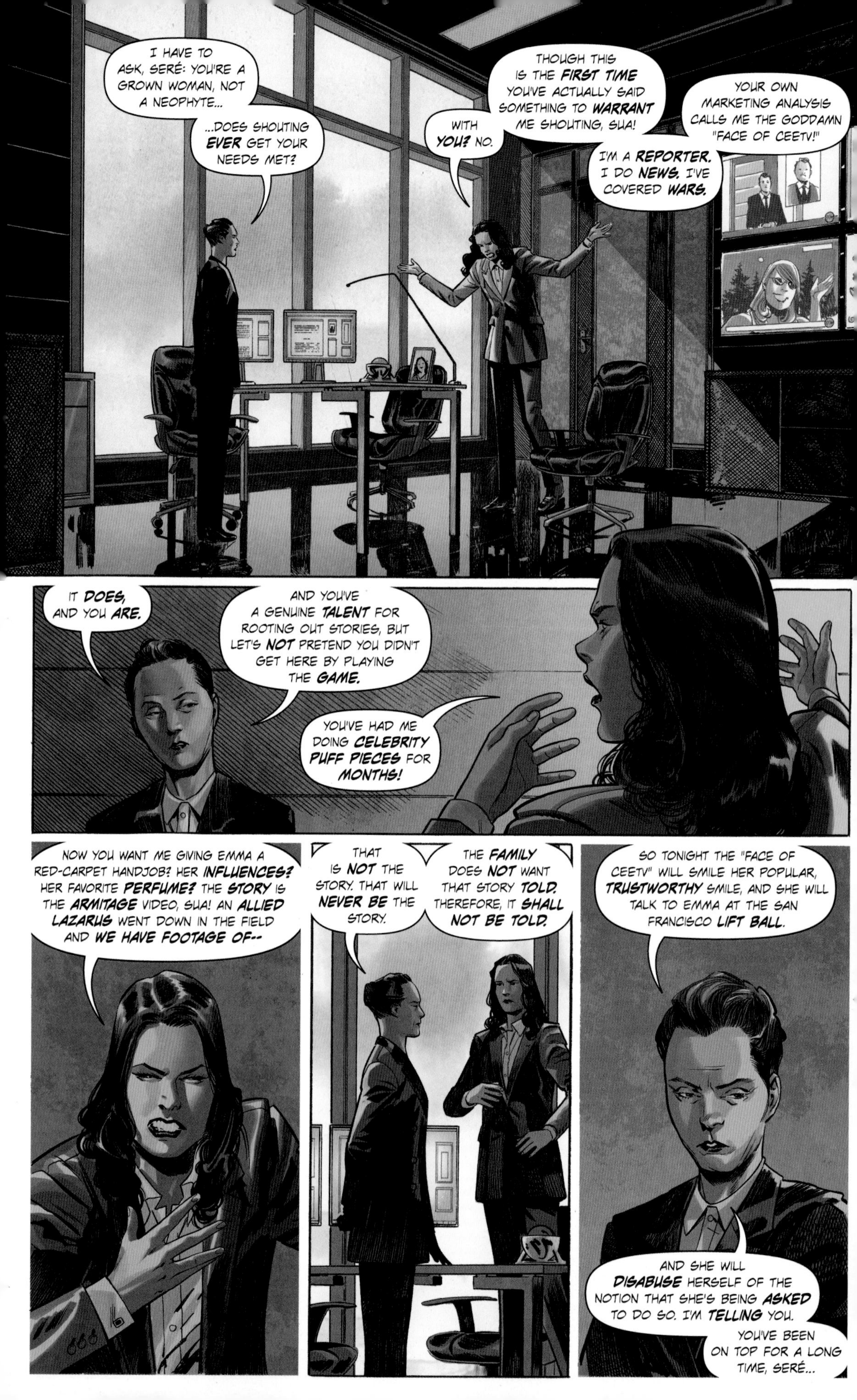
I HAVE TO ASK, SERÉ: YOU'RE A GROWN WOMAN, NOT A NEOPHYTE...
...DOES SHOUTING EVER GET YOUR NEEDS MET?
WITH YOU? NO.
THOUGH THIS IS THE FIRST TIME YOU'VE ACTUALLY SAID SOMETHING TO WARRANT ME SHOUTING, SUA!
YOUR OWN MARKETING ANALYSIS CALLS ME THE GODDAMN "FACE OF CEETV!"
I'M A REPORTER. I DO NEWS. I'VE COVERED WARS.
IT DOES, AND YOU ARE.
AND YOU'VE A GENUINE TALENT FOR ROOTING OUT STORIES, BUT LET'S NOT PRETEND YOU DIDN'T GET HERE BY PLAYING THE GAME.
YOU'VE HAD ME DOING CELEBRITY PUFF PIECES FOR MONTHS!
NOW YOU WANT ME GIVING EMMA A RED-CARPET HANDJOB? HER INFLUENCES? HER FAVORITE PERFUME? THE STORY IS THE ARMITAGE VIDEO, SUA! AN ALLIED LAZARUS WENT DOWN IN THE FIELD AND WE HAVE FOOTAGE OF--
THAT IS NOT THE STORY. THAT WILL NEVER BE THE STORY.
THE FAMILY DOES NOT WANT THAT STORY TOLD. THEREFORE, IT SHALL NOT BE TOLD.
SO TONIGHT THE "FACE OF CEETV" WILL SMILE HER POPULAR, TRUSTWORTHY SMILE, AND SHE WILL TALK TO EMMA AT THE SAN FRANCISCO LIFT BALL.
AND SHE WILL DISABUSE HERSELF OF THE NOTION THAT SHE'S BEING ASKED TO DO SO. I'M TELLING YOU.
YOU'VE BEEN ON TOP FOR A LONG TIME, SERÉ...

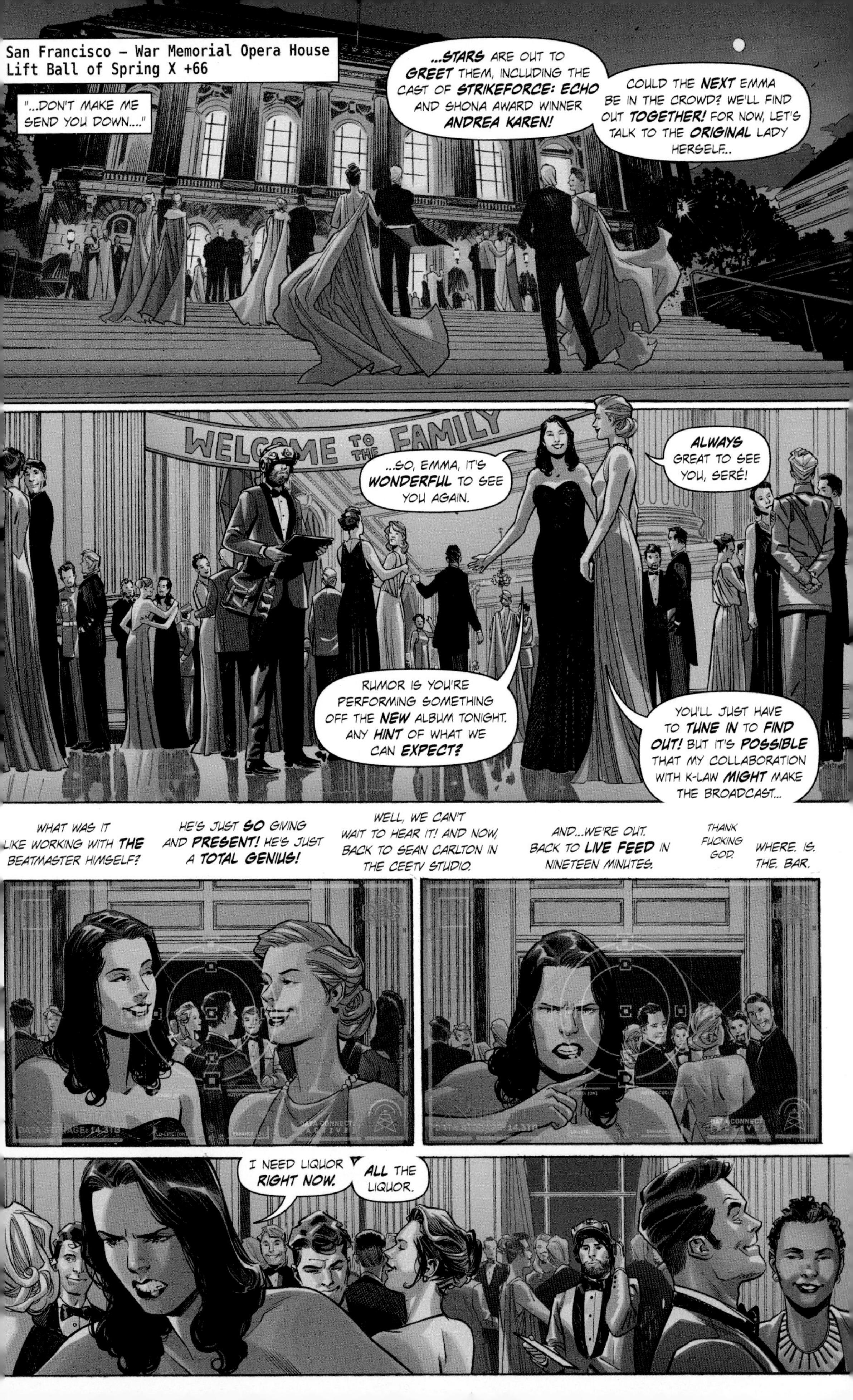
San Francisco – War Memorial Opera House
Lift Ball of Spring X +66
"...DON'T MAKE ME SEND YOU DOWN..."
...STARS ARE OUT TO GREET THEM, INCLUDING THE CAST OF STRIKEFORCE: ECHO AND SHONA AWARD WINNER ANDREA KAREN!
COULD THE NEXT EMMA BE IN THE CROWD? WE'LL FIND OUT TOGETHER! FOR NOW, LET'S TALK TO THE ORIGINAL LADY HERSELF...
WELCOME TO THE FAMILY
...SO, EMMA, IT'S WONDERFUL TO SEE YOU AGAIN.
ALWAYS GREAT TO SEE YOU, SERÉ!
RUMOR IS YOU'RE PERFORMING SOMETHING OFF THE NEW ALBUM TONIGHT. ANY HINT OF WHAT WE CAN EXPECT?
YOU'LL JUST HAVE TO TUNE IN TO FIND OUT! BUT IT'S POSSIBLE THAT MY COLLABORATION WITH K-LAW MIGHT MAKE THE BROADCAST...
WHAT WAS IT LIKE WORKING WITH THE BEATMASTER HIMSELF?
HE'S JUST SO GIVING AND PRESENT! HE'S JUST A TOTAL GENIUS!
WELL, WE CAN'T WAIT TO HEAR IT! AND NOW, BACK TO SEAN CARLTON IN THE CEETV STUDIO.
AND...WE'RE OUT. BACK TO LIVE FEED IN NINETEEN MINUTES.
THANK FUCKING GOD.
WHERE. IS. THE. BAR.
I NEED LIQUOR RIGHT NOW.
ALL THE LIQUOR.

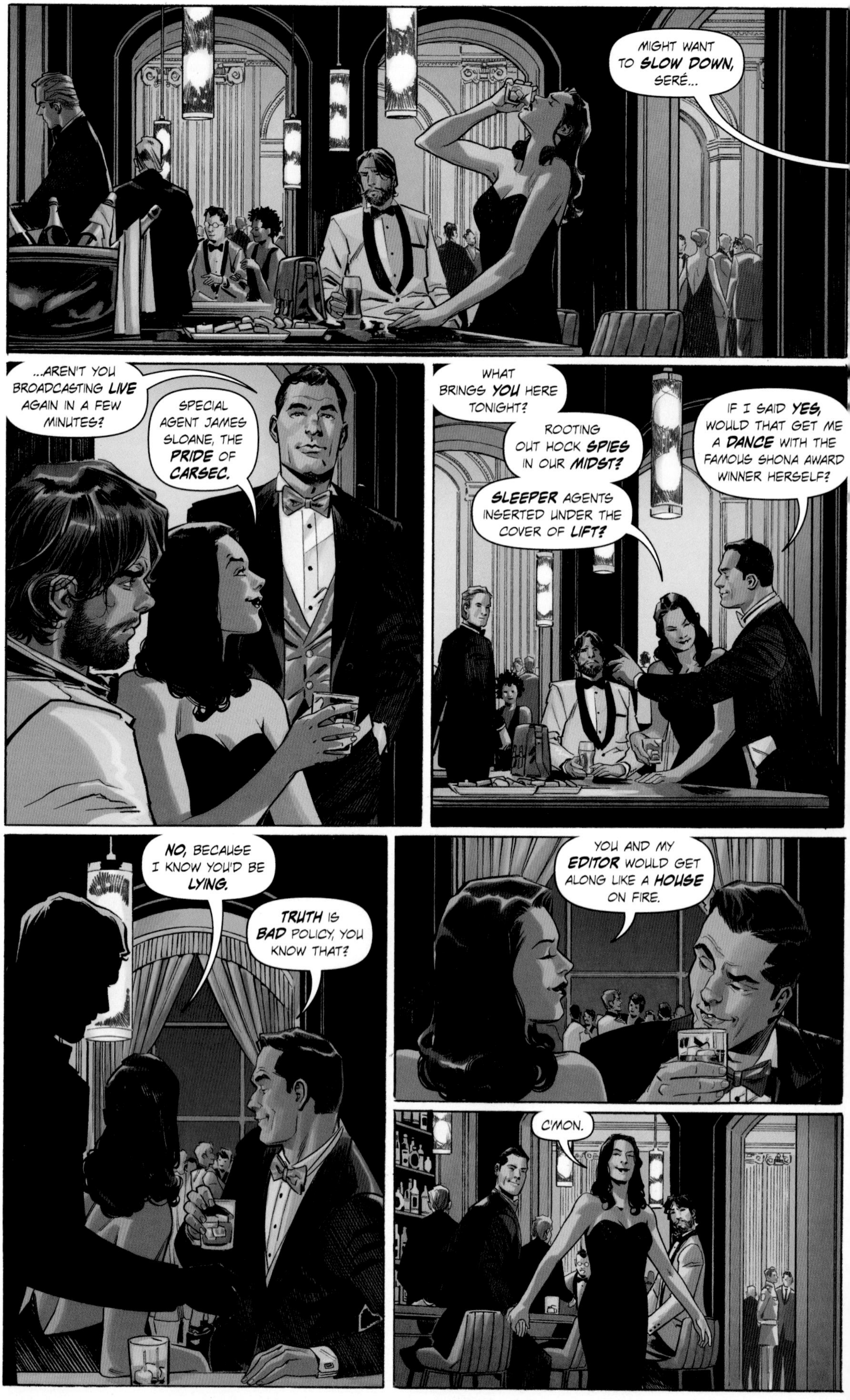
MIGHT WANT TO SLOW DOWN, SERÉ...
...AREN'T YOU BROADCASTING LIVE AGAIN IN A FEW MINUTES?
SPECIAL AGENT JAMES SLOANE, THE PRIDE OF CARSEC.
WHAT BRINGS YOU HERE TONIGHT?
ROOTING OUT HOCK SPIES IN OUR MIDST?
SLEEPER AGENTS INSERTED UNDER THE COVER OF LIFT?
IF I SAID YES, WOULD THAT GET ME A DANCE WITH THE FAMOUS SHONA AWARD WINNER HERSELF?
NO, BECAUSE I KNOW YOU'D BE LYING.
TRUTH IS BAD POLICY, YOU KNOW THAT?
YOU AND MY EDITOR WOULD GET ALONG LIKE A HOUSE ON FIRE.
C'MON.

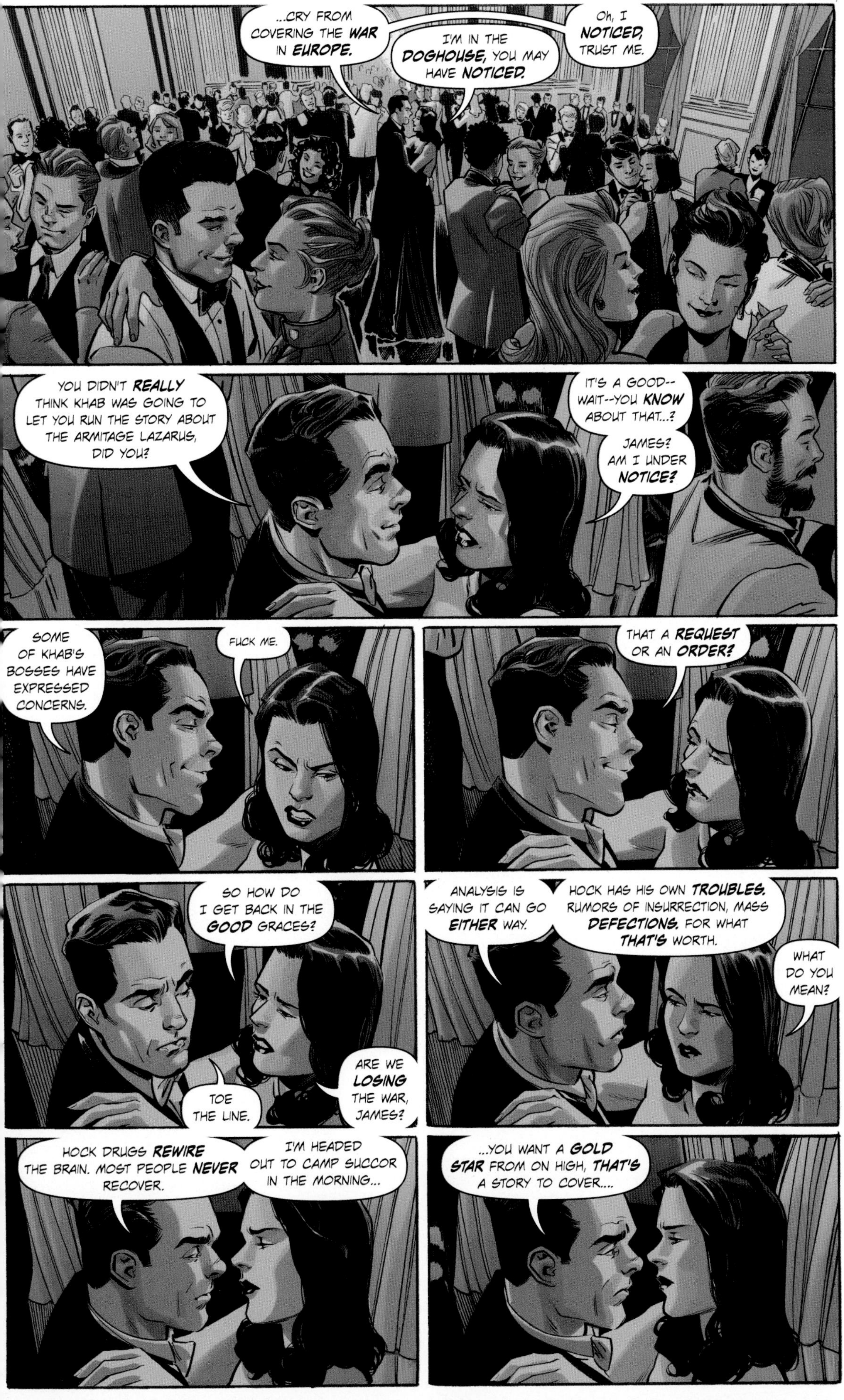

...CRY FROM COVERING THE WAR IN EUROPE.
I'M IN THE DOGHOUSE, YOU MAY HAVE NOTICED.
Oh, I NOTICED, TRUST ME.
YOU DIDN'T REALLY THINK KHAB WAS GOING TO LET YOU RUN THE STORY ABOUT THE ARMITAGE LAZARUS, DID YOU?
IT'S A GOOD-- WAIT--YOU KNOW ABOUT THAT...?
JAMES? AM I UNDER NOTICE?
SOME OF KHAB'S BOSSES HAVE EXPRESSED CONCERNS.
FUCK ME.
THAT A REQUEST OR AN ORDER?
SO HOW DO I GET BACK IN THE GOOD GRACES?
TOE THE LINE.
ARE WE LOSING THE WAR, JAMES?
ANALYSIS IS SAYING IT CAN GO EITHER WAY.
HOCK HAS HIS OWN TROUBLES. RUMORS OF INSURRECTION, MASS DEFECTIONS. FOR WHAT THAT'S WORTH.
WHAT DO YOU MEAN?
HOCK DRUGS REWIRE THE BRAIN. MOST PEOPLE NEVER RECOVER.
I'M HEADED OUT TO CAMP SUCCOR IN THE MORNING...
...YOU WANT A GOLD STAR FROM ON HIGH, THAT'S A STORY TO COVER....

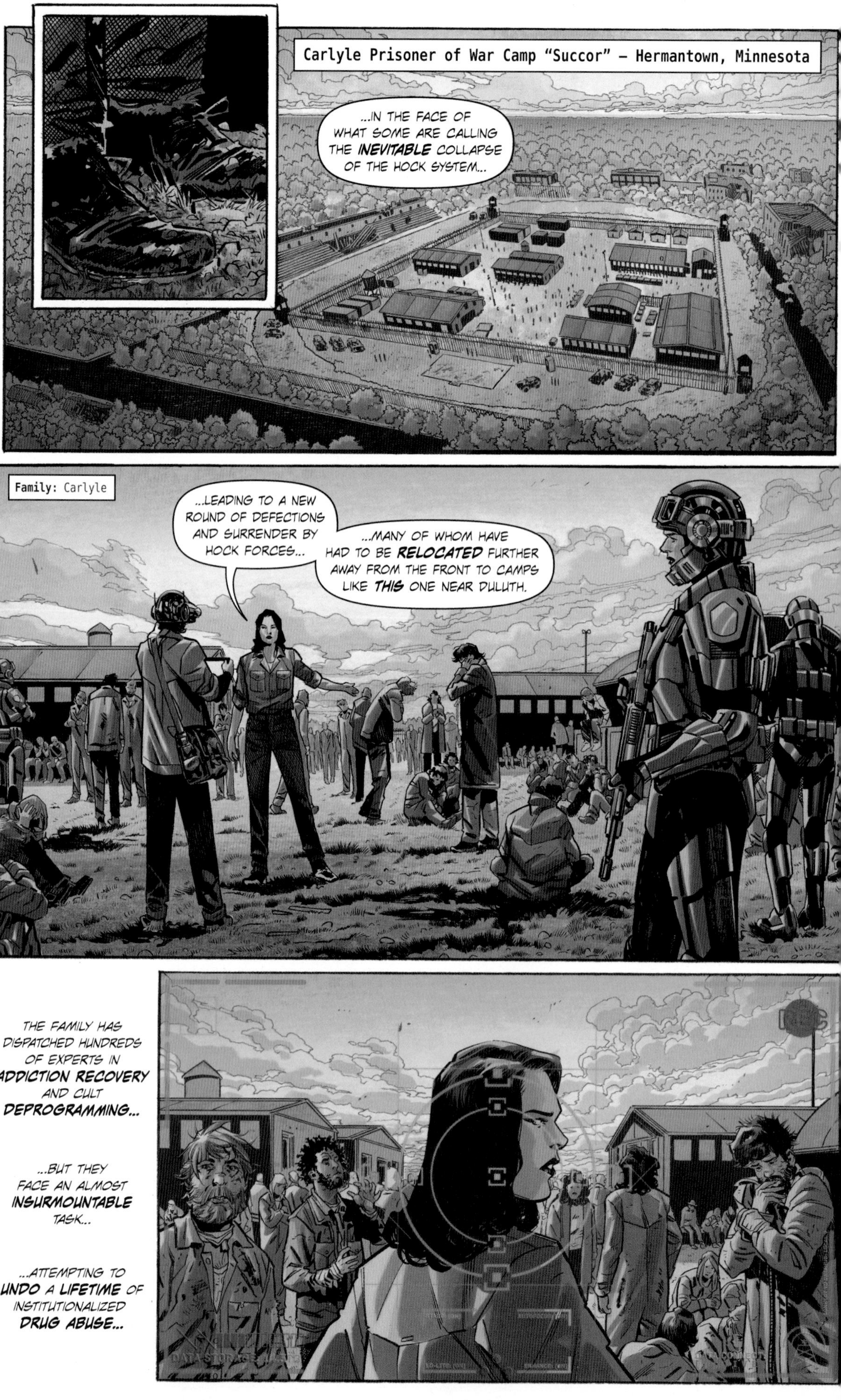
Carlyle Prisoner of War Camp "Succor" – Hermantown, Minnesota
...IN THE FACE OF WHAT SOME ARE CALLING THE INEVITABLE COLLAPSE OF THE HOCK SYSTEM...
Family: Carlyle
...LEADING TO A NEW ROUND OF DEFECTIONS AND SURRENDER BY HOCK FORCES...
...MANY OF WHOM HAVE HAD TO BE RELOCATED FURTHER AWAY FROM THE FRONT TO CAMPS LIKE THIS ONE NEAR DULUTH.
THE FAMILY HAS DISPATCHED HUNDREDS OF EXPERTS IN ADDICTION RECOVERY AND CULT DEPROGRAMMING...
...BUT THEY FACE AN ALMOST INSURMOUNTABLE TASK...
...ATTEMPTING TO UNDO A LIFETIME OF INSTITUTIONALIZED DRUG ABUSE...

...FOR DOCTOR HOCK DOESN'T SIMPLY **STEAL** THE **FREE WILL** OF THE MEN AND WOMEN WHO LIVE UNDER HIS RULE...

...HE TAKES THEIR **MINDS** AS WELL.

BEFORE THEY'RE EVEN **BORN,** HOCK **DOSES** HIS SUBJECTS WITH A PHARMACEUTICAL COCKTAIL THAT DEMANDS NOTHING LESS THAN **TOTAL** OBEDIENCE.

WITH DRUGS THAT **REWRITE** THE BRAIN, THAT CRUSH PERSONALITY, AND THAT DEMAND TOTAL **LOYALTY.**

THIS IS THE HOCK **LEGACY.**

SUFFERED BY **ALL** WHO HAVE THE SIMPLE MISFORTUNE TO HAVE BEEN **BORN** UNDER HIS **REGIME.**

THESE ARE THE FACES OF HIS FORGOTTEN VICTIMS.

MANY OF WHOM MAY **NEVER** RECOVER.

A CHILLING REMINDER OF THE **STAKES** IN THIS ONGOING **CONFLICT.**

I'M SERÉ COOPER, REPORTING FROM CAMP SUCCOR, OUTSIDE DULUTH.

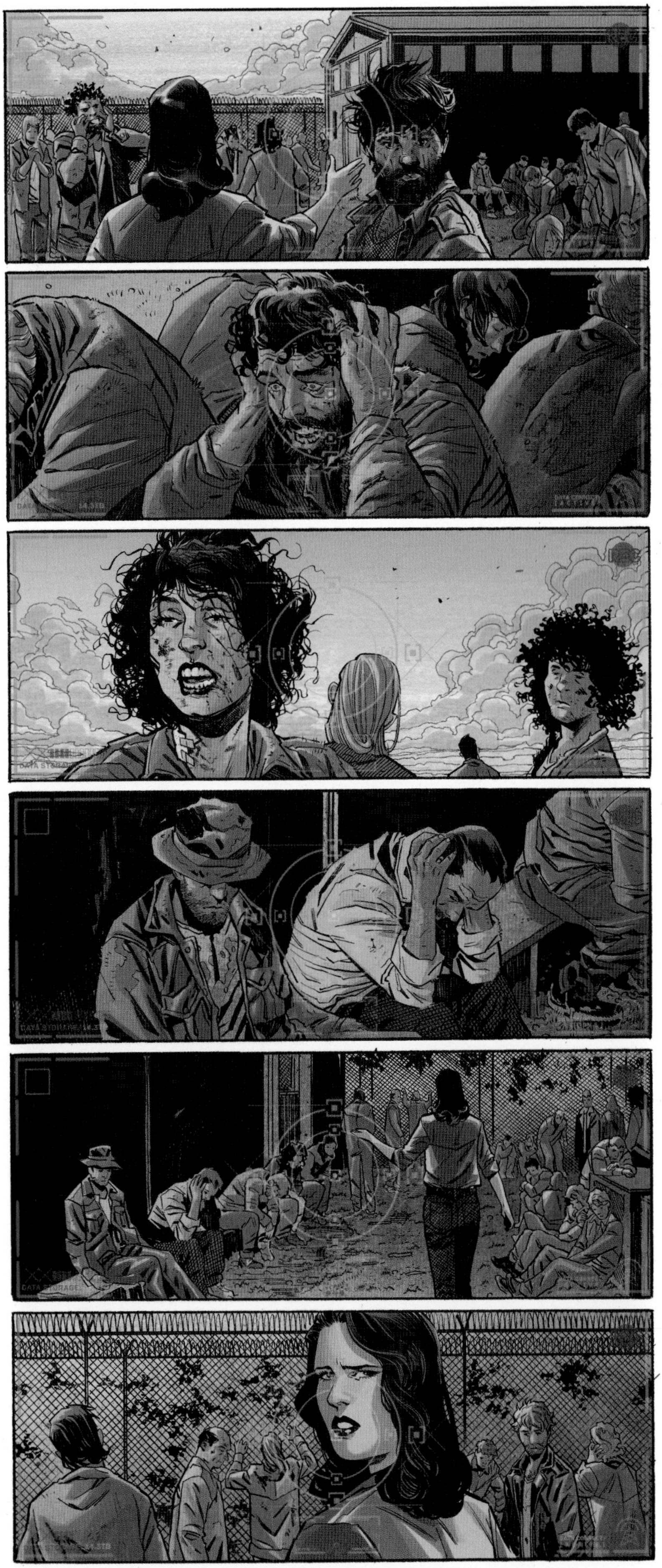

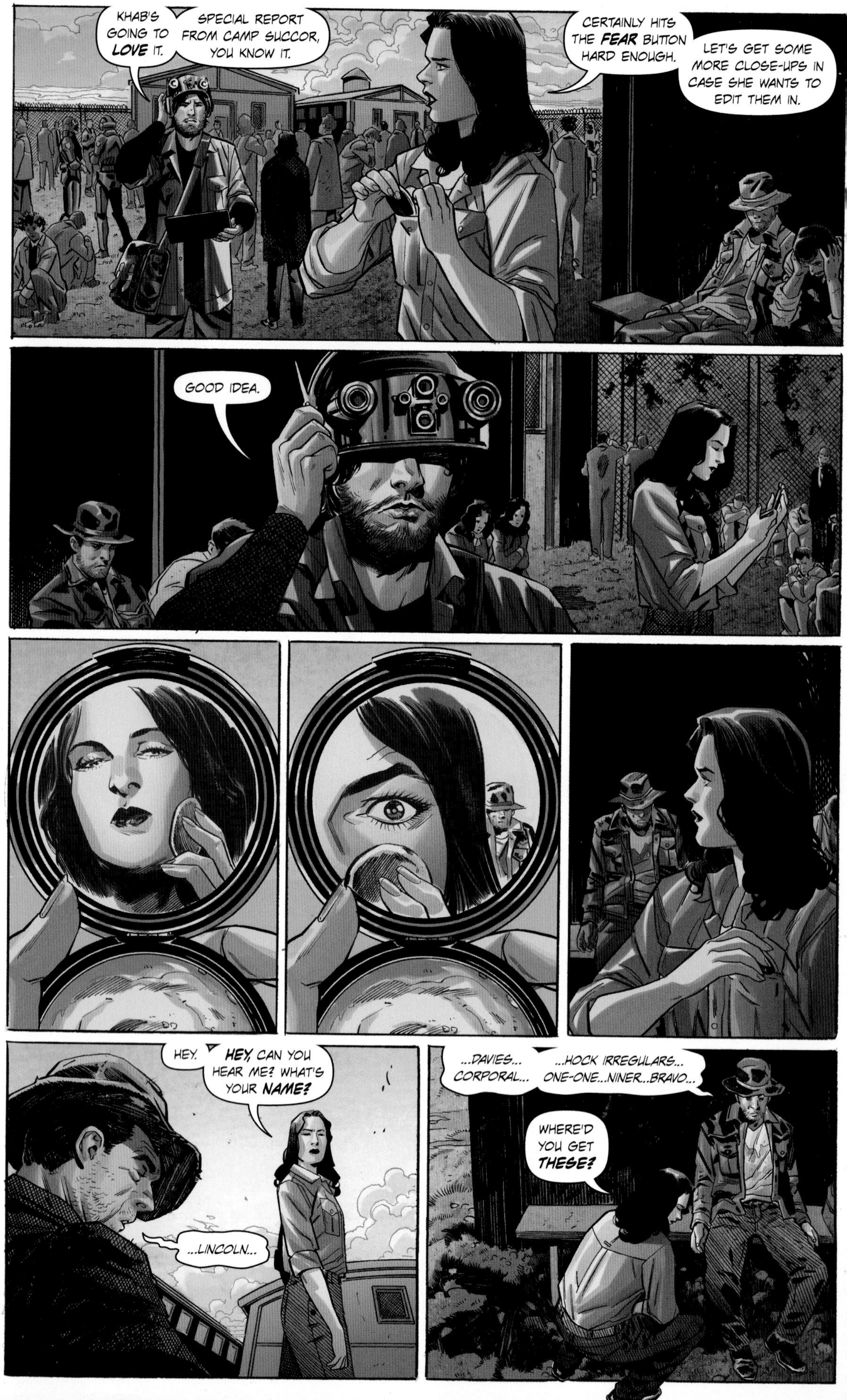
KHAB'S GOING TO LOVE IT.
SPECIAL REPORT FROM CAMP SUCCOR, YOU KNOW IT.
CERTAINLY HITS THE FEAR BUTTON HARD ENOUGH.
LET'S GET SOME MORE CLOSE-UPS IN CASE SHE WANTS TO EDIT THEM IN.
GOOD IDEA.
HEY.
HEY, CAN YOU HEAR ME? WHAT'S YOUR NAME?
...LINCOLN...
...DAVIES... CORPORAL...
...HOCK IRREGULARS... ONE-ONE...NINER...BRAVO...
WHERE'D YOU GET THESE?

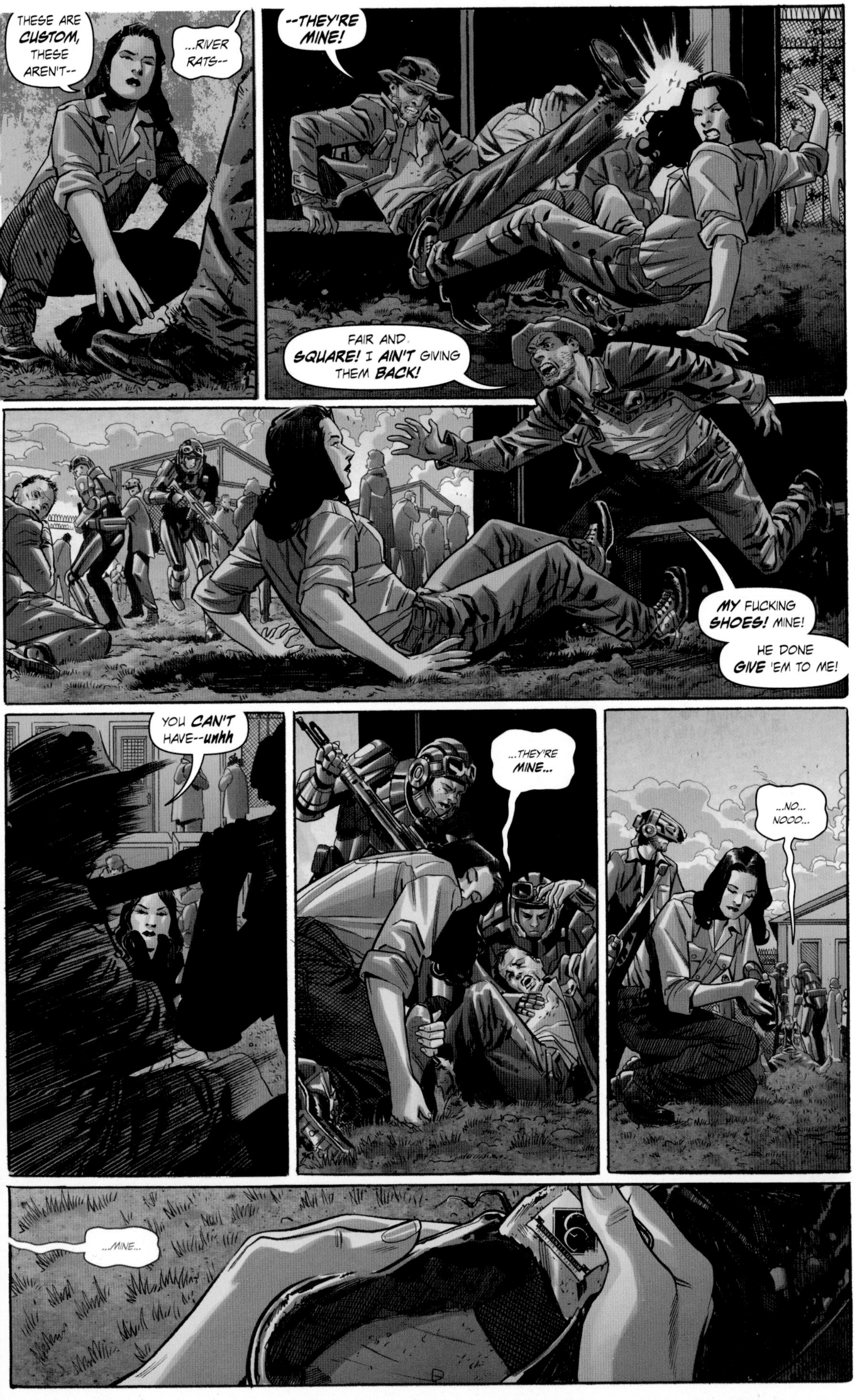
THESE ARE CUSTOM, THESE AREN'T--
...RIVER RATS--
--THEY'RE MINE!
FAIR AND SQUARE! I AIN'T GIVING THEM BACK!
MY FUCKING SHOES! MINE!
HE DONE GIVE 'EM TO ME!
YOU CAN'T HAVE--unhh
...THEY'RE MINE...
...NO... NOOO...
...MINE...

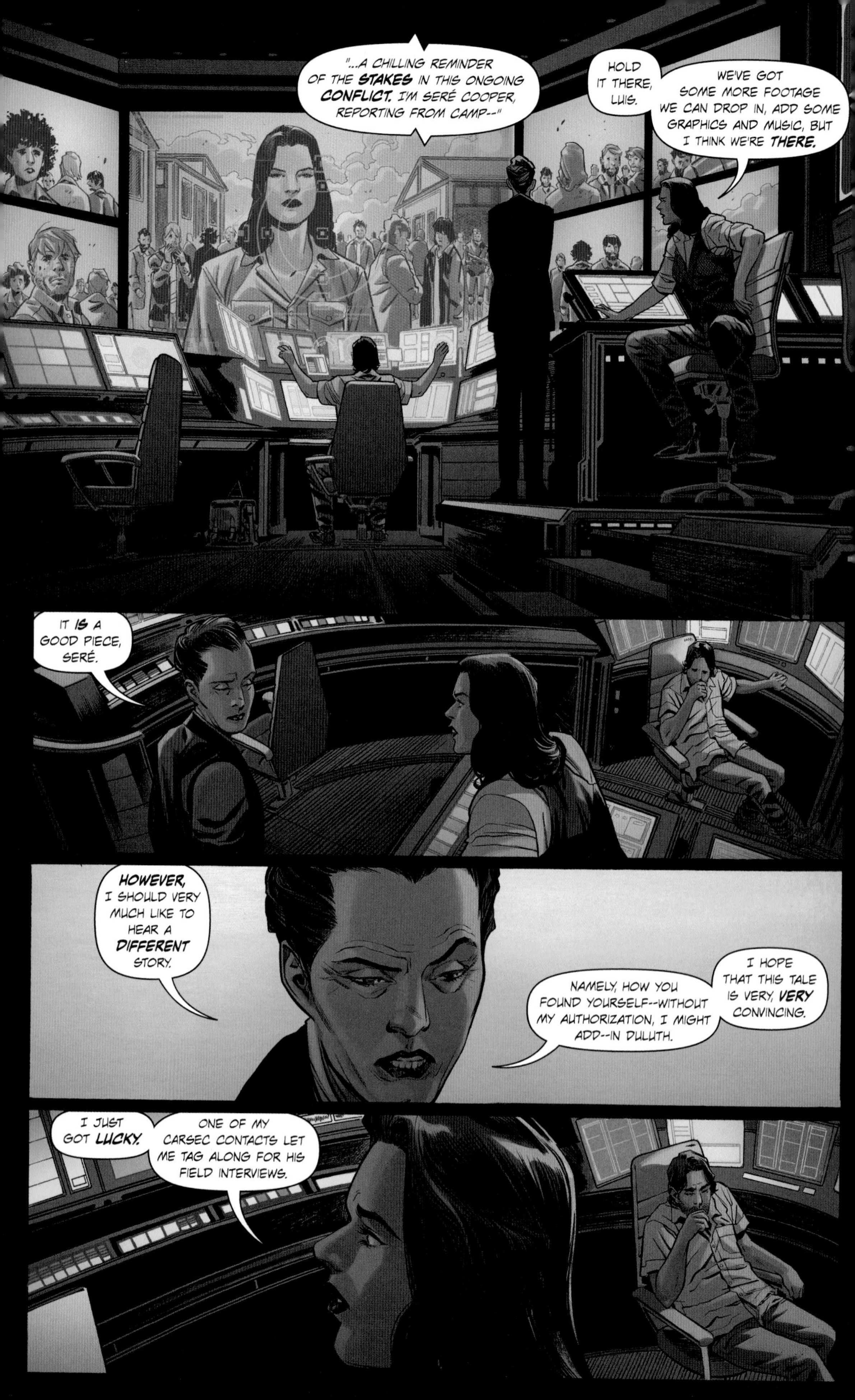
"...A CHILLING REMINDER OF THE STAKES IN THIS ONGOING CONFLICT. I'M SERÉ COOPER, REPORTING FROM CAMP--"
HOLD IT THERE, LUIS.
WE'VE GOT SOME MORE FOOTAGE WE CAN DROP IN, ADD SOME GRAPHICS AND MUSIC, BUT I THINK WE'RE THERE.
IT IS A GOOD PIECE, SERÉ.
HOWEVER, I SHOULD VERY MUCH LIKE TO HEAR A DIFFERENT STORY.
NAMELY, HOW YOU FOUND YOURSELF--WITHOUT MY AUTHORIZATION, I MIGHT ADD--IN DULUTH.
I HOPE THAT THIS TALE IS VERY, VERY CONVINCING.
I JUST GOT LUCKY.
ONE OF MY CARSEC CONTACTS LET ME TAG ALONG FOR HIS FIELD INTERVIEWS.

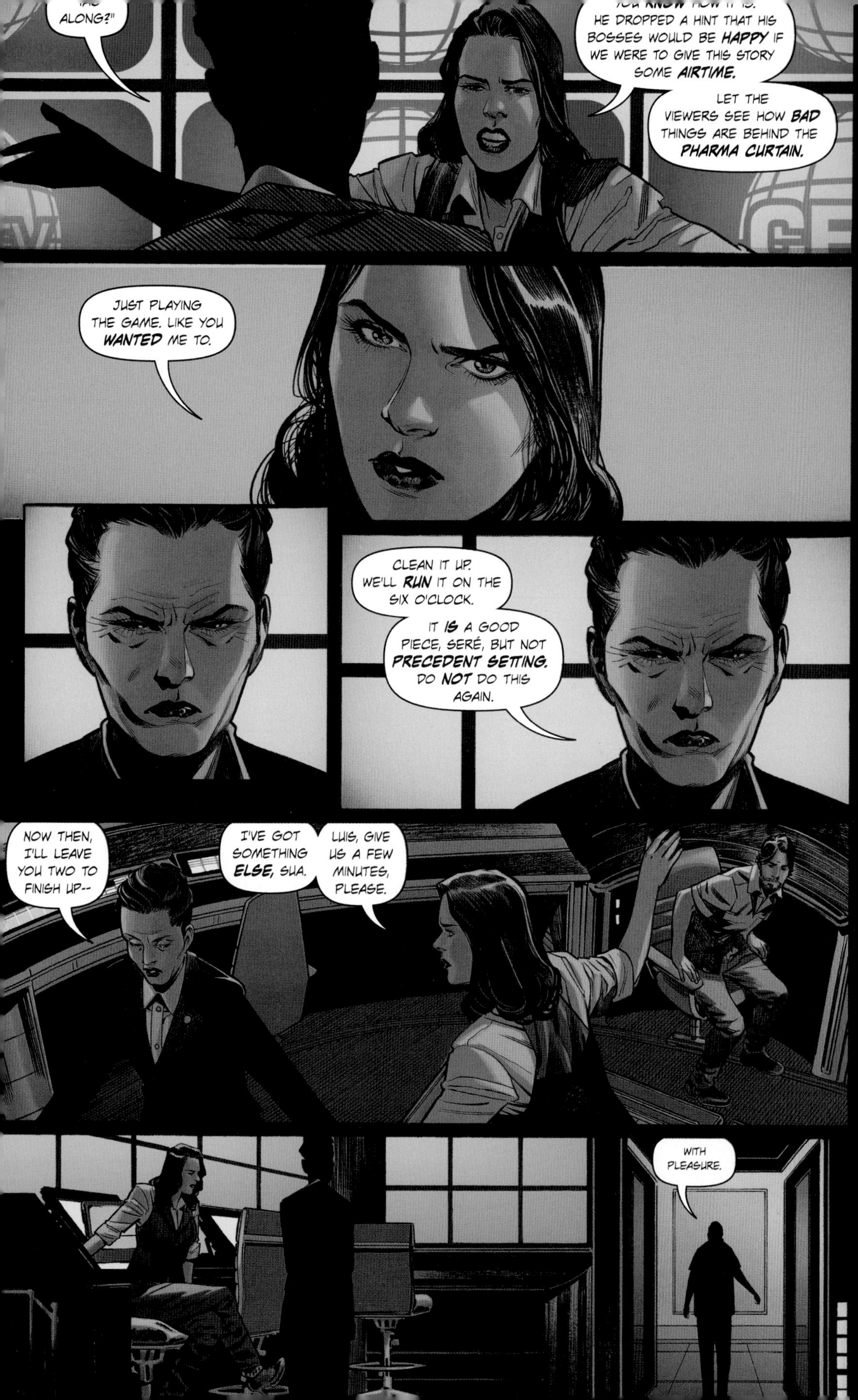
ALONG?"
HE DROPPED A HINT THAT HIS BOSSES WOULD BE HAPPY IF WE WERE TO GIVE THIS STORY SOME AIRTIME.
LET THE VIEWERS SEE HOW BAD THINGS ARE BEHIND THE PHARMA CURTAIN.
JUST PLAYING THE GAME. LIKE YOU WANTED ME TO.
CLEAN IT UP. WE'LL RUN IT ON THE SIX O'CLOCK.
IT IS A GOOD PIECE, SERÉ, BUT NOT PRECEDENT SETTING. DO NOT DO THIS AGAIN.
NOW THEN, I'LL LEAVE YOU TWO TO FINISH UP--
I'VE GOT SOMETHING ELSE, SUA.
LUIS, GIVE US A FEW MINUTES, PLEASE.
WITH PLEASURE.

THEY'RE CALLED THE **RIVER RATS,** HOCK MILITIA.

THESE GUYS ARE THE LOWEST OF THE LOW AS FAR AS HOCK'S MILITARY GO. SCAVENGE **ALL** THEIR GEAR.

THIS IS CORPORAL LINCOLN DAVIES, RIVER RAT. LIFETIME ON HOCK PHARMA HAS PRETTY MUCH **BAKED** HIM.

WHEN THEY CAUGHT HIM HE HADN'T EATEN IN A WEEK, HIS RIFLE WAS EMPTY AND HE WAS USING OLD SPORTS EQUIPMENT FOR BODY ARMOR.

AND HE WAS WEARING **THESE.**

SHOES **INSTEAD** OF COMBAT BOOTS.

HARDLY SURPRISING. YOU SAID THEY'RE SCAVENGERS.

LOOK AT THOSE SHOES, SUA. THEY'RE MADE BY CONSTANTI...

...AND CONSTANTI **ONLY** MAKES SHOES FOR THE **FAMILY** AND THEIR **PERSONAL** RETINUES.

MAYBE **ONE** IN A **MILLION** SERFS HAS A PAIR. **MAYBE.**

SO YOUR CORPORAL DAVIES KILLED A HIGH-RANKING SERF AND TOOK HIS SHOES.

UNFORTUNATE, YES. NEWSWORTHY, NO.

IF HIGH-RANKING, HOW COME WE **NEVER** HEARD ABOUT IT?

I DID SOME **CHECKING.** CONSTANTI USES **GENETICALLY ENGINEERED** LEATHER. EACH LOT CAN BE TRACKED BACK TO A **SPECIFIC** COW.

THIS LOT WAS FOR THE **FAMILY'S** USE

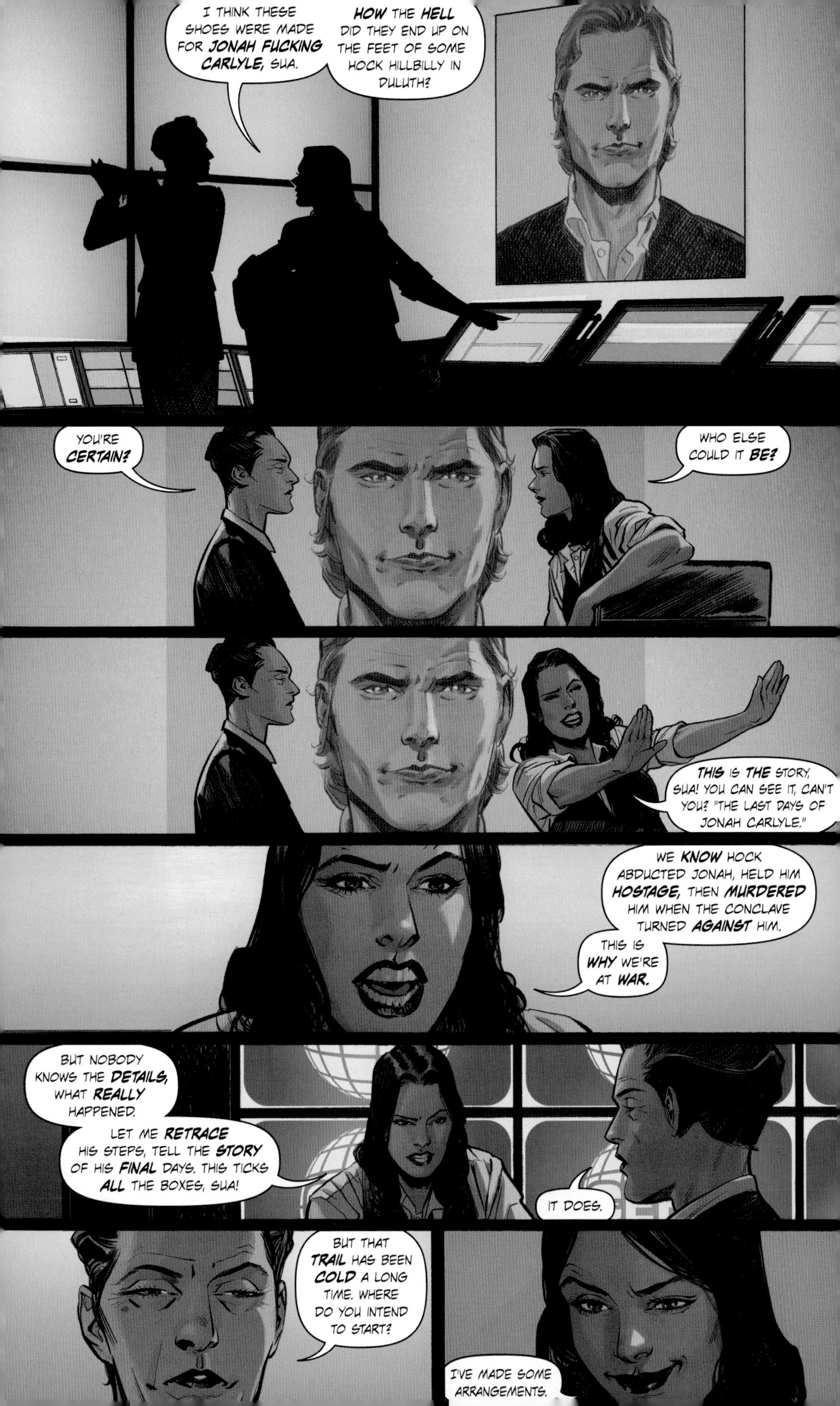
I THINK THESE SHOES WERE MADE FOR JONAH FUCKING CARLYLE, SUA.
HOW THE HELL DID THEY END UP ON THE FEET OF SOME HOCK HILLBILLY IN DULUTH?
YOU'RE CERTAIN?
WHO ELSE COULD IT BE?
THIS IS THE STORY, SUA! YOU CAN SEE IT, CAN'T YOU? "THE LAST DAYS OF JONAH CARLYLE."
WE KNOW HOCK ABDUCTED JONAH, HELD HIM HOSTAGE, THEN MURDERED HIM WHEN THE CONCLAVE TURNED AGAINST HIM.
THIS IS WHY WE'RE AT WAR.
BUT NOBODY KNOWS THE DETAILS, WHAT REALLY HAPPENED.
LET ME RETRACE HIS STEPS, TELL THE STORY OF HIS FINAL DAYS. THIS TICKS ALL THE BOXES, SUA!
IT DOES.
BUT THAT TRAIL HAS BEEN COLD A LONG TIME. WHERE DO YOU INTEND TO START?
I'VE MADE SOME ARRANGEMENTS.

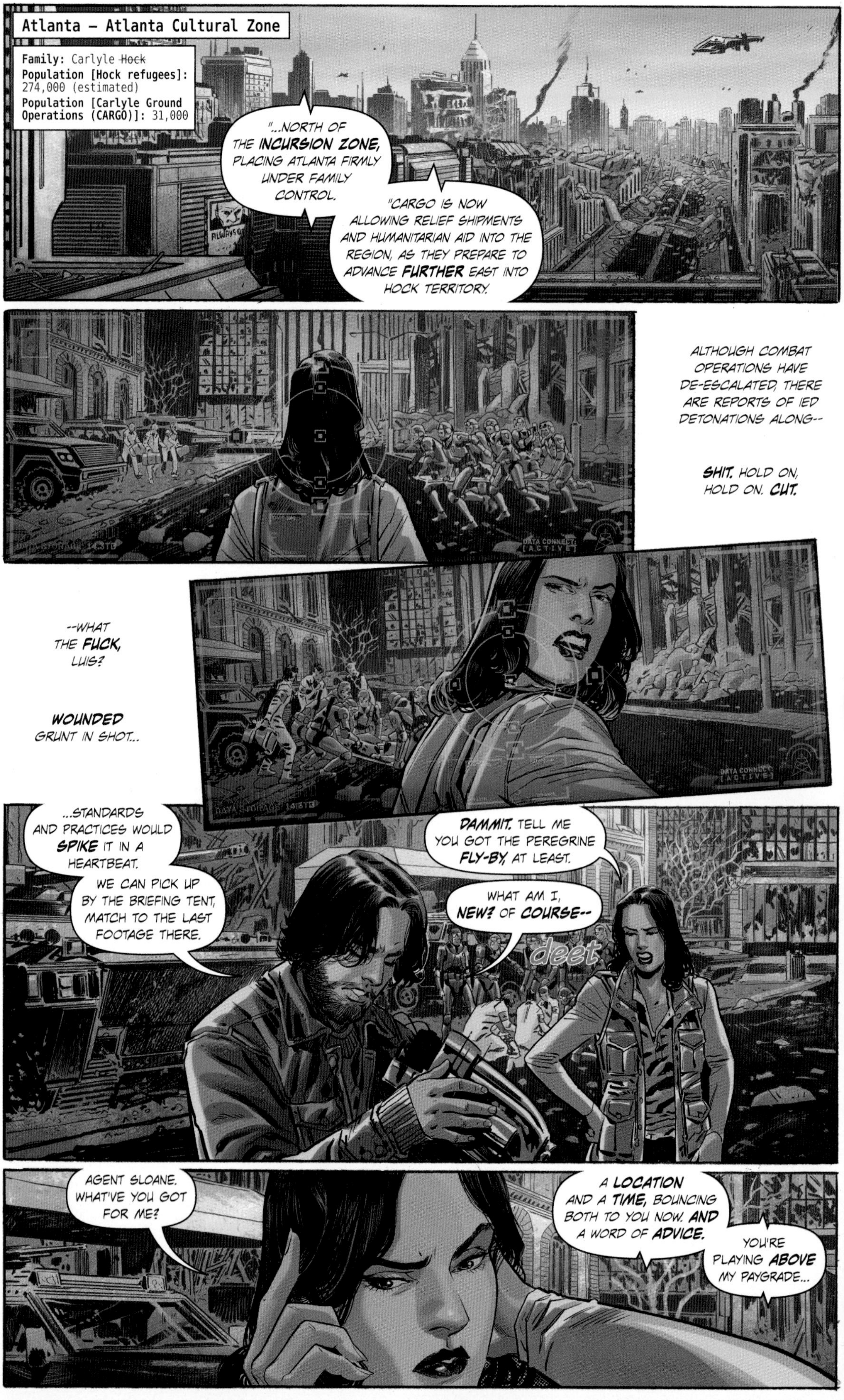
Atlanta – Atlanta Cultural Zone
Family: Carlyle ~~Hock~~
Population [Hock refugees]: 274,000 (estimated)
Population [Carlyle Ground Operations (CARGO)]: 31,000
"...NORTH OF THE INCURSION ZONE, PLACING ATLANTA FIRMLY UNDER FAMILY CONTROL.
"CARGO IS NOW ALLOWING RELIEF SHIPMENTS AND HUMANITARIAN AID INTO THE REGION, AS THEY PREPARE TO ADVANCE FURTHER EAST INTO HOCK TERRITORY.
ALTHOUGH COMBAT OPERATIONS HAVE DE-ESCALATED, THERE ARE REPORTS OF IED DETONATIONS ALONG--
SHIT. HOLD ON, HOLD ON. CUT.
DATA STORAGE: 14.3TB
DATA CONNECT: [ACTIVE]
--WHAT THE FUCK, LUIS?
WOUNDED GRUNT IN SHOT...
...STANDARDS AND PRACTICES WOULD SPIKE IT IN A HEARTBEAT.
WE CAN PICK UP BY THE BRIEFING TENT, MATCH TO THE LAST FOOTAGE THERE.
DAMMIT. TELL ME YOU GOT THE PEREGRINE FLY-BY, AT LEAST.
WHAT AM I, NEW? OF COURSE--
deet
AGENT SLOANE. WHAT'VE YOU GOT FOR ME?
A LOCATION AND A TIME, BOUNCING BOTH TO YOU NOW. AND A WORD OF ADVICE.
YOU'RE PLAYING ABOVE MY PAYGRADE...

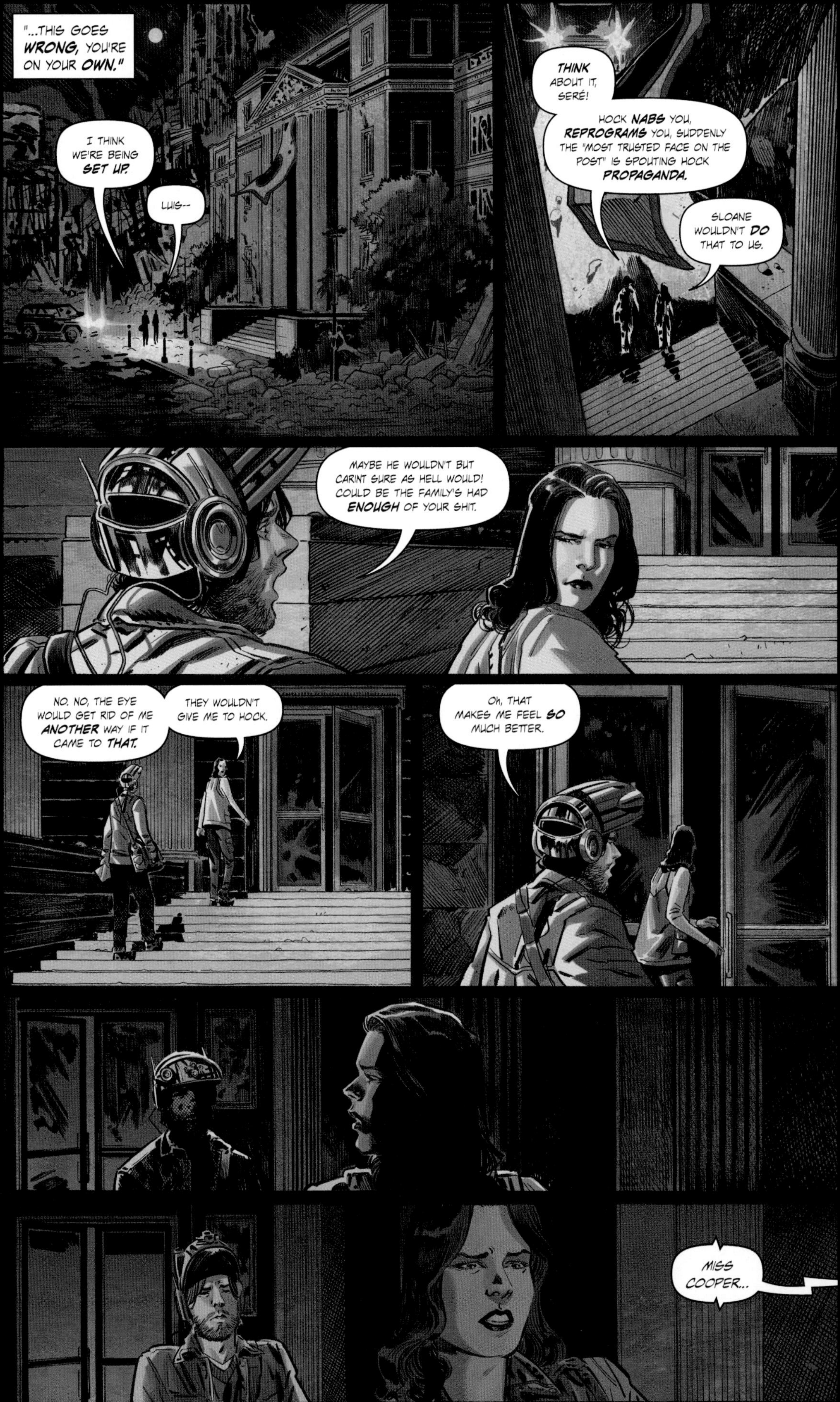
"...THIS GOES WRONG, YOU'RE ON YOUR OWN."
I THINK WE'RE BEING SET UP.
LUIS--
THINK ABOUT IT, SERÉ!
HOCK NABS YOU, REPROGRAMS YOU, SUDDENLY THE "MOST TRUSTED FACE ON THE POST" IS SPOUTING HOCK PROPAGANDA.
SLOANE WOULDN'T DO THAT TO US.
MAYBE HE WOULDN'T BUT CARINT SURE AS HELL WOULD! COULD BE THE FAMILY'S HAD ENOUGH OF YOUR SHIT.
NO. NO, THE EYE WOULD GET RID OF ME ANOTHER WAY IF IT CAME TO THAT.
THEY WOULDN'T GIVE ME TO HOCK.
Oh, THAT MAKES ME FEEL SO MUCH BETTER.
MISS COOPER...

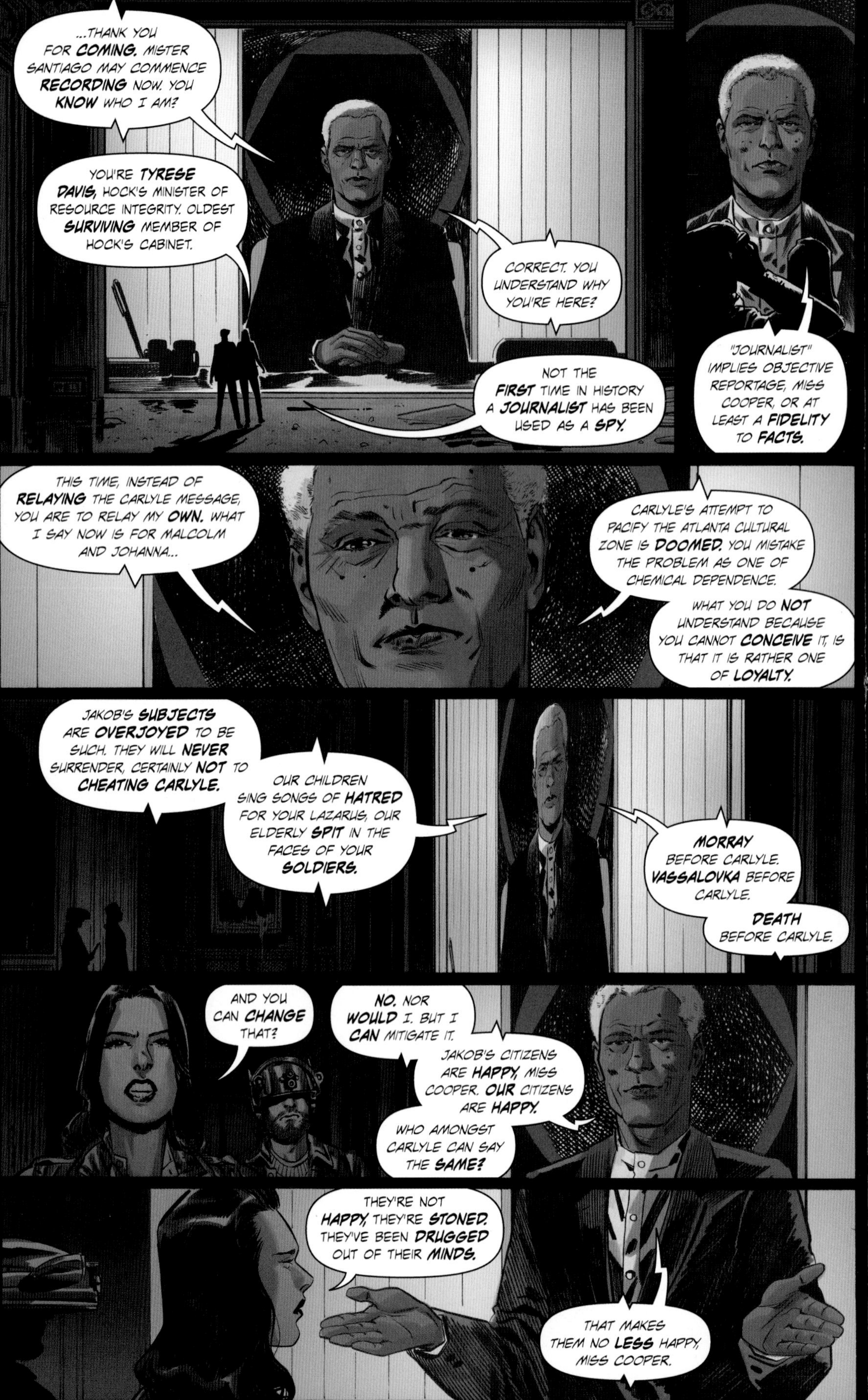
...THANK YOU FOR COMING. MISTER SANTIAGO MAY COMMENCE RECORDING NOW. YOU KNOW WHO I AM?
YOU'RE TYRESE DAVIS, HOCK'S MINISTER OF RESOURCE INTEGRITY. OLDEST SURVIVING MEMBER OF HOCK'S CABINET.
CORRECT. YOU UNDERSTAND WHY YOU'RE HERE?
NOT THE FIRST TIME IN HISTORY A JOURNALIST HAS BEEN USED AS A SPY.
"JOURNALIST" IMPLIES OBJECTIVE REPORTAGE, MISS COOPER, OR AT LEAST A FIDELITY TO FACTS.
THIS TIME, INSTEAD OF RELAYING THE CARLYLE MESSAGE, YOU ARE TO RELAY MY OWN. WHAT I SAY NOW IS FOR MALCOLM AND JOHANNA...
CARLYLE'S ATTEMPT TO PACIFY THE ATLANTA CULTURAL ZONE IS DOOMED. YOU MISTAKE THE PROBLEM AS ONE OF CHEMICAL DEPENDENCE.
WHAT YOU DO NOT UNDERSTAND BECAUSE YOU CANNOT CONCEIVE IT, IS THAT IT IS RATHER ONE OF LOYALTY.
JAKOB'S SUBJECTS ARE OVERJOYED TO BE SUCH. THEY WILL NEVER SURRENDER, CERTAINLY NOT TO CHEATING CARLYLE.
OUR CHILDREN SING SONGS OF HATRED FOR YOUR LAZARUS, OUR ELDERLY SPIT IN THE FACES OF YOUR SOLDIERS.
MORRAY BEFORE CARLYLE. VASSALOVKA BEFORE CARLYLE.
DEATH BEFORE CARLYLE.
AND YOU CAN CHANGE THAT?
NO. NOR WOULD I. BUT I CAN MITIGATE IT.
JAKOB'S CITIZENS ARE HAPPY, MISS COOPER. OUR CITIZENS ARE HAPPY.
WHO AMONGST CARLYLE CAN SAY THE SAME?
THEY'RE NOT HAPPY, THEY'RE STONED. THEY'VE BEEN DRUGGED OUT OF THEIR MINDS.
THAT MAKES THEM NO LESS HAPPY, MISS COOPER.

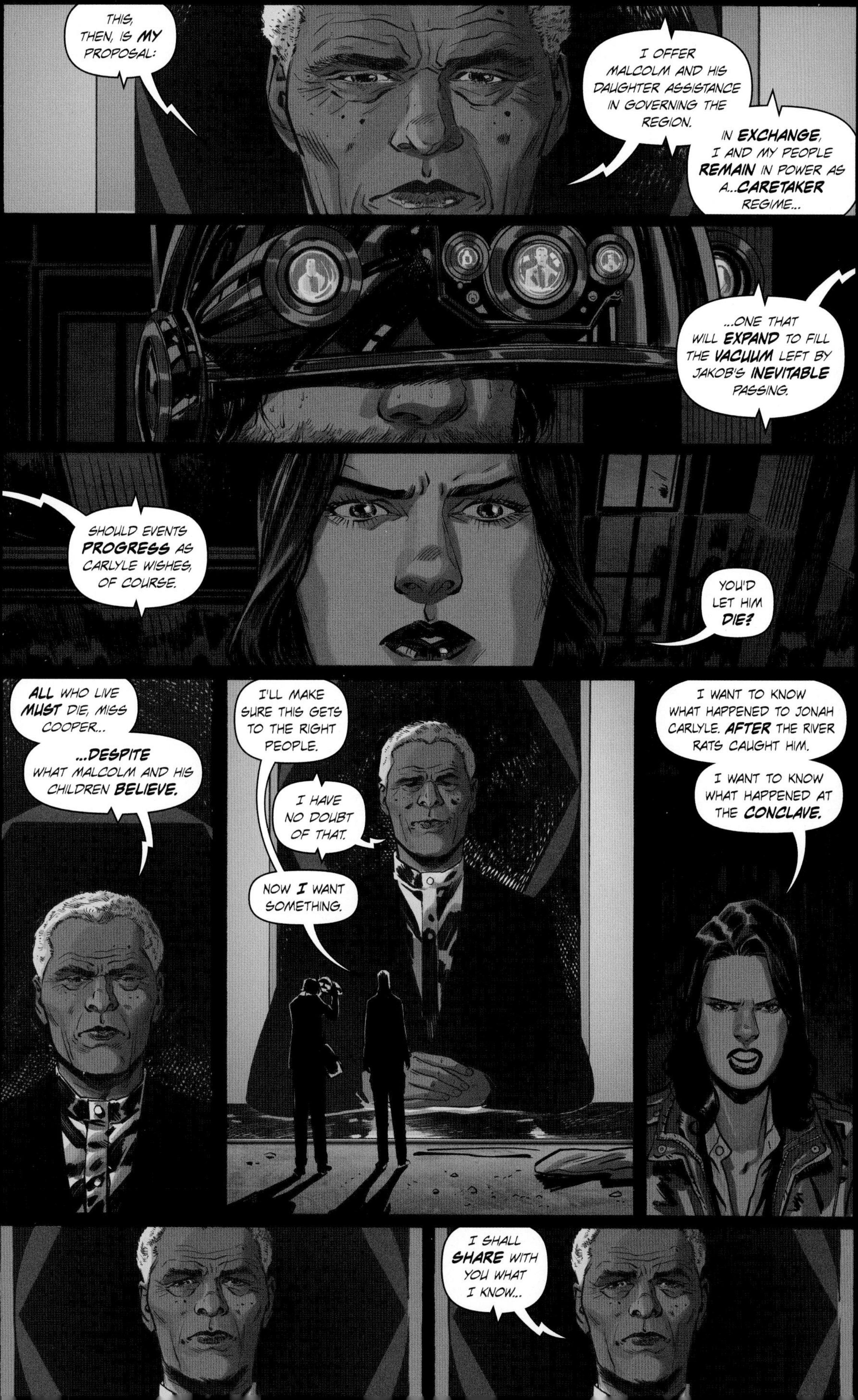
THIS, THEN, IS MY PROPOSAL:
I OFFER MALCOLM AND HIS DAUGHTER ASSISTANCE IN GOVERNING THE REGION.
IN EXCHANGE, I AND MY PEOPLE REMAIN IN POWER AS A...CARETAKER REGIME...
...ONE THAT WILL EXPAND TO FILL THE VACUUM LEFT BY JAKOB'S INEVITABLE PASSING.
SHOULD EVENTS PROGRESS AS CARLYLE WISHES, OF COURSE.
YOU'D LET HIM DIE?
ALL WHO LIVE MUST DIE, MISS COOPER...
...DESPITE WHAT MALCOLM AND HIS CHILDREN BELIEVE.
I'LL MAKE SURE THIS GETS TO THE RIGHT PEOPLE.
I HAVE NO DOUBT OF THAT.
NOW I WANT SOMETHING.
I WANT TO KNOW WHAT HAPPENED TO JONAH CARLYLE. AFTER THE RIVER RATS CAUGHT HIM.
I WANT TO KNOW WHAT HAPPENED AT THE CONCLAVE.
I SHALL SHARE WITH YOU WHAT I KNOW...

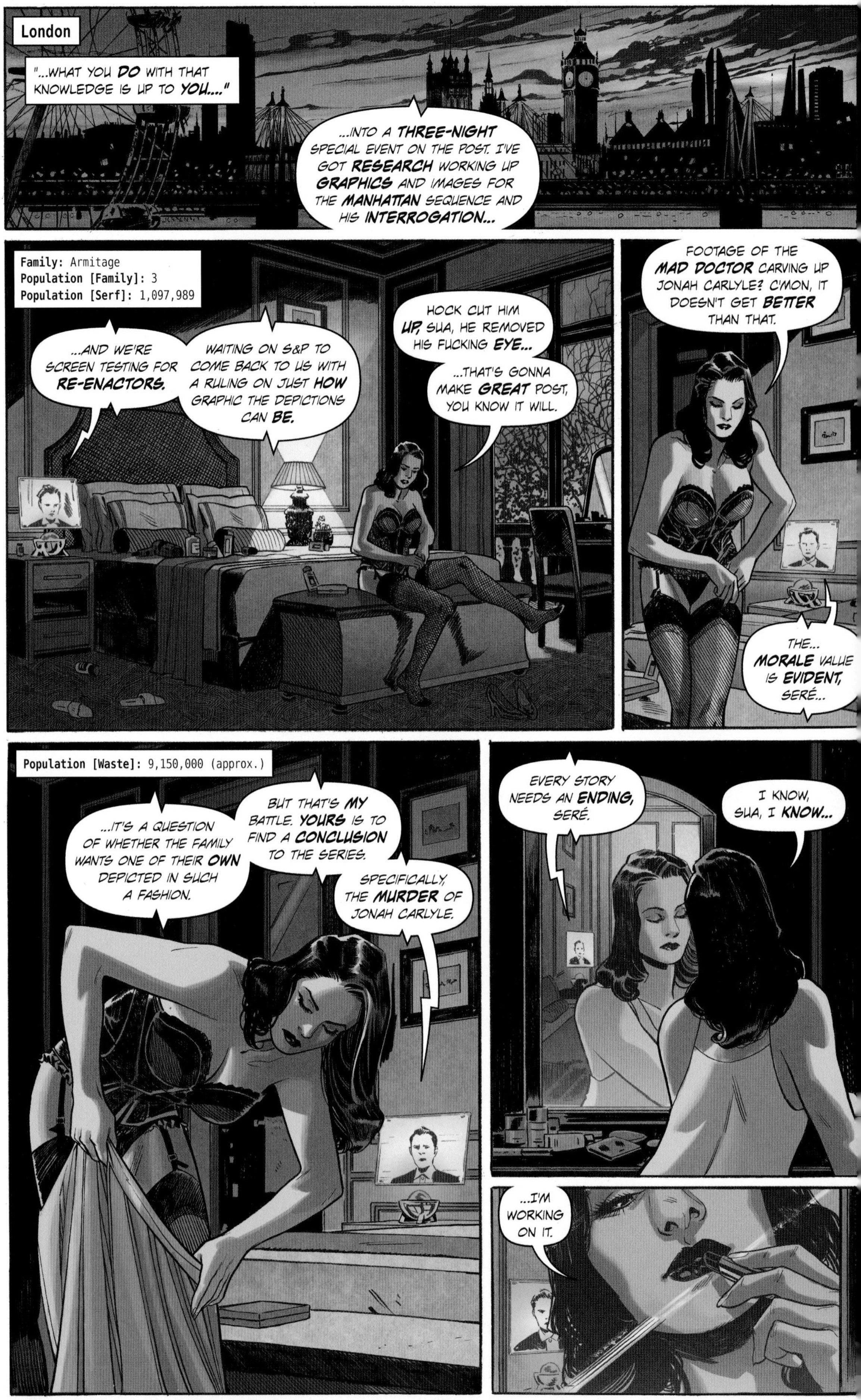
London
"...WHAT YOU DO WITH THAT KNOWLEDGE IS UP TO YOU..."
...INTO A THREE-NIGHT SPECIAL EVENT ON THE POST. I'VE GOT RESEARCH WORKING UP GRAPHICS AND IMAGES FOR THE MANHATTAN SEQUENCE AND HIS INTERROGATION...
Family: Armitage
Population [Family]: 3
Population [Serf]: 1,097,989
...AND WE'RE SCREEN TESTING FOR RE-ENACTORS.
WAITING ON S&P TO COME BACK TO US WITH A RULING ON JUST HOW GRAPHIC THE DEPICTIONS CAN BE.
HOCK CUT HIM UP, SUA, HE REMOVED HIS FUCKING EYE...
...THAT'S GONNA MAKE GREAT POST, YOU KNOW IT WILL.
FOOTAGE OF THE MAD DOCTOR CARVING UP JONAH CARLYLE? C'MON, IT DOESN'T GET BETTER THAN THAT.
THE... MORALE VALUE IS EVIDENT, SERÉ...
Population [Waste]: 9,150,000 (approx.)
...IT'S A QUESTION OF WHETHER THE FAMILY WANTS ONE OF THEIR OWN DEPICTED IN SUCH A FASHION.
BUT THAT'S MY BATTLE. YOURS IS TO FIND A CONCLUSION TO THE SERIES.
SPECIFICALLY, THE MURDER OF JONAH CARLYLE.
EVERY STORY NEEDS AN ENDING, SERÉ.
I KNOW, SUA, I KNOW...
...I'M WORKING ON IT.

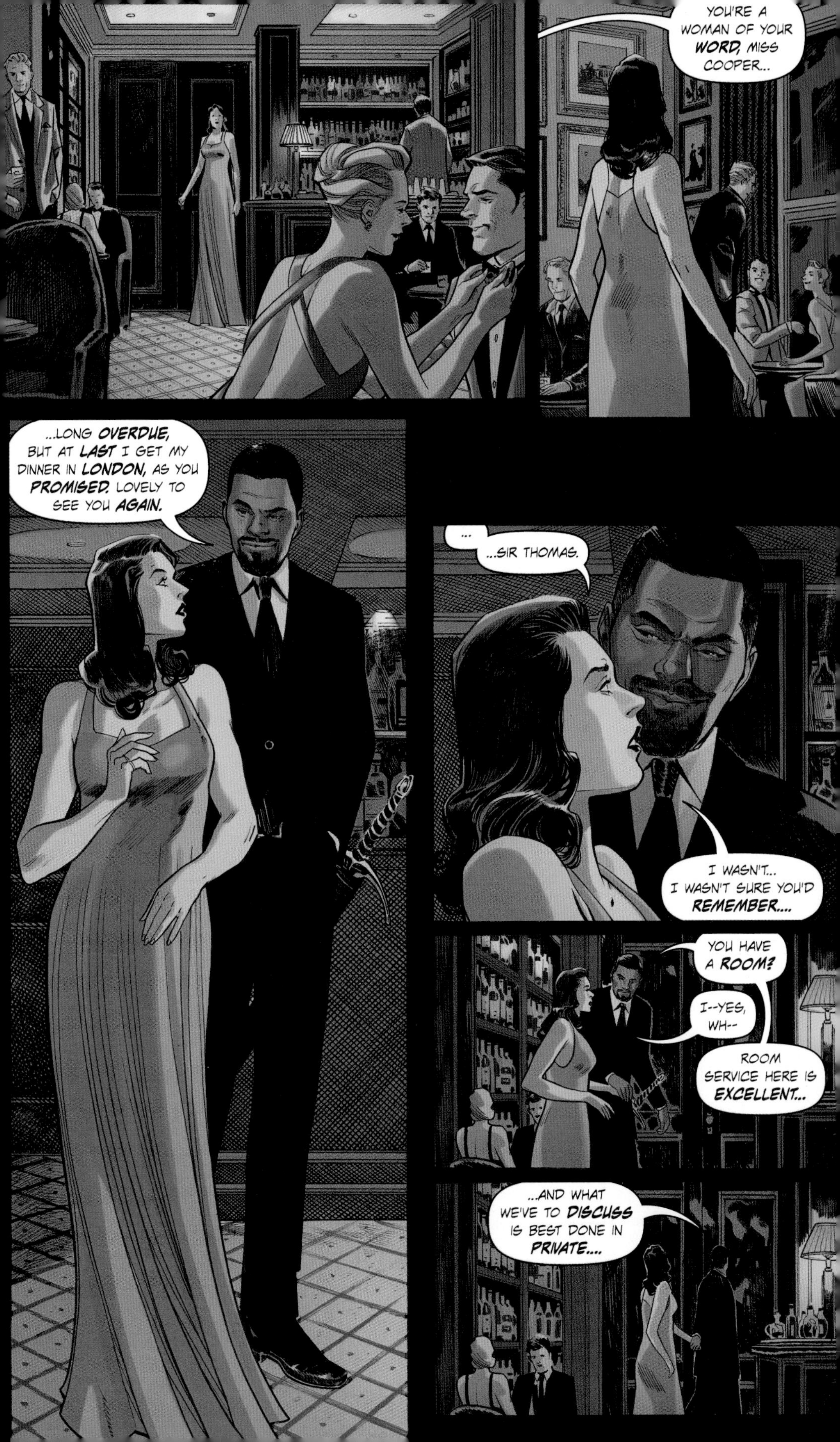
YOU'RE A WOMAN OF YOUR WORD, MISS COOPER...
...LONG OVERDUE, BUT AT LAST I GET MY DINNER IN LONDON, AS YOU PROMISED. LOVELY TO SEE YOU AGAIN.
...
...SIR THOMAS.
I WASN'T... I WASN'T SURE YOU'D REMEMBER....
YOU HAVE A ROOM?
I--YES, WH--
ROOM SERVICE HERE IS EXCELLENT...
...AND WHAT WE'VE TO DISCUSS IS BEST DONE IN PRIVATE....

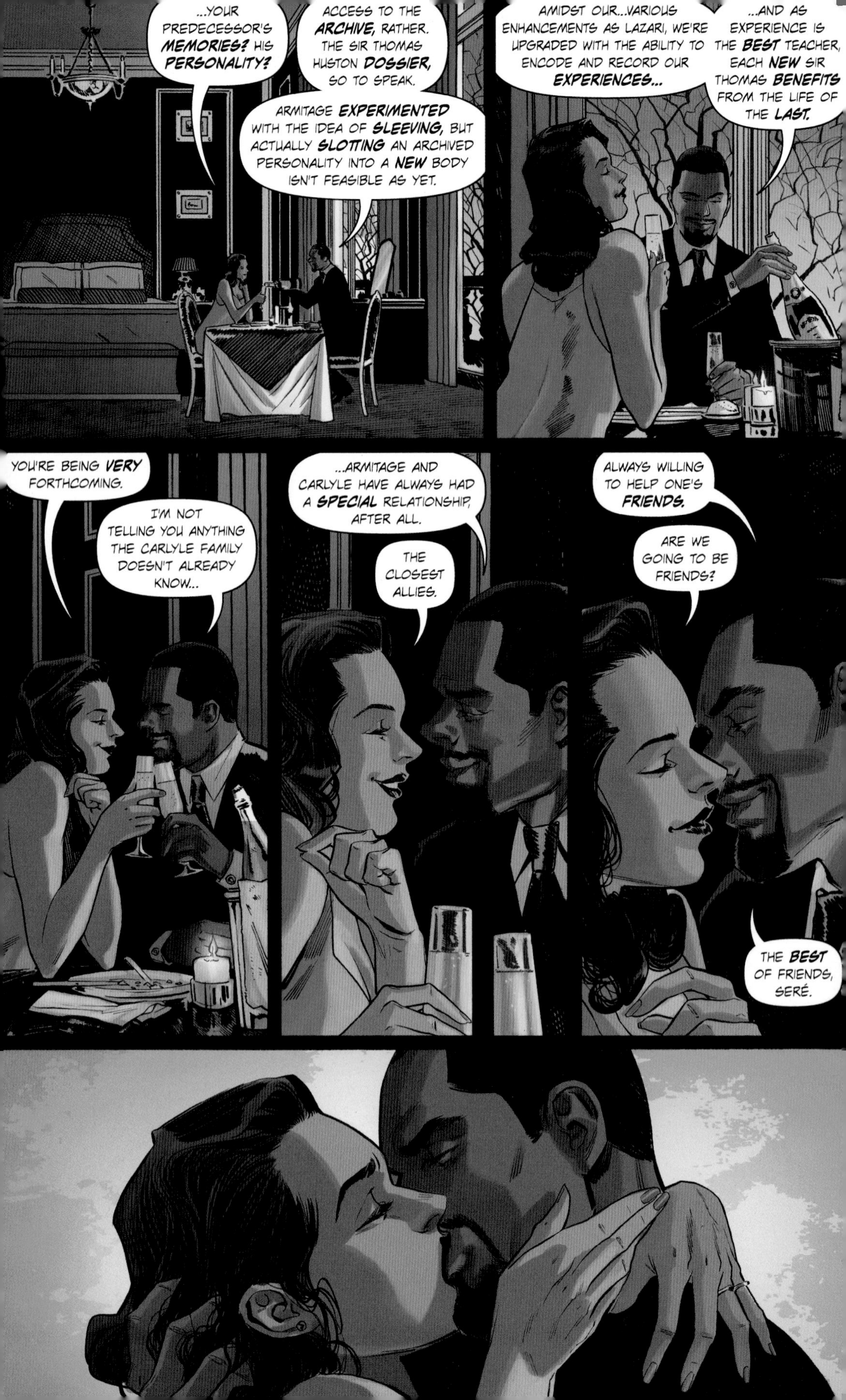

...YOUR PREDECESSOR'S MEMORIES? HIS PERSONALITY?
ACCESS TO THE ARCHIVE, RATHER. THE SIR THOMAS HUSTON DOSSIER, SO TO SPEAK.
ARMITAGE EXPERIMENTED WITH THE IDEA OF SLEEVING, BUT ACTUALLY SLOTTING AN ARCHIVED PERSONALITY INTO A NEW BODY ISN'T FEASIBLE AS YET.
AMIDST OUR...VARIOUS ENHANCEMENTS AS LAZARI, WE'RE UPGRADED WITH THE ABILITY TO ENCODE AND RECORD OUR EXPERIENCES...
...AND AS EXPERIENCE IS THE BEST TEACHER, EACH NEW SIR THOMAS BENEFITS FROM THE LIFE OF THE LAST.
YOU'RE BEING VERY FORTHCOMING.
I'M NOT TELLING YOU ANYTHING THE CARLYLE FAMILY DOESN'T ALREADY KNOW...
...ARMITAGE AND CARLYLE HAVE ALWAYS HAD A SPECIAL RELATIONSHIP, AFTER ALL.
THE CLOSEST ALLIES.
ALWAYS WILLING TO HELP ONE'S FRIENDS.
ARE WE GOING TO BE FRIENDS?
THE BEST OF FRIENDS, SERÉ.

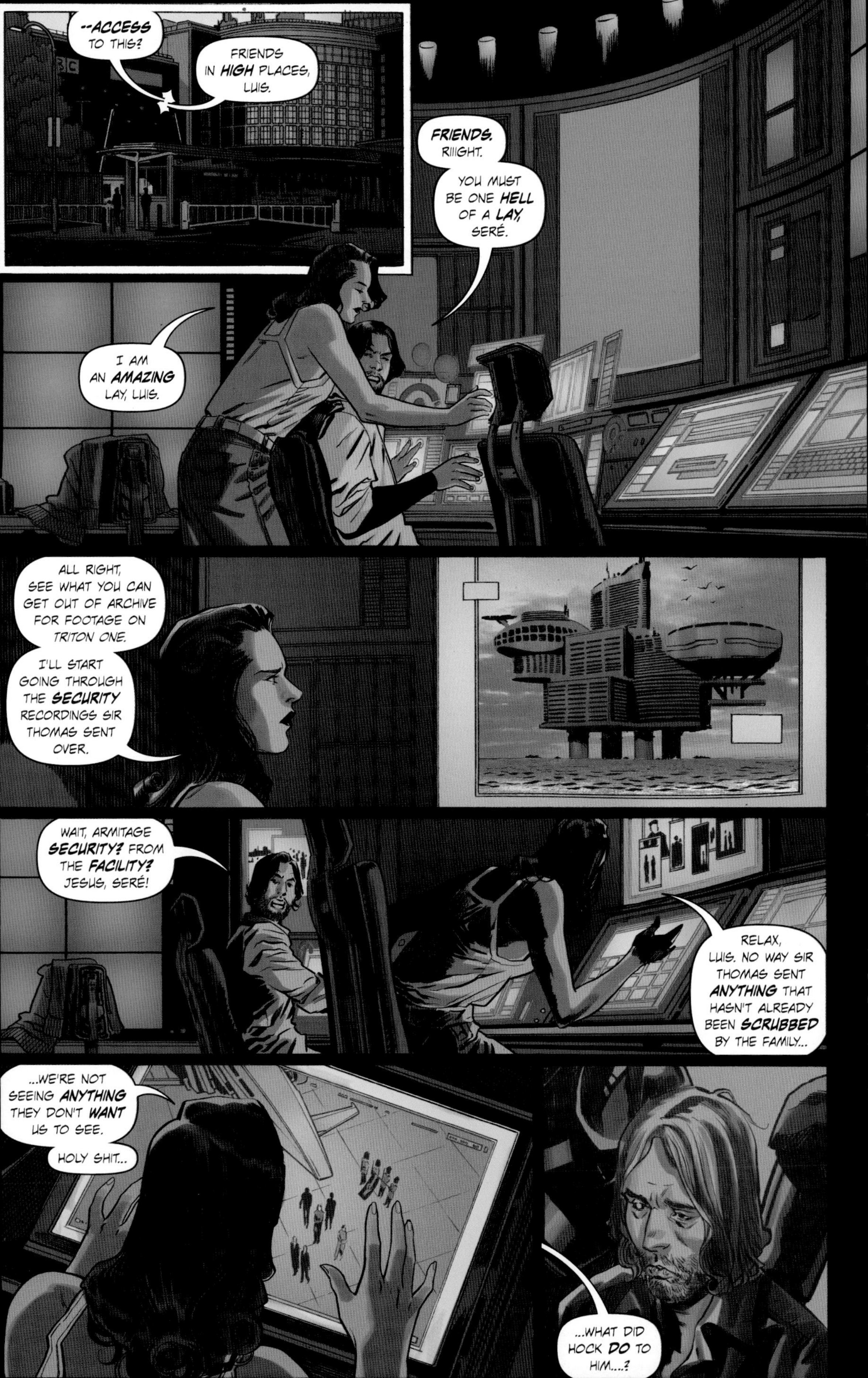
--ACCESS TO THIS?
FRIENDS IN HIGH PLACES, LUIS.
FRIENDS. RIIIGHT.
YOU MUST BE ONE HELL OF A LAY, SERÉ.
I AM AN AMAZING LAY, LUIS.
ALL RIGHT, SEE WHAT YOU CAN GET OUT OF ARCHIVE FOR FOOTAGE ON TRITON ONE.
I'LL START GOING THROUGH THE SECURITY RECORDINGS SIR THOMAS SENT OVER.
WAIT, ARMITAGE SECURITY? FROM THE FACILITY? JESUS, SERÉ!
RELAX, LUIS. NO WAY SIR THOMAS SENT ANYTHING THAT HASN'T ALREADY BEEN SCRUBBED BY THE FAMILY...
...WE'RE NOT SEEING ANYTHING THEY DON'T WANT US TO SEE.
HOLY SHIT...
...WHAT DID HOCK DO TO HIM...?

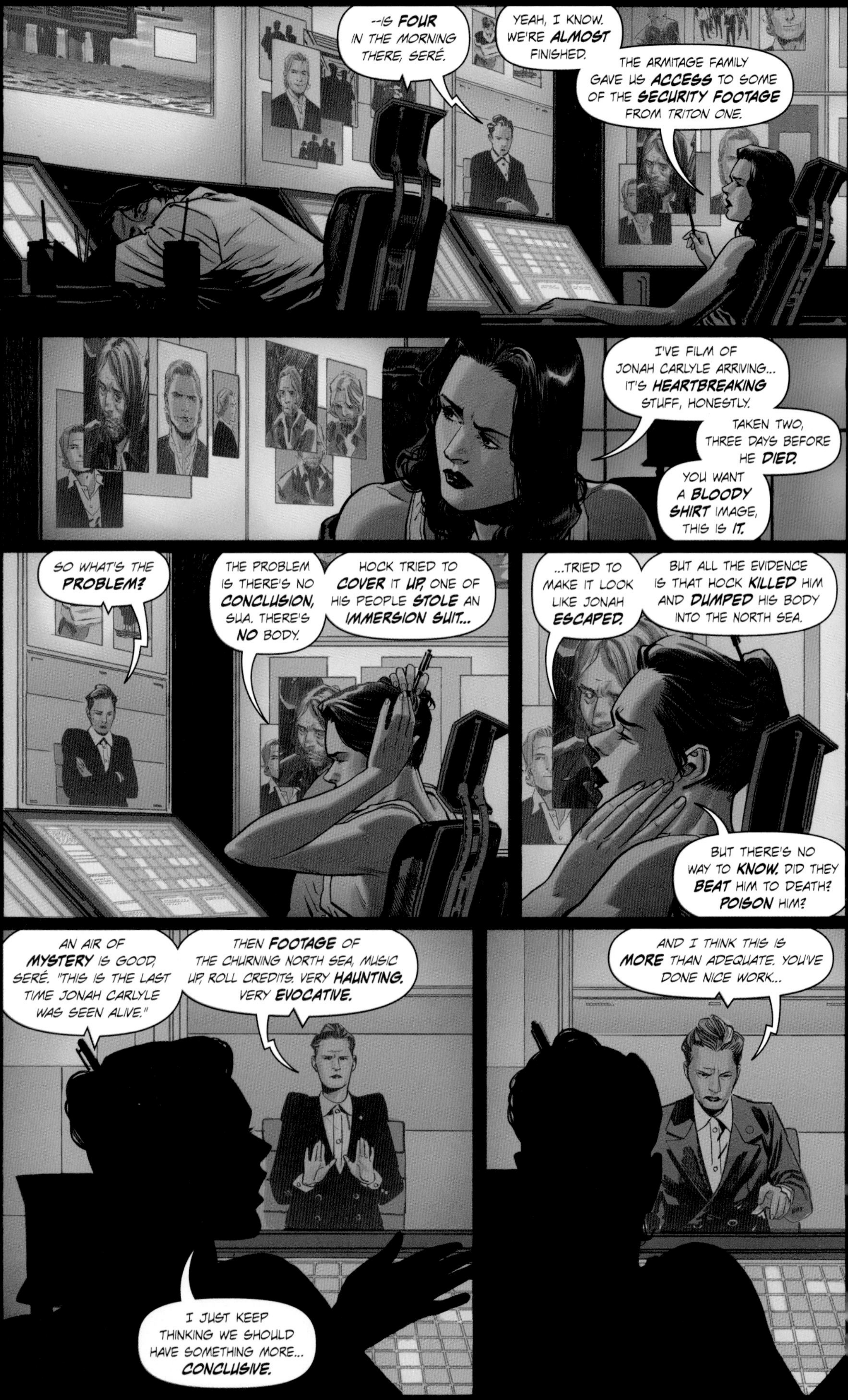
--IS FOUR IN THE MORNING THERE, SERÉ.
YEAH, I KNOW. WE'RE ALMOST FINISHED.
THE ARMITAGE FAMILY GAVE US ACCESS TO SOME OF THE SECURITY FOOTAGE FROM TRITON ONE.
I'VE FILM OF JONAH CARLYLE ARRIVING... IT'S HEARTBREAKING STUFF, HONESTLY.
TAKEN TWO, THREE DAYS BEFORE HE DIED.
YOU WANT A BLOODY SHIRT IMAGE, THIS IS IT.
SO WHAT'S THE PROBLEM?
THE PROBLEM IS THERE'S NO CONCLUSION, SUA. THERE'S NO BODY.
HOCK TRIED TO COVER IT UP, ONE OF HIS PEOPLE STOLE AN IMMERSION SUIT...
...TRIED TO MAKE IT LOOK LIKE JONAH ESCAPED.
BUT ALL THE EVIDENCE IS THAT HOCK KILLED HIM AND DUMPED HIS BODY INTO THE NORTH SEA.
BUT THERE'S NO WAY TO KNOW. DID THEY BEAT HIM TO DEATH? POISON HIM?
AN AIR OF MYSTERY IS GOOD, SERÉ. "THIS IS THE LAST TIME JONAH CARLYLE WAS SEEN ALIVE."
THEN FOOTAGE OF THE CHURNING NORTH SEA, MUSIC UP, ROLL CREDITS. VERY HAUNTING. VERY EVOCATIVE.
I JUST KEEP THINKING WE SHOULD HAVE SOMETHING MORE... CONCLUSIVE.
AND I THINK THIS IS MORE THAN ADEQUATE. YOU'VE DONE NICE WORK...

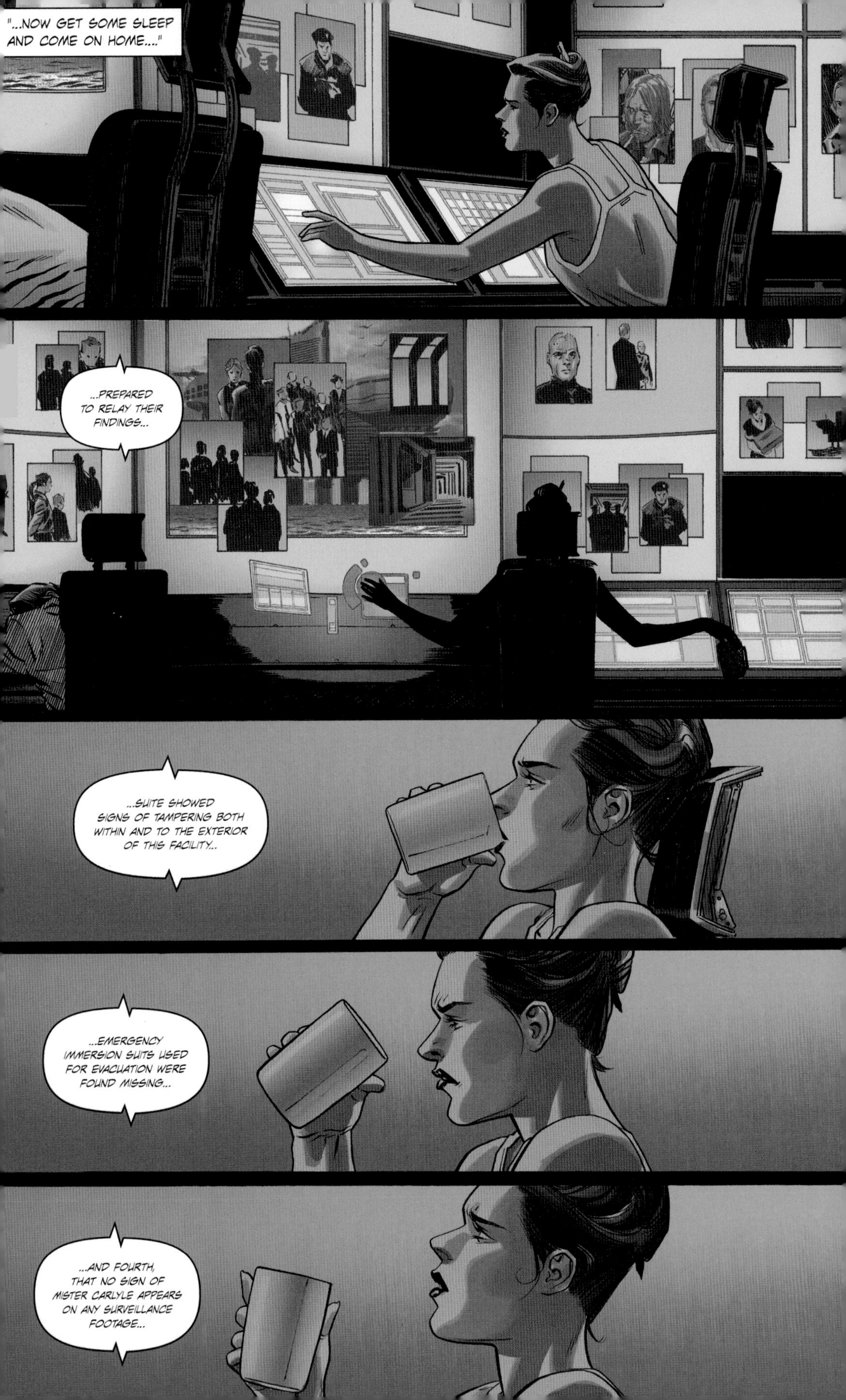
"...NOW GET SOME SLEEP AND COME ON HOME..."
...PREPARED TO RELAY THEIR FINDINGS...
...SUITE SHOWED SIGNS OF TAMPERING BOTH WITHIN AND TO THE EXTERIOR OF THIS FACILITY...
...EMERGENCY IMMERSION SUITS USED FOR EVACUATION WERE FOUND MISSING...
...AND FOURTH, THAT NO SIGN OF MISTER CARLYLE APPEARS ON ANY SURVEILLANCE FOOTAGE...

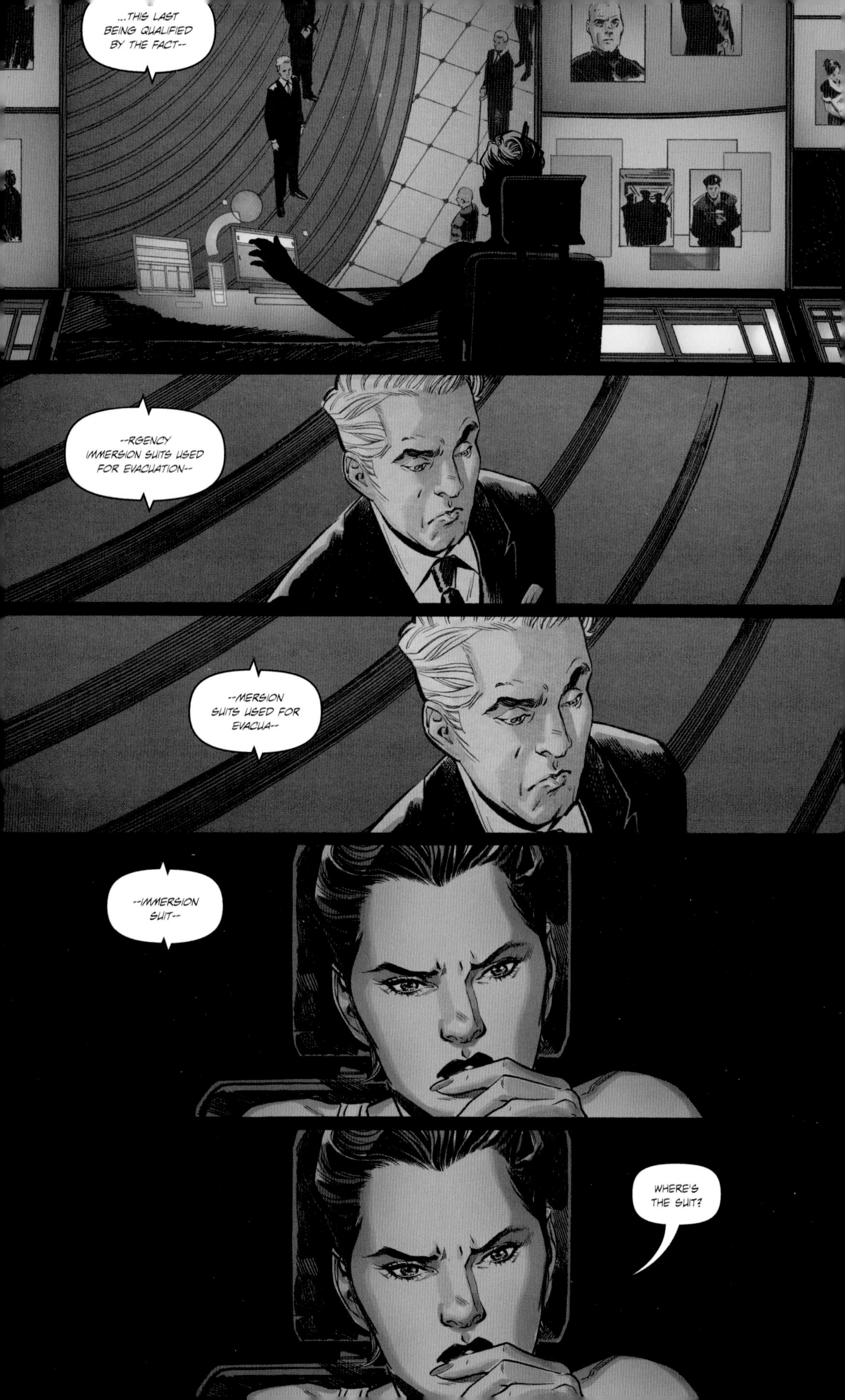
...THIS LAST BEING QUALIFIED BY THE FACT--
--RGENCY IMMERSION SUITS USED FOR EVACUATION--
--MERSION SUITS USED FOR EVACUA--
--IMMERSION SUIT--
WHERE'S THE SUIT?

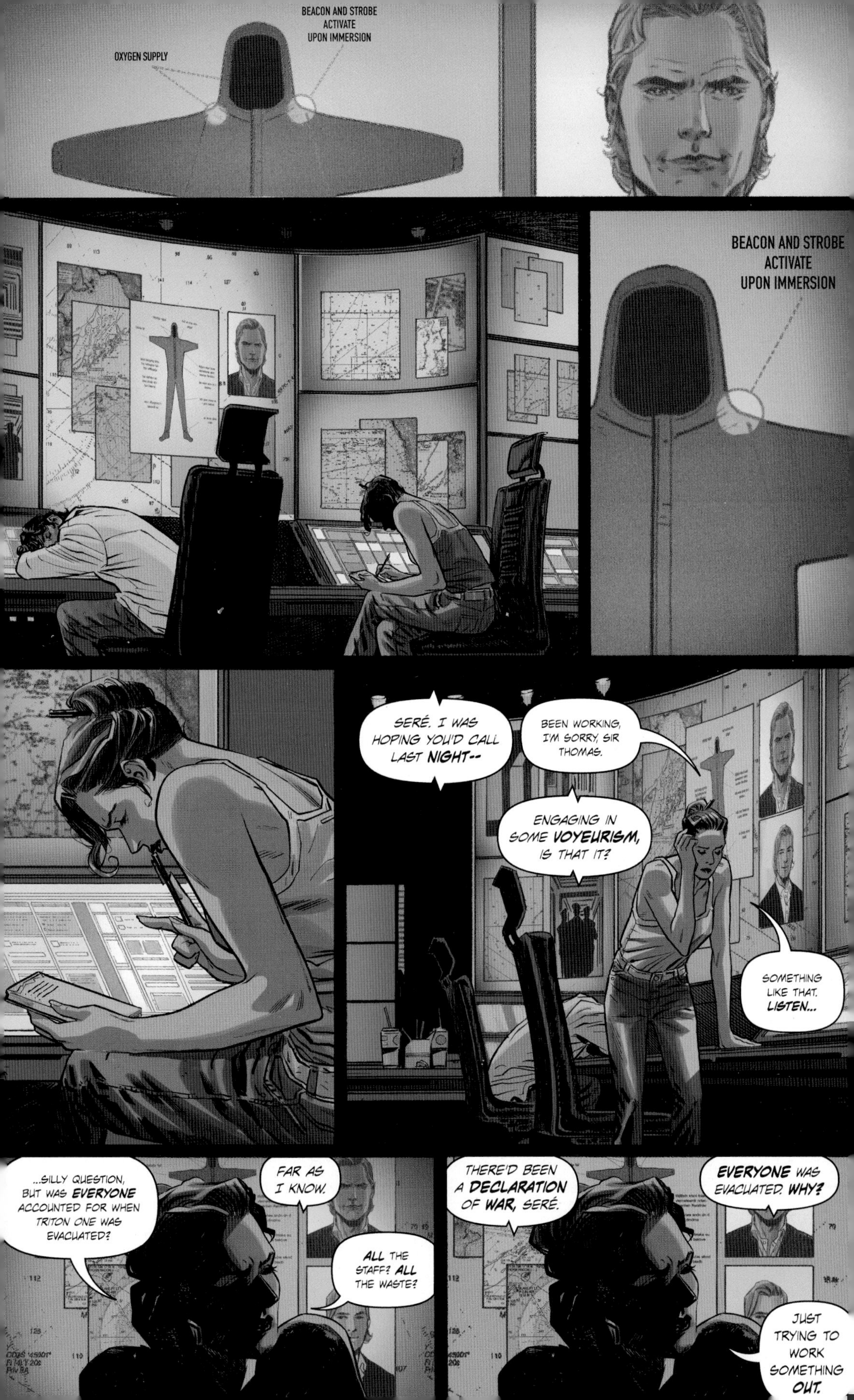
BEACON AND STROBE ACTIVATE UPON IMMERSION
OXYGEN SUPPLY
BEACON AND STROBE ACTIVATE UPON IMMERSION
SERÉ. I WAS HOPING YOU'D CALL LAST NIGHT--
BEEN WORKING, I'M SORRY, SIR THOMAS.
ENGAGING IN SOME VOYEURISM, IS THAT IT?
SOMETHING LIKE THAT. LISTEN...
...SILLY QUESTION, BUT WAS EVERYONE ACCOUNTED FOR WHEN TRITON ONE WAS EVACUATED?
FAR AS I KNOW.
ALL THE STAFF? ALL THE WASTE?
THERE'D BEEN A DECLARATION OF WAR, SERÉ.
EVERYONE WAS EVACUATED. WHY?
JUST TRYING TO WORK SOMETHING OUT.

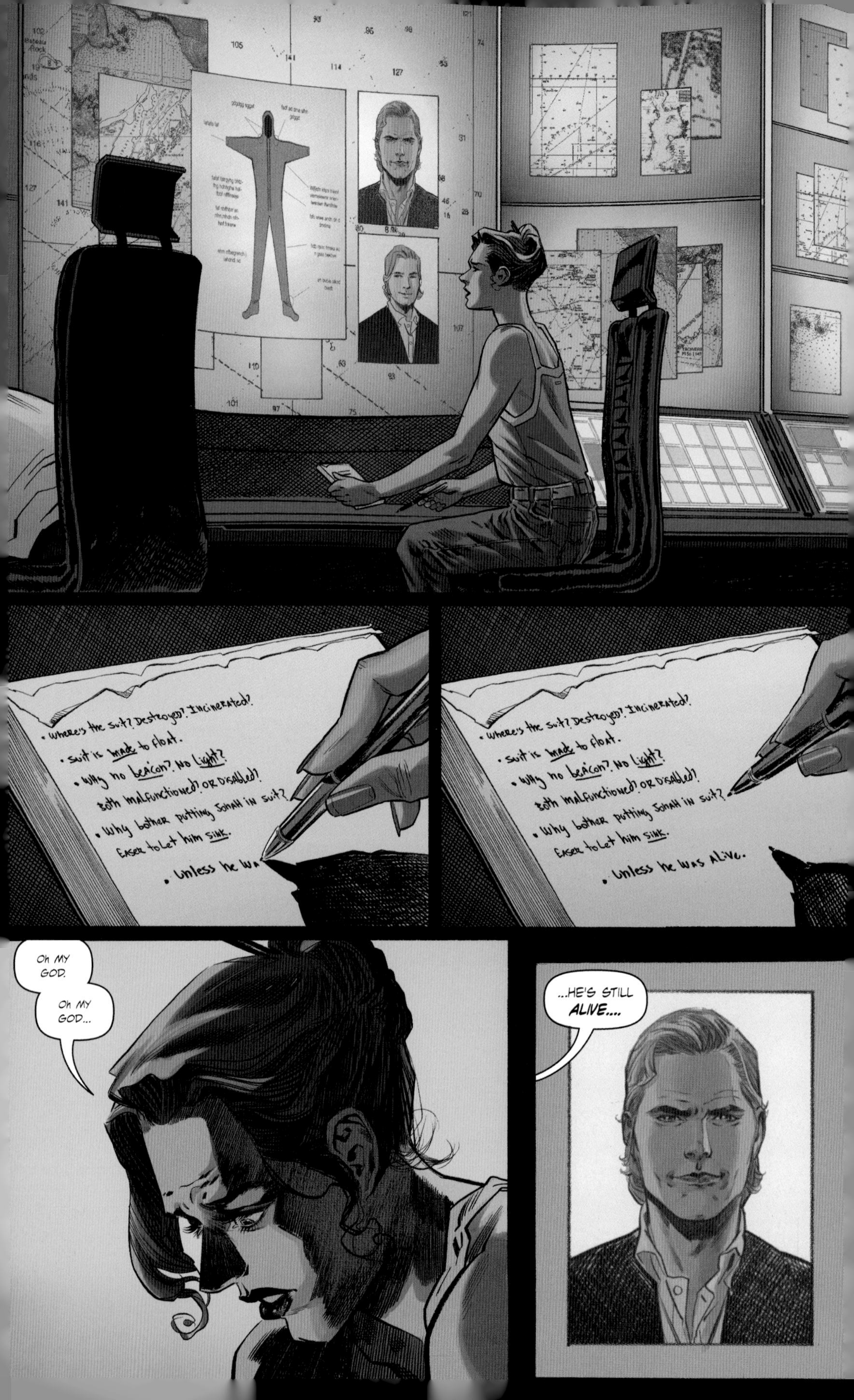

• Where's the suit? Destroyed? Incinerated?
• Suit is made to float.
• Why no beacon? No light?
Both malfunctioned? Or disabled?
• Why bother putting Jonah in suit?
Easier to let him sink.
• Unless he wa
• Where's the suit? Destroyed? Incinerated?
• Suit is made to float.
• Why no beacon? No light?
Both malfunctioned? Or disabled?
• Why bother putting Jonah in suit?
Easier to let him sink.
• Unless he was alive.
Oh my God.
Oh my God...
...He's still alive....

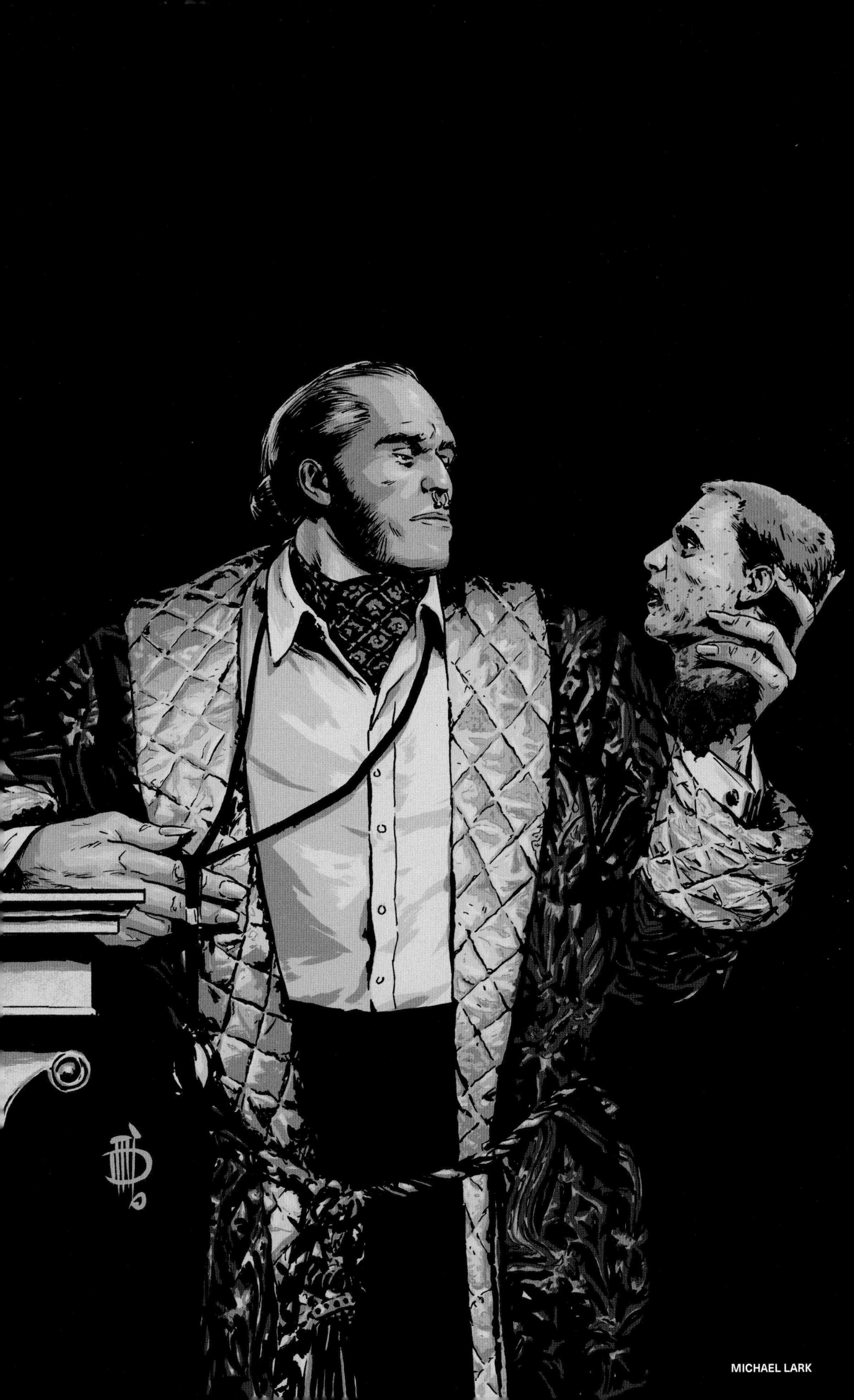

MICHAEL LARK

To each Family, their **LAZARUS** means different things.

To many, he or she is a symbol of
their **power**, an emblem of their mastery of **technology**.

To others, their Lazarus embodies the **strength** of their rule,
their **determination** to bend the world to their will.

But to every Family, the Lazarus is always one more thing: a **weapon**.

The **VASSALOVKA** Family Lazarus is the most feared of them all.

Met on the field of battle, he is inhuman not simply in size and strength and
speed, but in his savagery and remorseless destruction of all life he encounters.

He is, by design, a walking nightmare.

He is called **THE ZMEY**, also known as **THE DRAGON**.

In the spring of X +65, **Forever Carlyle** led
three other Lazari in an attempt to kill The Zmey.

They failed.

In X +66, the Lazari of **Nkosi** and **Meyers-Qasimi**
engaged in a joint operation to recover details of The Dragon's creation.
Despite the arrival of Vassalovka Special Forces, the data was recovered.

Whether this knowledge will prove
crucial to defeating The Zmey remains to be seen.

The Conclave War continues.

The Lazari fight for their Families.

And in the heart of
Vassalovka Territory, The Zmey sleeps in his lair....

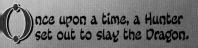

Once upon a time, a Hunter set out to slay the Dragon.

The Dragon was a beast of legend, spoken of in hushed tones (if he was ever spoken of at all) and the beast had cast, for many years, a dread pall across the length and breadth of the Motherland.

The Dragon knew nothing of mercy, it was said. The Dragon knew nothing of pity. The Dragon was beyond human concerns, and drew its only joy from the desecration of flesh, the piteous pleas of its prey, and the extinguishing of life, and with it, all hope.

"No more," the Hunter vowed. "Today, the Dragon dies."

And so the Hunter set off into the wilderness where it was said the Dragon made his home, to slay the beast once and for all.

Sebyan-Kyuyol Exclusion Zone,
Sakha Republic (former)

Family: Vassalovka

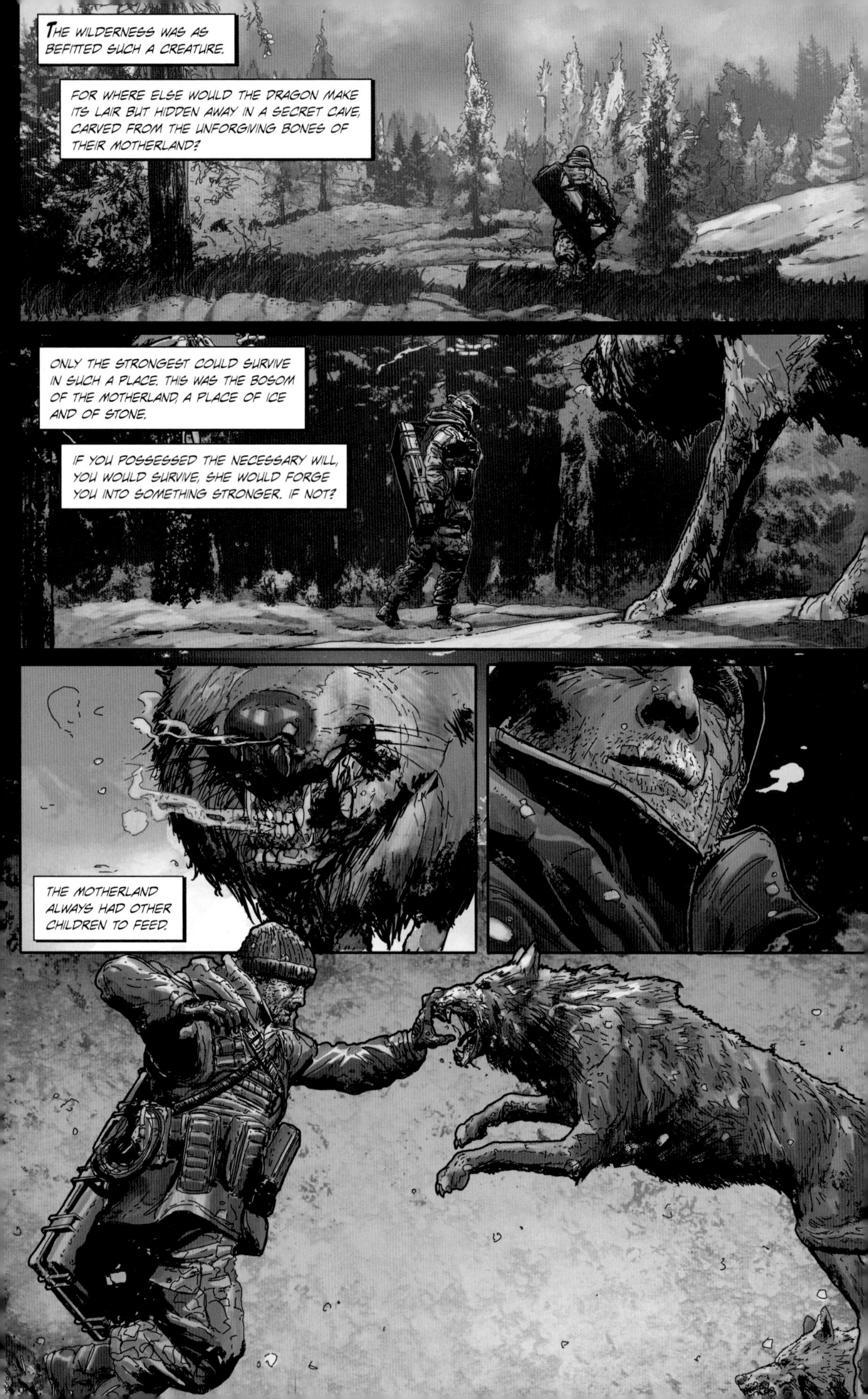
THE WILDERNESS WAS AS BEFITTED SUCH A CREATURE.
FOR WHERE ELSE WOULD THE DRAGON MAKE ITS LAIR BUT HIDDEN AWAY IN A SECRET CAVE, CARVED FROM THE UNFORGIVING BONES OF THEIR MOTHERLAND?
ONLY THE STRONGEST COULD SURVIVE IN SUCH A PLACE. THIS WAS THE BOSOM OF THE MOTHERLAND, A PLACE OF ICE AND OF STONE.
IF YOU POSSESSED THE NECESSARY WILL, YOU WOULD SURVIVE, SHE WOULD FORGE YOU INTO SOMETHING STRONGER. IF NOT?
THE MOTHERLAND ALWAYS HAD OTHER CHILDREN TO FEED.

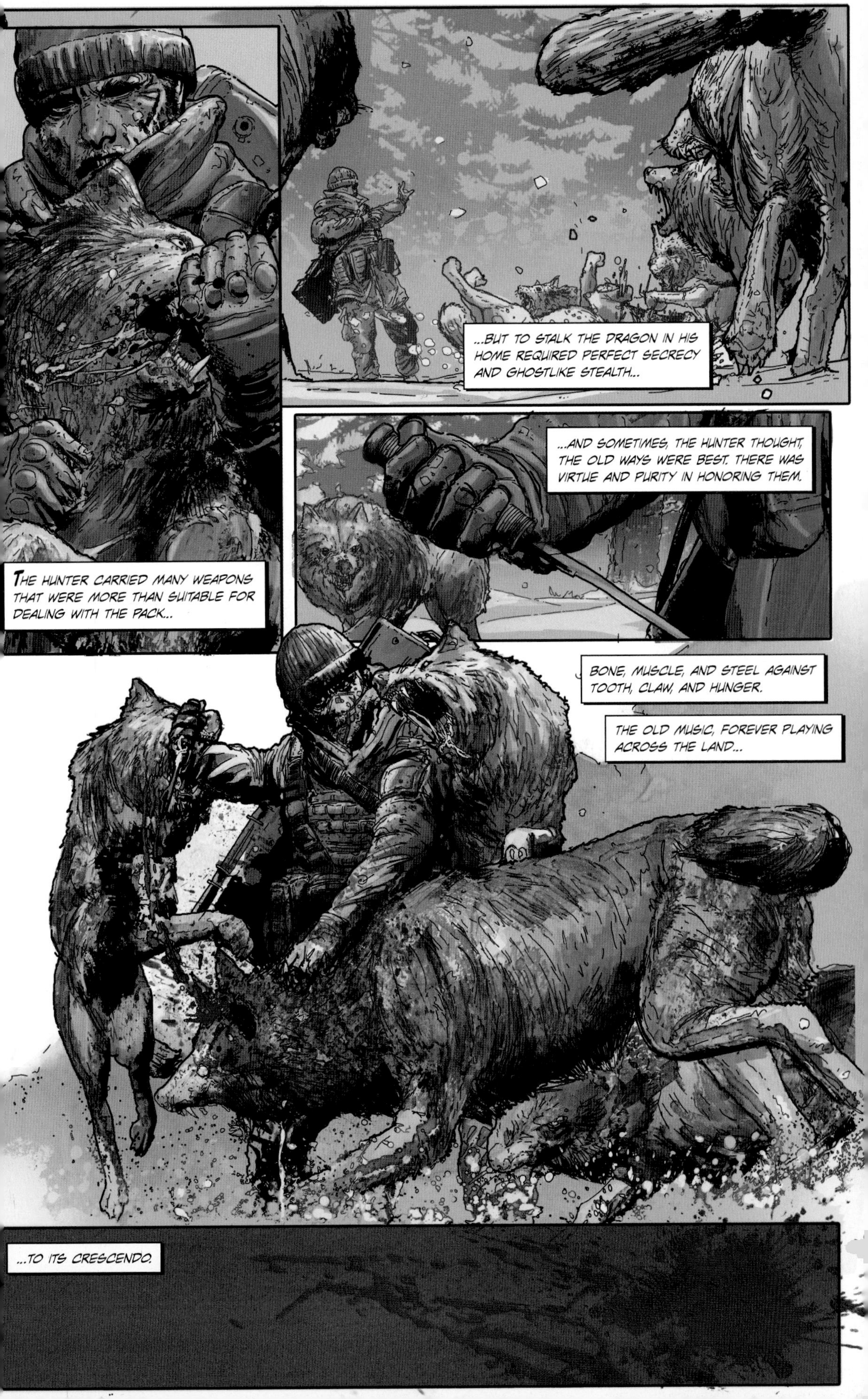
THE HUNTER CARRIED MANY WEAPONS THAT WERE MORE THAN SUITABLE FOR DEALING WITH THE PACK...
...BUT TO STALK THE DRAGON IN HIS HOME REQUIRED PERFECT SECRECY AND GHOSTLIKE STEALTH...
...AND SOMETIMES, THE HUNTER THOUGHT, THE OLD WAYS WERE BEST. THERE WAS VIRTUE AND PURITY IN HONORING THEM.
BONE, MUSCLE, AND STEEL AGAINST TOOTH, CLAW, AND HUNGER.
THE OLD MUSIC, FOREVER PLAYING ACROSS THE LAND...
...TO ITS CRESCENDO.

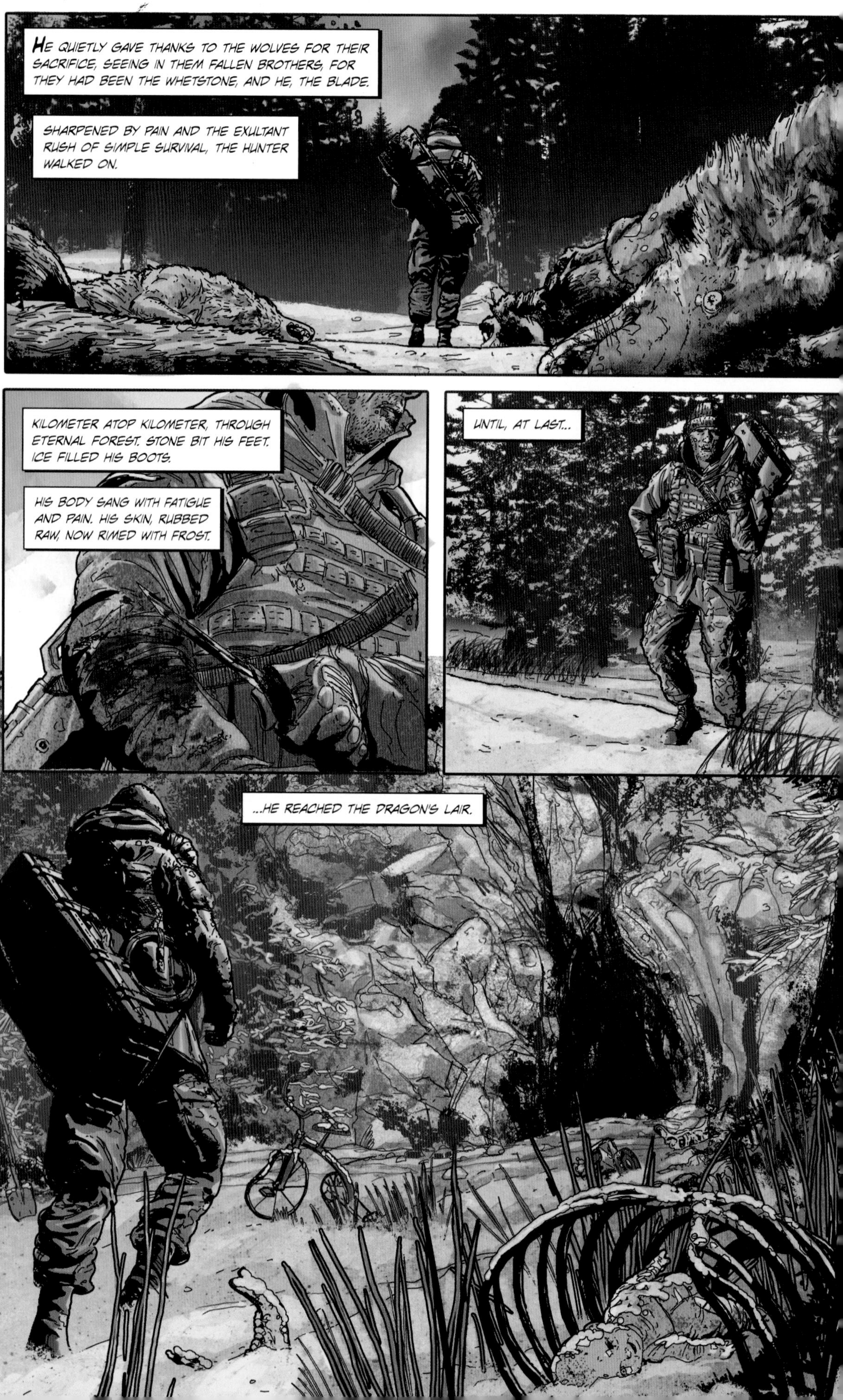
HE QUIETLY GAVE THANKS TO THE WOLVES FOR THEIR SACRIFICE, SEEING IN THEM FALLEN BROTHERS, FOR THEY HAD BEEN THE WHETSTONE, AND HE, THE BLADE.
SHARPENED BY PAIN AND THE EXULTANT RUSH OF SIMPLE SURVIVAL, THE HUNTER WALKED ON.
KILOMETER ATOP KILOMETER, THROUGH ETERNAL FOREST. STONE BIT HIS FEET. ICE FILLED HIS BOOTS.
HIS BODY SANG WITH FATIGUE AND PAIN. HIS SKIN, RUBBED RAW, NOW RIMED WITH FROST.
UNTIL, AT LAST...
...HE REACHED THE DRAGON'S LAIR.

ERE, AT THE MOUTH OF THE DRAGON'S
AVE, THE HUNTER PREPARED THE TOOLS
E WOULD NEED FOR HIS TASK.

IS WAS NO PACK OF WOLVES.
BEARD SUCH A BEAST AS
E DRAGON WITHIN ITS OWN LAIR
ARRIED UNTOLD DANGERS.

O SLAY THE DRAGON--OR INDEED, ANY OF ITS KIND, FOR ITS KIND
AS KNOWN AND FEARED AROUND THE WORLD--A SPECIAL WEAPON
AS NEEDED. A MAGIC WEAPON, FORGED FOR THIS PURPOSE ALONE.

THROUGH STEALTH AND GUILE, THE HUNTER
HAD LAID HANDS UPON SUCH A WEAPON,
THE ONLY ONE KNOWN TO EXIST.

IT HAD NEVER BEEN TESTED IN BATTLE.

THE HUNTER KNEW HE WOULD
HAVE BUT ONE SHOT BEFORE THE
DRAGON WOULD BE UPON HIM.

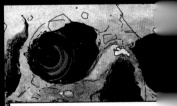

BUT THE HUNTER HELD HOPE, FOR
THE DRAGON HAD NEVER FACED A
WEAPON OF THIS KIND BEFORE. IT
WAS HIS ONE ADVANTAGE, AND THE
HUNTER HELD IT DEAR.

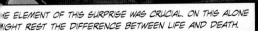

HE ELEMENT OF THIS SURPRISE WAS CRUCIAL. ON THIS ALONE
IGHT REST THE DIFFERENCE BETWEEN LIFE AND DEATH.

WITH A LAST LOOK AT THE EM
SKY, A LAST LUNGFUL OF THE CL
COLD AIR, THE HUNTER STEPPED
THE DARKNESS...

...AND, HIS HANDS STEADY AND HIS HEART COLD, BEGAN HIS HUNT IN EARNEST.

THE AIR WAS STILL, RANK WITH THE STENCH OF HIS QUARRY. THE HUNTER CONTROLLED HIS BREATHING, ONE STEP AFTER THE OTHER, EACH PLACED WITH CARE...

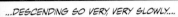

...DESCENDING SO VERY, VERY SLOWLY....

IN EVERY SHADOW LAY UNKNOWN MENACE. IN EACH CORNER, AMIDST THE DEBRIS OF THE BEAST'S LAIR, THE FEAR OF A PREDATOR LYING IN WAIT.

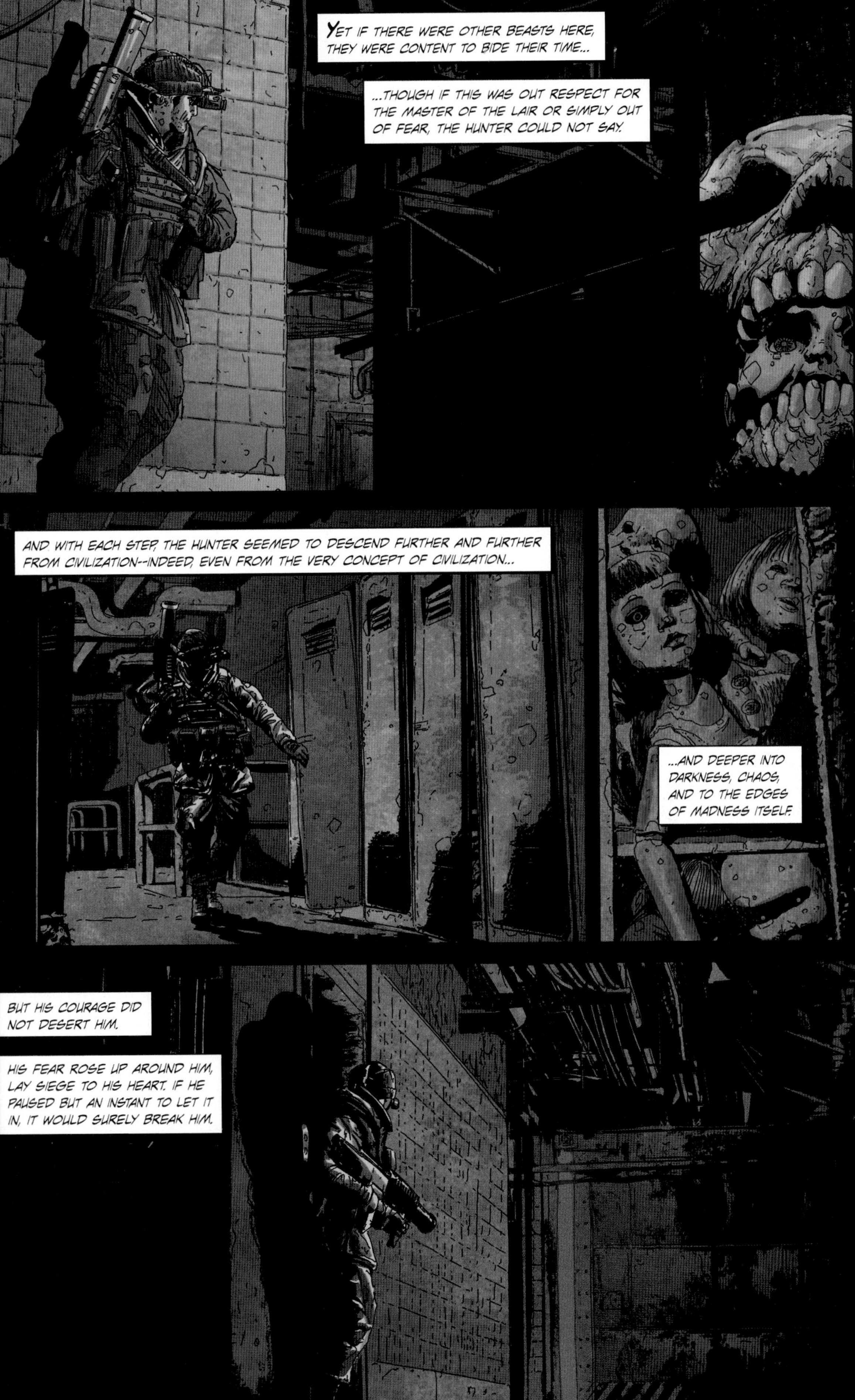
YET IF THERE WERE OTHER BEASTS HERE, THEY WERE CONTENT TO BIDE THEIR TIME...
...THOUGH IF THIS WAS OUT RESPECT FOR THE MASTER OF THE LAIR OR SIMPLY OUT OF FEAR, THE HUNTER COULD NOT SAY.
AND WITH EACH STEP, THE HUNTER SEEMED TO DESCEND FURTHER AND FURTHER FROM CIVILIZATION--INDEED, EVEN FROM THE VERY CONCEPT OF CIVILIZATION...
...AND DEEPER INTO DARKNESS, CHAOS, AND TO THE EDGES OF MADNESS ITSELF.
BUT HIS COURAGE DID NOT DESERT HIM.
HIS FEAR ROSE UP AROUND HIM, LAY SIEGE TO HIS HEART. IF HE PAUSED BUT AN INSTANT TO LET IT IN, IT WOULD SURELY BREAK HIM.

YET NOT LIKE THIS, NOT IN THIS DAMNED PLACE WHERE THE VERY WALLS ECHOED WITH THE BLOODLUST AND MADNESS THAT DROVE THE DRAGON.

THE HUNTER AND FEAR WERE OLD FRIENDS, AFTER ALL. A SEASONED SOLDIER, HE HAD FACED IT MANY A TIME BEFORE.

AS IF THE SCREAMS AND PLEAS OF ALL HIS VICTIMS WERE INTERRED WITHIN HIS LAIR.

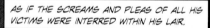

OTHERS WHO HAD COME ON THE SAME MISSION AS THE HUNTER.

OTHERS WHO HAD FAILED.

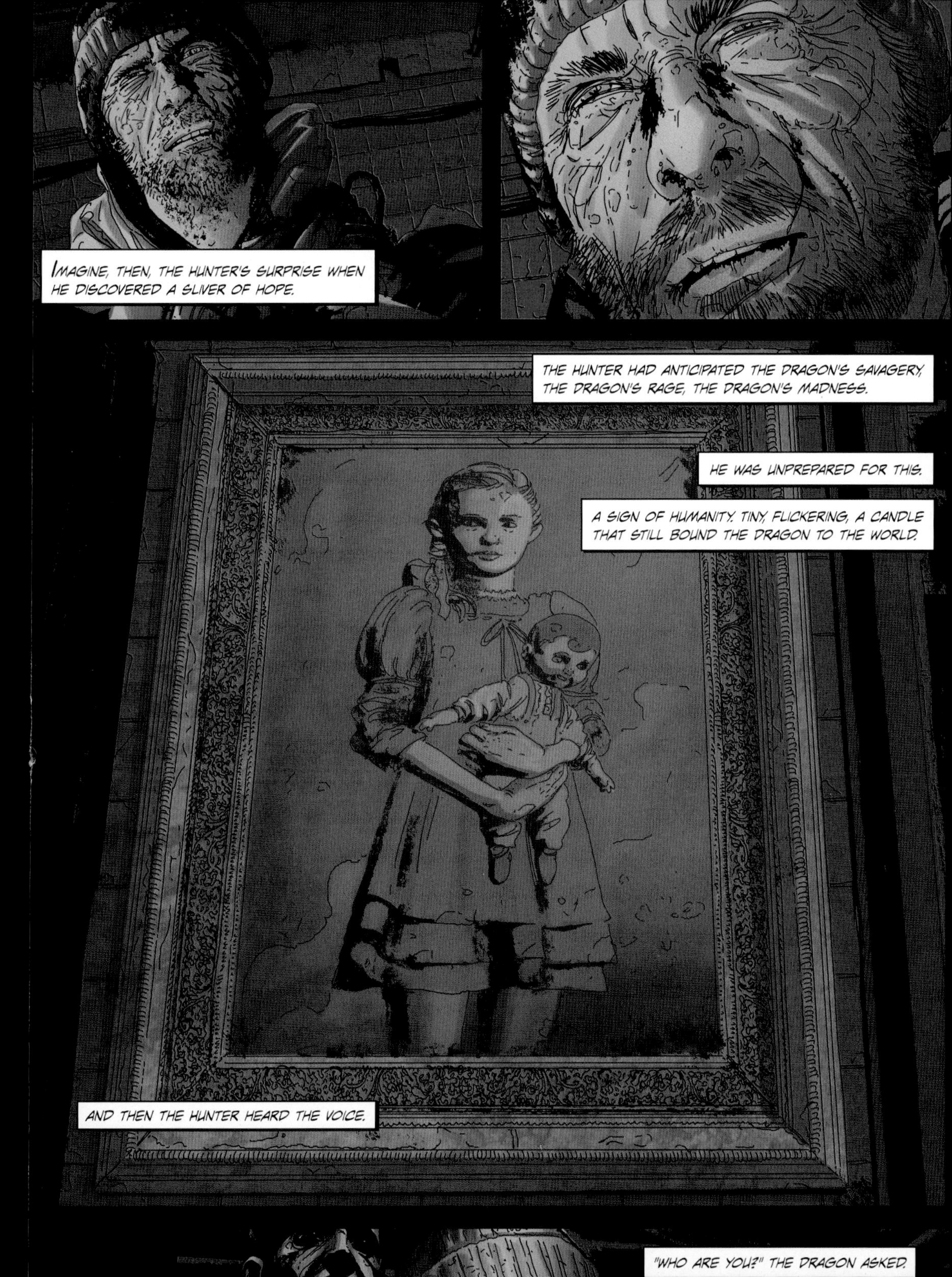
IMAGINE, THEN, THE HUNTER'S SURPRISE WHEN HE DISCOVERED A SLIVER OF HOPE.
THE HUNTER HAD ANTICIPATED THE DRAGON'S SAVAGERY, THE DRAGON'S RAGE, THE DRAGON'S MADNESS.
HE WAS UNPREPARED FOR THIS.
A SIGN OF HUMANITY. TINY, FLICKERING, A CANDLE THAT STILL BOUND THE DRAGON TO THE WORLD.
AND THEN THE HUNTER HEARD THE VOICE.
"WHO ARE YOU?" THE DRAGON ASKED.

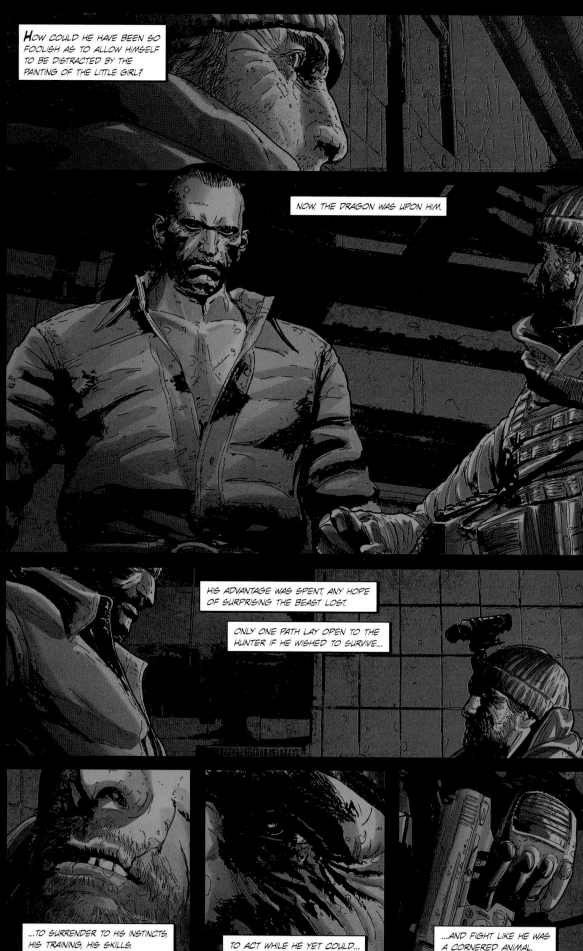

HOW COULD HE HAVE BEEN SO FOOLISH AS TO ALLOW HIMSELF TO BE DISTRACTED BY THE PAINTING OF THE LITTLE GIRL?

NOW, THE DRAGON WAS UPON HIM.

HIS ADVANTAGE WAS SPENT, ANY HOPE OF SURPRISING THE BEAST LOST.

ONLY ONE PATH LAY OPEN TO THE HUNTER IF HE WISHED TO SURVIVE...

...TO SURRENDER TO HIS INSTINCTS, HIS TRAINING, HIS SKILLS.

TO ACT WHILE HE YET COULD...

...AND FIGHT LIKE HE WAS A CORNERED ANIMAL.

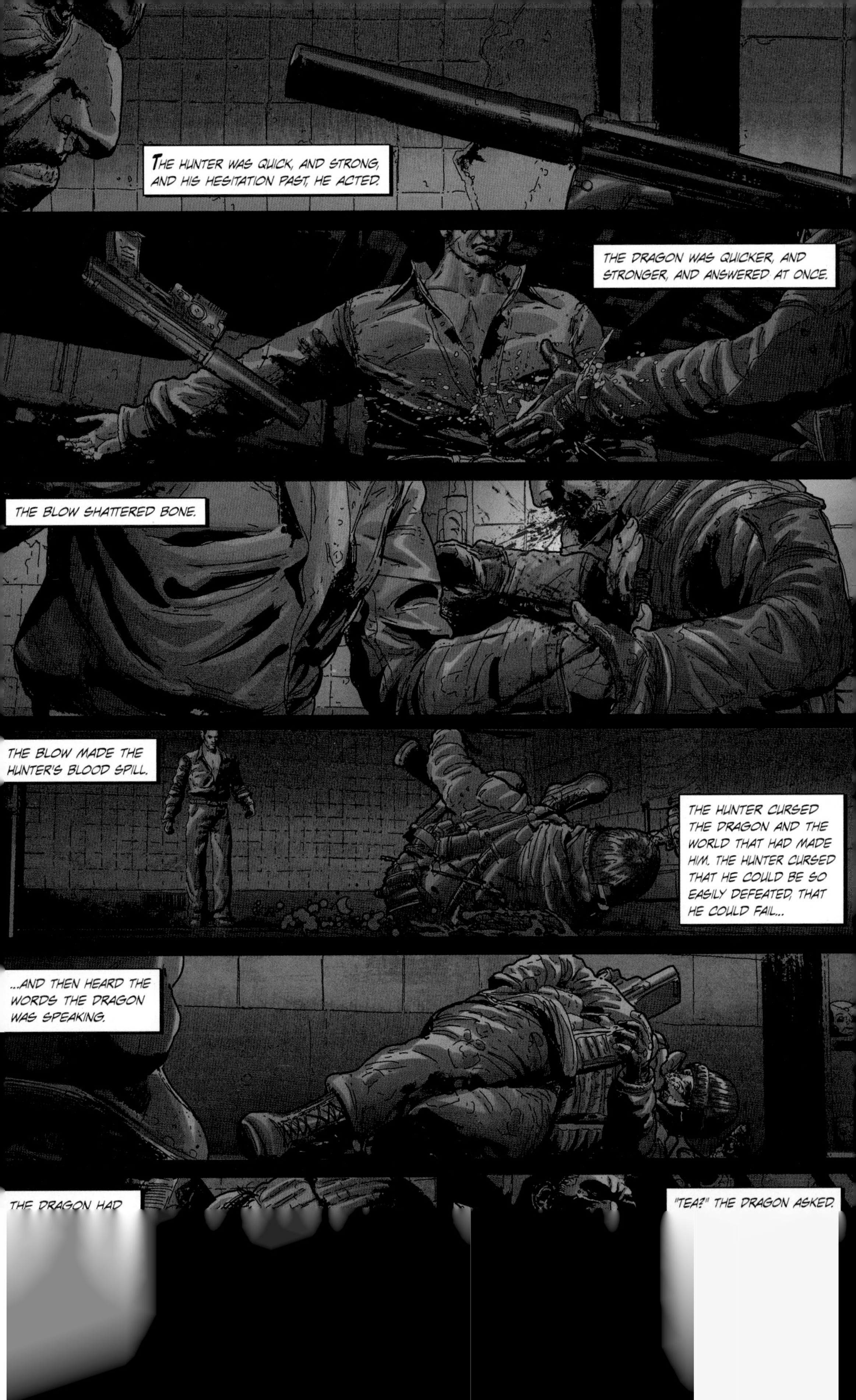
THE HUNTER WAS QUICK, AND STRONG, AND HIS HESITATION PAST, HE ACTED.
THE DRAGON WAS QUICKER, AND STRONGER, AND ANSWERED AT ONCE.
THE BLOW SHATTERED BONE.
THE BLOW MADE THE HUNTER'S BLOOD SPILL.
THE HUNTER CURSED THE DRAGON AND THE WORLD THAT HAD MADE HIM. THE HUNTER CURSED THAT HE COULD BE SO EASILY DEFEATED, THAT HE COULD FAIL...
...AND THEN HEARD THE WORDS THE DRAGON WAS SPEAKING.
THE DRAGON HAD
"TEA?" THE DRAGON ASKED.

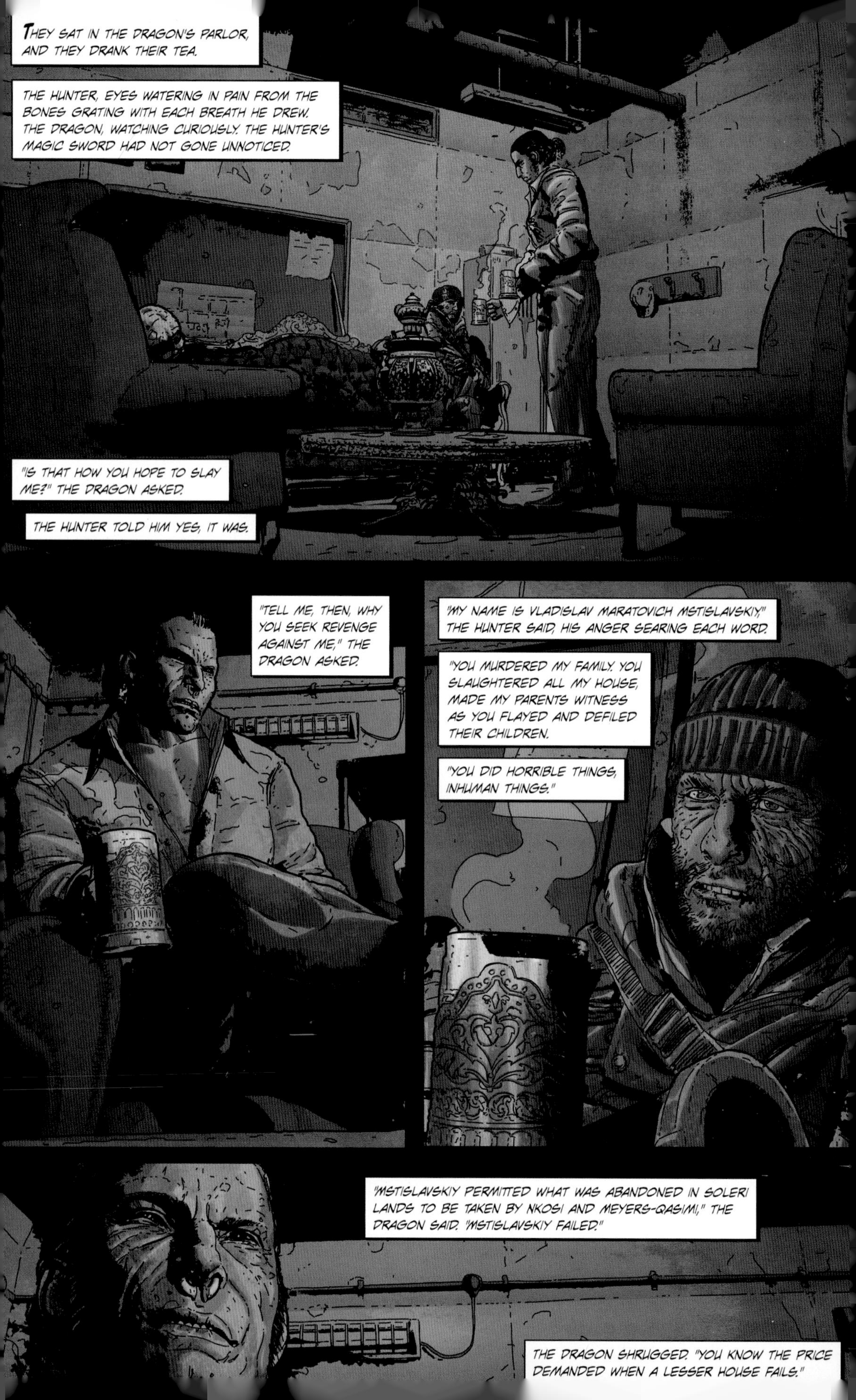
THEY SAT IN THE DRAGON'S PARLOR, AND THEY DRANK THEIR TEA.
THE HUNTER, EYES WATERING IN PAIN FROM THE BONES GRATING WITH EACH BREATH HE DREW. THE DRAGON, WATCHING CURIOUSLY. THE HUNTER'S MAGIC SWORD HAD NOT GONE UNNOTICED.
"IS THAT HOW YOU HOPE TO SLAY ME?" THE DRAGON ASKED.
THE HUNTER TOLD HIM YES, IT WAS.
"TELL ME, THEN, WHY YOU SEEK REVENGE AGAINST ME," THE DRAGON ASKED.
"MY NAME IS VLADISLAV MARATOVICH MSTISLAVSKIY," THE HUNTER SAID, HIS ANGER SEARING EACH WORD.
"YOU MURDERED MY FAMILY. YOU SLAUGHTERED ALL MY HOUSE, MADE MY PARENTS WITNESS AS YOU FLAYED AND DEFILED THEIR CHILDREN.
"YOU DID HORRIBLE THINGS, INHUMAN THINGS."
"MSTISLAVSKIY PERMITTED WHAT WAS ABANDONED IN SOLERI LANDS TO BE TAKEN BY NKOSI AND MEYERS-QASIMI," THE DRAGON SAID. "MSTISLAVSKIY FAILED."
THE DRAGON SHRUGGED. "YOU KNOW THE PRICE DEMANDED WHEN A LESSER HOUSE FAILS."

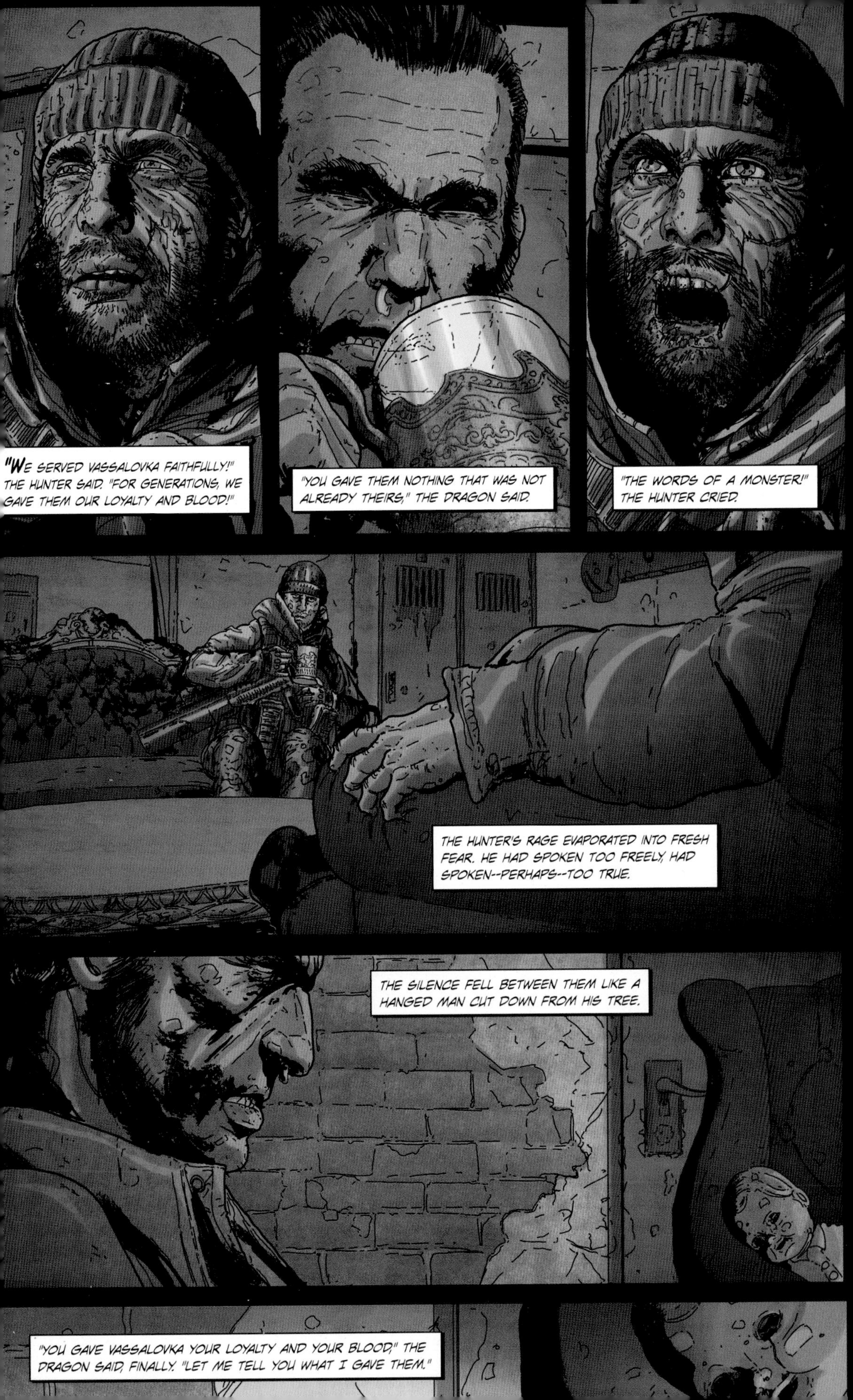
"WE SERVED VASSALOVKA FAITHFULLY!" THE HUNTER SAID. "FOR GENERATIONS, WE GAVE THEM OUR LOYALTY AND BLOOD!"
"YOU GAVE THEM NOTHING THAT WAS NOT ALREADY THEIRS," THE DRAGON SAID.
"THE WORDS OF A MONSTER!" THE HUNTER CRIED.
THE HUNTER'S RAGE EVAPORATED INTO FRESH FEAR. HE HAD SPOKEN TOO FREELY, HAD SPOKEN--PERHAPS--TOO TRUE.
THE SILENCE FELL BETWEEN THEM LIKE A HANGED MAN CUT DOWN FROM HIS TREE.
"YOU GAVE VASSALOVKA YOUR LOYALTY AND YOUR BLOOD," THE DRAGON SAID, FINALLY. "LET ME TELL YOU WHAT I GAVE THEM."

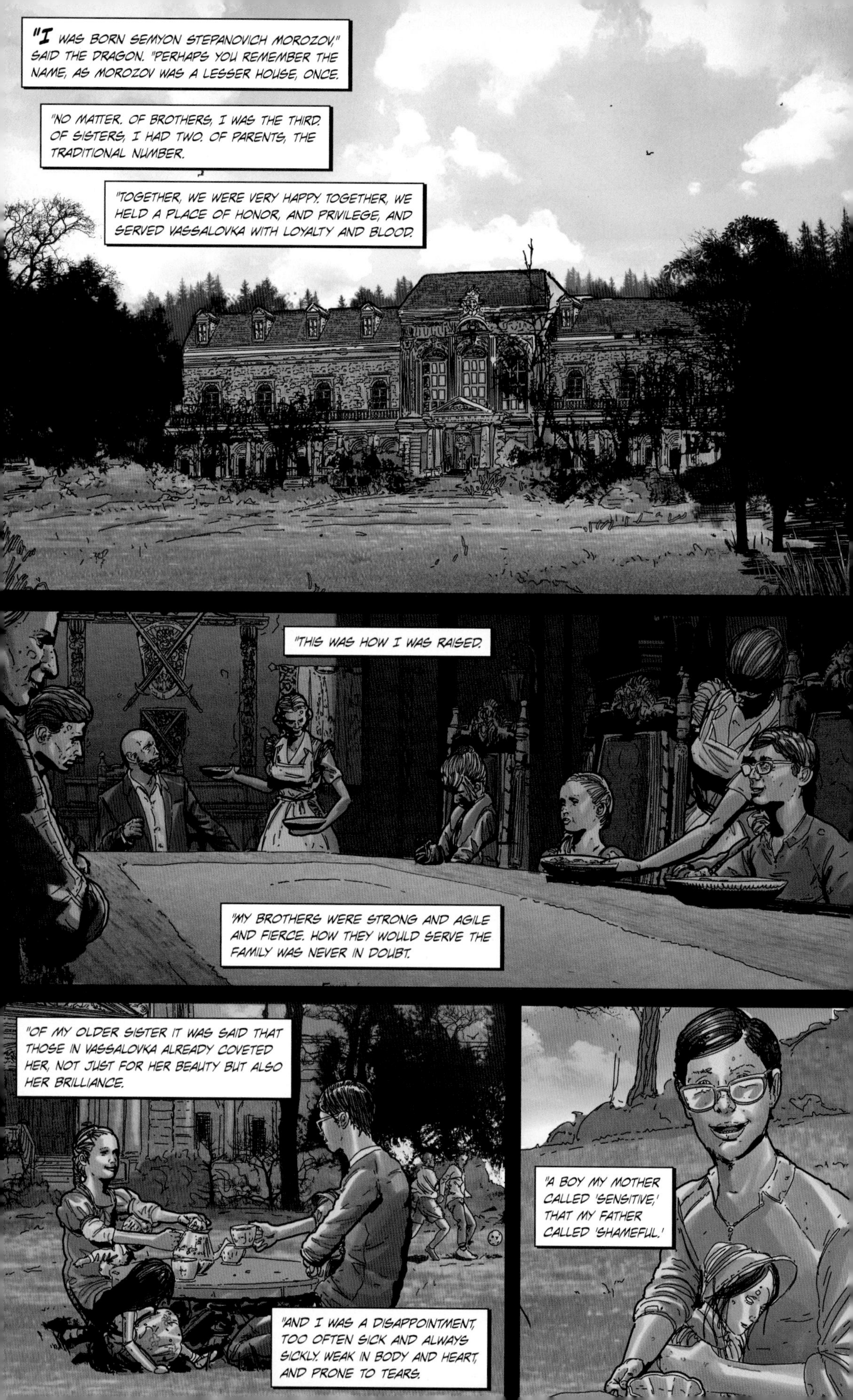
"I WAS BORN SEMYON STEPANOVICH MOROZOV," SAID THE DRAGON. "PERHAPS YOU REMEMBER THE NAME, AS MOROZOV WAS A LESSER HOUSE, ONCE.
"NO MATTER. OF BROTHERS, I WAS THE THIRD. OF SISTERS, I HAD TWO. OF PARENTS, THE TRADITIONAL NUMBER.
"TOGETHER, WE WERE VERY HAPPY. TOGETHER, WE HELD A PLACE OF HONOR, AND PRIVILEGE, AND SERVED VASSALOVKA WITH LOYALTY AND BLOOD.
"THIS WAS HOW I WAS RAISED.
"MY BROTHERS WERE STRONG AND AGILE AND FIERCE. HOW THEY WOULD SERVE THE FAMILY WAS NEVER IN DOUBT.
"OF MY OLDER SISTER IT WAS SAID THAT THOSE IN VASSALOVKA ALREADY COVETED HER, NOT JUST FOR HER BEAUTY BUT ALSO HER BRILLIANCE.
"AND I WAS A DISAPPOINTMENT, TOO OFTEN SICK AND ALWAYS SICKLY. WEAK IN BODY AND HEART, AND PRONE TO TEARS.
"A BOY MY MOTHER CALLED 'SENSITIVE,' THAT MY FATHER CALLED 'SHAMEFUL.'

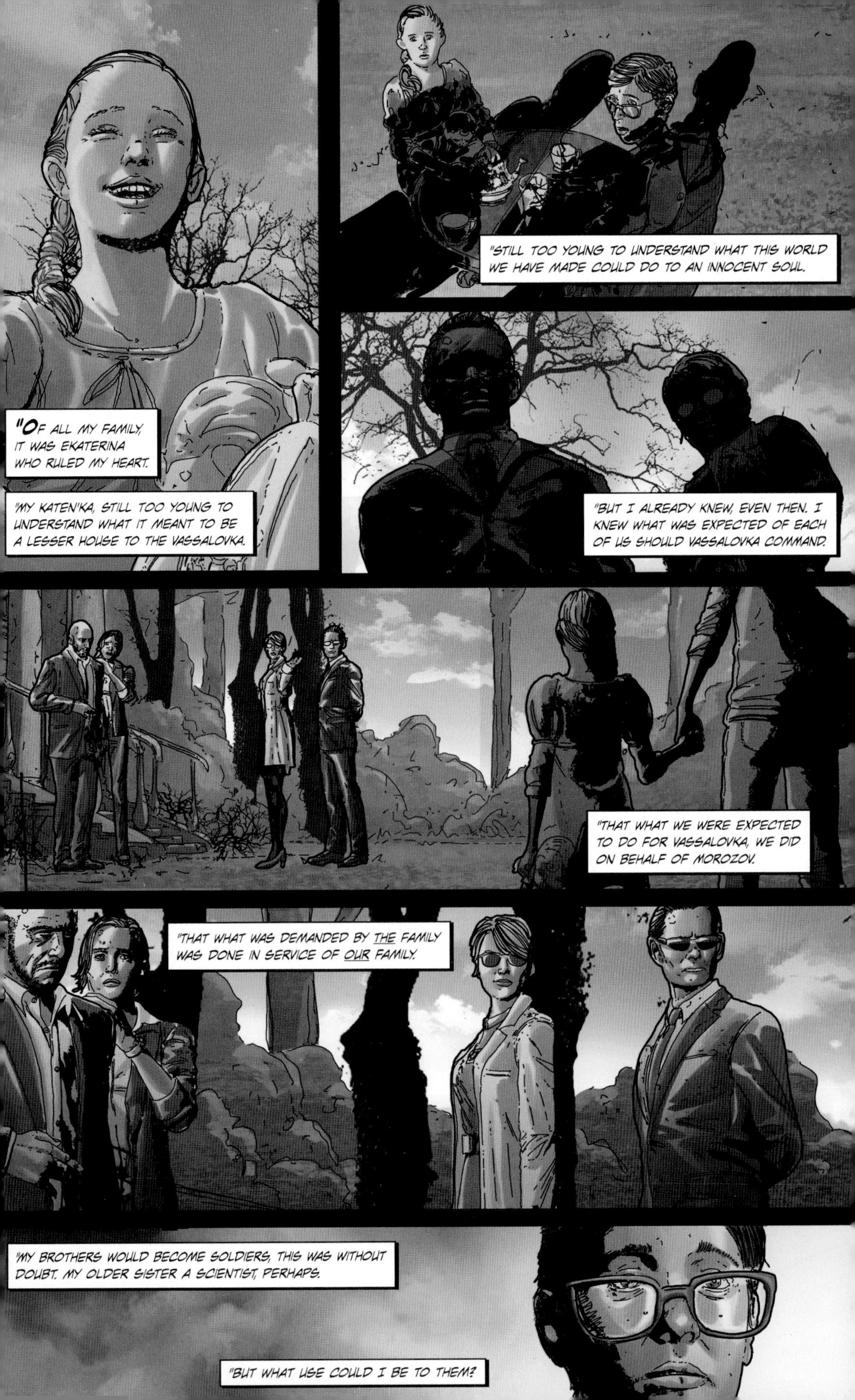
"OF ALL MY FAMILY, IT WAS EKATERINA WHO RULED MY HEART.
"MY KATEN'KA, STILL TOO YOUNG TO UNDERSTAND WHAT IT MEANT TO BE A LESSER HOUSE TO THE VASSALOVKA.
"STILL TOO YOUNG TO UNDERSTAND WHAT THIS WORLD WE HAVE MADE COULD DO TO AN INNOCENT SOUL.
"BUT I ALREADY KNEW, EVEN THEN. I KNEW WHAT WAS EXPECTED OF EACH OF US SHOULD VASSALOVKA COMMAND.
"THAT WHAT WE WERE EXPECTED TO DO FOR VASSALOVKA, WE DID ON BEHALF OF MOROZOV.
"THAT WHAT WAS DEMANDED BY THE FAMILY WAS DONE IN SERVICE OF OUR FAMILY.
"MY BROTHERS WOULD BECOME SOLDIERS, THIS WAS WITHOUT DOUBT. MY OLDER SISTER A SCIENTIST, PERHAPS.
"BUT WHAT USE COULD I BE TO THEM?

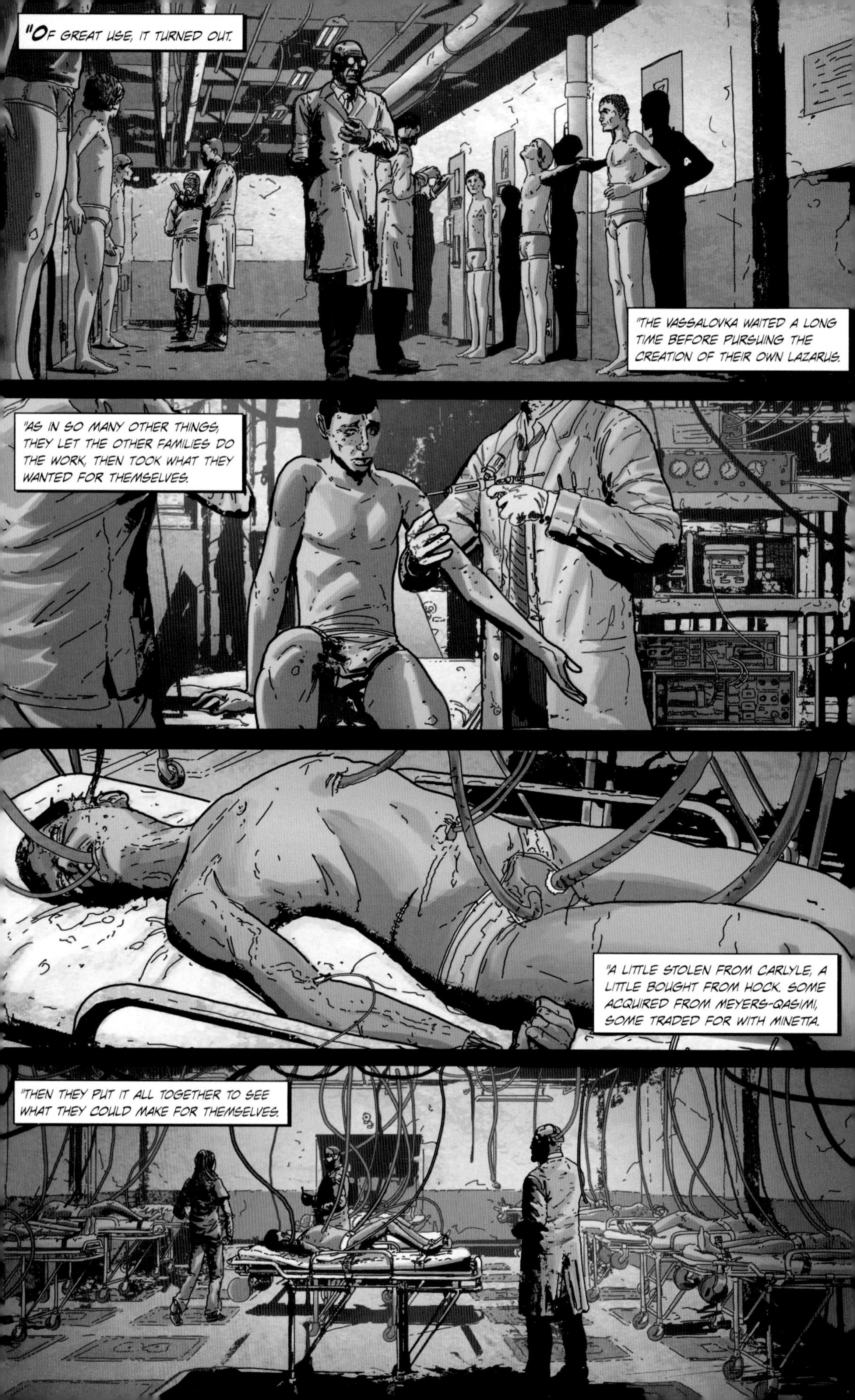
"OF GREAT USE, IT TURNED OUT.
"THE VASSALOVKA WAITED A LONG TIME BEFORE PURSUING THE CREATION OF THEIR OWN LAZARUS.
"AS IN SO MANY OTHER THINGS, THEY LET THE OTHER FAMILIES DO THE WORK, THEN TOOK WHAT THEY WANTED FOR THEMSELVES.
"A LITTLE STOLEN FROM CARLYLE, A LITTLE BOUGHT FROM HOCK. SOME ACQUIRED FROM MEYERS-QASIMI, SOME TRADED FOR WITH MINETTA.
"THEN THEY PUT IT ALL TOGETHER TO SEE WHAT THEY COULD MAKE FOR THEMSELVES.

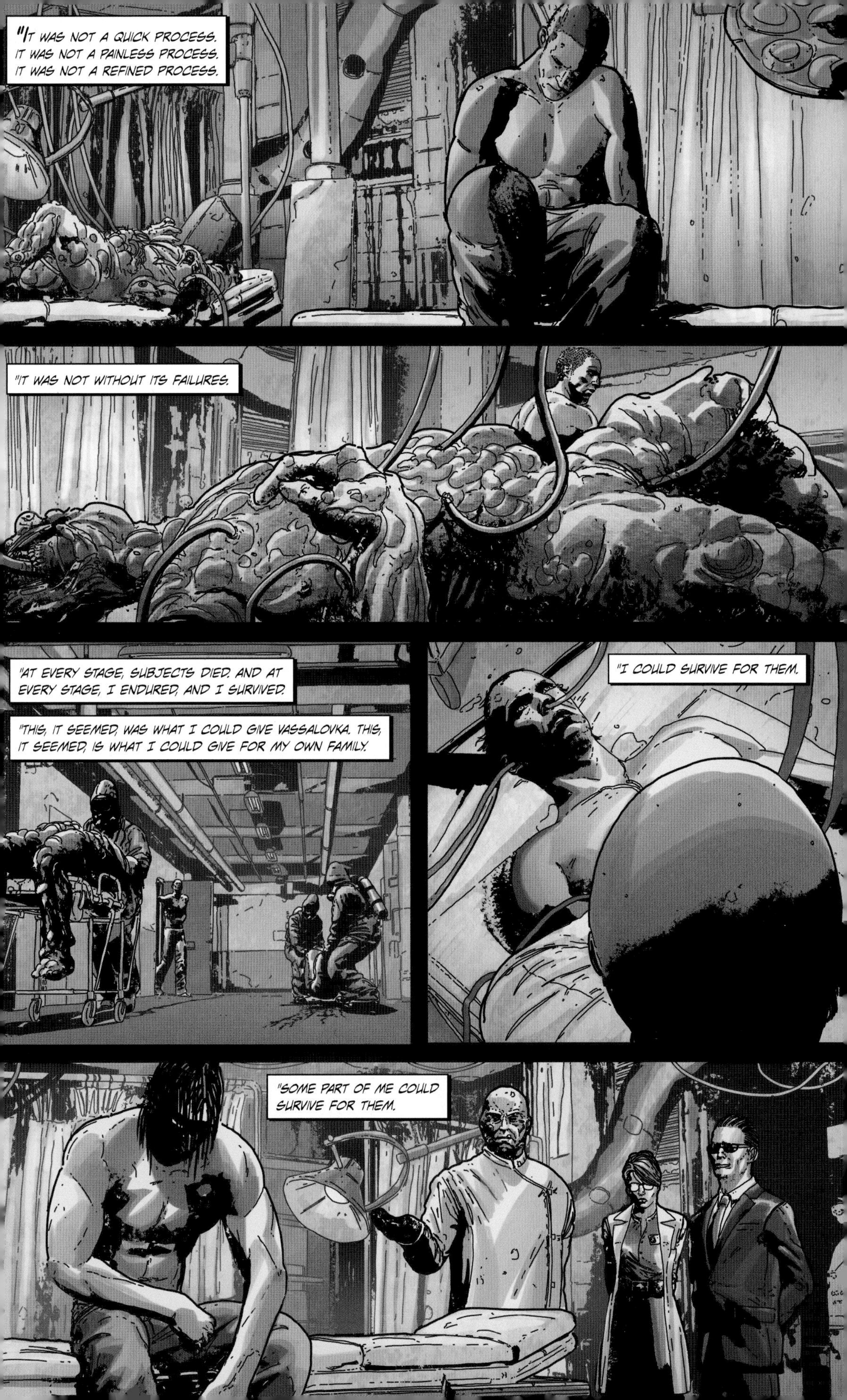

"IT WAS NOT A QUICK PROCESS. IT WAS NOT A PAINLESS PROCESS. IT WAS NOT A REFINED PROCESS.
"IT WAS NOT WITHOUT ITS FAILURES.
"AT EVERY STAGE, SUBJECTS DIED. AND AT EVERY STAGE, I ENDURED, AND I SURVIVED.
"THIS, IT SEEMED, WAS WHAT I COULD GIVE VASSALOVKA. THIS, IT SEEMED, IS WHAT I COULD GIVE FOR MY OWN FAMILY.
"I COULD SURVIVE FOR THEM.
"SOME PART OF ME COULD SURVIVE FOR THEM.

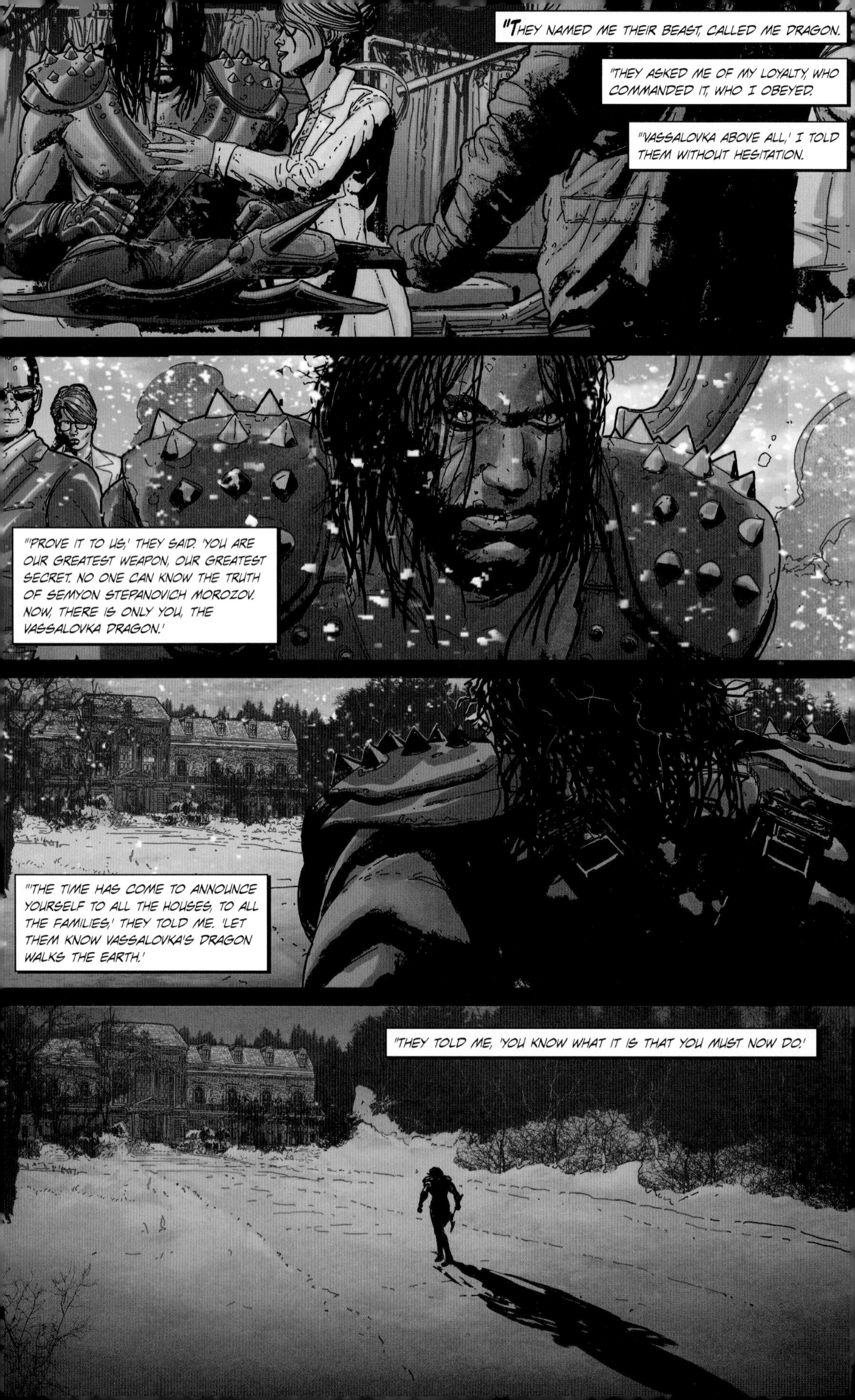
"THEY NAMED ME THEIR BEAST, CALLED ME DRAGON.
"THEY ASKED ME OF MY LOYALTY, WHO COMMANDED IT, WHO I OBEYED.
"'VASSALOVKA ABOVE ALL,' I TOLD THEM WITHOUT HESITATION.
"'PROVE IT TO US,' THEY SAID. 'YOU ARE OUR GREATEST WEAPON, OUR GREATEST SECRET. NO ONE CAN KNOW THE TRUTH OF SEMYON STEPANOVICH MOROZOV. NOW, THERE IS ONLY YOU, THE VASSALOVKA DRAGON.'
"'THE TIME HAS COME TO ANNOUNCE YOURSELF TO ALL THE HOUSES, TO ALL THE FAMILIES,' THEY TOLD ME. 'LET THEM KNOW VASSALOVKA'S DRAGON WALKS THE EARTH.'
"THEY TOLD ME, 'YOU KNOW WHAT IT IS THAT YOU MUST NOW DO.'

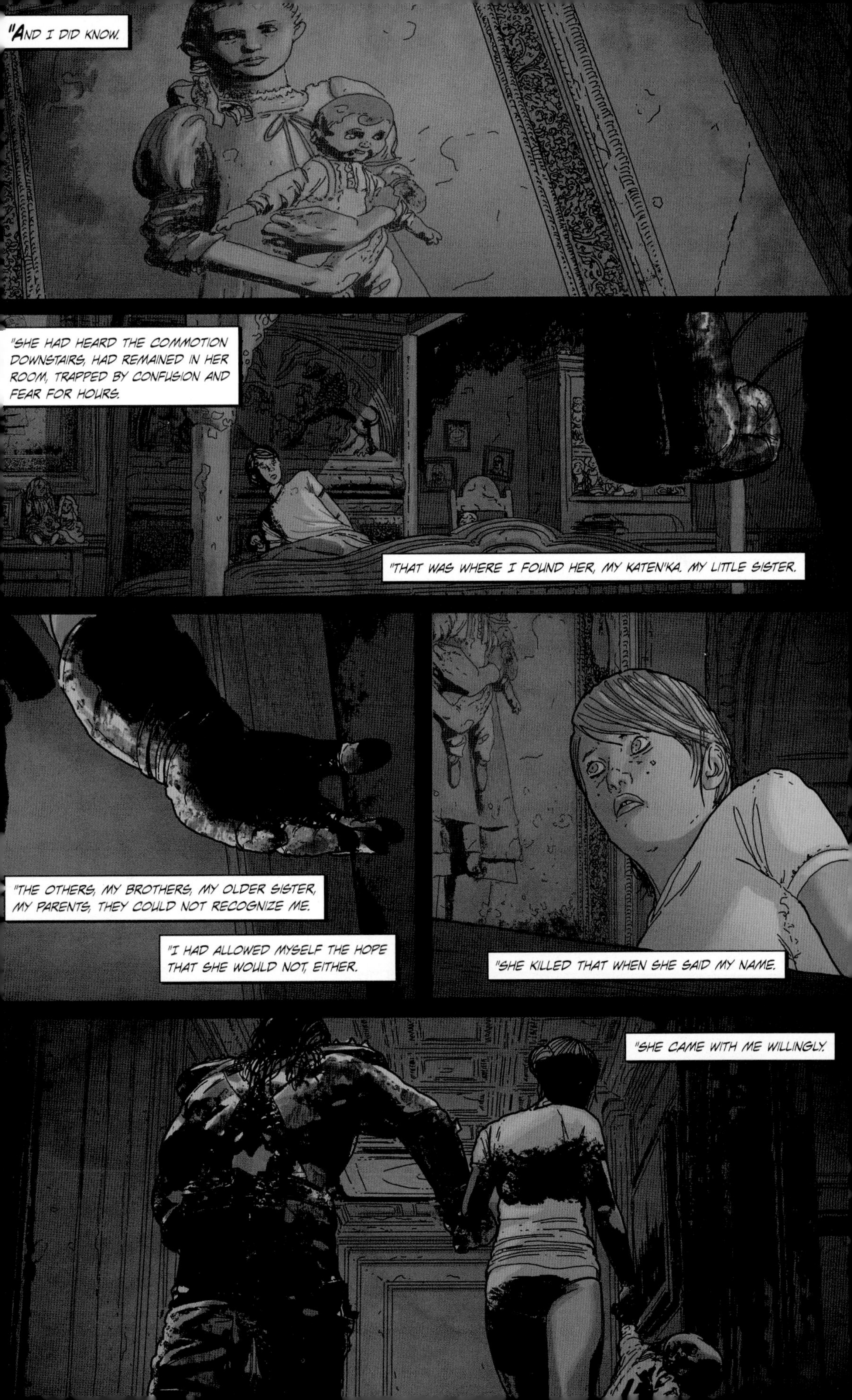
"AND I DID KNOW.
"SHE HAD HEARD THE COMMOTION DOWNSTAIRS, HAD REMAINED IN HER ROOM, TRAPPED BY CONFUSION AND FEAR FOR HOURS.
"THAT WAS WHERE I FOUND HER, MY KATEN'KA. MY LITTLE SISTER.
"THE OTHERS, MY BROTHERS, MY OLDER SISTER, MY PARENTS, THEY COULD NOT RECOGNIZE ME.
"I HAD ALLOWED MYSELF THE HOPE THAT SHE WOULD NOT, EITHER.
"SHE KILLED THAT WHEN SHE SAID MY NAME.
"SHE CAME WITH ME WILLINGLY.

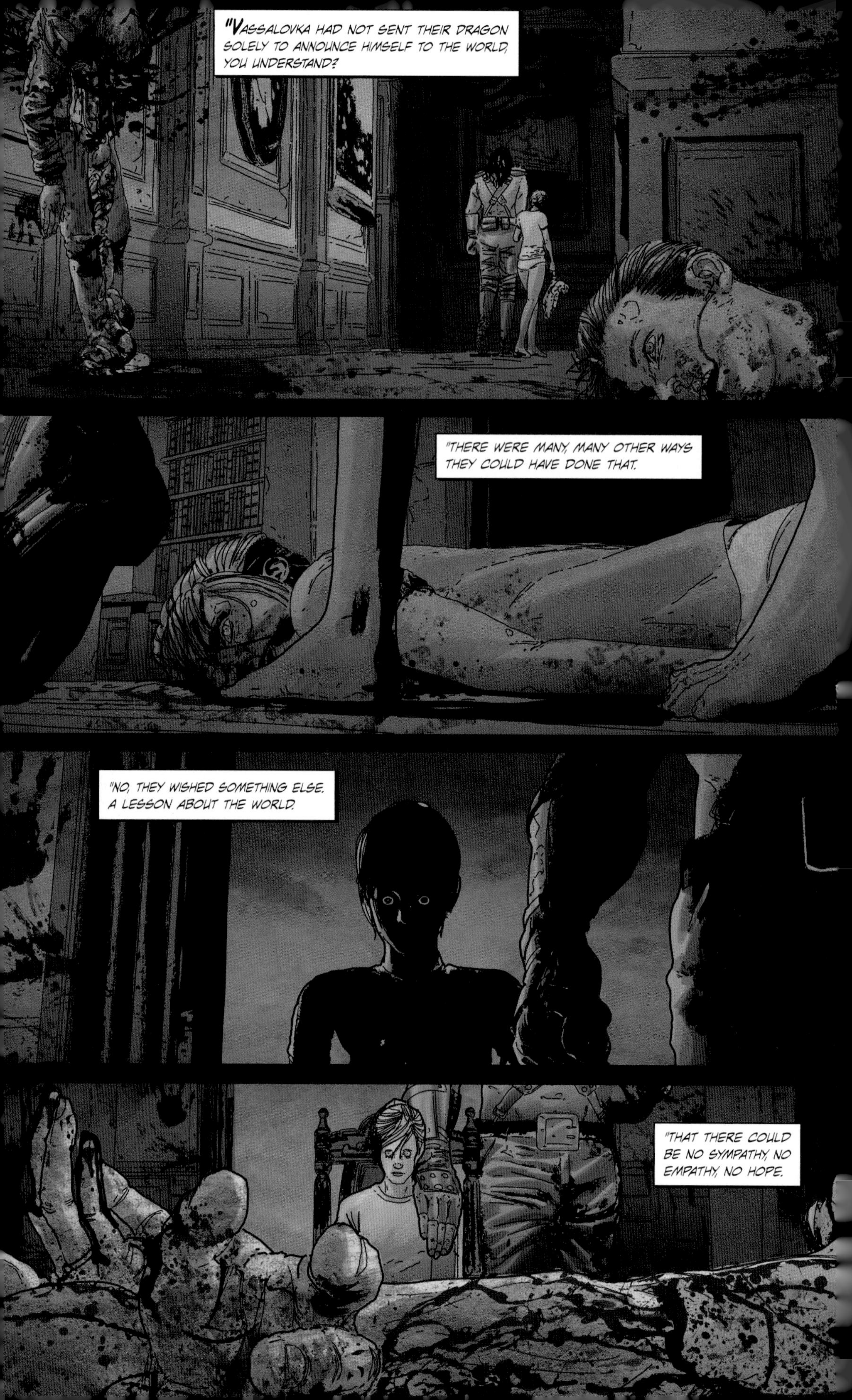
"VASSALOVKA HAD NOT SENT THEIR DRAGON SOLELY TO ANNOUNCE HIMSELF TO THE WORLD, YOU UNDERSTAND?
"THERE WERE MANY, MANY OTHER WAYS THEY COULD HAVE DONE THAT.
"NO, THEY WISHED SOMETHING ELSE. A LESSON ABOUT THE WORLD.
"THAT THERE COULD BE NO SYMPATHY, NO EMPATHY, NO HOPE.

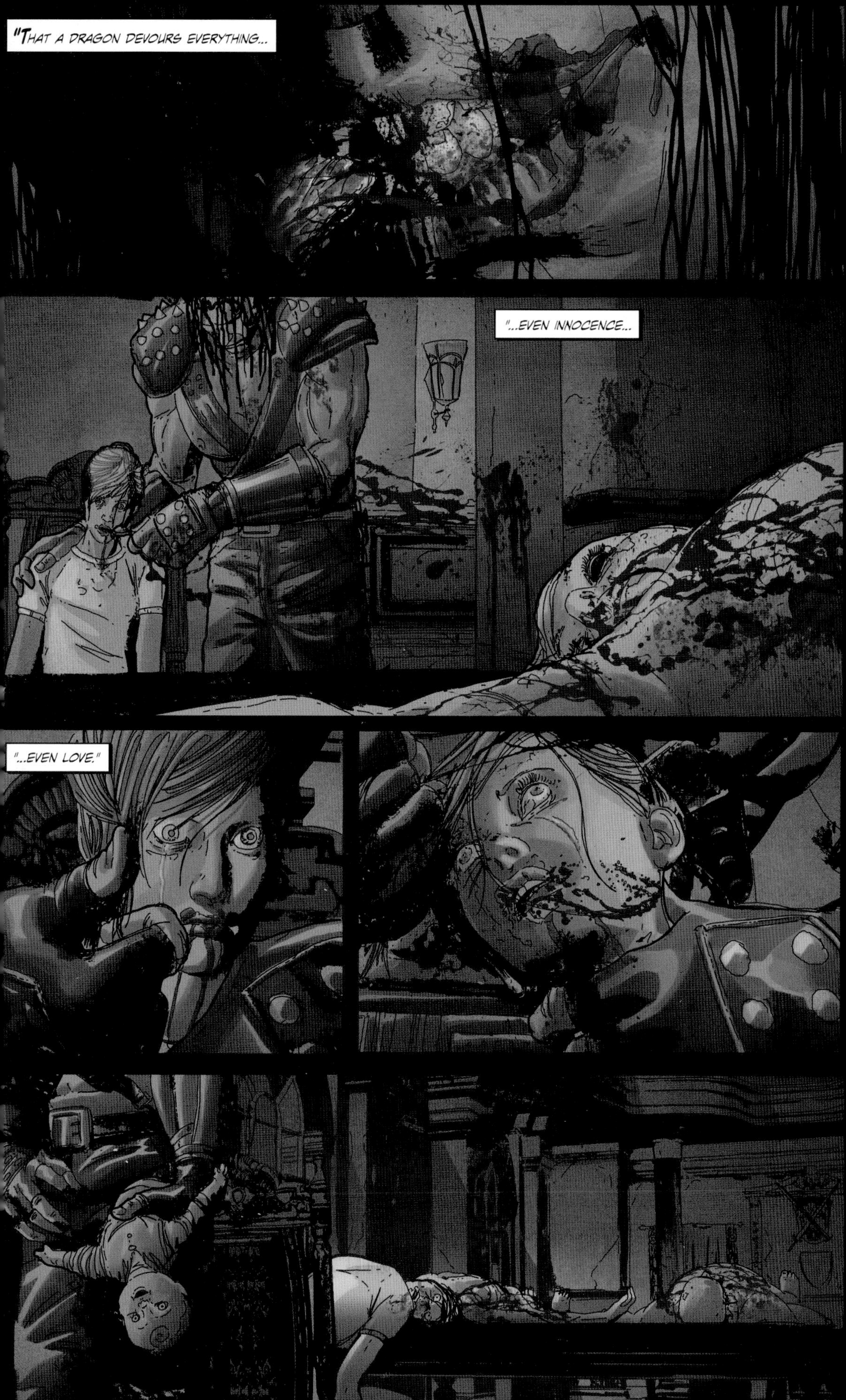
"That a dragon devours everything...
"...even innocence...
"...even love."

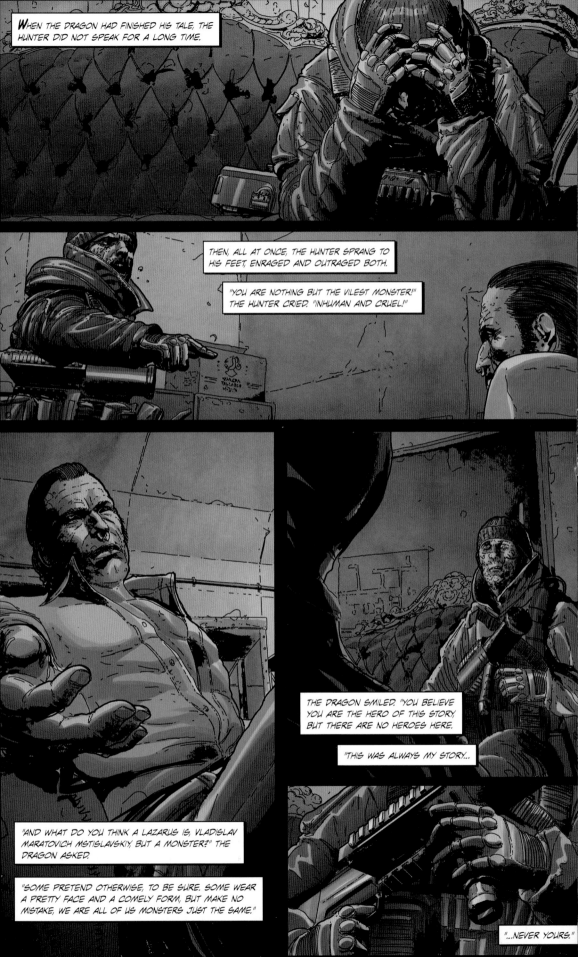

WHEN THE DRAGON HAD FINISHED HIS TALE, THE HUNTER DID NOT SPEAK FOR A LONG TIME.

THEN, ALL AT ONCE, THE HUNTER SPRANG TO HIS FEET, ENRAGED AND OUTRAGED BOTH.

"YOU ARE NOTHING BUT THE VILEST MONSTER!" THE HUNTER CRIED. "INHUMAN AND CRUEL!"

THE DRAGON SMILED. "YOU BELIEVE YOU ARE THE HERO OF THIS STORY, BUT THERE ARE NO HEROES HERE.

"THIS WAS ALWAYS MY STORY...

"AND WHAT DO YOU THINK A LAZARUS IS, VLADISLAV MARATOVICH MSTISLAVSKIY, BUT A MONSTER?" THE DRAGON ASKED.

"SOME PRETEND OTHERWISE, TO BE SURE. SOME WEAR A PRETTY FACE AND A COMELY FORM, BUT MAKE NO MISTAKE, WE ARE ALL OF US MONSTERS JUST THE SAME."

"...NEVER YOURS."

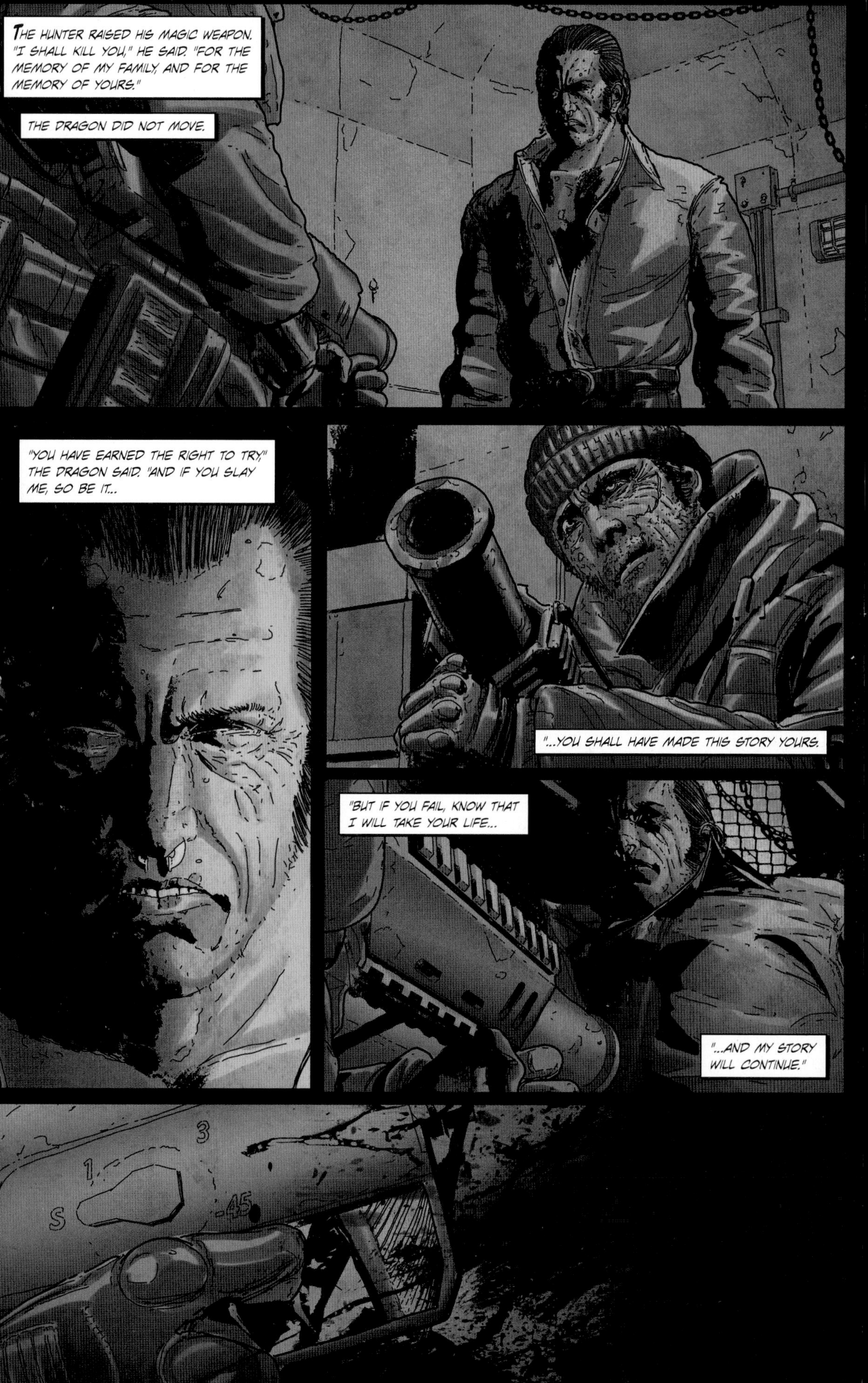
THE HUNTER RAISED HIS MAGIC WEAPON. "I SHALL KILL YOU," HE SAID. "FOR THE MEMORY OF MY FAMILY, AND FOR THE MEMORY OF YOURS."
THE DRAGON DID NOT MOVE.
"YOU HAVE EARNED THE RIGHT TO TRY," THE DRAGON SAID. "AND IF YOU SLAY ME, SO BE IT...
"...YOU SHALL HAVE MADE THIS STORY YOURS.
"BUT IF YOU FAIL, KNOW THAT I WILL TAKE YOUR LIFE...
"...AND MY STORY WILL CONTINUE."
3
1
S
45

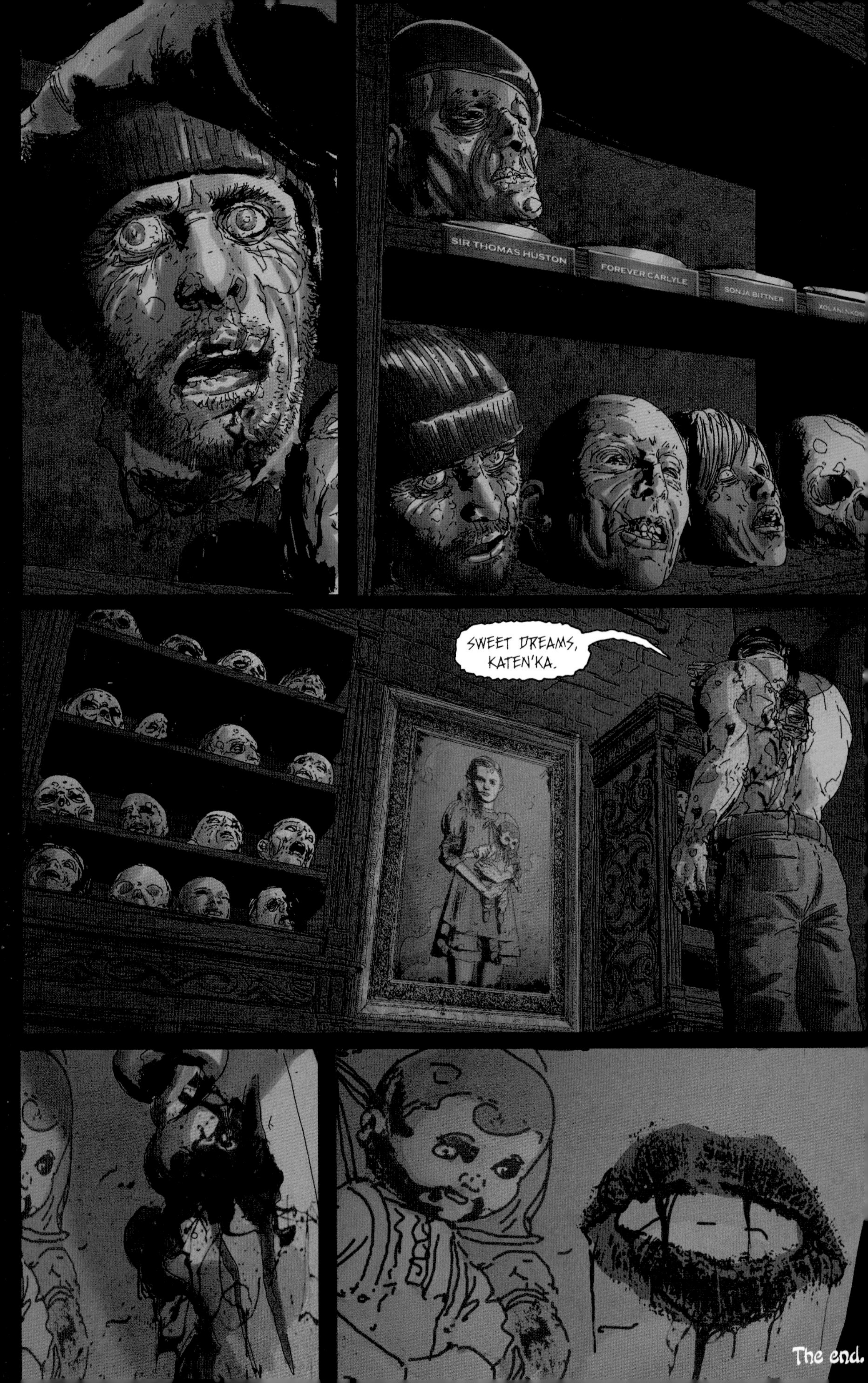
SIR THOMAS HUSTON
FOREVER CARLYLE
SONJA BITTNER
XOLANI NKOSI
SWEET DREAMS, KATEN'KA.
The end.

CARLYLE

ODERINT DUM METUANT

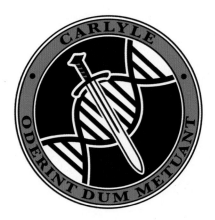

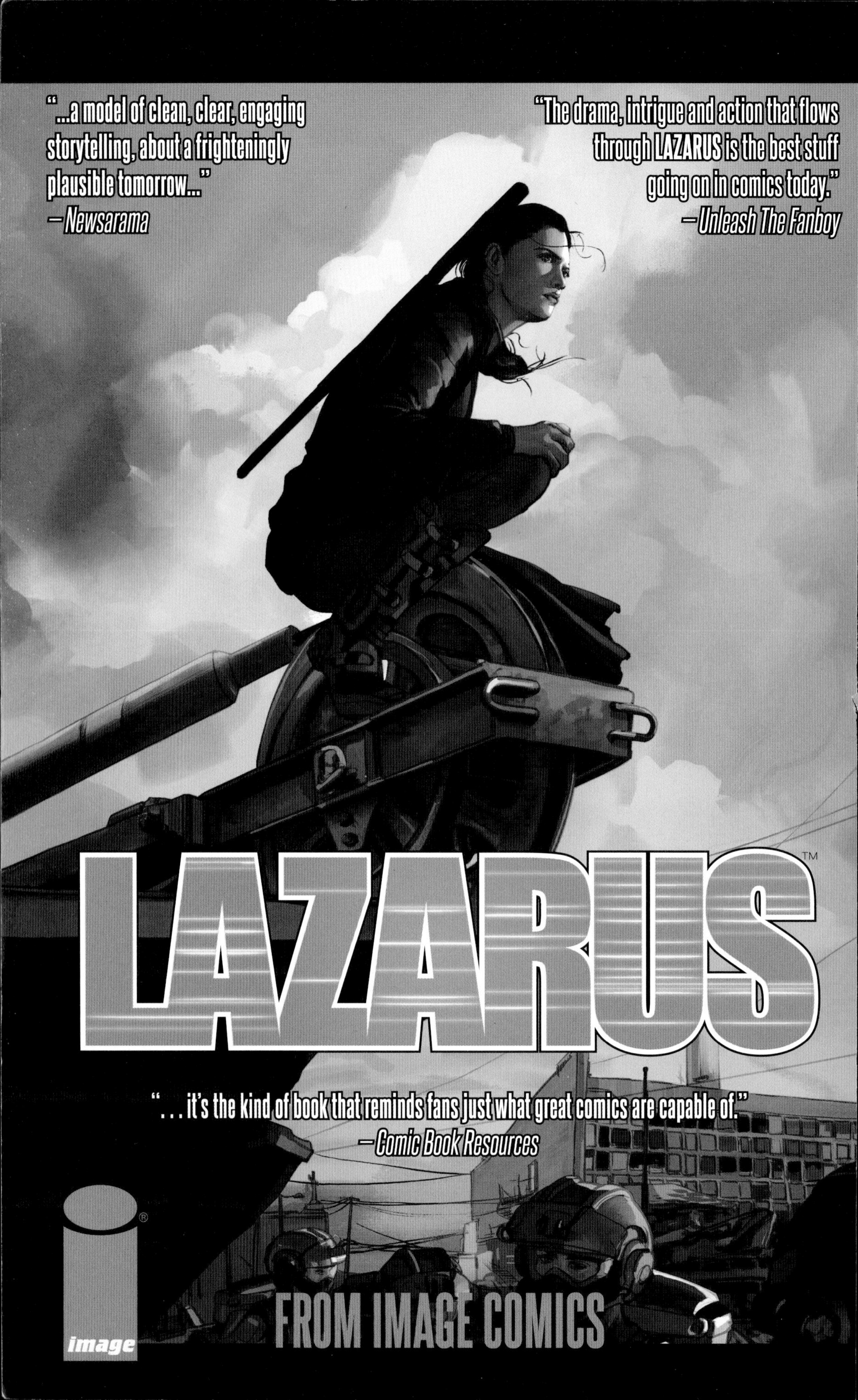
"...a model of clean, clear, engaging storytelling, about a frighteningly plausible tomorrow..."
— Newsarama
"The drama, intrigue and action that flows through LAZARUS is the best stuff going on in comics today."
— Unleash The Fanboy
LAZARUS™
". . . it's the kind of book that reminds fans just what great comics are capable of."
— Comic Book Resources
image
FROM IMAGE COMICS

AVAILABLE IN HARDCOVER...

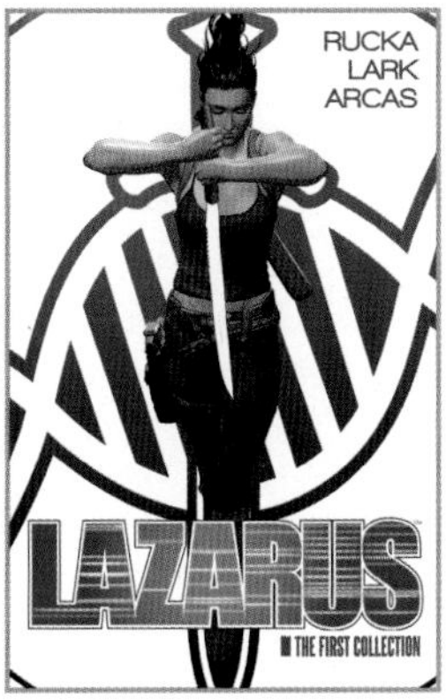
RUCKA
LARK
ARCAS
LAZARUS
THE FIRST COLLECTION

LAZARUS: THE FIRST COLLECTION HC
ISBN: 978-1-63215-183-4
DIAMOND ORDER CODE: SEP140626
RATED M/MATURE
SCIENCE FICTION/DRAMA
$34.99

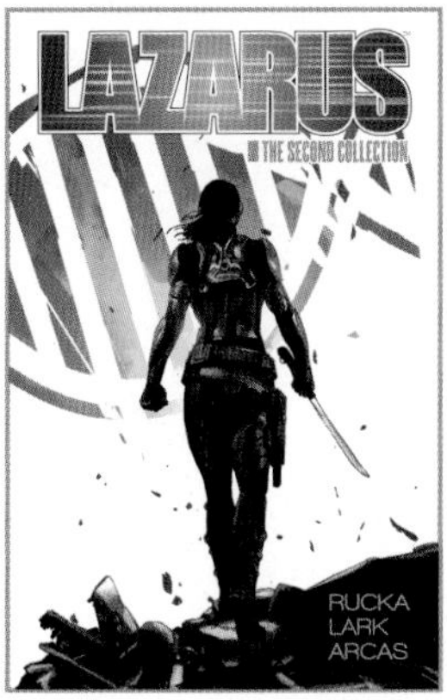
LAZARUS
THE SECOND COLLECTION
RUCKA
LARK
ARCAS

LAZARUS: THE SECOND COLLECTION HC
ISBN: 978-1-1632157225
DIAMOND ORDER CODE: FEB160687
RATED M/MATURE
SCIENCE FICTION/DRAMA
$39.99

...AND IN TRADE PAPERBACK EDITIONS.

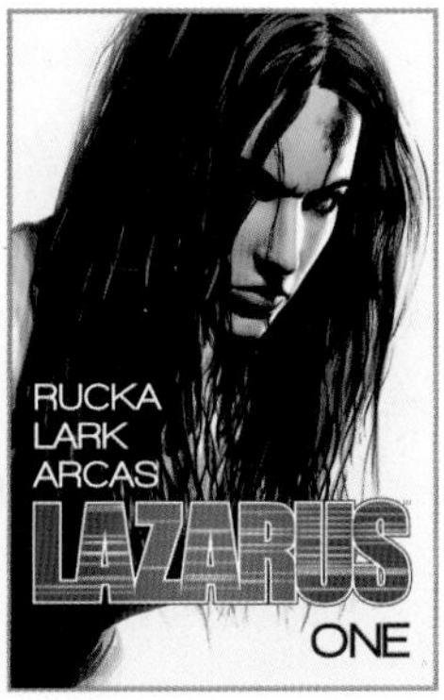
RUCKA
LARK
ARCAS
LAZARUS
ONE

LAZARUS VOL.1: FAMILY
ISBN: 978-1-60706-809-9
DIAMOND ORDER CODE: AUG130621
RATED M/MATURE
SCIENCE FICTION/DRAMA
$9.99

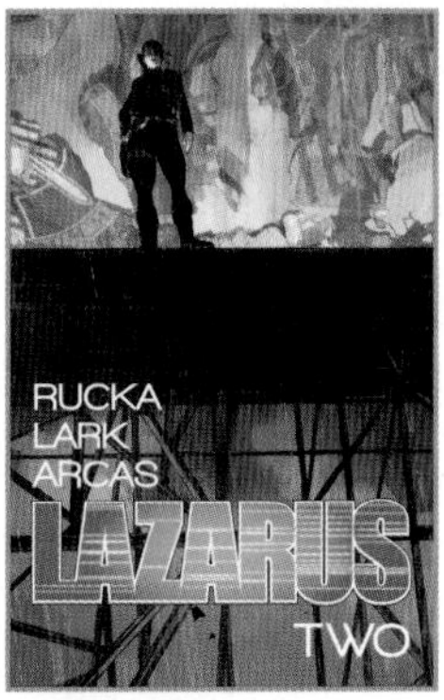
RUCKA
LARK
ARCAS
LAZARUS
TWO

LAZARUS VOL.2: LIFT
ISBN: 978-1-60706-871-6
DIAMOND ORDER CODE: FEB140527
RATED M/MATURE
SCIENCE FICTION/DRAMA
$14.99

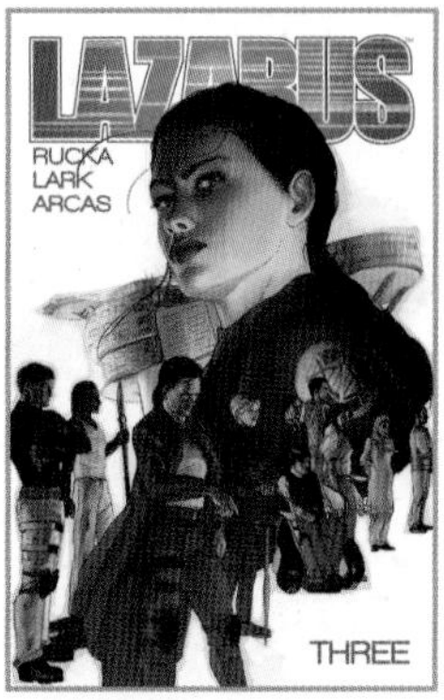
LAZARUS
RUCKA
LARK
ARCAS
THREE

LAZARUS VOL.3: CONCLAVE
ISBN: 978-1632152251
DIAMOND ORDER CODE: JAN150631
RATED M/MATURE
SCIENCE FICTION/DRAMA
$14.99

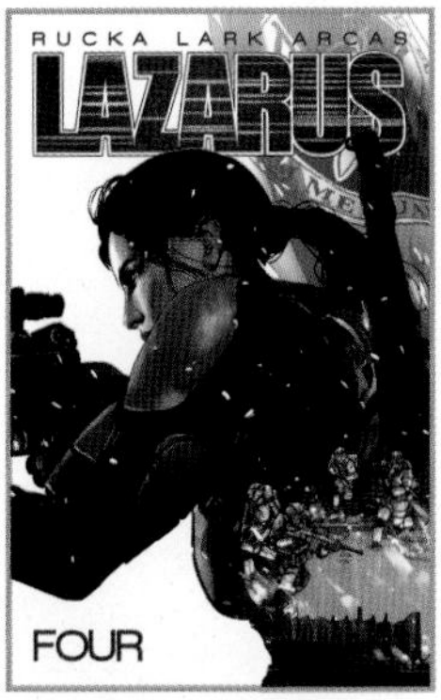
RUCKA LARK ARCAS
LAZARUS
FOUR

LAZARUS VOL.4: POISON
ISBN: 978-1632155238
DIAMOND ORDER CODE: NOV150672
RATED M/MATURE
SCIENCE FICTION/DRAMA
$14.99

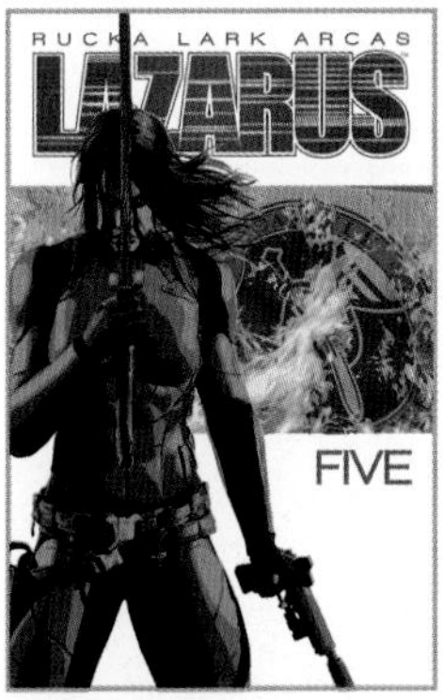
RUCKA LARK ARCAS
LAZARUS
FIVE

LAZARUS VOL.5: CULL
ISBN: 978-1534300248
DIAMOND ORDER CODE: DEC160811
RATED M/MATURE
SCIENCE FICTION/DRAMA
$14.99

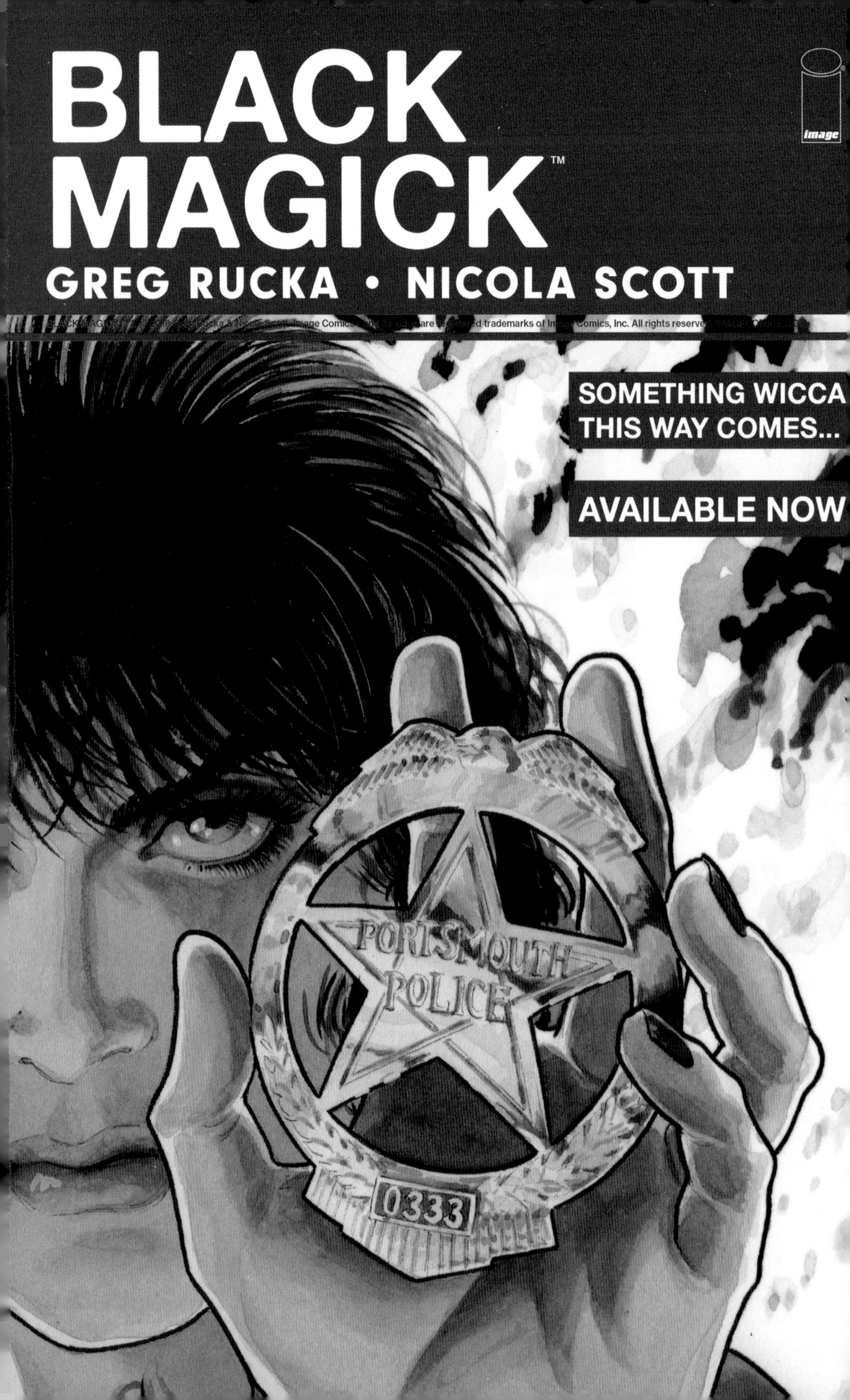
BLACK MAGICK™
GREG RUCKA • NICOLA SCOTT
image
trademarks of Image Comics, Inc. All rights reserved.
SOMETHING WICCA THIS WAY COMES...
AVAILABLE NOW
PORTSMOUTH POLICE
0333